DYNAMICS OF INTERNATIONAL POLITICS

Dynamics of International Politics

[For UGC-NET, M.A., UPSC and State Public Service Commission Examinations]

By

MANOJ SHARMA

ANMOL PUBLICATIONS PVT. LTD.

NEW DELHI - 110 002 (INDIA)

ANMOL PUBLICATIONS PVT. LTD.
4374/4B, Ansari Road, Daryaganj
New Delhi - 110 002
Ph.: 23261597, 23278000
Visit us at: www.anmolpublications.com

Dynamics of International Politics

First Published, 2004

ISBN 81-261-1921-7

PRINTED IN INDIA

Published by J.L. Kumar for Anmol Publications Pvt. Ltd., New Delhi - 110 002 and Printed at Mehra Offset Press, Delhi.

Contents

Preface

Dynamics of International Politics as a paper is being taught at the graduate and post graduate level in Political Science syllabus in almost all the Indian Universities. The various courses conducted by various institutions at the Central and State level too have been considered in respect of their syllabus, course contents and requirements. Thus the material presented here would be of interest as well as great use to the students of Political Science. This book has been especially designed for UGC-NET Examination, M.A. (Political Science) Students and other competitive examinations by UPSC and Public Service Commission of various States.

The major topics dealt in this book are—Emerging Issues of World Order; Emerging World Order; International Political Geography; Two World Wars; Emergence of Super Powers; Colonialism and Decolonialism; Balance of Power; Cold War; End of Cold War; Nuclear Weapons and Disarmament; Non-Alignment and Economic Development; New World Order etc.

Manoj Sharma

1

Emerging Issues of World Order

Asia which is more than fifty per cent of the world population and covers approximately thirty per cent of the earth surface till the dawn of the present century was under Western domination. The domination in the words of Sardar K.M. Pannikar took the form of "the dominance of maritime power over the land masses of Asia; the imposition of a commercial economy over communities whose economic life in the past had been based not on international trade, but mainly on agricultural production and international trade; and the domination of the people of Europe who held the mastery of seas, over the affairs of Asia."

With the turn of the century the Asian countries started aspiring for independence from foreign yoke. The First World War and the Russian Revolution had profound effect on Asia. The First World War upset the old equilibrium and the Western powers in general and Great Britain in particular began to lose their dominant position on the world stage. The growing national consciousness of the Asian people also contributed to this. The Russian revolution also had profound impact on the Asian minds. The Bolsheviks posed as champions of anti-Imperialism. But perhaps the greatest impact was made by Japan who embarked on invasion of Manchuria in 1931 and inaugurated a campaign of expansionism on mainland of Asia.

After World War II most of the countries of Asia gained independence and the vast empires held by Britain, France and the Netherlands were liquidated. The emergence of Asia in the mid-twentieth century became a major turning point in the contemporary history. This development according to Prof. Romein implied that

Asian revolution had been accomplished and Western domination was no longer feasible.

But Asia was not merely satisfied with political liberation. Soon it embarked on two other revolutions in the economic and social fields. In the economic sphere the Asian countries started the work of economic reconstruction with a view to stregthen the base of political independence. Countries like India, Burma and Ceylon adopted economic plans based on socialist ideology and are moving in the direction of extensive public investment and public sector. On the other hand, countries like Japan, Formosa, the Philippines and Pakistan have not been very active in planned economy.

Almost all the countries of Asia, with the exception of Japan have been traditionally underdeveloped and the principal occupation of the people in these countries is agriculture. The agriculture is in a very primitive stage and scientific facilities are not readily available. Except for Japan and in certain sectors in India, there was no significant industrial development in the Asian countries.

The poverty of Asians is another dominant feature of Asian life. The poverty leads to allied problems of malnutrition, disease and general lack of vigour and energy. Consequently in almost all the countries of Asia, the governments have devoted their main attention on the solution of these problems.

These countries are also faced with the problems of illiteracy. Majority of the children in the Asian countries do not get any education. This problem of illiteracy has been made more complex by the lack of facilities for higher and technical education. No doubt, in almost all the countries of Asia in recent years an effort has been made to introduce compulsory education up to a certain standard and facilities have been provided for higher education.

Thus we find that the Asian countries for the time being have been concentrating their activities in the social, economic and international political problems.

In the sphere of international relations these countries have followed the policy of peaceful co-existence. This policy was imperative in view of the fact that they want to concentrate their resources for their national reconstruction and development plans. They are convinced that too much of attention on defence and security questions certainly leads to diversion of attention from development.

This attitude of the Asian countries has gone a long way in consolidating the forces of peace and stability in the world. The Asian countries also have great interest in preserving the international organisation because they can hope to gain immensely from the socio-economic and welfare activities of this organisation. Therefore, the Asian countries have proved to be the greatest supporters of the U.N.

Another impact of the emergence of Asian countries is the growth of Pan-Asian movements. The common interests of the countries of Asia brought these countries together and a number of Asian Conferences were held. Two such conferences were held at New Delhi in 1947 and 1949. This was followed by Conferences at Cairo, Bandung and Accra.

But this feeling of Asianism did long not last. Soon the frontier problems and diverse national interests of the countries of Asia gave it a setback. This feeling of Asianism was further weakened by the political rivalry of the two Great Powers and the alliances created in this region. The two Super Powers (U.S.A. and Soviet Union) are trying to win the favour of the Asian countries because they are considered a vital element in the international power, political and ideological struggle. It can be hoped that the direction and course of the international relations will be determined for a considerable time by the role of the Asian countries.

ROLE OF ETHNICITY IN SOUTH ASIA

Following are the causes which made the countries of South Asia to co-operate with each other:

1. Importance of Bargaining Power. Economically backward countries of the region realised that they can improve their bargaining power *vis-a-vis* the developed countries only if they attain self-reliance through mutual co-operation. Hence, they supported the New International Economic Order.

2. Economical Considerations. The ecological considerations demanded greater cooperation among the South Asian countries. No country of the region could solve problems single-handed, these could be solved only if the countries of the region cooperated. For example, the problem of soil salinity in Bangladesh caused by tidal waters flowing inland could be solved only if India agreed to augment the waters of the Ganga river system.

3. Foreign Ministers Meeting (New Delhi, August, 1983). The foreign ministers of Bangladesh, Bhutan, India, Maldives, Nepal and Pakistan met at New Delhi. The foreign ministers signed a Declaration on South Asian Regional Co-operation. They expressed their concern about the common problems and aspirations of the people of South Asia. They emphasised the need to accelerating their economic and social development through regional co-operation. They expressed their concern about the common problems and aspirations of the people of South Asia. They emphasised the need of accelerating their economic and social development through regional cooperation.

4. Presence of European Navy in Indian Ocean. The presence of the naval forces of the European powers in the Indian Ocean is a serious threat to the freedom of the region. Therefore, the states of the region realised that the infighting between them will be exploited by outside powers.

Objectives of SAARC. They highlighted the following objectives of the South Asian Regional Co-operation based on the principle of sovereign equality, territorial integrity, political independence, non-interference in internal affairs of other states and mutual benefit—

(i) to promote welfare of the people of South Asia and improve quality of their life;

(ii) to accelerate economic growth, social progress and cultural development in the region and to provide all individuals the opportunity to live in dignity and to realise it among the countries of South-Asia;

(iii) to contribute to mutual trust, understanding and appreciation of another's problems;

(iv) to promote active collaboration and mutual assistance in the economic, social, cultural, technical and scientific fields;

(v) to strengthen co-operation with other developing countries;

(vi) to strengthen co-operation among themselves in international forums on matters of common interest; and

(vii) to co-operate with international and regional organisation with similar aims and purposes.

Slow Progress of SAARC. Over the years the progress in co-operation among SAARC countries has been quite slow due to following reasons:

1. ***Difference in the Approaches.*** It is argued that this war quite natural due to the different socio-economic character and varying geo political and strategic objectives of the countries of the region. For example, to start with, Bangladesh favoured co-operation in the economic sphere which could be subsequently extended to the social and cultures spheres. On the other hand Sri Lanka pleaded for more comprehensive co-operation and favoured extension of co-operation to the political fields as well. Pakistan wanted regional co-operation to be limited only to four out of the eleven areas identified in the Bangladesh Working Paper. India emphasised expanding co-operation in the cultural, infra structural, scientific and technological fields and refrained from making any reference to political or security objectives.

2. ***Different Attitudes on Institutional Framework.*** The members adopted different attitudes on the question of the institutional framework. Bangladesh consistently emphasised the need of evolving some institutional frame work. Sri Lanka emphasised the need of establishing an association for the purpose of promoting and safeguarding the interests of the participating member states. Nepal favoured an additional institutional framework for regional co-operation. India and Pakistan favoured institutional framework, which must

evoke enthusiastic response for an informal forum for consultation.

3. ***Ethnicity.*** Ethnicity problem is the greatest hindrance in progress of co-operation.

India's Relations with Neighbours

1. ***Nepal.*** Traditionally, ties between India and Nepal have been close. During 1995-96 two countries signed a treaty on the development of Mahakali rivers for harnessing of river waters for mutual benefit. The on-going economic liberalisation in both the countries as well as the stable foundations provided by the 1990-91. Treaty of Trade and Transit continued to have a positive impact on Indo-Nepal trade and economic relations. As on 31 December, 1995, out of a total of 247 joint ventrues. 95 are from India. India continued to play an active role in Nepals developmental efforts. Projocts being undertaken by India included the setting up of a medical College and institute at Dharan, the construction of 22 bridges on the Vast-West Highway in Western Nepal and surveys for east-west electric railway, outer ring road at Janakpur, broad-gauging of rail link between Raxaul and Sirsia.

2. ***Bangladesh.*** Relations with Bangladesh continue to be close and stable with regular interaction between the two Governments. The Bangladesh Government has continued its attempts at internationalising the issue of river water, the Prime Minister of Bangladesh raised the issue at the United Nations General Asembly in October, 1995. India believes this issue requires a bilateral solution and remains committed to holding constructive bilateral dialogue for arriving at a long-term, comprehensive arrangement on water sharing with Bangladesh, taking into account the requirements of both sides. A Rs. 30 crore credit agreement and an agreement on avoidance of double taxation are in force.

3. ***Bhutan.*** Relations with Bhutan, which have traditionally been close and cordial, continued to be marked by deep

mutual understanding. Close coopreation in the economic field has been a significant factor in reinforcing intimate bilateral links. Periodic exchange of views have fostered a traditionally friendly relationship. Bhutanese Foreign Minister and Planning Minister visited India during the year, King, Jugme Singye Wan hgchuk paid an official visit to India from 1 to 7 March 1996. Two agreements for bilateral development for the Tata Hydroelectric project and the Dungsum Cement Plant were signed during the visit. India continues to be closely associated with Bhutan's developmental efforts. Major projects such as hospitals, school, roads and bridges, transmission lines, electrification, survey projects are underway.

4. ***Maldives.*** India and Maldives share a close, cordial and friendly relationship. The Indira Gandhi Memorial Hospital, gifted to the Maldives by India, was jointly inaugurated by Prime Minister of India and President Maumoon Abdul Gayoom of Maldives on 15 and 16 April, 1995. The Minister of External Affairs visited Maldives in August, 1995, and co-chaired the 3rd Indo-Maldives Joint Commission. Both sides agreed to take steps to develop trade relations further and coopreate in the field of tourism.

5. ***Sri Lanka.*** A close understanding and cordality has been built up with the new Government in Sri Lanka. Friendly ties between the two countries were cemented through the visits of the Sri Lankan President to India in March, and May, 1995 India continues to favour a peaceful solution to the ethnic crisis in Sir Lankan within a framework of sovereignty and territorial integrity of Sri Lanka, without outside interference and through negotiations. Government of India has welcomed the proposals for devolution of power announced by President Kumaratunga in August 1995. Problems pertaining to fishermen from both countries straying into each other's territorial waters was discussed during the visits of Sri Lankan Foreign Minister and the Sri Lankan President to India.

6. ***Myanmar.*** India's relations with Myanmar also showed improvement during 1995-96. The first Indian Trade Fair was inaugurated by Minister of State for Commerce in Yangon in March, 1995. The Indo-Myanmar Border Trade Agreement was operationalised during the visit of Myanmar Minister of Commerce to India in April, 1995. The Myanmar Minister for Heavy Industries visited India from 16 to 21 October, 1995. India and Myanmar signed a Memorandum of Understanding to restore civil aviation links on 11 July, 1995.

7. ***Pakistan.*** Pakistan's unabated promotion and support to terrorism directed against India, its sustained efforts to internationalise the Kashmir issue and its intransigence on the resumption of bilateral dialogue with India, continued to prevent an improvement in bilateral relations. Pakistani and third country mercenaries continued to be inducted into the Indian State of Jammu & Kashmir by Al Faran group highlighted the brutal methods being adopted by terrorists operating in Jammu & Kashmir India has strongly urged Pakistan to give up its path of promoting and supporting terrorism and conduct inter-state relations as a responsible member of the international community. Pakistan continued its efforts to internationalise the Kashmir issue. Pakistan raised the issue in various international fora, including the Special Commemorative meeting of the UN General Assembly, 11th Non-Aligned Meeting and the Commonwealth heads of Government Meeting (CHOGM). Pakistan's moves were effectively thwarted. It was reiterated from all relevant international platforms that the State of Jammu & Kashmir is an integral part of the Indian Union.

Ethnicity and U.S. Approach. An interesting feature of Indo-Pak conflict in its international context is that while both the countries are members of the non-aligned movement their super power linkages were suspect in each other's eyes: they were seen as "pro-Soviet" India by Pakistan and a "pro-US" Pakistan by India. India's "pro-Sovietism" was of course not comparable to Pakistan's "pro-

Americanism" for obvious reasons. India's large resource base, its relatively well-grown capitalist class and the pluralistic nature of its politics sustained by democratic institutions leave limited scope for the Soviet Union to dominate Indian politics even though on strategic matters New Delhi's dependence on Moscow was considerable. Correspondingly, although there exists a clear perceptional gap between India and the United States on regional and global issues, there is little possibility of the Indian ruling elites adopting a position of out-right hostility to Washington.

Indo-Bangla Cleavage: Politics of Foreign Relations. The fall of Sheikh Mujibur Rahman marked the watershed in Indo-Bangla relations and the growth of religious fanaticism and Bangladesh's change of stance in foreign policy seriously impaired them. At the same time, economic hardships forced the country to look further field for possible aid-donors which indirectly contributed to misunderstanding between India and Bangladesh. In its 1977-78, development budget of Taka 1190 crores the aid component was Taka 805 crores which largely came from the West. Indian assistance was $ 111 million in 1971-72; it declined to $ 7 Million in 1975-76, and to naught in 1976-77.

Nepali Ethnicity. Many measures were adopted to boost the ethnic Nepalis at the cost of Indian Nepalis. For example, though the introduction of a system of weightage for the Nepalis ths governement reduced by 10 per cent the marks obtained at competitive examinations by candidates with Indian university degrees. The system affected the Terai people most because on account of their cultural linkages with India they preferred to send their children to Indian universities for higher education.

Ethnic Tangle in Sri Lanka. Both with regard to Sri Lanka politics as well as Indo-Sri Lanka relations, it may be said that much depends on the way The Tamil question is solved. The central issue is how and when the 'Tigers' are tamed. This issue has relevance for Indian politics as well more particularly for the politics of Tamil Nadu where the Assembly elections are to be held in the near future.

Radio Programmes Dropped. Radio programmes which were earlier broadcast in Nepali, Hindi and Newari, dropped the Hindi and

Newari programmes from 1965 onwards. This irked the Indian Nepalis particularly Phadnis writes: "The absence of Newari and Hindi from such broadcast has been a potential focus for agitation amongst the Newars as well as the Terai people.....[but], as regards the Newars, well entrenched as they are in the power structure, the language issue has in the main been the manifestation of a search for cultural identity rather than of ethnocentricity.

Settlement Policies in India. The Indian Nepalis also complained against the government's resettlement policies. They attributed the increased rate of migration from the hill region to the Terai to these policies and the tenure of land reform. For example, the Nepal government placed a ceiling on family hodings of land at 25 bighas (around 20 acres). But instead of distributing the surplus land in the Terai districts to the landless people of the area, the government allotted the land to the people from the hills, many of whom were ex-servicemen. In the same way, the deforested areas in the Terai were also allotted to people from the hills.

Dichotomy. The existence of a dichotomy between the people of Nepali origin and those of Indian origin overrides that between the Kathmandu valley and the hill region which could pose a challenge to the existing power pattern. It may be noted that this valley-hill dichotomy had surfaced during the 1979 referendum. In the wake of announcement of the referendum one Khagendra Bahadur Gurung convened a confrernce of "Mongoloid-origin People" in September, 1979. Claiming to repersent Mongoloid and martial ethnic groups like the Gurungs, Magars, Tamangs, Kiratis, and Sherpas, Gurung questioned the validity of Nepal's claim as a Hindu state. By implication he questioned the authority of the caste Hindus of the valley to rule. The conference also put forward several grievances with regard to the economic lot of the tribals and held that the privileged classes again meaning primarily the elites of the valley, were responsible for this. This pan-Tribalism, however, did not influence Nepal's politic much as was evident in the 1981 elections. Even the Consititution Commission which King Birendra had appointed in the aftermath of the referendum did not take the grievances of the "Mongoloid-origin People" too seriously.

Unequal Treatment. The Nepal government treated the Indian Nepalis unequally also on the question of language and education. In 1941, a National Education commission was set up which recommended that Nepali should be the medium of instruction in schools and colleges. Following this, the government undertook a programme to develop Nepali as the national language. this evoked serious protest in the form of a "save Hindi campaign in the Terai resulting in violence. In the 1959 elections, while agreeing that other languages should also be encouraged, most of the parties threw their weight in favour of Nepali as the national language. Following the dismissal of the Koirala ministry and the royal "take-over", the Second National Education Commission was set up in 1961. This commission endorsed the decisions of the first commission.

Nepali Support to GNLF. There has been no evidence of foreign financial support, meaning Nepali particularly, to the GNLF movement. It was, however, suspected that Ghising had contacts with Nepali businessmen in Nepal and pro-business politicians like H.B. Gurung. It was believed that under their influence he demanded the scrapping of Clause 7 of the Indo-Nepalese treaty of 1950 which allowed citizens of both the countries to travel, work and live without hindrance in either country. Ghising argued that since the ethnic Nepalis from Nepal entered India freely the *bona fide* Indian national of Nepali origin faced the problem of being identified as Nepali nationals and were, therefore, harassed by India authourities. The Indian government has itself taken measures to restict the movement of Nepalis in certain parts of India but we can see that in Ghising's demand there were issues which had larger implications for Indo-Nepal relations. In the case of the open border system, the Nepali government had indirectly demanded its abolition but India had never agreed. It was suspected that the abolition of the open border would severely affect the interest of Indian business community in Nepal and would correspondingly benefit the rising Nepali business class there.

Indian and Bhutan. In conclusion it may be said that Bhutan has not so far posed any serious challenge to Indian foreign policy and strategic planning, nor has it put forward an earnest demand for the revision of the 1949 treaty, but relations between the two countries cannot be taken for granted for too long. At the least, India must reconsider its premise that Bhutan should necessarily hold identical views on international and regional affairs. We have seen already that regarding Afghanistan and Kampuchea Bhutan has held views different from those of India. There are now indications that even on South Asian regional affairs Bhutan's position on certain vital issues is not identical with that of India. On the question of superpower involvement in South Asian affairs Bhutan probably continues to respect Indian sensitivities, but on the crucial question of declaring the region as a nuclear-free zone its position tends to oppose that of India and support Pakistan's.

DISINTEGRATION OF USSR

The former Soviet Union declined and disintegrated into a number of sovereign countries in 1991. This Was the outcome of the process of reform initiated by Mikhail Gorbachev after he took over as General Secretary of the Communist Party in 1985. As a result of the collapse of the mighty Soviet Union, came to an end of the one of the two superpowers, the first socialist country in the world and the leader of the eastern or communist bloc. This was end of an era. The end of the bipolar world and the end of the Marxist assertion that capitalism has germs fits own.

Background. The policy of Glasnost, initiated by Gorbachev, led to liberalisation of Soviet economy and free expression of dissent within the party and various organs of government. And once people got their freedom Gorbachev could not restrain them. Gorbachev was a communist and wanted to establish a free and democratic communist system. But this strategy failed. Events moved so fast and in such dramatic manner that Gorbachev lost control and with his resignation in 1991 as President the country over which he presided ceased to exist. When Gorbachev assumed the leadership of the CPSU in 1985, his reforms (Perestroika and Glasnost) were widely welcomed. In 1988, he introduced multi-candidate elections but within the one-party system. In 1988, Gorbachev was undisputed leader of the party and how clearly stated that there was no question of permitting any party other than .the CPSU. However, public opinion was fast turning in favour of muliti-party system. Following a massive demonstration on the eve of a plenary meeting of the CPSU demanding multi-party system, Gorbachev conceded the demand for end of communist monopoly. At the 28th Congress of the CPSU, the principle of multi-party system was accepted in principle.

Political Confusion. Meanwhile most of the East European countries had decided to discard communism and assest their "independence" from "Soviet Control'. As soon as East European allies opted for 'independence', many of the Union Republics, like Lithunia, Estonia, Latvia and others began demanding complete sovereignty and secession from the Soviet Union. Till 1990, demand for secessions had been made by parliaments of different Union Republics and the movement for secession had been gaining momentum, Soviet leadership appeared to be faced with a serious threat and therefore in a confused state. Gorbachev insisted on the referendum to ascertain the wishes of the people of each Union Republic wanting to secede. However, confusion persisted as Gorbachev came under sharp criticism with the conservation communist accusing him of leading the country to disintegration and the radicals charging him with continuing the existing model.

Amendment of Constitution in December, 1990. This was done by yet another major amendment of the constitution in December, 1990. The fourth session of the Congress of People's Deputies, held in December, 1990, created a presidential type of government in the former USSR. Though the terms was not used in the constitution, it was largely based on the American pattern, minus the system of checks and balances.

Isolation of Gorbachev. But by the end of 1990, President Gorbachev was fighting heavy odds almost single-handed. Most of his trusted colleagues including Foreign Minister Sheverdnadze had resigned, while some were forced to quit. In mid-1991, Soviet Union was in economic chaos and political uncertainty. The demand for secession by Baltic Repblics gained momentum. Since Armenia and Moldavia were also demanding secession, Gorbachev proposed in April, a fresh Union Treaty to bind the remaining nine republics.

These nine republics agreed to remedy the economic crisis in meeting of their leaders with Gorbachev.

Monopoly of Power. During Gorbachev's absence from Moscow—he was holidaying with his family in Crimia—a coup was staged against him by a group led by Vice-Preesident Yanagev, Prime Minister Pavlov and the KGB Chief. Gorbachev was removed from power and put under house arrest. There was an eminent threat to the position of Boris Yelstin as well who had won the Russian presidency by a big margin in July 1991 presidential election of Russian Republic and had proceeded with total liberalisation of economy there.

The August Coup. The economic situation remained grim and in August, 1997 diehard communists decided to remove Gorbachev from power and re-establish orthodox communist amendment, were scrapped. In the new, short lived set up, President Gorbachev was executive head of the state with reduced powers.

Emergence of Yelstin. Yelstin emerged as hero who got Gorbachev back to power. But this had weekened Gorbachev who had to take all such steps as were desired by Yelstin. The organs of state power, based on 1988 constitutional amendments, were scrapped. In the new, short-lived setup, President Gorbachev was executive head of the state with reduced power. Moreover, soon after the abortive coup of August, 1991, the authority of the central government became so weak that the republics freely began taking their own decision. The oft-repeated idea of new union treaty was given up. In September, 1991, three Baltic Republics, Lithuania, Latvia and Estonia unilaterally declared their independence which was soon accepted by international community and the Russian Federation (while still USSR) recognised the sovereignty of three Baltic Republics.

Formation of CIS and Final Act of Disintegration. The final act of disintegration began when early in December, 1991, three of the Republics namely Russia, Ukraine and Belarus met and decided to set up a Commcnwealth of Independent State (CIS). All other republics were also invited to join it. The idea soon caught up as one after the other all the Republics declared their indepedence and eventually 11 of them because member of the CIS. This meant loose union of former republics of the Soviet Union Gorbachev found that he had become irrelevant and resigned. With his resignation as President of the USSR on December 21, 1991 the once mighty Soviet Union ceased to exist as one soverign nation and Russia became the principal successor of the former Soviet Union and was recognised as such by the international community. It got the permanent seat in the U.N. Security Council with the power of veto. All other former republics were by 1992, admitted to the membership of the United Nations.

CAUSES OF DISINTEGRATION IN USSR

Here we can see the following Causes of disntegration in USSR:

1. Failures of the Past Communist Regimes. The good work done by the great revolutionary Lenin was in way lost by criminally misguided rule of Stalin. The Soviet leadership after Stalin failed to accomplish any worthwhile reforms. Stalin has after been called a 'dictator'—even a butcher, under whose rule hundreds of thousands of Soviet people were shot dead simply because he suspected them on one imaginary account or another. There was hardly any democracy. Stalin and his secret police Chief Beria governed ruthlessly with an iron rod. There was complete secrecy in not only decision-making, but also day-to-day administration. When Second World War ended and cold war began with the emergence of two power blocs, the Soviet camp of East-European countries was said to be under an "iron curtain". Thus situation was sought to be changed by Stalin's successor, but their success was only partial. The Soviet leadership even after Stalin failed to accomplish any worthwhile reform. In fact Brezneb era was marked by stagnation. Where Gorbachev assumed leadership in 1985, there was stagnation, shortage of consumer goods and absence of true socialist democracy.

2. Gorbachev's Policy of Reforms. Gorbachev's policy of reforms as embodied in terms like Perestroika (socio-economic restructuring), Glasnost (openness) had been enthusiastically accepted by a vast majority of Soviet people by 1988. Such reforms were expected to correct the distortion of socialism and stagnation in economy. But while Gorbachev continued to swear by Lenin, entire Soviet history was being rewritten. Glasnost had bacome visible even in Soviet judiciary and it was by 1999 delivering blows at Stalin's legacy of bureaucratised economy and dictatorial politics. Indeed, Glasnost had given first opportunity to the Soviet people to enjoy the freedom to criticise their past as well as present rulers. Political democracy, though not in Western Liberal sense, had been established in the Soviet Union by important amendment in the constitution and adoption of a new electoral law, economic restructuring was also vigorously pursued in all embracing and comprehensive way. But all this also gave the critics the opportunity to point out obvious contradictions in the whole process and gave the people a resolve to change the entire system at the earliest.

Demand for More Democratisation. Democratisation was being anxiously awaited by the Soviet people for 70 long year. Gorbachev gave them, in the name of Lenin, what was denied by Lenin and his successors. An open public involvement with different view points resulted in a revolutionary change in Soviet polity. For 70 years, people were told to elect their representatives but were given no choice. They had been told that they were sovereign but all their actions were controlled by the party. They were promised democracy but were not allowed to express their views freely. And they were granted several political rights but they could not hold even peaceful demonstrations. All this had changed by 1988-89. The election law of 1988, for the first time, gave freedom to the people to demonstrate, express their views, defeat offical candidates.

HUMAN RIGHTS

There are certain rights of the individuals which are inherent in his personality. Such rights are called as Natural Rights. Man is moral and rational being and this very state entitles him to the enjoyment of certain, rights, which are called as Human Rights. These rights are derived from the inherent dignity of the human person and they should be available to man every where and at all times. These rights are necessary condition for the development of human personality and without them man would really not be man. The ideal of human rights and fundamental freedom is universally accepted and this problem never received so much attention as to day. The Declaration of the Rights of Man following the American and French Revolutions contained fundamental human rights. The Declaration of American Independence, 1776 stated: "We hold these truths to be self-evident, that all men are created equal, that they are endowed by their Creator with certain inalienable rights, that among these are life, liberty and pursuit of happiness." The French Declaration of the Rights of Man, 1789 emphasised the concepts of "liberty, equality and fraternity." In 1941 in his message to American Congress, President Roosevelt laid stress on 'Four Freedoms, of Man and said, "We look forward to a world founded upon four essential freedoms—freedom of speech and expression, freedom of worship, freedom from want and freedom from fear." Right from the Atlantic Charter till the end of the Second World War in their wartime conferences the Allied Powers laid particular stress upon the human rights and fundamental freedoms. In the Declaration of the United Nations of 1942, the United Nations put on record that 'complete victory over enemies is essential to defend life, liberty, independence and religions freedom and to preserve human rights and justice in their own lands', But unfortunately, while it is accepted in principle, it seems to be ignored in practice. There are very few states where the human rights and fundamental freedoms are available, otherwise in most of the states people are deprived of it. They are the cases of racial and religious discrimination in general and the problem of apartheid in particular. Again, there is economic and political exploitation. In totalitarian regimes and dictatorships people are deprived of their political rights and freedoms. In 1971 inhuman and barbaric cruelties, and genocide committed on the people of Bangladesh moved the very conscience of mankind. The policy of apartheid pursued in South Africa has been condemned by all. The General Assembly has repeatedly condemned this policy as a 'crime against humanity.'

THE UNITED NATIONS AND HUMAN RIGHTS

Even before the end of Second World War the Allied Powers expressed the hope that after the victory in the war, efferts would be made for the protection of human rights in every state. In Dumbarton

Oaks Conference of 1944 the emphasis was laid on the promotion of human rights and fundamental freedoms.

The representatives gathered at the San Francisco Conference demanded that the declaration of human rights should be included in the U.N. Charter itself. Though a separate declartion of human rights does not find place in the Charter but the specific mention of the human rights has been made in the Charter at various places.

The Preamble to the United Nations Charter refer to the determination of the United Nation's 'to affirm faith in fundamental human rights, in the dignity and worth of the human person, in the equal rights of men and women.'

Under Atricle 1, one of the purposes of the United Nations is to achieve international co-operation 'in promoting and encouraging respect for human rights and for fundamental freedoms for all without distinction as to race, sex, language or religion.'

Under Article 13 it is the duty of the General Assembly to assist 'in the realisation of human rights and fundamental freedoms for all without distinction as to race, sex language or religion.'

Under Article 55 it is provided that the United Nations shall promote 'universal respect for, and observance of human rights and fundamental freedoms for all without distinction as to race, sex language or religion.'

Under Ariticle 62 it is the duty of the Economic and Social Council 'to make recommendations for purpose of promoting respect for, and observance of human rights fundamental freedoms for all.'

According to Article 68 the Economic and Social Council is required to set up commissions for the promotion of human rights.

It is for the first time that the provision in regard to the protection of human rights and fundamental freedom has been made in the U.N. Charter. Under the Charter the United Nations is empowered only to encourage the promotion of human rights and fundamental freedom, but has no power to take any binding measure in this regard. The Charter deals with the human rights and the fundamental freedoms but it does not give any precise definition of there rights or a clear acknowledgement of the principle of their observance. In fact, the Charter aims at the voluntary co-operation of the states in achieving this objective. There is no doubt that the provisions of the Charter in regard to human rights have absolutely no binding authority but at the same time the protection of human rights has ceased to be the exclusive jurisdiction of states and has become the concern of the United Nations. According to Oppenheim, "It cannot of the that the provisions of the Charter on the subject signify a full and effective guarantee of the inalienable rights of man on the part of international society. In particular, these are absent from the Charter Clauses embodying either a more parse definition of these rights or a clear acknowledgment of the principle of their observance... Whatever these may be, the observance of fundamental human rights in so far it is the subject-matter of local obligations, ceases to be one of exclusive domestic jurisdiction of states and has become a matter of legitimate concern for the United Nations and its members."

UNIVERSAL DECLARATIONS OF HUMAN RIGHTS

The United Nations Commission on Human Rights was asked to prepare a draft on the general principles governing the human rights. After two and half years of painstaking labour the Commission on Human Rights prepared a draft of the 'Universal Declaration of Human Rights,' as a common standard of achievement for all peoples and all nations. This declaration, the first of its kind in history, was approved by the General Assembly on December 10, 1948. This declaration is the first international definition of the rights of man. It is, therefore, 10th December, is commemorated every year as Human Rights day.

The Declaration of Human Rights contains 30 Articles including the preamble. The Preamble stresses the 'dignity and worth of the human person.'

Article 1. All human beings are born free and equal in dignity and rights.

Article 2. Every one without any distinction is entitled to all the rights and freedoms set forth in this Declaration.

Article 3. Every one has the right to life liberty and the security of person.

Article 4. No one shall be held in slavery or servitude; slavery and slave-trade shall be prohibited in all their forms.

Article 5. No one shall be subjected to torture or to cruel, inhuman or degrading treatment or punishment.

Article 6. Every one has the right to recognition everywhere as a person before the law.

Article 7. All are equal before the law and are emitted to equal protection of the law.

Article 8. Every one has the right to an effective remedy by the competent national tribunals for acts violative of the fundamental rights granted to him by the constitution or by law.

Article 9. No one shall be subjected to arbitrary arrest, detention or exile.

Article 10. Every one is entitled in full equality to a fair and public hearing by an independent and impartial tribunal.

Article 11. Every one charged with a penal offence has the right to be presumed innocent until proved guilty according to law in a public trial. No one shall be held guilty of any penal offence which did not constitute a penal offence at the time when it was committted.

Article 12. No one shall be subjected to arbitrary interference with its privacy, family, home or correspondence, nor to attacks upon his honour and reputation.

Article 13. Every one has the right to freedom of movement and residence within the borders of each state.

Article 14. Every one has the right to seek in other countries asylum from persecution.

Article 15. Every one has right to nationality. No one shall be arbitrarily deprived of his nationality nor denied the right to change his nationalty.

Article 16. Men and Women of age, without any limitation due to race nationality or religion, have the right to marry and to found a family.

Article 17. Every one has the right to own property and no one shall be arbitrarily deprived of his property.

Article 18. Every one has the right to freedom of thought, conscience and religion.

Article 19. Every one has the right to freedom of opinion and expression.

Article 20. Every one has the right to freedom of peaceful assembly and association.

Article 21. Every one has the right to take part in the government of his country with equal access in public service.

Article 22. Every one has the right to social security and is entitled to realization of the economic, social and cultural rights indispensable for his dignity and the free development of his personality.

Article 23. Every one has the right to work, to free choice of employment, to just and favourable conditions of work and to protection against unemployment. Every one has the right to equal pay for equal work. Every one who works has the right to just and favourable remuneration.

Article 24. Every one has the right to rest and leisure, including reasonable limitation of working hours and periodic holidays with pay.

Article 25. Every one has the right to adequate standard of living, including housing, medical care and security in the event of sickness, widowhood and old age.

Article 26. Every one has the right to education.

Article 27. Every one has the right to take part in the cultural life of the community and to share in the scientific advancements and its benefits.

Article 28. Every one is entitled to social and international order in which the rights and freedoms set forth in this Declaration can be fully realized.

Article 29. Every one has duties to the community in which alone the free and full development of his personality is possible. In the exercise of his rights and freedoms, every one shall be subjected to due recognition and respect for the rights and freedoms of others and just requirements of morality, public order and general welfare.

Article 30. Nothing in this Declaration may be interpreted as implying for any state, group, or person any right to engage in any activity or to perform any act aimed at the distruction of any of the rights and freedoms set forth above.

The Universal Declaration of Human Rights is a historic event of great importance for the mankind. It is an international. 'Magna Carta' of all men everywhere. According to Dr. Charles Malik of Lebanon, this Declaration was not simply a resolution but the part of U.N. Charter itself. About the Declaration, American representative in the United Nations observed: "In giving our approval to the declaration to-day, it is of primary importance that we keep clearly in mind the basic character of the document. It is not a treaty ; it is not an international agreement. It does not purport to be a statement of law or of legal obligation. It is a declaration of specific principles of human rights and freedoms, to be stamped with the approval of the General Assembly by a formal vote of its members and to serve as a common standard of achievement for all peoples of all nations." According to Palmer and Perkins, "The declaration is merely a statement of principles, not a legally binding instrument; but it has become one of the best known of international documents, and it has often been referred to in resolution of the U.N., the specialized agencies, regional arrangements and other international orgainsations, and in national constitutions, legislations, and court decisions. It is a beacon light for all mankind, even though it has been honoured more often in the breach than in the observance."

However, it must not be forgotten that no machinery has been provided to enforce the provisions of this Declaration. The states cannot be compelled to enforce this Declaration. Oppenheim remarks. "The Declaration is not an instrument which is legally binding either directly or indirectly" In 1948 the Commission on Human Rights tried to make this Declaration binding on the states but this could not be possible as it would have provided an opportunity to the majority states in the U.N. to interfere in the internal affairs of the other states. Although the Declaration is only in the form of a recommendation to the states, yet the U.N. General Assembly has condemned the states which have violated the declaration. The General Assembly has a number of times condemned South Africa for its policies of apartheid. Lacking in binding and legal force the Declaration, nevertheless, presents a moral ideal before the states in very clear terms. The states can hardly afford to ignore the world orgnisation and the world public opinion.

INTERNATIONAL COVENANTS ON HUMAN RIGHTS

The United Nations not only made a Declaration of human rights but it also took steps in the direction that they are effectively implemented by the states. With this view the General Assembly in 1951, requested The Commission on Human Rights to prepare draft of two covenants, one on 'Civil and Political Rights' and the other on 'Economic, Social and Cultural Rights.' The purpose of these covenants is to give more precise definition of the human rights and make necessary provision for their observance. These covenants, after being approved by the General Assembly, were to be submitted to the U.N. members as treaty, and it would be binding upon all states that ratified it. On 16th December, 1966, the General Assembly adopted and opened for signature, ratification and accession three International Covenants on Human Rights—*(a)* International Covenant on Civil and Political Rights ; *(b)* International Covenant on Economic, Cultural and Social Rights; and *(c)* The Optional Protocol to the International Covenant on Civil and Political Rights.

The principles proclaimed in the Declaration of Human Rights have been embodied in a number of International Conventions, binding upon the states which ratify them; and in some cases the international machinery necessary to ensure the application of the Conventions has been established. The important conventions adopted by the General Assembly are—Convention on Genocide (1948), Conventaion on the Political Rights of Women (1952), Convention on Slavery (1956) and Convention on the Elimination of Racial Discrimination (1965). On 20th November, 1959 the General Assembly unanimously approved the 'Declaration of the Rights of the Child.' This Declaration contains a number of human rights and fundamental freedoms that are provided in the Universal Declaration of Human Rights of 1948.

The U.N. has been able to do lot for the promotion of human rights and fundamental freedoms. The General Assembly has repeatedly declared that the policies of apartheid pursued by the Government of South Africa are a negation of the U.N. Character and constitute a crime against humanity. From 1952 to 1960, the General Assembly made repeated appeals to the South African Government to revise its policy on this question in accordance with the principles of the U.N. Charter. In its resolutions adopted in 1963 and 1964, the Security Council called on all states to implement an arms embargo against South Africa. In 1965 the General Assembly appealed to all states to stop their economic collaboration with South Africa. In 1970, the General Assembly made a General appeal for contributing moral, political and material assistance to the people of South Africa in their legitimate struggle against apartheid. The General Assembly established the United Nations Trust Fund for South Africa to provide legal assistance, relief and education to the oppressed people of South Africa, March 21, is celebrated as "International Day for the Elimination of Racial Discrimination." The General Assembly designated 1968 as the "International year for Human Rights." and 1971 as the "International year for Action to combat Racism and Racial Discrimination."

In spite of whatever has been done by the United Nation for the protection and promotion of human rights. It has not yet become a reality with regard to its universal obseravance. There is no U.N. machinery to provide any assistance in case there is any violation of human rights. The interpretation and very implementation of these have been left to the concerned states. Owing to the differences in

the values and attitudes of the states, it appears difficult to achieve a uniform standard of human rights.

The Universal observance of human rights would promote the ideals of freedom, justice and peace in the world. It would also help in the advancement of international co-operation and good-will. But this has given a great set back to anti-democratic, imperialist and colonialist forces. It is hoped that the states would be more and more inclined to fulfil their obligations under the Charter to promote respect for, and observance of human rights and freedoms in deference to the world public opinion.

Strictly speaking, human rights are concerned with the individual states and it is their concern to make provision of fundamental rights and freedoms for their citizens. Every sovereign states by it own laws provides for the relationship between the state and its citizens, It is the domestic jurisdiction of every state and the same is determined by its municipal law. The United Nations cannot compel the states in regard to the fundamental rights and freedom as it would be an interference in the domestic affairs of the states. Though the states which have ratified the international covenants on human rights are bound by it, but the question of interpretation and the very implementation of these rights rest with the individual states. In the prevailing international system it is a moot question whether the scheme of fundamental rights will really be implemented by the sovereign states. Human rights constitute a universal ideal and it is suggested, that this can realised only by the establishment of a world government. For universal enforcement of human rights, perhaps, it appears necessary to exercise binding authority upon the states and to impose some limitation on their sovereignty. Since this does not seem feasible, the only course available is to rely upon the force for moral pressure and the constant reminder of the rights embodied in the Universal Declaration of Human Rights and the obligations under the Charter in this regard. However, the world organisation is no completely unconcerned about this question as the protection of human rights has ceased to be exclusive jurisdiction of states and has become the legitimate concern of the United Nations and its members.

IMPACT ON WORLD POLITICS

One of the outstanding events of the mid-twentieth century has been the emergence of Asia and Africa. The countries in these two sub-continents emerged from the prison-cells of colonial rule and form the obscurity imposed by the foreign rules. Between 1945 and 1960 almost one quarter of the world's population won political indepedence in these two continents. The collapse of colonialism marked the dawn of a new era.

But all these states, with the exception of Japan, are suffering from the chronic of poverty, unemployment, illiteracy and disease. These problems were mainly the creation of the Colonialism which involved the capture of overseas markets for raw material and compulsory dumping of manufactured goods.

Most of the Afro-Asian countries on the eve of their independence were poor, lacked factories of their own, had insufficient roads and railways and poor communications. Most of the people were illiterate and there were very few institutions of higher learning. Their banking system was very poor. They exported only raw materials, ores or some stable products. Mostly the exploitation of these sources of export was in the hands of the foreign companies.

After their independence most of the Afro-Asian countries embarked on the path of achieving democracy and liberation in the economic and social sphere. Majority of the countries embarked on national economic re-construction programmes with a view to achieve speedy development of their economies. Though majority of the countries like India, Burma and Ceylon in Asia and Guinea, Mali, Congo, Tanzania and the U.A.R. in Africa, have planned their development on socialistic lines, some other countries have stood against socialism. Thus the Asian and African sub-continents are witnessing a contest between socialism and capitalism.

Impact of Afro-Asian Resurgence on International Politics. The emergence of Afro-Asian countries has exercised profound influence on international politics.

(1) In the first place it gave death blow to imperialism. The independence of these countries gave a further stimulus to

liberation movements in other parts of the world. The race relations were also transformed into international relations. Earlier the racial problems were concerned as falling within the domestic jurisdiction of the state concerned. However, the Afro-Asian group by raising it quite frequently at the U.N. elevated it to the status of international problem.

(2) Another noteworthy feature is that in the international sphere most of the Afro-Asian countries are following the policy of peace and co-existence. This policy was an imperative need for them in view of the fact that they want to concentrate their resources for their national re-construction and development plans. These countries are convinced that involvement in power politics will certainly imply diversion of funds from development projects and will delay their development.

(3) The emergence of Afro-Asian countries have also strengthened international fraternity and narrowed down the sphere of exploitation. Both in Asia and Africa it gave rise to what is known as Pan-Asian and Pan-African movements. A number of conferences of the Asian and African states were held at New Delhi, Cairo, Bandung, Addis Ababa, Accra, etc. The common problems of these states were discussed and ways were explored to achieve quick development by mutual co-operation in these conferences. This unity of the Afro-Asian countries has been amply demonstrated by their co-operation in the United Nations.

(4) In the fourth place the awakening of Asian and African countries has strengthened the causes of neturalism in international politics..This concept was first evolved by the Asian countries and India played a leading role in this direction. Later the African countries also adopted this policy. It may be noted that there are certain states in these two sub-continents, which are still following either of the two blocs. But the number of the non-aligned countries is large. This policy of non-alignment was also dectated by

self-interests. The states of Asia and Africa are so much preoccupied with their nation-building and economic development projects that they had of necessity to keep out from bloc politics.

(5) In the fifth place with the independence of Afro-Asian countries there was an influx of new states in international relations, which has greatly complicated it. As Prof. Vernon Mackay says, "This striking increase obviously complicates international relations. It creates not only substantive problems but organizational difficulties for all the foreign offices of the world. It brings forth a large group of untrained and inexperienced diplomats dealing with unfamiliar tasks. "

(6) Lastly, the emergence of the Afro-Asian group in the United Nations has greatly affected the working of this world body. The states of these two regions have placed too much reliance on U.N. and sought solution of their multifarious problems through this forum. These states have depended on the U.N. particularly for the social and economic welfare activities. The Special Fund and the Technical Aid Programmes undertaken by the world body to accelerate the modernization process in these two continents are the examples in sight. These states have strengthened the basis of the U.N.O. by frequently and repeatedly pleading their loyalty to the U.N. Charter and the Universal Declaration of Human Rights. The attitude of the two Super Powers in the United Nations has also been greatly affected by the presence of such a large number of Afro-Asian countries. Both these powers try to win over these countries on the various issues because they are considered a vital element in international body. This Super Power's rivalry has also divided the Afro-Asian fraternity and solidarity against the colonialism.

❐

2

Emerging World Order

The post-war period witnessed the emergence of cold war in international relations. It continued to be the hallmark of the international system between 1945-70. In 1970s, a detente came to replace it. It produced several important and positive changes in the international system by way of producing agreements over several ticklish problems. However, this detente proved to be a short lived phenomenon and towards late 1970s a new cold war came to characterise international relations. It brought into operation several confrontations and disputes between the USA and the USSR, and produced several 'proxy wars' between them. 'Star War' programme of the USA and lack of progress towards disarmament and North-South dialogue over NIEO, kept the world divided and stained. The scene, however, started changing in mid 1980s more precisely since 1985 when Mr. Mikhail Gorbachev came to power in the USSR. Acting under the concepts of Perestroika and Glasnonst, he initiated several bold steps towards the promotion to peace, security and development, and the replacement of cold war with a new, positive and extensive detente between East and West.

The Breakthrough. A major breakthrough came in the form of INF Treaty between the USA and the USSR. Thereafter, the international system started changing rapidly and within 3 years it registerd several big development. These developments became instrumental in giving an end to the cold war. The liberalisation secured by the countries of eastern Europe, the emergence of Latvia, Estonia, Lithuania as independent states, the rise of several independent sovereign republics in the territory of the erstwhile USSR, rise of Russia as the successor state of the erstwhile USSR and its close relations with the USA and other Western Powers, the demolition of Berlin wall and the unity of West Germany and East Germany into a unified Germany, the invigorated role of the UN in the Post-Golf war era of international relations the end of wars in Afghanistan and Cambodia, emergence of West Asian peace process, recognition of Israel by several states including India, some success towards arms control and disarmament as reflected by the INF, START-I, START-II and the chemical weapons conventions, new international co-sciousness in favour of environment protection, preservation and securing of human rights, protection of international peace and promotion, spirit of peaceful coexistence and mutual cooperation of development, have been the new positive realities of international relations.

From Cold War to Post-Cold War International System. The following can be recorded as the major developments of the international relations of this last decade of the 20th century which fully reflect the end of cold war.

1. Relations between the USA and Russia have become warm and co-operative. Cold war strains and tensions replaced by regular, active and productive bilateral contacts co-operation for development in place of confrontation and conflict has come the develop. Between 1986-90, six summit level talks (Geneva, Reykjavik, Washington, Moscow, Malta and Washington) were held between the USA and the erstwhile USSR. There appeard a regular pattern of by continued contacts and negotiations at other levels.
2. Liberalisation and democratisation have come to characterise the political systems of Eastern European Countries—Poland, Czechoslovakia, Hungary, Romania and Bulgaria. East Germany willingly merged with the democratic West Germany to form one single united Germany. Within a short span of time (last few months of 1989 and early months of 1990) these states, acting under the impact of Perestroika and Glasnost in the erstwhile USSR, registered

a vital movement towards democracy and liberalism and against authoritarian socialism. These changes brought a new warmth and closeness in the relations between the Western and Eastern European states. As a result, ideological conflict between 'democracy' and 'socialism' got virtually ended and a new era of co-operation among all the European states emerged.

3. The biggest symbol and manifestation of cold war in Europe—the Berlin wall, got demolished. The people of 'two Germanies' began meeting as Germans. East Germany West Germany became a single state in 1991. Both the USA and the erstwhile USSR accepted the unification of Germany as a natural development.
4. Since the signing of INF Treaty in 1987, progress in the spheres of Disarmament and Arms control became a possible and attainable reality. START-I, START-II, the agreement to eliminate chemical weapons a self-imposed ban on nuclear tests have been very welcomc developments. Arms race appears to be getting diluted.
5. A new and welcome realisation in favour of international peace, security and development has come to dominate contemporary thought and relations.
6. Efforts are now on to give a new positive health to international economic relations. Uruguay Round of negotiations are designed to achieve the objective.
7. In 1990 the Soviet Union withdrew from Afghanistan. A good change in the US policy towards Afghanistan made its appearance. Iran-Iraq war came to an end. Namibia became independent and became 160th member of the UN. The two Koreas are inching towards a union, Nelson Mandela became free. ANC began getting bigger and bigger support in its fight against the apartheid in South Africa. NAM came to be an association of friends with similar in perceptions towards major international problems and issues. The vision of a non-nuclear, non-violent world by 2010

caught the imagination of the world. Things began getting stabilised in Central America. The 'Capitalist West' began giving economic aid to former 'Socialist East'. The UN started a more active and positive role in international relations. Kashmir issue began getting a maturer response from the USA and several other states of Europe. Peace movements started gaining a good ground. Some of the local wars came to an end.

8. The Middle East, which had been a big flash point, in the past, has been witnessing a peace process since September, 1993. PLO and Israel are now putting their heads together to iron out their differences as well as to stablise the peace process. Israel and Jordan have signed a peace accord and a similar one is expected between Israel and Syria. An Agreement on the issue of return of Golan heights to Syria is expected to be signed in near future.

9. The Angolan Peace Accord of November, 1994 had again given strength to the forces of peace.

10. NPT got an indefinite extension on May 11, 1995. The CTBT got a worldwide recognition. Now these must be followed up by a comperhensive global pact in favour of nuclear disarmament. Without it NPT & CTBT are bound to remain incomplete and discriminatory. The world is trying to bring home this fact to the nuclear powers.

11. The collapse of the USSR and the dependence of its successor state Russia on the USA and other western powers for foreign aid, paved the way for a big increase in the role of the USA as the sole surviving super power in world politics. The increased role and power of the USA began getting reflected in its dominance over the decision-making by the UN Security Council. However, in the process, the peace-keeping role of the United Nations got strengthened. It got engaged in peace keeping operations in several different parts of the globe from Cambodia to Somalia.

12. The end of cold war and several other changes which came to characterise international relations of late 1980s influenced a change in the role of NAM in world politics. The new environment of international relations gave additional strength to several international movements—the Planet Protection Movement, the Environment Protection Movement, the Arms Control and Nuclear Disarmament Movement, Human Rights Movement and above all the movement for liberalisation, democratisation and decentralisation. A new emphasis on globalisation and the growing commitment to preserve peace and use it for securing rapid around development have gained a good ground.

Commenting upon the new changes and the new thinking in international relations, Rasheed-ud din Khan has well observed (World Focus April, 1990): "Never in the history of international relations since the 1815 Concert of Vienna, such dramatic and drastic changes have taken place that have altered radically the basic premises of inter-state policies and indeed of global politics. Never have the principles of co-existence of diverse socio-political systems, in peace and co-operation with each other, been underlined as the only genuine and realistic basis of international politics, as has been done as a consequnce of the Gorbachev phenomenon since 1986."

As the humankind head for the 21th century the international system of last decade of the phenomenal 20th century shows the following new welcome features:

1. A new faith in peaceful coexistence and peaceful international intercourse among all members of the international community.
2. A vigorous commitment to international peace, security and development.
3. Increased awarenes towards the need for nuclear disarmament and arms control. INF, START and chemical weapons elimination agreement, fully reflect this new awareness. The acceptance of the ideal of a non-nuclear

non-violent world in the 21st century is emerging as a new positive reality.

4. Rejection of politics of Cold War and confrontations in favour of politics of peaceful co-exitence and co-operation for mutual development.
5. Increasing efforts towards international economic co-operation and development though global as well as regional institutional devices and processes. Functionalism has gained a new strength in relations among nations particularly of a region.
6. Rejection of the concepts of Balance of Terror, Nuclear deterrence and Mutually Assured Destruction in favour of a commitment to mutually assured survival through phased disarmament.
7. Increased awareness among the developing countries to secure their due rights thourgh South-South co-operation and attempts at equitable relations between the North and South.
8. Emphasis upon global economic development for securing the emergence of a unified, integrated, organic, inter-dependent world of shared peace and prosperity.
9. A new faith in the UN as a global institution catering to the developmental and other needs of the international community.
10. Emergence of a large number of well functioning international and regional functional orgainsations, agencies and associations.
11. Increasing faith in peaceful methods of conflict resolution in international relations.
12. Real globalisation of international relations and end of the era of a divided Europe.
13. Final end of Cold War in international relations, emergence of a maturer stable and enduring detente among former adversary states, end of ideological conflict between Western

(capitalist) Europe and Eastern (Socialist Europe, slow but definite progress towards disarmament and arms control, end of several local wars Iran-Iraq war, Angolan war, Afghanistan crisis), emergence of effective peace processes in Cambodia, Central American states, an Lebanon, the successful operation of the UN Peace keeping operations in various parts of the world, the emergence of strong world public opinion in favour of environment protection, development of peaceful technology, denuclearisation, human rights and widespread co-operation among all states for socio-economic-cultural development of the world, all have combined to give the contemporary international system a healthy look and health.

14. Warsaw Pact is dead. NATO too is bound to change despite the US decision to continue and expand it and keep unified Germany within its fold. Russia has become partner of NATO.
15. Rise of strong peace movements, planet protection movements, environmental movements and movements against apartheid, poverty and disease, have again given a new positive direction to international relations.

STRUGGLE OF AFRICAN PEOPLE

The African continent which was described as a 'dark continent' because it remained away from the pale of civilization , awoke in the post-World War II period. Most of the countries of this region have not only gained freedom but are also playing an important role in the international politics.

Awakening of Africa. The awakening of the African people in the present century was largely due to rise of extreme nationalism in Africa. The active participation of the Africans in Second World War and the divisions whithin the ranks of the Western powers in the post-World War II period encouraged them to overthrow the yoke of colonialism and imperialism. In addition as a result of education the African people developed a strong desire to assert themselves and attain independence.

Struggle Against France. The Africans under the control of France started struggle for independence soon after the Second World War was over. France had carved out an extensive colonial empire in Africa in the 19th century and always treated as a source of her economic and military power. Broadly speaking the African territories under French control fell into three categories. Firstly there were territories like Tunis and Moracco which were protectorates of France. They began to agitate for independence after Second World War. In Moracco, the Sultan, who used to be a puppet in the hands of the French Resident, assumed leadership of the Freedom movement and gained independence for his country after much resistance. Likewise Tunisia under Habib Bourguiba's leadership waged a struggle against French colonialism and earned an autonomous status in 1951.

But most violent agitation for freedom was launched by the Algerians. France was not willing to grant freedom to Algeria because of her strong economic interests in the territory. Further a large number of French men had settled down there and were not willing to withdraw on account of their strong economic interests and dominant position there. On the other hand, the Algerians were determined to overthrow the French. This resulted in long drawn out war between the French forces and freedom fighters. Despite all the repressive measures taken by the French, including bombardment of Algerian villages, the struggle continued to gain momentum. The Bandung Conference of 1955, also extended full support to the Algerian Movement for freedom. Thereafter the Moslem Algerians further stepped up their agitation. General De Gaulle tried to resolve the problem through use of force as well as negotiations but did not succeed. Ultimately as a result of plebiscite held in 1962 the people of Algeria voted for their independence and Algeria emerged as an independent country.

Struggle Against British. In The Post-World War II period the African countries under the control of British had not to wage that fierce struggle as they had to do against the French. The British realized that in the changed context it was not possible to keep the Africans under countrol for all times. Therefore, they adopted a policy of co-operation towards the Africans and began to prepare them for ultimate independence. Most of the African territories under their control were granted independence through negotiations. It may be observed that the British policy towards African colonies was more pragmatic and greatly contributed to the good-will which characterises her relations with these former colonies.

Struggle Against Belgium. Congo had to wage a bitter struggle against Belgium to gain independence. However, her problems assumed new dimensions after the Belgium withdrawal in 1960. As the people of Congo were not fully prepared to bear the responsibilities of self-government, the country was thrown into throes of civil war. The things were further complicated due to secession of province of Katanga. The violence and lawlessness increased to such an extent that the very existence of the country was threatened. The presence of the Belgian troops in country further aggravated the situation. In view of the fast deteriorating situation in the country the UN Security Council adopted a resolution for despatch of peace forces in Congo. The General Assembly directed the member states to refrain from any action that would impede restoration of order in Congo and appealed to the Congolese people to achieve unity through peaceful means. A Commission was appointed to restore peace among the rival political parties in Congo and bring the civil war between Congo and Katanga to an end.

Problems Confronting African States. Though the countries of Africa gained independence this did not mark an end to their problems. They are still confronted with numerous economic, social and political problems. Some of the problems which have confronted the independent countries of Africa are as follows:

Fristly, most of the African countries have tended to adopt new ideas and institutions which are often at variance with their traditions and beliefs. This has created a feeling of insecurity among the people who are not able to reconcile the new values and old traditions.

Secondly, independence of African people has greatly affected the outlook of the people and they have been asserting themselves more effectively.

Thirdly, the attainment of independence and adoption of new outlook has led to transformation of the social system of these countries and has left a deep impact on the life style of the people.

Fourthly, the emergence of African countries has given a serious set back to the policy of racialism which was a dominant feature of the colonial era. Now the African people are not willing to tolerate racialism any where and have extended full support to movements directed against policy of apartheid.

Fifthly, a strong Pan-African feeling has grown in the African countries which is highly dangerous bacause it tends to promote aggressive nationalism.

Sixthly, in most of the African countries monolithic governmental systems have made appearance because people are keen to achieve fast development. This has given set back to democratic forces and fostered dictatorial regimes.

Seventhly, the newly independent African countries have shown desire to force closer unity amongst various African countries so that they may become a force to be reckoned with in the international sphere. However, they have not been able to achieve much success in this direction because of social, economic and political differences among various countries of the region.

RESURGENCE OF AFRICA

The resurgence of Africa, (which was popularly designated as 'the Dark Continent') in the post-World War II period is one of the most important developments of the post-World War II period. The African continent which cover in one fifth of the land area of the globe and inhabited by nearly two hundred million people was almost entirely divided between four major colonial powers—France, Britain, Belgium and Portugal. Before First World War even Germany and Italy possessed certain colonies in Africa.

In the post-World War II period with the decline of imperialism and attainment of independence by large number of Asian states, the

Africans also felt the urge for liberty and built up pressure to free themselves. Between 1955 and 1970, most of the African countries attained independence. In the year 1960, alone 13 African states got independence. In 1968 also about 39 African states were given independence. Thus we can say with prof. Palmer and Perkins that "the emergence of Africa is a very recent development...A new Africa has emerged, an Africa of many independent states".

Problems Confronting African States. The attainment of independence by the African states did not solve all their problems. In fact they were confronted with numerous problems. As Palmer and Perkins has said, "As Africa emerges into the modern world, it is hampered by barriers of geography and of ignorance, by racial tensions, and social dislocations by the legacy of the past, by the problems arising from the struggle for racial equality, economic betterment and political independence, and by the effects of conflicts among the great powers and of the general international situation". The major problems which confronted the African states at the time of their independence, and to some extent even now, are as follws:

1. ***Nationalism.*** Nationalism in Africa emerged as a reaction against the rule of western powers, but considerably differs from the western nationalism. Often it is characterised by tribalism which has hampered the process of self-government. This also stands for elimination of aparthied, which had resulted in second class citizen status for the Africans in their own home-lands. In other words African nationalism lays emphasis on political as well as cultural aspects.
2. ***Lack of Political Awakening.*** Most of the African people at the time of independence lacked political awakening and consequently were not fit to manage their own government affairs. Their ignorance, poverty, and socio-cultural heritage also proved a great stumbling block in their way. As a result the democratic institutional could not work successfully in Africa because these were superimposed and were not evolved from within.

3. ***Failure of Democratic Institutions.*** Apart from the illiteracy and economic backwardness of the people which hampered the smooth working of democratic instutions, the predominance of tribalism has also greatly contributed to the failure of democracy and encouraged growth of miilitary dictatorship.

4. ***Tribalism.*** Another important problem which confronts the African countries is the problem of tribalism. The African society is composed of several tribes and sub-tribes which are often hostile to each other. This hostility has not only influenced the politics of these states but also resulted in frequent civil wars and revolutions.

5. ***Strong Separatist Tendencies.*** In most of the African countries strong separatist tendencies have been a common feature. This is largely the outcome of feeling of tribalism prevailing in these countries. Generally the tribesmen are intolerant of each other and are not willing to make any compromise. This has made the African society weak and incoherent and prevented it from playing an effective role in the elimination of poverty.

6. ***Border Disputes.*** Most of the African countries are involved in border disputes. These disputes are largely the result of the narrow policies adopted by the imperialist powers who tried to crave out countries on the basis of their influence and control. As a result often they created artificial geographical boundaries which gave rise to disputes among these states after they attained independence.

Efforts at Unity. Despite presence of various internal and external problems the African states have felt the need of co-operation to attain political stability and economic development. In fact the African leaders began their efforts to forge some sort of unity in the beginning of the present century when the first Pan African Conference was convened in London in 1900. In 1909 Dr. William Du established to National Association for the Advancement of the Coloured People to promote Pan Africanism. The First World

War provided a further fillip to African nationalism. After the war frequent conferences were held to take strong action against the strength and weaknesses of the Africans. These conferences were held at Paris (1919), Lisbon (1923), and New York (1927).

In the post-World War II period with the decline of imperialism and colonialism, most of the African countries attained independence. As they were keen to play an effective role in the international forums they tried to forge some sort of unity among themselves. This resulted in the formation of various orgainsations so that the African could raise a united voice and fight against exploitation.

Accra Conference 1958. The lead in the direction of forging untiy among the African states was taken by Kwame Nkrumah of Ghana. He convened a conference of the African states at Accra in December, 1958, which was attended by about 200 delegates from 28 states. At this conference these delegates discussed wide range of subjects of common interest and pledged to work for the independence of subjugated people of Africa and promote feeling of national unity among African. However, the objective of Africa unity could not be achieved because the different states of African motivated by their parochial interests refused to accept a common policy. In fact the African states got divided into two groups—Casablanca Group and Monrovia Group. The former group contained states like Ghana, Egypt, Algeria, Morocco, Mali and Guinea which were in favour of a free policy. These states agreed to co-operate with each other and set up a permanent secretariat, a military command and a common market. The other group consisted of states like Nigeria, Sierra Leone, Liberia, Libya, Ethiopia, Tunisia, Togo and Somalia. This group held a separate convention at Liberia. The formation of these two groups greatly undermined efforts at African unity.

Addis Ababa Conference. The next bid to bring about African Unity was made at the Addis Ababa (capital of Ethiopia) in May, 1963. This Conference was attended by 30 African states. The Conference emphasised the need of mutual co-operation among African states and called upon them to end imperialism in Africa. The Conference also decided to form the Organisation of African Unity (OAU), which became "by far the most significant and comprehensive organisation for African unity". The member of this organisation pledged to *(i)* extend utmost co-operation in the attainment of national independence of all African territories still under foreign domination; *(ii)* refrain from interfering in the internal affaris of one another; *(iii)* adopt pacific means for the settlement of disputes; *(iv)* respect the sovereignty and territorial integrity of one another; *(v)* follow the policy of non-alignment in their international relations. For the attainment of the above noted objectives it provided for an elaborate organisation consisting of the Assembly, the Council of Minister, the Secretariat, the Commission of Mediation, Conciliation and Arbitration and the Specialised Commissions.

The OAU has played an important role in promotion of African unity and almost all the states except South Africa and Rhodesia, have extended full co-operation to this organisation. It has not only tried to promote social and economic co-operation among the states of Africa but also rendered great serivce in creating a feeling to belonging to Africa. In the subsequent years the oraganisation played improtant role in resolving disputes between various African states *viz.*, Kenya-Somalia boundary dispute. Over the years the OAU has emerged as symbol of African resurgence.

IMPACT OF EMERGENCE OF AFRICA ON INTERNATIONAL POLITICS

The emergence of large number of African states from the yoke of colonial rule in the post-World War II period has lifted a deep impact on the course of international relations, though during the initial years of their independence the African states were not able to play as effective role as was expected of them due to their social, economic and political backwardness, but over the years they have come to play a significant role in international politics. This became possible because Africa is indispensable to all the big powers. In view of its vast reserves of raw materials, nutural resources and strategic importance no big power eager to establish its dominance over world, can afford to ignore the African states. No wonder both the Super Powers have tried to increase their influence in Africa and undermine the influence of their opponent.

The African states, like most of the newly independent countries of Asia and Latin America, have elected to keep aloof from power politics and adopted policy of non-alignment. This has greatly contributed to the strengthening of the non-alignment movement and reduction of tension between power blocs.

The African states in co-operation with the Asian states have laid emphasis on promotion of world peace. They have expressed open faith in disarmament, peaceful co-existence and international co-operation. The Afro-Asian countries on account of their numerical strength have been able to exercise profound influence on the activities of the United Nations.

The African states have lodged strong protests against policy of racial discrimination being pursued by the White regime of South Africa and inspired the anti-racialist elements all over the world to raise their voice against it.

Finally, the states of Africa have greatly enhanced the importance of the United Nations by expressing their full faith in the world body. They have repeatedly expressed their faith in the United Nations and pledged their loyalty to the UN Charter and Universal Declaration of Human Rights.

Hence we can say that the emergence of Africa has left a deep impact on international politics.

❑

3

International Political Geography

The roots of Political Geography reach back into ancient history. Plato (427 B.C.-347 B.C.) in his 'Republic' pointed out certain considerations, such as the relationship of state and land etc., which are of great importance for the modern political geographers. Julius Caesar (100 B.C.-44 B.C.) in his scholarly work Gallic Wars, Herodotus, the Greek scholar, Hecataeus, 'the father of ancient geography', Strato, Ptolemy and later geographers in the middle ages conceived the relationship between earth and man as they had imagined the relationship between man and stars. As such, all these scholars continued the slow develpoment of this subject. However, in all instances lack of documentation prevented these scholars from presenting this subject in a systematic way. As such during this period the evolution of Political Geography was an unnoticed part of the developmemt of the subject. However, it was only in the middle of the 17th century when a systematic attempt was made to establish the science of Political Geography. However, the history and development of Political Geography can be broken down in different centuries starting from 17th century.

POLITICAL GEOGRAPHY IN THE SEVENTEENTH CENTURY

In the middle of 17th century Dr. William Petty maintained that geography played a significant part in politics. His first word 'Town Survey' consists of the geographical development of towns. In this work Petty recognised the science of Political Geography. His other great work 'Political Arithmetic' was fully devoted to research on the inter-play between states and their geographical environment and comprises elements of political geography. His famous work 'Hiberniae Delineatio' was the first atlas of a whole country to be compiled in the field. His other works the 'Political Anatomy of Ireland', 'Treaties on Ireland' and the 'Essays in Political Arithmetic' are still today useful sources for the building of political geography. The theories which he depicted in these works deal with the state's geographical spheres of influence with population density, capital cities and the factors controlling man's activities. These are still today some of the major problems with which the modern political geographers are concerned. Petty's politico-geographical analyses and theories offered a superbly original conception of the geographical background of the like of a state. His ideas provide thought for further research in the field.

POLITICAL GEOGRAPHY IN THE EIGHTEENTH CENTURY

In the 18th century, Immanual Kant, the founder of modern geography, in the series of his lectures at the University of Konigsberg, defined the field of geography and futher sub-divided the subject, which he termed as Political Geography. As a consequence of the series of lectures Kant has been regarded as the father of Political Geography. His politico-geographical ideas produced great results among the Germans. The most noteworthy of his German disciples were Friedrich, Heinrich. Von Trcitschke, Alexander Von. Humboldt. Karl Ritter and Friedrich Ratzal. These German political geographers recognised the state's vital interest in matters relative to both space relations and power. Kant, in fact, played a vital role towards the development of political geography in the 18th century.

POLITICAL GEOGRAPHY IN THE NINETEENTH CENTURY

Perhaps the first systematic treatment of political geography was the publication of Ratzal's 'Politische Geographie'. Ratzal developed Political Geography to a great extent. He believed that the state was a union of the people and land, and was a spatial organism that grew in accordance with the processes of any other living organism. Ratzal made a close study of the earth, and its peoples and he felt that a close relationship existed between man and earth. This is the reason that he asserted, "Every state is made up of a portion of territory and humanity." He sought to determine the value of the soil and of the factors of physical geography in relation to the state. He regarded the soil as kind of Moloch 'ruling the destinies of the people with a blind brutality; the people must live upon soil allotted them by fate: there they must die in obedience of its laws.' Prof. Goblet remarks, "If Ratzal had written nothing but aphorisms of that sort his name would already have been forgotten, but political geography, which he served so well in other respects has atoned for them."

Prof. Ratzal conceived space as a political force of great importance. He believed that great size confers all rights and virtues upon states and particularly upon the German Empire. He asserted that frontiers were dynamic and reflected on the expansive force of aggressive countries. He also asserted that boundary questions often led to war because a boundary might be an obstacle to the growth of the state. Ratzal thus, took each problem systematically and treated it scientifically. His teachings were cultivated vigorously in Germany and later on were carried to many other countries. In Germany Political Geography became a political instrument of the state.

POLITICAL GEOGRAPHY IN THE TWENTIETH CENTURY

The real development of political geography was made during the 20th century and that too after World War II. However, in some of the states like Germany political geography developed immensely even in the early stages of the 20th century. However, for our convenience we shall note the history and development of political geography in different countries in the present century.

In Germany in the earlier stages stages of the 20th century, political geography became a political instrument of the state. German political geographers recognised the state's vital role in matters relating to both space relations and power. At the end of the First World War Germany received a crushing defeat. Soon after their defeat the German political geographers felt that political geography had declined with the defeat of the German Army. As such, there was a great need for a new name of the old subject in Germany. The German geographers found a new name 'Geopolitics' for the subject of Political Geography, the world which Kjellen had coined in Sweden the "adoption of the new term, Geopolitik" remarks George Renner, "fooled the German public into believing that here was something new, dynamic, and portentous os success: it enabled the German geographers themselves to escape the moral censorship of their science, and to side-step their own scientific consciences." After Kjellen's death in 1922, Karl Haushofer became the leading protahonist of Geopolitik.

The organisation for research of Geopolitics was estblished under the name Institute of Geopolitics (Institut fur Geopolitik). The institute worked under the direction of Karl Haushofer and his son Albert Haushofer. This institute attracted many political geographers. These scholars developed a considerable amount of Geopolitical data. "The basic, incontestable truth is that Haushofer directly in some instances, indirectly in others, co-ordinated, integrated, and rationalized the whole field of comparative geography for the use of the Fuehrer." As time went on the institute became an instrument for statecraft and a tool of the state. Edward Walsh remarks, "Geography, particularly war geography, became a national pre-occupation which influenced and moulded public opinion in post-war Germany from elementary school to university seminar, from street corner and book store to factory, club, beer hall, and dinner table." As such a considerable development of political geography was made in Germany.

In Great Britain, Sir Halfred Mackinder and James Fairgrieve were the outstanding political geographers who promoted the growth of political geography. Mackinder, who became the founder of the contemporary school of British Geography, contributed a number of standard works towards the development of political geography. The great works of Mackinder drew the attention of many geographers, who agreed with Mackinder that geography played a significant role in politics. Mackinder separated economic geography from political geography. The great efforts of Mackinder towards the development of political geography led to the establishment of the Royal Geographical Society in England. From the teachings of Mackinder and Herbertson the British School of Regional Geography was born.

In the United States, in the early part of the twentieth century economic geography was much developed by the American geographers. World War-I, however, drew some attention of the American geographers to political geography. However, not until World War II did the subject really achieve a standing in the United States. During the World War, the Americans became aware of the existence of political geography. As a result of this war numerous geographers in the U.S.A. were set to work plotting bombing objectives, analysing the concentration of enemy industries, rail roads and population etc. Scores of geographers were also engaged in topography and map study. Eventually, many army officer candidates were required to study Political Geography as a preparation for military leadership. It may be noted here that during the World War the Americans, because they had previously never heard of geopolitics, found that the whole field of knowledge concerning political geography was of recent origin. However, after World War II political geography as a subject of study within the academic environment achieved prestige in the United States. Among the outstanding political geographers of the U.S.A. who have considerably contributed to the development of the subject are Isaiah Bowman, Derwent Whittlesely, Nicholas J. Spykman etc.

After World War II political geography grew rapidly throughout the world. As a subject of study in the academic field it has now gained much popularity. It has now been recognised as a distinct field of study. This is perhaps the reason that some of the Indian Universities have introduced it as a separate paper in the post-graduate level. In countries like the U.S.S.R., France, Switzerland, political geography has been recognised as a distinct field of study. Its growth in these countries is very impressive. However, in some of the countries in the world it is still unrecognised as distinct field of study.

STAGES OF DEVELOPMENT OR EVOLUTION OF INTERNATIONAL POLITICS

As an academic discipline, the study of International Politics gained recognition and popularity only in the inter-war period. It was in 1919 that the first Chair of International Relations, called the Woodrow Wilson Chair, was founded at the University of Wales and two eminent historians Alfred Zimmerhn and C.K. Webster got the honour of being its first two occupants. This event marked a starting point in the development of International Relations as a subject of study.

However, the phenomenal growth in its popularity got underway only in the post-1945 period. The two World Wars of unprecedented and catastrophic magnitude, a considerably large number of more limited conflicts, a rapid increase in the number of sovereign nation-states, a growing interdependence among nations, emergence of a number of supra national and non-state actors, and the continuing threat of a final and ultimate holocaust have been the dominant factors of the period. These factors have forced men to attempt a clearer view and understanding of the complex field of international relations. To theorise the behaviour of states at international level with a view to strengthen the chances of peace against war, stability against anarchy and order against chaos, has been a major concern of the humankind.

The Four Stages of Evolution. Since the emergence of the new consciousness among the scholars to theorise international politics, the study of international relations has passed through several stages of development Kenneth W. Thompson has systematically analysed the development of international relations and has discussed its evolution in four stages :

(1) The Diplomatic History Stage,

(2) The Current Events Stage,

(3) The Law and Organisation Stage, and

(4) The Contemporary Stage.

FIRST STAGE

The Diplomatic History Stage. The first stage in the evolution of the subject stretched upto the end of the First World War and was dominated by the historians. "Before World War I," writes Schleicher, "there was almost no organised study of international relations either in American universities and colleges or elsewhere—although Paul S. Reinsch was pioneering in the field when, in 1900 he lectured on World Politics at the university of Wisconsin." In the few courses that existed there, initial efforts were little more than unsystematic and often superficial attempts to discuss a wide variety of current problems which differed greatly in the level of their importance.

The impact of World War I and its aftermath on the study and teaching of the subject was tremendous. The importance and necessity of the study of relations among nations was realised and this influenced the decision to provide an order to the attempt by establishing departments and chairs in various universities.

To begin with, the study was dominated by diplomatic historians and the attention was focussed on the study of history of diplomatic relations among nations. The scholars concentrated on the study of past history of political and diplomatic relations among nations. They adopted a chronological and descriptive approach and made no attempt to draw universal principles from their study of historical facts. Diplomatic historians enjoyed the monopoly and the relations and interactions among nations were presented as historical descriptions without reference to how various events and situations fitted into the general pattern of international behaviour. They also ignored the necessity of relating the present with the past. Their attempts brought to light certain interesting and important facts about past international relations but at the same time these failed to provide any meaningful help to the study of relations among nations during the inter-war years. This partial and one-sided approach did not render any material help towards the formulation of principles or theories of international relations. The descriptive and chronological studies conducted by the diplomatic historians did not satisfy either the need for the study of the relations of their time or the demands of the future development of the subject.

SECOND STAGE

The Current Events Stage. The experiences of war-time relations gave a new turn to the study of International Politics. The creation of the Woodrow Wilson Chair of International Relations at the University of Wales opened a new era in the study of the subject. The study of current events and problems came to be regarded as the central theme of international relations. The review of newspapers, periodicals and journals was considered to be the right and necessary step for understanding the day to day relations among nations. The scholars emphasised the need for the interpretation of current developments and problems at international level. An attempt was made to overcome the shortcomings of the first stage and replace the historical bias by attempts to concentrate upon the present.

However, in itself this second stage was almost as much incomplete, partial and inadequate as was the first stage. The first stage had been concerned with the study of past without relating it to the present. Similarly the current events stage was concerned with the present without attempting to trace the historical roots of the problems and events in the past. This stage also lacked an integral view of international relations in as much as it concentrated only on the study of present without any significant reference to the past. The unrelated approach adopted of this stage, consequently, failed to provide much help towards the development of an understanding and theorising of relations among nations. The failure to establish links with the past and the inability to assess the future possibilities made this stage a short lived stage.

THIRD STAGE

The Legal Institutional Stage. The third stage, which developed simultaneously with the second stage, constituted an attempt to reform the nature and content of international relations in future through the development of international law and institutions. Shocked by the sufferings inflicted by the First World War, the scholars adopted an idealistic outlook which focussed attention upon the task of reforming international relations by institutionalising these through the development of international institutions like the League of Nations and by codifying the rules of International Law—the body of rules governing the relations among nations. The Fourteen Points listed by President Wilson of the United States were together regarded as a Charter of Reforms for relations among nations. The Paris Peace Conference and the subsequent establishment of the League of nations gave strength to the optimism that it was possible and desirable to make efforts towards the improvement of international relations.

For this purpose the Legal-Institutionalists proposed three alternative approaches:

(1) Creation of supranational institutions for replacing the competitive and war prone system of territorial states.

(2) Securing a legal control of war by creating new international norms (Int. Law) for deterring the initiation of war and should it occur, its destructiveness.

(3) By eliminating weapons through global disarmament and arms control, peace should be strengthened.

The study of international relations at this third stage was influenced by the faith in goodness of human relations and consequently it sought to study and improve international law and institutions. War was looked upon as both a sin and an accident which was to be eliminated through institutionalisation of relations. It was believed that all international problems could be solved by developing a system of international law and by successfully working international organisations. The scholars at this stage were infused with a spirit of emotional and visionary reformism under the influence of which they sought to reform the future of international relations. The establishment of an ideal international society free from war came to be adopted as the ideal.

The approach at this stage was again partial and incomplete. It concentrated upon future without realising the importance of the past and present. It made no attempt to base the study of international relations upon an understanding of the past history and the current problems which faced the nations during the inter-war years. It ignored the hard realities of international relations and instead adopted an idealistic approach which was soon found to be superficial and inadequate. The outbreak of Second World War in 1939 proved the visionary and unhelpful nature of the third stage. No doubt this approach rightly stressed the need for strengthening peace at international level, yet the solution that it offered was almost utopian. The scholars were putting the cart before the horse by attempting to develop legal institutions and organisations without first trying to understand the true nature of international relations. Morgenthau has rightly remarked that, "Between the two World Wars, the scholars were concerned not with the understanding of the true nature of international relations but with the development of legal institutions and organisational devices which would supersede the type of international relations then existing."

Since the focus at this stage was narrow, the law and organisation approach failed to provide a durable basis to the highly dynamic international relations. The rise of dictatorships, aggressive nationalism and certain other factors, like the economic depression of the 1930s, made the matters worst for both the League of Nations and International Law.

FOURTH STAGE

The Contemporary Stage. Between 1919-1939 the study of international relations passed through three main stages—The Diplomatic History, The Current Events and Law and Organisation or the Political Reformism stages. All these three approaches were inadequate and partial. The first was past oriented, the second was obsessed with current problems and the third concentrated on idealistic reformism. None of these could provide a meaningful direction to the study of international relations.

Post-War Stage. ***(a) The Need for Theory-Building.*** The fourth stage in the study emerged after the end of Second World War. The deterioration in international situation which resulted into the outbreak of the Second World War in 1939 amply proved the shortcomings of the approaches of inter-war period. The need for new approaches capable of examining and explaining relations among nations was felt in a big way. The deep changes produced by Second World War and its impact upon the power structure at international level further made the task of developing new approaches to the study of international relations a really challenging task. A number of scholars came forward to meet the challenge and in the process there was initiated the fourth stage in the study of International Politics, which continues to constitute the present stage of the study of international relations.

(b) Emphasis Upon Study of All Factors and Forces and not only Institutions. In the fourth stage of development, the emphasis was shifted from law and organisations to the study of all factors and forces which condition and shape the behaviour of nations in the international environment. It was realised that there existed regular patterns in international behaviour which were far away from idealism. The role of power found acceptance as an incontrovertible fact of international relations. This realisation led to the emergence of political realism which advocated the study of International Politics as the struggle for power among nations. The emphasis came to be upon the study of the determinants and working of foreign policies. Further, the process of conflict-resolution at international level was accepted by many scholars as the field of research. The understanding of international relations through a realistic and objective study came to be accepted as the purpose of study. It was accepted that the aim was not to praise or condemn but to understand the nature of international issues. In place of the Institutional Approach, the Entity Oriented View came to be accepted. This view stressed the study of units of international relations. Study of international environment and the nature of interactions among the nations came to be a popular direction in the study of the subject.

(c) The Main Concern in Post-War Period. Since 1945, considerable progress has been secured in this direction. Many useful theories and approaches have come to be developed. The beginning was made in the late forties by the development of a Realist Model of International Politics particularly as formulated by Hans Morgenthau. Morgenthau's Realist Model advocated the study of International Politics as struggle for power among nations. It advocated National Power, National Interest and Foreign Policy as the fundamental units of study. The main concern came to be the study of:

(i) the motivating factors of foreign policies everywhere,

(ii) techniques of conduct of foreign policies, and

(iii) mode of resolution of international conflicts.

The study of international institutions now came to be conducted not from the legal and moral perspective but from the political perspective. For example the United Nations was viewed as a "political organisation designed not as a substitute of power politics but as an appropriate mechanism within which the direct national rivalries are compromised through normal processes."

In an age which had witnesses two World Wars within a short duration and which was witnessing the super power rivalry and cold war in international relations, it was natural for the Realities to define international politics as struggle for power in which each nation tried to secure the goals of its national interest by the use of power.

The 'realistic' posture of the Realists made it a power approach in the post-war years. But soon there appeared fissures which gradually fragmented the school. There emerged a strong difference of opinions over such questions as : Were alliances devices of peace or destabilisations? Did arms increased security or risks? Was cold war a blessing because it avoided the hot war or a curse since it kept the world on the brink of war? Did ideological conflicts serve or undetermine the national interest? It was felt that these questions cannot be answered on the basis of a theory. These needed empirical analysis and answers. Hence Behaviouralism or scientific approach which stood for empirical methods started becoming more popular than Political Realism.

(d) Emergence of Behaviouralism in International Politics. Under the impact of Behavioural Revolution in Politics, the political scientists studying international relations started formulating new approaches and methods for the study of international politics. The development of scientific approach in International Politics came as another landmark in the post-1945 development of the study of the subject. The inter-disciplinary focus as advocated by the Behaviouralists found favour with a large majority of scholars studying international relations. The scientific study of the substantive issues and problems of international relations came to a most popular direction. Along with this, the drive towards the development of more and more sophisticated methods and tools for the study of relations among nations appeared. All these attempts revolutionised the study of international relations. Considerable efforts were made toward the development of scientific theories of international behaviour.

Thus, in this fourth stage of the development of International Politics, there has come to be a big change. Its study has become and is still becoming, more and more systematic.

However, the highly complex nature and vast scope of international relations has kept limited the drive towards the development of universally acceptable theories and approaches. Diversity continues to characterise the field of study. "The scientific school", observes David Singer, "has produced more promise than performance." Nevertheless it must be accepted that it has made the study of the subject highly popular. The emergence of Post-behaviouralism and the acceptance of relevance (values) and action as the goals has now secured a combination of the Historical Tradition with the Scientific method of study. Systems Analysis, the Peace Research Approach, the World Order Approach and several other ideological a strategic perspectives have made the scope of study vast and the task of theory-building a challenging one. International Politics today continues to retain some of the classical directions but at the same time it has broken many old barriers and developed a host of new terms, concepts, approaches, methods, perspectives and theories. In fact, in this fourth stage of development International Politics is fast heading to be an autonomous discipline.

❐

4

Two World Wars

FIRST WORLD WAR

For about half a century before the out-break of First World War no major conflict or clash took place between the Western powers, even though all the major European powers, with the exception of England, continued to arm themselves. As a result of this race for armament a feeling of tension, rivalry and hostility prevailed among various European powers. This feeling of hostility and distrust ultimately burst out in the shape of First World War when Archduke Ferdinand, the heir to the Austrian throne was murdered. Actually the causes responsible for the outbreak of First World War lay much deeper and can be studied under following headings :

1. Secret Alliances. The basis of the First World War was the secret alliances. The Foreign Departments of the European powers had woven a fabric of crafty diplomacy around them.

The secret alliances and rival power blocks were a kind of curse of the age. It divided Europe into two hostile camps. In 1879 Germany made a secret alliance with Austria-Hungary. In 1882 A.D. Italy also became a party to the alliance which came to be known as Triple Alliance. Bismarck through his stroke of crafty diplomacy did not allow France and Russia to come closer to each other. In 1890 A.D. after the downfall of Bismarck Russia and France came closer to each other.

Kaiser William II adopted a comprehensive policy of world domination. It made England and other rival powers antagonistic to Germany. Edwards, a famous historian says: "After the death of Bismarck his Triple Alliance was confronted with the Triple Entente and the rivalry between the two was one of the causes of the Great

World War of 1914-18 which shattered the German Empire in the long run."

2. Militarism. The main causes of the World War was the compulsory military training. Almost all the administrative work was being done on a military basis. All the powers of Europe were increasing their naval strength. It led to a sprit of rivalry among the European powers. They were building warships and looking suspiciously at one another.

Eighty-five per cent of the national income of Germany and France was spent on war preparations. In 1913 the permanent strength of French army was 9 to 10 lakhs of soldiers whereas the permanent strength of Germany was eight lakhs and seventy thousand. Destructive weapons were made due to the scientific progress in that age.

3. Violent Forms of Nationalism. All the European countries loved their own individual nations. Germany was so blinded by this nationalistic zeal that it laboured under the idea that it was the world's best nation. Hence, she could not tolerate the rise of France. In the same manner England did not like the idea that other nations should make greater naval advance. All the nations, to foster their own interests, decried the other nations. Obsessed with the idea of nationalism, Russia and Serbia took upon their shoulders the task of the protection of the Slavaces and France on the other hand was getting mad for regaining Alsace and Lorrain.

4. False Propaganda. Almost all the papers of all the countries were freely indulging in false propaganda pouring venom against one another in their columns. Sometimes the disputed questions were discussed in such a manner that it made an injurious impact on the minds of the people.

5. Thirst for Colonies. All the European countries craved for the colonial expansion abroad. It created rivalry among them. Germany and England were at daggers drawn, in this respect, with each other.

6. Lack of International Sovereignty. Sings of chaos were visible all over Europe. There was no sovereign power to crush it down. All nations deemed themselves to be free agents and would do anything they liked with impunity. They even did not hesitate to violate international laws. There was no set policy of any nation. In order to gain their selfish ends they unscrupulously made pacts which made people lose faith in them.

7. Ignoring of Public Opinion. Public Opinion was ruthlessly ignored and violated in the European kingdoms. Only a few top officers were looking after the administration of their countries. The legislatures remained supremely ignorant about certain secrets of vital importance. Even the cabinets remained ignorant of the secret alliances formed in those days. The Parliament of England could not know about the negotiations made by Sir Edward Grey upto 1912 A.D., and they were made in 1906. Due to the secret alliances the people were terribly depressed. It created in them lack of faith in their own government.

8. Germany Acted on the Prussian Policy. The Prussian Policy embodied the saying that he who succeeds, is never in the wrong. Victory was rated much higher than spiritualism. It was said and a good war follows every cause. Germany acted on such principles and policies. The German leaders said that "after bloody victories the world will be healed by being Germanised."

Besides, the Germany believed that goods could only come out of German culture. Germany due to this feeling could not work in cooperation with England.

9. French Feeling of Revenge. Germany was badly trampling France under her heels. In 1871 she had snatched away Alsace and Lorrain from the French possession. It made the latter itch to avenge the loss. France wanted to snatch them back from Germany. National sentiments were beign awakened in France. In Morocco, Germany opposed France.

10. Policy of Austria. Austria always opposed Serbia in the Balkan Peninsula. Serbs lived in Austria. Hence, Austria apprehended that the Serbs might not rise in revolt against her on witnessing the rising glory of the kingdom of Serbs. They might not try to annex their kingdom to Serbia. Alexander, the ruler of Serbia, always maintained goods relations with Austrria though the Serbs did not like that attitude, but after his death, Peter, his successor, thought it wiser to cultivate friendship with Russia.

Austria had captured Bosnia and Herzegovina in 1908 A.D. In this manner she had violated the Treaty of Berlin. Many times Serbia had to accept terms of Austria which were unjust downright. Austria prevented Serbia from advancing towards Agean Sea in the Balkan wars.

11. Germany and the Eastern Policy. When Germany failed to achieve world supremacy in the country of European nations, she veered to have her sway in the east First of all the cultivated friendship with Turkey. She started expanding her influence in that region. She followed the Austrian policy in Balkan Peninsula. She opposed the policy of Russia. Germany asked Turkey to permit her to built Berlin-Baghdad Railway. It became a positive menace for the British Possessions in India. It became necessary for Germany to cultivate friendship with Austria without which the railway project could not materialise. It led Germany to crave for Austrian friendship. The other nations of Europe opposed the project.

12. Desire of Italy. The Italians wanted to possess the places near Trieste Harbour. Italians lived there, but they were under the rule of Austria-Hungary. A movement was launched in Italy to have the said places.

13. Immediate Cause of War. The immediate cause of war was the assassination of Prince Archduke Francies of Austria in Serajevo. The relations between Austria-Hungary and Serbia were already strained. In 1909 A.D. these relations grew all the more bitter. Bosnia and Herzegovina were getting ready to become independent. The Government of Serbia was giving help to both. A lot of propaganda was in the air against Austria-Hungary. As ill luck would have it, the Prince of Austria along with his royal consort, went over to Serajevo, the capital city of Bosnia. Completely overtaken by a blind spasm of zeal, some revolutionaries assassinated him and his wife.

Beginning of War. England and Germany did not want that war should become a world issue, but the President of France making a pact with Russia convinced her that she would help her in the war against Austria. Therefore, Germany declared war against France. England did not want to fight, but she could not help jumping into the conflagration of war siding with France and Russia.

It is a debatable question as to who should be held responsible for igniting the war. According to Ferdinand Scherille, the responsibility for igniting war, in a lesser or greater degree, devolves upon all the five powers—Austria, Germany, England, Russia and France, who while participating in it, made it a world war. Chancellor Bethmann Hollweg of Germany before declaring war criticised the foreign policy of the English, and held England responsible for it.

He roared out in the Lower House of Germany convincing the people that war was the immediate necessity of the time. He said "We are entering war with a clear conscience and the opportunity for reaping advantages of our hard labour for decades together has at last come to us. I am repeating the words of Kaiser. Our fleet is ready and the German army is already in the field."

In the same way Lord Asquith said in the British Parliament before he made the declaration of war. "We are fighting for two causes:

1. To preserve the solemn international obligations.
2. To see that no small or weak nation is preyed upon by the arbitrary will of a strong nation."

In short the Great War was a result of the animosities among the European powers, disturbances in the East, Franco-German hostility, hostility of Germany against Russia, England set against Germany, Russia set against Austria and the mutual animosity of Austria and Serbia. Austria declared war on 28th July, 1914 and immediately despatched her armies to invade Serbia.

RESULTS OF FIRST WORLD WAR

Following were the main results of the First World War:

1. Economic Loss. In this war thirty-two kingdoms on the side of the allies, and four kingdoms on the side of the axis had taken part. Only fourteen kingdoms remained neutral in the Great War. Two crore soldiers of Germany and four crores those of the allies took part in the war. The great economists of the world opine that some 58,50,000,000 rupees were spent in the course of warfare. It is said that even the entire wealth of the British empire cannot match the figures spent on this war, and the entire wealth of America of 1918 could not come up to the astronomical figures spent in this war. The average expenditure in the Great War ran to 80 crores of rupees per day, and in the last year it shot up to 84 crores rupees per day. Both sides had got involved in a debt of 40,000 crores; the big countries in particular, in 1918.

2. Human Destruction. George Bernard Shaw says that war is a necessary evil. To crave for world peace while involved in war is merely an empty dream. In the backstage of the adventure of war the vast destruction of man is hidden. These was vast destruction of humans in the Great war. It is presumed that in four years during which the war raged some eighty lakh people were killed. Ordinarily we can say above one crore and thirty lakh people were wounded. And nearly sixty lakhs of them were rendered invalid being fatally injured. 30 lakh soldiers of Germany and her allies were killed, and eighty lakhs were wounded.

Besides the combatants, civilians also had to lose their lives due to sea and air operations. It is surmised that among the civilians 692 Americans and 20,620 British citizens were drowned by German submarines. Three crore and twenty lakh persons were killed and met an unknown doom in the war. Those combatants who were killed in the war were all young. In this way all the nations had to suffer heavy losses. Such a destructive war had never occurred on the earth before.

3. Political Consequences

(a) Though the revolutions of 1830 and 1848 had sown the seeds of democracy in Europe, yet in Germany, Russia and Turkey the old monarchs were ruling and were vastly interested in preserving the tone of monarchy. But the great war saw the end of autocracy of the Monarchs. Kaiser William II, the Emperor, of Germany, left the throne and fled away to Holland. Now a democratic form of government was set up in Germany. Imitating her the German satellites too followed suit and established the democratic form of governments in their countries. In 1925 the Sultan of Turkey had also to tender resignation. He had to abdicate the throne. There also the democratic form of government was set up. In Russia the old grandeur and luxury of the crown was still going on, but at the time of the World War there took place a revolution. The crown had to surrender to the new forces and the people's government was established in that country.

(b) Due to the end of autocracy democracy set in Europe. Before this the concept of monarchy was being supported by the people, but with the leaving of the throne by the Emperor of Germany the democratic form of governments were set up in the kingdoms of Europe. Republics were established in Russia, Czechoslovakia, Germany, Austria, Poland, Lithuania, Latvia, Esthonia etc. In many kingdoms of Asia and Africa democratic forms of governments were set up. Due to the Great War the peoples of the world got an opportunity to take part in the political affairs.

(c) After the Great War all the nations saw the meteoric rise of the national sentiments. Now the people were of the opinion that the civilisation, culture and modes of living of the people should determine the formation of their country. The nations must be based on the concept of nationalism. Great emphasis was laid on the concept of nationalism in the Fourteen Points of Wilson, but the selfish members of the Peace Conference did not translate them into practice. But some nationals acted upon them in totality.

(d) The rulers, during the days of Great War, had behaved arbitrarily ignoring the importance of democracy. Efforts were being made for establishing world peace. Some autocrats putting on the mask of patriotism issued orders according to their own whims, which ultimately proved baneful for their country. Even after the end of war there were some who opposed the concept of democracy. Thus the reaction against democracy also came in the wake ot war. After the French Revolution the concept of liberty, equality and fraternity became current. The political rights of the people increased a great deal.

(e) Before the beginning of the war the rising militarism of Germany was taken to be the enemy of world peace. For that very reason the allies made a pact among themselves of destroy the power of Germany. Many restrictions were imposed on those nations after the war so that they may not enhance their military power. Yet, all the powers believed that military strength should be increased for development of their country. It was for that reason that the allies did not reduce their military stregth even after the Great War was over.

(f) During the Great War the nations came into contact with one another. Pacts and blocks were formed among them, and it gave rise to the sentiments of internationalism. The Industrial Revolution and the progress of science brought the kingdoms of the world closer to one another.

4. The Evolution of the League of Nations. The most significant result of the Great War was the establishment of the League of Nations. It was established with a view to solving the difficulties of the nations after the war. But as ill luck would have it Nazism, Fascism and Bolshevism made Germany. Italy, Russia and Spain to invest all the powers in a single ruler called a Dictator.

5. Economic Consequences of War

(a) Dearness of the Commodities. After the great war the prices went up spiralling which led to abject conditions of the people, Starvation stalked the world. At that time capitalism was evolved and the government restricted the prices of the commodities.

(b) Increase in the Taxes. The currency notes came into being because of the necessity of fabulous amounts required to the spent on war. Huge taxes were imposed on the people. Paper currency was introduced.

(c) ***The State Control of Trade and Socialism.*** Till then the entire trade was in the hands of the private sector, and the traders did not hesitate in selling and buying according to their personal whim. Capitalism was boosted up, and the personal capital increased much. The capitalists started exploiting the people which created great discontent among them.

(d) ***The Importance of Labourers Increased.*** At that time the importance of the labourers was also enhanced. Organising themselves they started agitating for their demands. For replenishing the war equipment many mills and factories were, established, and thousands of people worked in them. The workers of these factories were given all kinds of facilities. Hence, during the days of the war they also exploited the circumstances. They launched movements for the recognition of their rights and succeeded in extracting many rights from the mill-owners.

(e) ***Exchange of Debts and Loans.*** Almost all the kingdoms of the world took part in it. They raised loans from all possible quarters for maintaining their armies and ships. Devaluation came in the wake of War, and an economic crisis occurred in the European countries due to a fall in currency.

6. Social Consequences of War

(a) ***Feeling of Fraternity.*** Till now racialism was the name of Europeans. The English thought themselves to be of superior blood. In the same way French and Germans suffered from a self-pride on grounds of racial superiority. All the countries were gripped in the colour complex of white and black. Africans and Indians were looked down upon because of their being black. But in the wake of the Great War the evil came to an end to a certain degree. People of almost all the races participated in war. The Indian soldiers worked shoulder to shoulder with the whites of European countries. Africans also helped the Britishers.

(b) ***Progress in the Sphere of Women.*** Till now the world of a woman was confined to within the four walls of her home. She knew nothing beyond the domestic chores. Since many persons joined the war and crores of them were killed in the battlefields, now women were employed by the factories to keep them running smoothly. It expanded the scope work for women. They also started taking part to the political movements.

(c) ***Evolution of Atheism.*** The Great War made a tremendous impact upon Europeans. Christianity held its sway all over Europe. Christians laid great emphasis upon fraternity. But the Great War shattered all the religious dogmas. Politics came to eclipse religion. Even the pious veered from their religious course of thinking and thought to plans to destroy the opponents. It became a pious duty of all to destroy other nations and enhance the glory of their own. Under such circumstances the god-fearing attitude of the people was metamorphosed and atheism replaced their former mode of thinking. It gave birth to deceit among the people. The crafty diplomacy held its sway in the domain of politics. People thought in terms of discomfiting others in the sphere of politics. They looked at one other with a suspicious eye. They had no faith in the integrity of the people.

(d) ***Colonial Expansion, Imperialism and Evolution of Capitalism.*** As a result of the Great War the tendency of colonial expansion was generated among the European nations. Due to the aggressive form of nationalism all the nations were desirous of expanding their kingdoms. At that hour capitalism took birth. The mill-owners started having control on the prices of manufactured articles. It made a bad impression upon the politics of the world. The capitalism started harassing the workers.

(e) ***The Scientific Progress.*** Tremendous impact of war was made on science. Many inventions took place in that period. It revolutionised human life all over the world.

Ships, submarines and aeroplanes changed the entire technique of war. Some lethal gases were invented which reduced the duration of war. Had the modern scientific inventions not been used in the warfare, the war would have continued for a very long period.

(f) ***Lack of Education.*** Many institutions had to be closed down during the days of war. People had lost the human element and became diabolical in their attitude towards life. They adopted some evil ways in fighting the war. The young students were asked to join under conscription. Military training was made compulsory in the institutions.

SECOND WORLD WAR

Though invasion of Poland by Germany was the immediate cause for the out-break of World War II (like the Sarajevo Murder which led to First World War) The real causes for the out-break of the war were much deeper and varied in character.

1. Follies of Victors at Versailles. The germs of the Second World War were contained in the Treaty of Versailles concluded in 1919. This treaty was based on the spirit of revenge and Germany was forced to sign the treaty at the point of bayonet. She was not only deprived of her colonies, territories and natural resources but was also burdened with reparations which were beyond her capacity to pay. While analysing the injustice inherent in the Treaty of Versailles Carr observes: "Nearly every treaty which brings a war to an end is, in one sense, dictated peace; for a defeated power seldom accepts the consequences of its defeat willingly. But in the Treaty of Versailles the element of dictation was more apparent than in any previous peace treaty of modern times." This element of dictation and humiliation gave rise to the spirit of revenge and Germany started looking for an opportunity to tear off the Versailles treaty. The Nazi movement in Germany and the rise of Hitler gave a ray of hope to the German people. Soon after assuming power Hitler started demolishing the structure elaborately raised by the Treaty of Vesailles. Had the treaty of Versailles been drafted with a foresight and Germany meted with a lenient treatment, the Second World War might have been averted. Hence, the short-sighted and selfishness of the victor powers was the root cause of World War II.

2. Rise of Fascism in Italy. The rise of extreme nationalism in Italy in the shape of Fascism was also responsible for World War II. Mussolini, the Fascist leader glorified war, He said: "War alone bring upto their highest tension all human energies and puts the stamp of nobility upon people who have the courage to meet it." Italy began to think of reviving the glory of the Old Roman Empire. She annexed Abyssinia and annexed it, in Spain the Italian volunteers were able to place General Franco in the saddle. To strengthen her position Italy joined the Anti-Comintern Pact in 1937 and concluded a ten years alliance with Germany in 1939. Both the countries agreed to help each other if any one of them was involved in war.

3. Japanese Imperialism. Japanese imperialism was another cause of war. After World War I Japan secured many concession at the Peace Conference, which were to some extent taken away from her by the Washington Conference of 1921-22. But she was determined to dominate the Far East. In 1931 Japan intervened in Manchuria and in spite of League's opposition occupied it. In 1937 Japan started an un-declared war against China and captured her cities one after another. When the World War II started the Chinese war was still on. Japan had already joined Berlin Rome-Tokyo Axis, which gave a further impetus to Japanese programme of expansion and conquest. A war was inevitable under the circumstances.

4. Failure of Collective Security. After World War I the League was created with a view to eliminate war as an instrument of policy. League suffered an early blow when U.S.A. could not join League. Even other states who accepted membership of the League showed indifference to the principle of collective security. The coercive machinery of the League as not adequate to cope with the task entrusted to it. The economy sanctions were useless against a determined aggressor and further the states were not willing to apply the economic sanctions because it hit their economy adversely. Japan was the first country to hit the collective security system when she occupied Manchuria and attacked China. League failed to check Japan. When League censured Japan for her invasion of China, she left the League. Encouraged by Japan, Italy occupied Ethiopia in 1935 and Albania in 1936. Though League imposed economic sanction upon Italy the other members did not apply them. In 1936 German defined the Treaty of Versailles and re-armed herself. In 1938 she occupied Austria and Czechoslovakia by force. The League remained silent. In 1939 Russia attacked Finland, though this led to her expulsion from the League.

As the League failed to maintain international peace, the countries of Europe lost faith in its efficacy and entered into mutual political and military alliance.

5. Failure of Disarmament. Another cause, intimately connected with the above cause, was the failure of disarmament. Article 8 of the Covenant had enjoined on the members to take steps for the reduction of national armaments to the lowest point consistent with national safety. But as the League members had no faith in the system of Collective Security guaranted by the League, they entered into a race of re-armament. Due to mutual distrust of the members the various Conferences for Disarmament both within and outside the League failed the achieve much. Apart from Germany, who was compulsorily disarmed the only other country to reduce arms was England. After 1935 even Germany introduced conscription in violation of the Treaty of Versailles. The other totalitarian stats also followed the principale of 'guns before butter'. This race for armaments had disastrous result for the security of peace loving countries.

6. Attitude of Western Powers Towards Russia. Western power continued to treat Russia as an outcast. They were scared of Bolshevism and encouraged the Fascist and Pro-Fascist politicians in the west against Bolshevik expansion. The Western powers failed to realise that the Fascist aggression was directed not only against Russia but also against them. It was a folly on the part of the Western powers to have spurn the offers of friendship and truce made by Russia. Ultimately Russia got frustrated with the attitude of Western powers and concluded a no war pact with Germany.

7. Ideological Conflict. Another basic cause of World War II was the ideological conflict between Fascist states Germany, Italy and Japan and Democratic States Great Britain, France and U.S.A. Mussolini commenting about the ideological conflict remarked, "The struggle between the two worlds can permit no compromise—Either we or they." This conflict was inevitable due to their different approach. While the democratic countries stood for maintenance of *status quo*, the Fascist states were keen to expand. Japan was land hungry and was determined to establish her supremacy in the Far East. Germany and Italy also wanted to expand their territories. This inevitably involved a clash with the powers who were not willing to sacrifice their colonial empires.

8. Policy of Appeasement. The policy of appeasement adopted by England and France towards the 'Dictators' also contributed largely to the outbreak to World War II. The protagonist of appeasement policy felt that the dictators had a real cause of grievance. If their grievances were removed they would leave others alone. This policy of appeasement was also partly due to their desire to divert Germany towards Russian Bolshevism, of which they were mortally afraid. Therefore, Germany was allowed to rearm, to remilitarize the Rhineland, and capture Asturia and Czechoslovakia.

Thus the Second World War was the outcome of the follies of the Victors, rise of Fascism in Italy, Japanese imperialism, collapse of collective security, failure of disarmament, ideological conflict and the policy of appeasement pursued by Great Britain and France. Above all it was due to the ambitions of Germany who wanted to rule over the whole of the world.

CAUSES SECOND WORLD WAR

Following causes were responsible for the out break of Second World War in 1939:

(1) Unjust Treaty of Versailles. The Treaty of Versailles was made after the end of the First World War, and in this treaty Germany was insulted flagrantly. She was given no opportunity to have deliberations on any issue. Her empire was torn limb by limb. Her naval and military power was destroyed. Her national sentiments were crushed. It led to the flaring up of the wounded prestige of Germany.

(2) Imperialistic Interests. Imperialism was also one of the factors which contributed to the breaking out of the Second World War. Many kingdoms considered themselves weak, though they were militarily sound, when they viewed themselves in the light of their empires. Germany, Italy and Japan were such countries. From the point of view of militarism they were in no way inferior to Britain, America and France, but like them they did not command vast expanses of empire. Hence, imperialism was growing at their hearts. In order to pacify that hunger Italy captured Abyssinia and Japan captured Manchuria. Prompted by their successes.

(3) Rise of Hitler in Germany. The main cause of the Second World War was the establishment of Nazism by Hitler who while assuming all powers declared the regeneration of Germany. It made France and other countries of Europe anxious for their own security.

(4) Problem of Saar Valley. German armies had devastated the France where trade and industry had come to a standstill. As an act of revenge Germany had also to lose Saar, an industrial part of the country. It was kept under the supervision of the League of Nations for fifteen years under a Commission, and at the end of the specified period it was to be decided through a plebiscite whether she wanted to remain under Germany or to get away from her.

(5) Mixture of Different National Sentiments. After the First World War there was not even a trace of nationalism on the map of Europe as planned by the victors of the war. The races with entirely different cultures and modes were placed under such countries whose cultural outlook and language were entirely different from them. Many places inhabited by Germans were amputated from Germany, and placed under such powers where they could not possibly develop their culture and personality.

(6) New Ideologies. After the First World War, in various kingdoms, democratic set-up was introduced, but after some time revolutions like Bolshevism in Russia, Nazism in Germany and Fascism in Italy took place. Communism, Nazism, and Fascism churned the whole of Europe.

(7) Economic Crisis. After the First World War nationalism set in everywhere. All loved to use the indigenous goods, manufactured in their own countries. They patronised their own stuff and it shocked the industries of the big countries. At that time Germany declined to pay war repartations. Under those circumstances war became inevitable for running their mills and factories, so that the manufactured goods might be used.

(8) Rejection of Treaties. In the Peace Conference of Paris all the nations of the world had decided to make arrangements for their safety against wars. The strength of militry was fixed for all the individual countries, and they were forbidden to maintain more than what was prescribed. But with the rise of Nazism in Germany these conditions were flagrantly violated. First of all Hitler declared that he was not going to accept the conditions laid down in the Treaty of Versailles and the Peace Conference of Paris. Germany, thereafter withdrew herself from the League of Nations and captured Czechoslovakia and Austria.

(9) Failure of the League of Nations. The main cause of these Second World War was the failure of the League of Nations. Germany, Japan and Italy captured Austria, Manchuria and Abyssinia respectively. Weaker nations appealed to the League of Nations to prevent such aggressions, but it turned a deaf ear to their request.

SECOND WORLD WAR WAS INEVITABLE

The Second World War inevitable form of international conflicts born out of the instincts of preservation of imperialistic security. The following were the causes of it:

(1) Due to the phenomenal rise of Italy, Germany and Japan in the fourth decade of Twentieth Century (1931-1940) the problem of finding out new markets for the industrial goods, and to inhabit the rising populations erupted which could be solved by the policy of colonial expansion. This could only be achieved through invasions. Mussolini, the maker of the modern Italy, made a treaty with Hitler in 1936 through which it was decided that they would keep the level of their individual policies at par with each other.

In this manner Rome-Berlin Axis was made. The same year Germany and Japan made a treaty against Russia which also bore the signature of Mussolini. It created a new axis which was called Rome-Berlin-Tokyo axis. Gradually one by one, they gave up the membership of the League of Nations and formed a powerful block.

(2) At that time peace of Europe depended upon these two conflicting blocks. Every international problem increased hostilities between the two. In 1936 the Revolution of Spain made these blocks all the more hostile to each other, and the victory of General Franco was treated as the victory of Hitler and Mussolini. In order to fulfil his ambition. Mussolini captured Albania and Abyssinia.

In order to fulfil his imperialistic ambitions Hitler adopted a fierce policy, more aggressive than that adopted by Mussolini. He captured Czechoslovakia, Sudetanland and Austria one after the other. Encouraged by his series of conquests he placed a demand for a corridor from Poland to Danzing. France opposed it. England in support of the French move tried to curb the imperialistic designs of Hitler. As a result of it Hitler declared the non-aggression pact made with Russia on 23rd August 1939, which electrified the entire world.

As a matter of fact the First World War and the circumstances following in its wake made the Second World War inevitable. It could not be prevented in any way. Some nations did try to prevent it, but the other nations construed it to be their weakness, and that gave them an opportunity to enhance their imperialistic activities. Hence, these big nations started annexing the smaller ones to their kingdoms. Almost all the nations were busy manufacturing arms and ammunition on a large scale. Some countries, particularly the fascists, had made the military training compulsory. In this way Second World War became inevitable.

NATURE AND RESULTS OF THE SECOND WORLD WAR

This war was quite different from the wars which were fought face to face. Such scientific weapons were used in it, that they devasted all what they hit. Though the First World War also saw the use of scientific weapons but by now they had all the more been modernised, and the complexion of war had undergone a sea change. The First World War was merely a child's play as compared to the Second World War. Hence, it was presumed that party would win ultimately which could employ the most devastating weapons of war. Hitler had stored such weapons in a large quantity and depending upon them he had ignited the war. His policy of weapons is called in history as Blitzkrieg. The initial success in war for Hitler was due to his use of these scientific weapons. But gradually the allies too adopted the same tactics and impeded the progress of Hitler. Consequently, the hurling of the scientific weapons by the former, and the marvellous turn out of the weapons by them, succeeded in destroying the vast armies of Hitler his big factories and bases. It was a war of bombardments.

MAIN EVENTS OF THE SECOND GREAT WAR

1. Attack on Poland. On 1st September 1939 Germany invaded Poland because her unjust demands were not met by her. Before the invasion Germany and Russia had entered into a secret pact. Germany attacked Poland with all the air, land and naval forces at her command Poland failed to cope with the well equipped armies of Germany. Within a fortnight Germany captured Warsaw, the capital of Poland. On the other side Russia also attacked Poland, and both of them occupied her.

2. Russian Conquest of Finland. Russia wanted to capture Finland. She made a request to the government of Finland to give her certain ports and islands. When the latter refused to part with them, she invaded her and captured the places by force.

3. Conquest of Denmark and Norway. Germany invaded Norway on 9th April, 1940 and established a new government there. The same day Germany attacked Copenhagen, the capital of Denmark with the result that the former captured the latter. These victories led to the resignation of Chamberlain, the Prime Minister of England, and Churchill came into power.

4. Fall of Holland and Belgium. On 10th May, 1940 Germany invaded Holland. On 14th May the Dutch surrendered. Though they fought well and bravely yet they could not face the devastating weapons of the German command. Holland was captured by Germany. The Queen of Holland fled and took refuge in England. Germany invaded Belgium also. Germany attacked many cities of Belgium. On 27th May, 1940 the armies of Belgium had to surrender. The armies of the allies and Great Britain could pass with great difficulty through the port of Dunkirk.

5. Defeat of France. On 3rd June, 1940, Germany made a three-pronged attack against France. On 9th June, she succeeded in breaking the French Defence Line. She launched a four-sided attack on Paris. On 10th June Italy also declared war against France and invaded her. On 10th June Paris was captured by Germany. France surrendered on 22nd June, and an armistice was announced. The conditions of the armistice were strange. The armistice took place in the same railway compartment in which Germany herself had signed the papers in 1918 when the treaty was made with the allies.

6. War With Britain. The naval power of Germany was weaker than the naval power of Britain. Hence the former did not attack the latter by sea. On 8th August, 1940, air attacks were commenced. In the beginning Germany started bombarding the harbours of England, and after that London also became its target. Many German airships, perished in the war, and the tempo of her air attacks also dwindled after some time. Germany started laying magnetic mines in the path of the British harbours.

7. The Defeat of Yugoslavia and Greece. Hitler's attention was drawn towards Iran and Egypt. Hitler sent word to Greece that she must give some parts of her territory to him. Greece did not yet know that she had already been attacked. Italians had started the operation. The Greek armies fought very gallantly. German armies came to Italy's rescue. Meanwhile Germany made treaties with Hungary, Rumania, and Kangoria. Yugoslavia declined to have a pact. Germany attacked her on 6th April 1941 and within eleven days she succeeded in defeating her. Then she attacked Greece. The Britishers went to the rescue of Greece, but Germany succeeded in capturing her.

8. War in Syria, Iraq and Iran. Hitler craved to capture all the three countries, because that could provide him foothold for defeating Britishers. Germany wanted to increase her influence in Syria so that in future she might be able to capture her. But she could not succeed in her aim because Syria came under the sway of the Britishers. Germany also desired to take Iraq, and she succeeded partly because the ruler of that region, Rashid Ali, was sympathetic towards Germany. Many Germans went to Iraq, but the Britishers succeeded in capturing her too. Germany also tried to take Iran but Russia from the north and England from the south invaded her. Germany failed in her efforts.

9. Invasion of Russia. Germany was an avowed enemy of Russia. She considered her inimical to the European culture and Christianity. She wanted to capture the fertile tracts of Ukraine, her mines and oil wells. Hitler presumed that after the outbreak of war between Russia and Germany. Britain would stood to make peace with him. With that aim in view Hitler sent Hess to England, but could not succeed in his attempts. Still Germany made a three pronged attack against Russia on 22nd June, 1941.

Germany caputred Ukraine very soon. On 25th October German armies reached near Moscow and they fiercely attacked Moscow and Leningrad. Russian armies too fought gallantly and succeeded in their defence. When the winter set in Germany attacked Crime and captured her. After some time the Russian army started routing the German forces.

10. War of Africa. At that time England sought to put an end to the Italian possession in Africa. She succeeded in liberating Libya, Somaliland and Ethiopia from the clutches of Italy. Later on Germany despatched her armies to Africa. German General Rommel succeeded considerably as he defeated the British armies.

11. War in Europe. In the beginning of the summer of 1942 Germany invaded Russia. German armies reached Stalingrad successfully. On the other side Rommel was scoring victories in Africa, but soon the allies started defeating him. They captured Sicily. At the same time a movement was launched in Italy against Mussolini. He was taken prisoner.

12. Japan and America Entered the War. Japan wanted to dominate whole of Asia. She made an air attack on Pearl Harbour in 1940. The invasion put America to a great loss. Japan soon made air attacks on Shanghai, Hongkong, Malaya and Singapore, and sank two British ships. Japan again invaded philippine islands, and captured it. After that Japan captured Singapore. She also captured the New Guinea islands, and after some time captured. Sumatra, Java, Borneo and Bali islands. On 8th March, 1942, she captured Rangoon also. After capturing Burma she invaded India also from the north-east side but failed in her attempts. Latter on American and British armies took Burma in their possession.

13. End of War. British and American armies entered France through north-western border and started making invasions upon Germany. France was liberated. German armies were routed from Belgium, and then they freed Holland. In November 1944, the allies invaded Germany through land forces. German armies faced the enemies with great courage and gallantry. From the other side Russian armies entered Germany after winning many battles. The Russian armies liberated Czechoslovakia, Rummania, Austria etc., from the clutches of Germany, and invaded Berlin, the capital of Germany.

RESULTS OF THE SECOND WORLD WAR

(1) The vast destruction of material wealth and loss of human lives during the Second World War could not be reckoned even by the mathematicians, economists and statisticians. But it is definite that the nations which participated in the war, must have spent not less than one lakh crore rupees. Great Britain had to suffer in the vicinity of 2,000 crores *i.e.*, one fourth of the entire national wealth of Russia was sent in the war. No one has been able to compute the loss of countries like Germany, France and Poland, etc. In this devastating war nearly one and a half crores of people were killed on both the sides.

(2) The second result of the war was that the European sovereignty was wiped away from Asia. At the end of the Second World War India, Ceylon, Burma, Malaya and Egypt enjoyed the

fruits of independence. British sovereignty came to an end in these countries. The possessions of France, Holland and Portugal in Asia ceased to exist, and the countries under them became free one by one.

(3) As a result of the Great War, the leadership of the world slipped off the hands of Great Britain and came to rest in those of Russia and America. Britain after liquidating her possessions could establish happy contacts with Pakistan, Ceylon, Burma and Egypt, and through that she could maintain a balance of power in the world largely dominated by Russia and Ammerica. Britain still commands a dignified position in the political sphere of the world. The scientific progress made during the World War invented atom bombs and many other destructive weapons which make a man shiver. The entire human race stands jeopardised lest it might become extinct any day. Nations like France, Italy and Spain could not afford to remain isolated from the world politics and sought to make contacts with powers like America.

The entire globe seemed to be divided by two different ideologies, that of America and Russia. Eastern Europe, China and other countries of south-east Asia have come under the Russian influence. On the other hand countries like Pakistan, Egypt, Arabia and Africa were largely influenced by the free American thinking.

IMPACT OF SECOND WORLD WAR

Under the impact of two world wars which took place during a short period of history, the nature of International Politics underwent a big change in the second half of the 20th century. Under the impact of the Second World War, particularly the changes that it produced in the power structure at the international level as well as due to the emergence of several new factors, the nature and content of international politics underwent a big, rather a total and revolutionary change. This, however, does not mean that there appeared a total break with the past. The influence of past exists, certain old dimensions continued to be operative but the approach and style of international relations of post-1945 era came to be different from the past. As an academic discipline, International Politics ushered out of the age of history, legal-institutionalism and reformism and entered the era of the study of all the factors and forces which condition and shape the relations among nations. It came to be characterised by a large number of new approaches, models, concepts and theories. It began its march towards the achievement of a universal recognition as an autonomous subject of study. This change came not by itself but by reasons of deep and far reaching changes in the structure and functioning of the international system which took place under the impact of the Second World War and several other developments.

The impact of the Second World War, on the international relations can be discussed as under:

1. Recognition of the Role of Power in International Relations. In the post-war period the factor of power came to be accepted as an incontrovertible fact of international politics. It was realised that a nation always uses power to secure the goals of her national interest and that the role of power in international relations is direct and nature of interactions among nations reflect a continuous struggle for power. To analyse international politics as a struggle for power or as a set of interactions involving power, came to be a very popular approach in International Politics. This necessitated the drive to evaluate National Power and National Interest. Since, it was through its foreign policy that a nation sought to exercise its power for securing the goals of national interest, the study of foreign policy also came to be a vital part of the study of International Politics. Further, the recognition of the role of power led to a rejection of idealistic view of politics.

2. End of the Traditional International Power Structure. The Second World War destroyed the old power structure in international relations and replaced it with a really new power structure. Before the war, only European nations, particularly England, France, Germany and Italy, were the major actors in world politics. The USA used to follow isolationalism and the USSR after 1917, remained fully occupied with the process of internal consolidation of the socialist system. The Second World War destroyed the old power system:

(i) Germany and Italy became very weak as a result of their defeat in war.

(ii) England and France also became weak powers due to the heavy war losses suffered by them.

(iii) Europe lost its position as the epicentre of international politics and instead became a continent faced with a serious problem of economic reconstruction.

(iv) The war destroyed the balance of power system in Europe and there appeared a power vacuum.

(v) A weak Europe set the stage for the liberation of Asian and African countries from the clutches of imperialism and colonialism.

(vi) The weakened position of formerly powerful European nations paved the way for the emergence of two newcomers—America and the USSR, as the two super powers.

These changes in power structure as well as certain other related changes produced a big change in the nature of international politics of the post-war period.

3. Emergence of Bipolarity. The emergence of cold war led to the organisation of their respective camps by both the USA and the USSR. The USA floated a large number of bilateral and multilateral alliances like NATO, SEATO, CENTO, ANZUS etc., for consolidating the democratic anti-communist countries under its own leadership. The USSR countered the move by organising the communist countries into the Warsaw Pact. These developments led to the emergence of two hostile camps—The US Bloc and the Soviet-Bloc, or the anti-communist axis and the Communist axis in world politics.

4. Decolonisation and Rise of New Sovereign States in International Relations. The world political map underwent big and rapid changes in the post-war period. After the World War II, the weakened position of the European imperial powers and the strengthened spirit of national self-determination and liberation among the imperialised nations became instrumental in securing a big decline, rather liquidation, of colonialism and imperialism in world politics. The anti-imperialism, anti-colonialism movement began registering a stupendous success.

After the end of Second World War in 1945, several nations of the world, particularly Asian and African nations, were successful in overthrowing the yoke of colonialism and imperialism and in securing their independence. There came to be big increase in the number of sovereign states in the World. Rise of new sovereign states in Asia, Africa and Latin American began giving a completely new look to the world map and international relations. The U.N. membership was only 51 in 1945, and within 25 years it registered a three fold increase. This big increase in the number of sovereign states made international relations highly complex and problematic. The problem of multi-state interest became a fact of post-war, international relations. Management of conflict became more difficult. The predominance of small nations and their commitment to preserve their identity and national interests came as new developments in international relations. The end of European domination of other continents gave a truly global dimension to international relations.

5. Emergence of Cold War. The emergence of the USA and the USSR as two super-powers with strong ideological rivalry led to the emergence of Cold War in post-war international relations. After the war, the USA decided to use its superior economic and military position for filling the power vacuum in Europe and for this end decided to win over the European nations through the grant of economic aid under the Marshall Plan. It also adopted the policy of fighting the menace resulting from the rapid spreading of communism. 'Containment of Communism' and 'Massive Retaliation' became primary aims of the US Foreign Policy. Such an American attempt was thoroughly opposed by the USSR and it also decided to extend its influence in Europe. The success that it achieved in exporting the communist system to most of the East European countries emboldened it. The emergence of China as a communist power in 1949 gave further strength to Soviet-led communist movement. The USSR adopted the policy of challenging the US policies. In the process, there developed a cold-war in world politics which made international peace a risky and unstable one.

6. A Healthy Trend Towards Democratisation of Foreign Policy and International Relations. The end of Second World War rejeced the thesis of authoritarianism in favour of democracy and under its influence the formulation and implementation of foreign policy became democratic in nature and style. The strength that public opinion, pressure groups and political parties acquired within the domestic politics of every nation, acted as a source of big change in the making of foreign policy. Upto the end of 19th century, the foreign policy of a nation was formulated by a class of professional experts—the diplomats and the statesmen. It used to be a close preserve of the Foreign Office and Diplomacy. The democratisation of politics, however, made foreign policy an object of discussion and subjected it to the influence of the common man National public opinion, press and world public opinion came to be important factors of foreign policy. The whole society got associated with the formulation of foreign policy of a state. The changes in the nature, content and working of foreign policies of various nations resulted in a big change in the nature of post-war international relations.

The process is still on. World public opinion or national public opinion or both can force a change in direction and working of the foreign policy of any nation, whether big or small. The U.S. decision to withdraw from Vietnam, besides other factors, was also influenced by world public opinion. Iraq had to withdraw from Kuwait due to an internationally supported collective security war. It has been the world public opinion which has been checking the adoption of aggressive and narrow nationalistic policies by the members of present day international community. Today, no state can afford to support war and armament race or imperialism for fear of adverse world public opinion. Similarly, domestic public opinion has come to be an important factor of foreign policy decision making. Many examples can be quoted to prove this point. In 1962, Mr. Krishna Menon had to resign under pressure of domestic public opinion. Pakistani foreign policy continues to keep up the Kaşhmir issue under pressure of domestic public opinion. The pro-Israel content of U.S. foreign policy is determined by the strength that Jews enjoy in American public opinion. Further, the change in the role of the personnel—professional diplomats and military men, has been a source of big change in the nature of International Politics. The open conference diplomacy has given a new look and content to relations among nations.

7. The Age of Technology. In the post-1945 years, man's ability to use the knowledge of scientific inventions for the welfare of humankind got greatly enhanced. It was because of this fact that 20th century came to be described as the age of technology. Science and Technology began playing a big role in changing the scenario of International community. As a result of technological revolution, there began appearing a revolutionary development in spheres of industry, transport, communication, agriculture and military. The resultant economic growth became instrumental in producing big changes in the nature of international relations. The change in the concept of war from simple war to total war gave a new dimension to international relations. The revolutionary development in the fields of transport and communication increased the scope and frequency of relations among nations. The rapid technological development in the developed countries of the North made these countries economically and militarily stronger enough to maintain a neo-colonial control over the newly emerged developing countries. Their monopoly over advanced technology and the disinclination to share its benefits with all other nations made a sharp division among nations, the developed and the under-developed or developing.

8. Loss of Relevance of Balance of Power. Between 1815-1914, Balance of Power acted as a regulator of international relations. It suffered a death blow in the First World War. It was revived in 1919, with a new mechanism like the League of Nations. But it again flopped in 1939 when the Second World War broke out.

After the end of the Second World War several big structural changes in the International system as well in the Balance of Power system reduced the operationability of this device. The rise of two super powers, transformation of war into a total war, the emergence of nuclear weapons, the establishment of the United Nations, the emergence of the process of decline of imperialism-colonialism and several other such factors made Balance of Power system almost obsolete.

9. The Birth of Nuclear Age. The end of the Second World War came with the use of atomic weapons by the USA against Japan. It symbolised the beginning of nuclear age in International Politics. The coming of nuclear weapons, as a part of the revolutionary development in the military technology, came to be the most significant development of the first half of the 20th century. For the first time several countries came to acquire means capable of destroying the entire world. Since then the nuclear factor has come to be a vitally important factor which has changed the complexion of international relations in many ways:

(i) ***Over Kill Capacity of the Super Powers.*** First, it has divided the nations into nuclear nations and non-nuclear nations—the former enjoying superiority in power relations over the latter. The two super powers enjoyed, as Max Lerner observed, the capacity of "over kill". Both, the U.S.A. and U.S.S.R. could destroy the entire world but no other nation individually or collectively could destroy or defeat the super powers. The nuclear powers came to live with a highly dangerous and risky situation.

(ii) ***Defencelessness of the Non-Nuclear Nations.*** Secondly, the non-nuclear nations found themselves in a state of defencelessness because they had no means to defend their sovereignty and protect their people against a possible nuclear attack by any nuclear power. This state of defencelessness changed the concept of sovereignty and the state became unable to protect the life and property of the people.

(iii) ***Balance of Terror in Place of Balance of Power.*** Fourthly, the traditional concept of balance of power became obsolete in the face of the fact that it became impossible to create a preponderance of power against any aggressor backed by a nuclear power. The Balance of Power got replaced by Balance of Terror.The latter could, however, secure peace because nations feared the recourse to war as a means of settling disputes. This balance of terror was very dangerous and risky. A small misunderstanding or wrong judgment or even an accident could have caused a totally destructive nuclear holocaust.

(iv) ***Transformation of War into Total War.*** Thirdly, Nuclear weapons changed the nature of war from simple war to total war. These made the war totally destructive. No nation whether nuclear or non-nuclear, could hope to survive a future war since it was going to be a thermo-nuclear war.

(v) ***Less Possibility of Disarmament.*** Fifthly, the coming of nuclear weapons reduced the chances of disarmament and arms control. Instead, it gave an increased momentum to the development of more and more sophisticated nuclear weapons.

(vi) ***Use of Power Became More Difficult.*** Sixthly, Nuclear weapons made it difficult for the statesmen to assess the amount of force that could be used for securing the goals of national interest. Previously they could regard war as the ultimate means for securing the purpose but now they found it very difficult, if not impossible, to take into consideration war as a means of achieving their desired end. In 1945, only two atomic bombs were actually used. The big destruction caused by them however, prevented men from using the nuclear weapons. The world public opinion became totally against the use of these weapons and as such the policy makers of nuclear nations got in a dilemma, they had the means to destroy the enemy but they dared not use these. The Soviet decision to yield ground during the Cuban Missile crisis of 1962 and the US decision to withdraw from Vietnam supported such a logic.

10. Increasing Interdependence among Nations. After the end of the Second World War, international relations began developing a truly global character in which each nation began finding its national interests inseparably bound up with the interests of other nations as well as with international peace, security and development. This realisation and the interdependent nature of modern became instrumental in giving a vital and welcome strength to the cause of peaceful and cooperative international relations. Peace became a cherished value and it gave a purpose to International Politics—to find ways and means for securing and strengthening stable and durable peace in the world. The emergence of trends towards international integration, regional cooperation for development and increasing international cooperation came to be new and very hopeful developments of post-1945 period.

11. A Strong Desire for Peace. The two World Wars within a short span and the possibility of a much more destructive, rather totally destructive, Third World War made humankind highly conscious of the need for preserving and strengthening international peace and security. The urge for securing peace became stronger than ever before. There appeared a welcome peace movement in international relations. This encouraged nations to work for mutual welfare and development. They became highly conscious of the need for development through mutual cooperation and good will.

12. Need for a New Theoretical Order. The increased importance of International relations and their growing complexity together created a new interest among the political scientists to take up a serious and systematic study of international relations for building a theory of International Politics. Many scholars, writers and political scientists got engaged in developing new approaches, methods and theories for ordering their research in international politics. Under the influence of Behaviouralism, they started attempting hard to devise theories for interpreting and analysing facts of politics among nations. They were quite successful in their attempts and these helped International Politics to march on the road to get acceptance as an autonomous subject. In the words of Palmer and Perkins, "The new interest in theory, both normative and empirical, general and analytical, may be a sign that a discipline of international relations is at last beginning to emerge." The urge for analysing the relations among nations made international politics very popular and it became very helpful in securing a theoretical order in international politics. The formulation and execution of foreign policy began becoming more systematic than ever before.

AMERICAN-SOVIET RELATIONS

The First World War made Great Britain a second rate-power while the first position went to France. The Second World War degraded Great Britain still further while the prestige of France was totally destroyed. The U.S.A. Which had by the Second World War entered the international arena, emerged as the top-ranking power in the world. By the end of the Second World War, Soviet Union competed with the U.S.A. in prestige and power. The history of international-events after the Second World War is, in fact, a history of relations between the U.S.A. and the Soviet Union. It is because only these powers emerged as big powers while all other nations only revolved round them. This is what is termed as bipolarisation in the world.

Soviet-American Relations. The Soviet-American relations, after the Second World War, can be discussed under seven periods. They are:

1. The Stalin Era;
2. The Khrushchev Era;
3. The Brezhnev-Kosygin Era;
4. The Nixon Era;
5. Carter Era;
6. Reagan Era; and
7. Gorbachev Era.

1. The Stalin Era. The relations between the Soviet Union and the U.S.A., immediately after the Second World War, developed into one of hostility on account of the differences over various world issues. In the words of Palmer and Perkins: "For at least eight yeras, until 1953 post-war Soviet foreign policy was characterized by growing hostility to the West, by increasing tendencies towards non-co-operation and isolation, by consolidation of the Soviet orbit, and by general intransigence." They further said that, "These tendencies were encouraged by the Soviet re-interpretation of national interests, especially the means to security, and the strong reaction of the leading States of the non-Communist world to Russian moves and techniques." There was open conflict in their relations and the cold war turned into hot war in Korea. There was every possibility of this war turning into total war as China also joined North Korea. This conflict is clearly represented in the words of Philip, who said: "Post-Yalta shift from limited co-operation to an attitude of sharp rivalry."

2. The Khrushchev Era. Stalin's death in 1953, however, brought a qualitative change in the the Soviet-American relations. The Russian leadership became more co-operative and flexible towards the non-communist States also. They began to champion the theme of peaceful co-existence. Truce in Korea was signed in 1953, and in Indo-China in 1954. Eisenhower's 'atoms-for-peace' proposals were well-received and Russia herself advocated significant proposals on disarmament and the control of atomic energy. Molotov went to the extent of proposing a European Security Pact in March, 1954 which the U.S.A. could join.

The 20th Congress of the Communist Party of the Soviet Union held in 1956 proved a land-mark in the new look towards the West. At the Congress, Khrushchev "revealed an ideological flexibility and capacity for fresh manoeuvre in striking contrast with the rigidity of the later-day Stalinism." Khrushchev emphasised peaceful co-existence and the reduction of international tension. U.S.S.R. and the U.S.A. concluded three Pacts in 1963. The first related to the establishment of in 'hot-line' between Washington and Moscow in order to have direct link for discussion over the problems. The second aimed at their co-operation in certain programmes in the outer-space. It aimed at their co-operation in nuclear test ban treaty. This treaty was perhaps the most significant landmark in the Soviet-American relations. This treaty prohibited unclear tests except the underground ones. This was a major break-through in the quest for an end to the nuclear arms race. Both Soviet Union and America voted together perhaps only once in history against Israel to withdraw her forces from the Suez.

But according to Palmer and Perkins, "In actuality Soviet policy under Khrushchev alternated between a soft and a hard line at different periods, on different issues, and in different parts of the world." It was Khrushchev who threatened to precipitate a major crisis over Berlin in 1959. Again, in 1960 he walked out of the 'Paris Summit' conference in protest against the U-2 incident. U-2 was an American reconaissance aeroplane that was hit down by Soviet Union while flying over her territory. He even went to the extent of shoe-waving in the General Assembly and advocated the 'troika' proposal in place of the one Secretary General of the United Nations. He even asserted in January, 1961 that in case the Western powers continue to be stubborn 'we will adopt decisive measures.' The Cuba crisis showed the height of tension in Soviet American relations. The warning by Kennedy, however, had a sobering effect on Khrushchev who dismantled the nuclear warheads in Cuba. This really averted a potential threat to world peace and security. It is evident that thereafter Khrushchev never dared take any precipitating act during the Kennedy administration. He, however, reverted to hard line after Kennedy's assassination.

3. The Brezhnev-Kosygin Era. Khrushchev's fall in October, 1964 was caused, among other things due to his "softness" in dealing with the United States. Consequently, the new leadership appeared to adopt a hard line in its relations with the United States and other Western countries. It tried to reap harvest out of the France-American differences created by De Gaulle. It tried to enhance the Russian prestige at the cost of the United States in the 'Third World' and also in the Communist world. They tried to bring India and Pakistan together after the Indo-Pak war of 1965 through the Tashkent Declaration. This was conspicuously an effort to take Pakistan away from the U.S.A.

This trend, however, was soon reversed when Kosygin signed a historic treaty with West German Chancellor, Willy Brandt on August 12, 1970 agreeing on the inviolability of the frontiers of all States in Europe. In June, 1972, the Foreign Ministers of Soviet Russia, United States, Great Britain and France activated the Berlin accord. This act virtually enabled both the States to ensure detente in Europe, at least. The policy of confrontation and cold war changed into that of co-operation and understanding. As a result thereof, the non-proliferation treaty of 1968 was signed by them.

4. Nixon Era. The next phase in the Soviet-American relations started with the Nixon era. It was President Nixon of U.S.A. Who stole the march in relationship with Soviet Russia. This era came to achieve its full implications, in collaboration with Kissinger by the the middle of 1971 when Nixo adopted aggressive policy for the establishment of peace in the world. The era of the Soviet leaders was eclipsed by the activities of the Nixon administration in the world arena. The visit to China in February, 1972 of Nixon was followed by a visit to the Soviet Union in May, 1972. They held discussions on the basic problems of Soviet-American relations and the then international situation. The discussions covered a wide range of questions of mutual interest. Both the side were guided by their desire to strengthen peaceful relations with each other and to place these relations on the firmest possible basis. They make earnest effort to remove the threat of war and to create conditions which promote the reduction of tension in the world and strengthening of universal peace and international security. As a result of the progress made in negotiations, a number of significant agreements were reached. These are:

Treaty on the Limitation of Anti-Ballistic Missiles System. Both the sides agreed in reducing the danger of nuclear war and therefore signed a treaty for the Limitation of ABMs (Anit-Ballistic Missiles) under which each party undertook to limit the anit-ballistic missiles systems, and not to deploy ABM system for a defence of the territory of its country, and not to provide a base for such a defence, and not to deploy ABM system for the defence of an individual region.

Agreement on Limitation of Strategic Armaments. The parties undertook not to start construction of additional fixed land-based inter-continental ballistic missile launchers after July 1, 1972 and also not to convert land-based launchers for light ICBM's (Inter-Continental Ballistic Missiles) or for ICEM's of older types developes prior to 1964, into land based launchers for heavy ICBM's types deployed after that time. This was a concrete expression of the intention of the two sides to contribute to the relaxation in international tension.

Agreement on Co-operation in the Field of Medical Science and Public Health. The parties undertook to develop and extend mutually beneficial co-operatation in the field of medical science and public health particularly in co-ordinated scientific research programme and other activities in health, exchange of specialists, organisation of colloquial scientific conferences and lectures, and exchange of information. Under this treaty, the initial reserach efforts will concentrate on health problems concerning the whole, like cancer, heart disease, and the environmental health sciences.

Agreement on Co-operation in the Exploration and Use of Outer Space for Peaceful Purposes. The parties undertook to develop co-operation in the fields of space meteorology, study of national environment, exploration of near earth space, the moon and the planets, space biology and medicine and in particular to take appropriate measures to encourage and activate the fulfilment of the summary of the results of discussions on space co-operation between the Academy of Science U.S.S.R. and the NASA. (National Aeronautics and Space Administration) of U.S.A. The first joint docking experiment of the two countries plotted spacecrafts, with visits by astronauts and cosmonauts to each other's spacecraft, was contemplated for 1975.

Agreement on Co-operation in the Field of Environmental Protection. Both the parties undertook to develop co-operation in the filed of environmental protection on the basis of equality, reciprocity and mutual benefit. This co-operation will be aimed at solving the most important aspects of the problem of the environment, particularly air pollution, water pollution associated with agricultural production, influence of environment change on climate, etc. This will contribute to the preservation of a healthy environment not only in the respective countries, but also throughout the world.

Agreement on Co-operation in the Field of Science and Technology. Both the sides undertook to assist and develop scientific and technical co-operation between the two countries on the basis of mutual benefit, equality and reciprocity. The co-operation in science and technology will mean exchange of scientists and specialists, exchange of scientific and technical information and documentation, joint research, development and testing, and exchange of research results and experience. A Soviet-US Joint Commission of Scientific and Technical Co-operation will be created for identifying and establishing co-operative programme.

Agreement on the Prevention of Incidence on and over the Sea. Both the parties undertook to instruct the commanding officers of their respective ships to observe strictly the letter and spirit of the international regulations for preventing collisions at sea. This agreement will diminish the chances of dangerous accidents.

Review of World Situation. Besides these agreements, the international situation was also discussed to reach understanding regarding certain areas.

Disarmament Issues. The two sides not with the satisfaction their joint and parallel actions which helped the conclusions of treaties which curb the arms race or ban some of the most dangerous types of weapons. Both the sides regarded the Convention of Prohibition of the Development, Production and Stock-piling of Bacteriological and Toxic Weapons and on their destruction as an essential disarmament measures.

The Middle East. They affirmed their support for a peaceful settlement in the Middle East in accordance with the Security Council Resolution No. 242. They also confirmed their desire to contribute to Jarring Mission and to play their part in bringing about a peaceful settlement.

Indo-China. Both the sides put their respective standpoint to the continuing war in Vietnam and the situation in the area of Indo-China as a whole. The Soviet side stressed its solidarity with the struggle of the people of Vietnam, Laos and Cambodia for their freedom, independence and social progress. The U.S.A. emphasised the need to bring an end to the military conflict as soon as possible. Peace in Vietnam has been brought about. Cambodia has fallen into Communist hands. Laos has also broken with the United States confirming Communist influence.

Strengthening the United Nations. They regarded the United Nations an instrument for maintaining peace and security in the world which discourages conflicts and develops International co-operation. They pledged to do their best to support the United Nations in the interests of world-peace.

5. Carter Era. President Carter's utterances during and soon after election gave a new hope to the world that there will be less of tension in the world. The detente arrived at will be worked in its true spirit. The world will be made free of arms race. But all these hopes were soon dashed to the ground. President Carter insisted that he will stick to upholding Fundamental Rights of the people all over the world. Soviet Union took it as an American excuse in interfering with the communist systems. This had created a tension in Soviet-American relations.

President Carter had expressed has desire that the Indian Ocean should be completely demilitarised. But actually we find that the Diego Garcia base in the Indian Ocean is being allowed to remain as it was. This had given a chance to Soviet Union not to go by Carter's word. They took counter-measure in getting base in Ethopia. The United States accused that Soviet Russia's policy in Africa will lead to more tension in international politics. So, during the Carter administration relations between Russia and America again got strained. On the positive side, we can say that SALT II (Strategic Arms Limitation Treaty) had been signed between U.S.A. and Soviet Russia. This is indeed a remarkable achievement for peace in the world.

6. Reagan Era. Regan era was in fact an extension both of the Nixon and Carter eras in the sense that he had followed the Carter policy with respect to China and Russia and Nixon Policy with respect to South Asia. It was a result of the pursuit of this policy that a kind of Sino-U.S.-Pak axis came into existence.

7. Gorbachev Era. President Reagan became more popular at the end of his eight-year Presidency than when it began. He had started out as the coldest of cold was warriors but ended embracing the Russians and forgot to refer to them as the "evil empire."

It was all due to the efforts of Gorbachev who emerged as the most innovative leader on the international stage. It was in 1988 that the world as it had been set in since the late forties was changing too fast and too drastically. Tension decreased and drastic steps were taken to arrest the destruction of the global environment. There was end of the Iran-Iraq war; Soviet forces began to withdraw from Afghanistan; signature and implementation of the Intermediate Range Nuclear forces started; first step was taken to end war in Angola and secure the independence of Namibia; new efforts started to resolve the old problems of Kampuchea, Western Sahara and Cyprus; reapproachment between China and the Soviet Union started. Above all, it was the year when man actually began to destroy weapons. Americans went to the Soviet Union and watched missiles being dismantled and Russians went to America and did the same. American doctors impected Soviet mental hospitals where the Russians were accused of depositing their political prisoners.

What happened in the Soviet Union under Gorbachev was indeed breath taking that led, in effect, to the end of cold war. At home, he pursued the twin policy of Glasnost (openness) and Perestroika (restructuring) and became the most important leader of his time. By what he proclaimed at the UN General Assembly in December, 1988, he made himself the most innovative leader on the international stage as well. He pleaded that the world cannot be left to be regulated by the Super Powers alone. There should be multilateral co-operation to resolve pressing global issues. He gave a new impetus to arms control by declaring that the Soviet Union would unilaterally cut back Soviet armed forces by half a million men in the next two years, reduce Soviet conventional armaments substantially and to withdraw troops from Eastern Europe. He made a forthright disclosure of the details of Soviet armed strength. The Soviet Union unveiled its plans to dismantle chemical weapons from 1989. At London, in April, 1989, he declared that the Soviet Union has decided to halt production of all weapons-grade enriched uranium from that year.

President Bush, on May 29, 1989 at Brussels, proposed a 20 per cent cut in US cambat troops in Europe as a part of a new NATO offer in negotiations with the Warsaw Pact in Vienna. On May 31, in West Germany, he said it was time to end the cold war and issued a challenge to the Soviet Union: "Let Europe be whole and free". Bush called on Moscow in re-uniting the divided city of Berlin and reconciling East and West. Let Gorbachev tear down the Berlin Wall and join the West in making the city a centre of commerce in Europe.

Collapse of Soviet Union. In July, 1991 was signed at Moscow between Soviet Russia and united States the Strategic Arms Reduction Treaty under which 30 per cent cut would be applied to the nuclear arsenals of both the countries. They also agreed to do something to secure nuclear disarmament by other countries as well otherwise everything they are doing would become useless.

However, the policy of liberalisation adopted by Gorbachev led to collapse of Soviet Russia at home by December, 1991. The East European countries all went their own way and adopted non-Communist governments. The Warsaw Pact was given a good bye in April, 1991.

On the international stage Soviet Union existed no more. And the international stage has been occupied by the United States as single prominent actor.

CONSEQUENCES OF THE WAR ON INTERNATIONAL POLITICS

Such an eventful happening has had far reaching consequences for future world. The end of the War brought in many consequences. These were:

(1) Origin of Cold War and Conflict Among the Allies. The most remarkable result of the Second War was the end of the war-time alliance and co-operation among the Allies. The United States, Britain and France in close collaboration with Soviet Russia entered war against the Fascist powers. The Western powers including the United States and Soviet Russia entered into a close alliance forgetting their ideological differences. In fact, the United States and the Soviet Union came very close to each other. But after the end of the war, the war-time co-operation and friendship among the Allies dried up. Soviet Russia and the United States emerged from the war with more power and influence. Since the end of war, opposition and dispute between Soviet Russia and the Western powers power had grown up in place of war-time co-operation and understanding. Under the leadership of these two powers, the world had been spilt up into two rival blocs varying with each other for world leadership. This gave rise to bipolarity. Each bloc tried to win areas of influence and allies in all parts of the world. Militray pacts were also signed. Without leagally going to war, both the blocs tried to fight war by proxy in areas such as Middle East and Indo-China. The hostility (opposition) between these two rival blocs has been termed 'cold war'. Cold war means war of nerves. It is not actual war. It is a war in which the rival States try through all means, short of actual war, to gain supermacy at the cost of the rival State.

(2) International Problems. As a result of the war, Europe has lost its dominance over the rest of the world. It has been turned into a problem-ridden continent. Various problems that arose immediately at the close of the war have undermined the political unity and oneness of Europe. The rival blocs have kept it divided. As an outcome of the war, various problems arose which demanded immediate solution. The more pressing of these included the rehabilitation of millions of refugees; economic and cultural reconstruction of Europe; the capture and trial of the war criminals; the elimination of Nazism from Central Europe; the creation of an atmosphere helpful to the development of democratic institutions in Germany and the neighbouring regions; the drafting of peace treaties with the former enemy states; problem of atomic bomb and its reaction on international relations; perparation, restoration of world-trade; territorial readjustment; the rival claims of different races; disarmament and the rising nationalism in Africa and Asia.

(3) A Big Loss of Human Lives. It has not been possible to ascertain even today the extent of the loss both in human and material resources on account of the Second World War. However, it has been estimated that 5.4 crore persons lost their lives while 9 crores were injured and 2.8 crore disabled. Of the victorious States, Britain, France and Russia particularly sustained incalculable loss.

(4) Importance of Europe as a Trouble Spot. Both the World Wars were fought in Europe. This made the world statesmen realise the importance of Europe as a tension area in world affairs. The statesmen began to make efforts to avoid conflict in Europe. They saw in Europe as the only sport that could lead to world war. This has led to a spirit of securing peace in Europe. But the two blocs continued their skirmishes on other spots such as Indo-China and West Asia.

(5) A Great Change in the Balance of Power. There has been a great reorientation of the balance of power as result of the Second World War. The power and position of Germany and Italy in Europe underwent a great change. France had become weak and the former power and prestige of Britain had been greatly undermined. On the other side, Soviet Russia and the United States emerged from the war as the leading power of the world. Germany lost her political integrity and remained divided into two parts upto 1991. In Eastern Germany, a Communist Government had been installed while a democratic Federal Republic had been established in Western Germany. Consequently, mutual enemity of the two parts of Germany and the question of their unification had created a great complication in the present day international politics. After the World War, the situation in Europe was made worse by ideological considerations. Immediately after the war, almost everywhere in Eastern Europe, there began Communist movement. Poland, Rumania, Yugoslavia, Bulgaria, Czechoslovakia and Finland all came whithin the Soviet influence; As a result of the war, the independence of the States like Estonia, Latvia, Lithuania etc., had disappeared and Russia domination had been established in this hemisphere. Again, as an outcome of the war, Italy has been reduced to a third grade power. Italy has lost her African colonies and she had been compelled to surrender some parts of her own territory to Yugoslavia and Greece. Besides, monarchy has been abolished in Italy and a republican government has come into being. France has got back the two principalities of Alsace and Lorraine. But the former power and prestige of France has been largely undermined. Immediately after the war, anarchy and disturbances had swept Italy and France and communist activities had assumed a violent form in these two countries.

(6) Impact of the Second World War upon Asia and Africa. The impact of the second World War also fell upon Asia and Africa. Most of Asia was involved in the Second World War. Throughout the continent, the post-war years witnessed a restless and surging nationalism aimed at bringing to an end the Asiatic colonialism of the weakened Western powers. During the period between the two World Wars, Revolutionary movements in the Asian countries against the mastery of Europe assumed an Extensive nature and in many cases the ruling western powers were compelled to concede various facilities to their governed. But after the War, the nationalist movements in the Asian countries were transformed into armed revolt and many countries of this continent secured political independence or right of self-rule one after another. Consequently, the structure of European mastery collapsed. In August, 1947 independent India and Pakistan Came into existence, in 1949 Indonesia achieved independent, Burma and Ceylon (now Sri Lanka) also gained independence. Thereafter, Malaya and Singapore became independent. Four independent states came into existence in French Indo-China, *viz*, Vietnam, Vietminh, Cambodia and Laos. In 1949, Communist rule was established in China. Korea was divided into two parts—in Northern Korea Communist regaime had been established in collaboration with Communist China and Russia. In South Korea the influence of the United States had gained ground.

(7) Spread of Socialism. As a outcome of the World War, everywhere in the world, socialism has made a remarkable progress. In the under developed countries of Asia and Africa, serious attempts are being made to formulate economic plans based upon socialistic principles. In the Asian and African countries the governments have been taking great interest in regard to political and economic reconstruction.

❐

5

Emergence of Super Powers

SUPER POWERS IN SOUTH ASIA

Rivalry Between U.S.A. and U.S.S.R. The growing rivalry between U.S.A. and Soviet Union and China encouraged the outside powers to intervene in the affairs of South Asia. U.S.A. interfered in Pakistan due to its conflicts with India and Afghanistan. Soviet Union and China interfered in the region due to conflict between various countries. Therefore it was realised by the countries of the region that to prevent interference by outside powers they must co-operate with each other.

Vietnam Problem. Vietnam was the most important component of the Franch Indo-China empire. Due to her humiliating defeat in Europe during World War II, the Franch authority in Indo-China received a serious blow. After the fall of France in 1940, the Japanese moved in Indo-China. Under the Postdam agreement after the War, China occupied northern Indo-China down to the parallel and the British occupied the remainder.

Vietnam Nationalist Liberation Movement, 1941. A nationalist liberation movement was started in Vietnam, under Mr. Ho Chi Minh, the veteran Communist leader. In 1941 he called a Congress of Vietnamese nationalists from which the League for the Independence of Vietnam emerged. He also set up an under-ground organisation and built an army. When Japan surrendered, Ho Chi Minh set up the People's Liberation Committee of Vietnam. On August 22, 1945 he succeeded in setting up a provisional government in Vietnam.

Indo-China War, 1946. As France was anxious to retain her control over the Indo-China Empire, the Franch started re-conquering Vietnam from the south-northward after their installation in southern

Indo-China. Ho Chi Minh demanded complete freedom and the unification of the three provinces of Vietnam-Tonking, Annan and Cochin-China. The Franch refused to accept this demand of the Vietnamese and conceded freedom only within the Franch Union. No agreement could be reached and ultimately developed into a crisis. The Actual fighting broke out after the Franch bombardment on Haiphong in November, 1946. In December, Giap launched an offensive against the Franch in Tonking.

End of Franch Control. The Franch opened negotiations with Bao Dai, who agreed to the Franch proposal for independence within the Franch Union. He was appointed the head of the new Franch dominion composed of Tonking. Annam and Cochin-China. Great Britain and U.S.A. recognised the government of Bao-Dai. On the other hand, China and Russia recognised the Ho Chi Minh's Viet Minh Government.

Military Disaster of Franch, 1954. The Franch continued the war in Vietnam with the American money and American pressure. As the war progressed the hope of Franch victory in Vietnam became very dim. In France a campaign started for ending the war and opening negotiations with Ho Chi Minh. However, U.S.A. insisted on Franch to adopt a bolder plan to crush the Viet Minh. Under Navarre Plan Franch tried to build up military superiority based upon massive deliveries of American aid. It was wrecked by the brilliant offensive of Giap at Dien Bien Phu. On the night of May 6,1954 Giap won a decisive victory resulting in a military disaster for Franch. U.S.A. wanted "to use air and navel power in Indo-China" because she felt that the loss of Indo China would mean loss of entire South-East Asia.

The Geneva Agreement, 1954. On April 23, 1954. The Geneva Conference met to conclude armistice agreements covering Vietnam, Laos and Cambodia. It was attended by Cambodia, Laos, Democratic Republic of Vietnam, Soviet Russia, People's Republic of China, Vietnam, United States and Great Britain. In all eleven documents were signed at the Geneva Conference.

The Geneva Agreement decided for the partition of Vietnam. While the north went to the democratic Republic of Vietnam the south went to the Saigon Government. The partition was only a provisional arrangement. To unify Vietnam a free general election by secret ballot was to take place in July, 1956 under the supervision of the International Commission. The two smaller states of Laos and Cambodia were to be free of all foreign troops. There were to be no foreign military bases in the two zones of Vietnam. Franch was to withdraw her troops from Cambodia, Laos and Vietnam. The Governments of Conference also agreed to "respect the sovereignty and independence, the unity and the territorial integrity". of Cambodia, Laos and Vietnam. To supervise and control, Vietnam an international Control Commission was set up consisting of India, Poland and Canada.

Vietnam after Geneva Agreement. The Ganeva Conference had proposed that the two governments of Vietnam should discuss the arrangements for holding elections in the country. The Franch troops were withdrawn before the deadline but the Diem government feared that free elections would go against it. Therefore, with the support of U.S.A., it refused to participate in the consultative conferences and thus wrecked the prospects for the conduct of free elections. However, from the very beginning the Democratic Republic of Vietnam tried to faithfully follow the Geneva Agreement, and insisted on holding the proposed elections.

Political Instability in South Vietnam. There has been no political stability in South Vietnam since 1963. There were as many as nine coups. These frequent changes in government were mainly due to the attempt of the young army to help the Government of South Vietnam so that it can stand against the pressure from North Vietnam. U.S.A. sent military advisers to help the South Vietnamese government to fight the Communist danger.

US Backing of Diem Regime. Adopting the policy of backing of Diem regime U.S.A. undertook the military build-up of South Vietnam, as the nationalist alternative to the Viet Minh. The Diem government became extremely unpopular due to its anti-Buddhist policy. In Saigon frequent demonstrations were staged by the Buddhists against the anti-Buddhist policy of Diem government. In December 1960 a National Liberation Front of South Vietnam was formed in Cochin-China with the object of overthrowing the camouflaged colonial regime of American imperialism and the dictatorial regime of Diem and to institute a government of National Democratic Union. NLF built up a strong organisation and established control in the greater part of the country side in Cochin-China. In 1963, the Diem government was overthrown by a popular revolt and Diem was murdered along with his brother.

American Offensive. United States resorted to air attacks against North Vietnam after the Tonkin Gulf incident on the plea that Vietcong (National Liberation Front of South Vietnam) was being replenished with arms and men from North Vietnam. Thus the civil war in South Vietnam was gradually encouraged into a Big American war against Vietnam. As the American bombardment posed a serious threat to peace in South-East Asia, Russia warned that "The Soviet Union will be compelled, together with its allies and friends, to take further measures to ensure the security and strengthen the defence capacity of the Democratic Republic of Vietnam". Going a step further China publicly offered to help North Vietnam. In September, 1965. President Johnson of U.S.A. agreed to stop bombing and hold cease-fire dialogue if Hanoi stopped aid to Vietcong. But U.S.A. continued bombardment as there was no response from Hanoi.

EFFORTS TO SOLVE VIETNAM PROBLEM

Following efforts were taken to solve the Vietnam problem:

1. ***Bombing Stopped (December, 1965).*** U.S.A., stopped the bombing in the hope of some solution, but the government of North Vietnam laid down certain conditions for withdrawal of all troops from South Vietnam and negotiations with the Vietcong as the sole representative of the people of South Vietnam.
2. ***Direct Confrontation (April, 1966).*** Senator Mansfield of U.S.A. proposed 'direct confrontation' across a peace table, between the United States, China, North Vietnam and 'essential elements' from South Vietnam. The proposal was accepted by the government of U.S.A. It was promptly rejected by the North Government.

3. ***New Peace Plan (March, 1967).*** The then Secretary-General of the United Nations, formulated a new peace plan envisaging a cease-fire to be followed by a new Geneva Peace Conference in March, 1967. It was accepted by U.S.A. but rejected by North Vietnam on the plea that the U.N. had no right to interfere in the internal affairs of Vietnam.
4. ***Bombing Called Off (March, 1968).*** President Johnson of U.S.A. called off all U.S. bombing raids in North Vietnam with the exception of a small supply route area.
5. ***Meeting Agreed (April, 1968).*** The North Vietnamese government conveyed its willingness to meet the American representatives to consider the possibility of bringing an end to the fighting.
6. ***Peace Dead Lock (May 13, 1968).*** Harriman of U.S.A. and Thuy of North Vietnam met but the peace talks were deadlocked because both the sides reiterated their known stands and neither side showed any sign of making a concession that could end the stalemate.
7. ***Eight Point Peace Plan (May, 1969).*** President Nixon suggested an Eight Point Peace Plan, for a mutual and phased withdrawal of all foreign troops from South, Vietnam within twelve months and internationally supervised cease-fire line. Peace plan also envisaged free elections to determine the political future of South Vietnam earliest possible release of the prisoners of war and observance the Geneva Accord of 1954. North Vietnam insisted on total unconditional withdrawal of all American troops from South Vietnam and rejected peace plan.
8. ***Revolutionary Govt. (June, 1969).*** A provisional revolutionary government was set up in 'liberated' areas of South Vietnam. However, both U.S.A. and South Vietnamese government refused to recognise this 'illegal' government.
9. ***26 Men Committee (September, 1969).*** Ho chi Minh, the President of North Vietnam, died. He was succeeded by a 26-man committee, which continued the struggle.

10. ***Pulling Out Troops (December, 1969).*** President Nixon decided to pull out about 50 thousand American troops out of Vietnam by April 1970, and end up the residual force by 1972. However, this was not actually implemented.

11. ***Five Point Peace Plan (October, 1970).*** Nixon proposed a Five Point Peace Plan, which proposed *(i)* an internationally supervised standstill cease-fire throughout Indo-China, with both sides holding their present positions, *(ii)* Broadening of the Peace talks of Paris to include Loas. Cambodia as well as North and South Veitnam, *(iii)* Further withdrawal of the U.S.A. Forces, *(iv)* A political settlement to meet the aspirations of South Vietnamese, *(v)* Unconditional and immediate release of all prisoners of war held by both sides. The peace plan was rejected on the ground that it constituted an 'electoral gift certificate' legalising the American war of aggression in Indo-China.

12. ***Unlimited Cease-fire (January 24, 1973).*** A simultaneous announcement was made in Washington and Hanoi that U.S.A. and North Vietman had agreed on an unlimited cease-fire which was to begin on Sunday, January 28, 1973. Within sixty days of the case-fire the U.S.A. would withdraw all American troops stationed in South Veitnam and North Vietnam would release all Americans held by it as prisoners of war.

13. ***Formal Agreement (January 27, 1973).*** The Vietnam cease-fire agreement was formally signed in Paris by United States, Democratic Republic of Vietnam (North Vietnam), South Vietnam representing the P.R.G. The chief provisions of this agreement were *(i)* the cease-fire will continue indefinitely, *(ii)* All American prisoners of war in Indo-China would be released within sixty days of the cease-fire, *(iii)* All U.S. military personnel in South Vietnam would be withdrawn within sixty days; *(iv)* South Vietnamese troops and the forces of the P.R.G. would remain where they were at the time of cease-fire. *(v)* An international conference to acknowledge the signed

agreements to guarantee the ending of the war, and to maintain peace would be held within 30 days of the signing to the cease-fire; *(vi)* U.S.A. pledged not to continue its military intervention in the internal affairs of South Vietnam *(vii)* U.S.A. and other foreign countries involved in the war agreed to dismantle their military bases in South Vietnam within sixty days: *(viii)* U.S.A. and North Vietnam recognised the right of the people of South Vietnam to self-determination. The South Vietnamese were to decide their political future through genuinely free and democratic elections under international supervision; *(ix)* Saigon regime and the N.L.F. pledged that they would achieve national reconciliation and accord.

Four International Bodies. Four international bodies were set up for ensuring compliance of these terms: International Conference on Indo-China, The International Commission of Control and Supervision, a Four-Party Joint Military Commission and a Two-Party Joint Military Commission. After the withdrawal of American troops, the Saigon government could not withstand the National Liberation Front's onslaught. South Vietnam opted for union after N.L.F. assumed power in South Vietnam in the elections held in June, 1976. Thus the two Vietnamese were merged and the Republic of Vietnam was born.

Super-Powers *Vs* SAARC. To encounter the intrusive role of the superpowers the South Asian countries founded a regional organisation called SAARC (South Asian Association for Regional cooperation.) Its achievements were as follows:

1. ***Consultation Among Leaders.*** Since its establishment SAARC has raised high hopes of peace despite despite the slow progress of regional cooperation in South Asia. Its periodical meetings provide an opportunity for private consultation among the leaders of various member states. For example, the meetings of Dhaka and Bangalore provided an opportunity to the leaders of India and Pakistan and India and Sri Lanka respectively to iron out their differences

and greatly contributed tc the reduction of tension between these states.

2. ***New Confidence.*** The SAARC establishment does provide an instrument that might build new confidence by solving non-controversial, non-political problems. If that confidence can be built up the chances for solving the region's political, other than by military means, will have considerably improved.

3. ***Regional Cooperation.*** The countries of South Asia have come to realise that it is in their mutual interest to pool their knowledge and experience and their past differences should not be permitted to hamper their realisation.

Super Powers and Non-Alignment Movement. While explaining India's interpretation of non-alignment Shri Nehru himself said, "When freedom is menanced or justice threatened or aggression takes place, we cannot be or shall not be neutral." To act as a missionary of peace, India adopted a policy of non-alignment, positive decision to keep aloof from militarist pacts. India reserved the right to judge every international issue on its merit and to express her view freely and frankly without any fear and favour.

RECENT DEVELOPMENTS IN ARAB-ISRAEL CONFLICT

Rival Positions. It is proper to make an assessment of the rival stances of the Arabs and the Israelis.

Arab Policy. The Arabs tend to divide the process of attaining their objectives into two phases. For Israel's withdrawal to the 1949 armistic lines, Egypt and Jordan would probably agree to cease belligerency (Syria is less willing on this point), while true peace would reamain conditional on the settlement of the Palestinian problem, *i.e.*, the fulfilment of the Palestinian's demands. The pactical implication of these demands is the liquidation of Israel and the establishment in its place of an allegedly democratic Palestine State. The idea of liquidating Israel has surfaced even though the actual verb "to liquidate" is now rarely used explicity. Its meaning, however, is implied in the demand for the retoration of the 'rights' of the Palestinians.

Syrian Demand. Khalid Bakdash, Secretary General of the Syrian Communist Party, expressed the demand for Israel's annihilation in a speech at the National Congress November, 1971 as follows:

> "The solution to the Palestine problem lies in the struggle for the right of the Arab nation to return to its homeland and to achieve self-determination there. At present, this slogan is satisfactory. Determining the final detailed character of the Palestine problem is difficult...." Thus, when the Palest inians, or a majority of them, return to the country (many having been outside), and the Jews are forced to restrore their former property, new conditions will develop, in which will lie the Arab solution to the problem.

Lessons of October War. The October war taught the Arabs lessons of a mixed nature. They realized the impossibility of a military solution to tne dispute because of Israel's power. They also realize that Israel cannot defeat them thanks to their own strength and the intervension of the Great Powers.

In short, generally speaking, the Arab States may be ready for some kind of settlement with an emaciated Israel, assuming or hoping that the reduction in size will weaken it. Israel will suffer shocks and dissension, the Palestinians will continue the fight, and the essential end will come.

Arab Position. Harkabi believes that throughout the course of events Arab position has evinced a considerable degree of consistency, combined with a trend towards moderation in the presentation of the Arab case, but not necessarily in its contents. Arab behaviour in the conflict has been rather rational, they have adjusted to situations they could not change, and thus postponed the implementation of their ultimate objective.

Israels Policy. In the face of the Arab challenge two political approaches emerge in Israel. The first conceives of only limited withdrawal. In political jargon this attitude is termed 'hawkish'. Its proponents are alive to the internal perils which would be set an emaciated Israel and more so to the dangers to its very existence from without which it nedeed to make major withdrawal. Therefore, proponents of limited withdrawal advocate that a line of consolidation be delineated from which no further withdrawal be made regardless of circumstances. In all versions of this concept the line runs at a considerable distance from the pre-1967 armistice lines. It underates the significance of Israel's international problem if it sticks to the present boarders. Some prominent Israelis who take "hawkish" position seek support among those U.S. circles who are inclined to take a stronger stance towards the U.S.S.R.

The 'Dovish' Approach. The second position is more pragmatic. The "dovish" approach recognizes the need for more considerable withdrawal even approaching the pre-1967 lines. It cherishes the hope that in return for such concessions a permanent settlement with the Arab States may be achieved, an that the support and aid of the United States could be enlisted to register such a settlement. This approach undertakes the vehemence of the Arab position and its persistence and is thus willing to make concessions and to withdraw. It is more pessimistic about the effect of international isolation on Israel's capacity to resist, and optimistic about the chances of bringing the Arabs to a settlement under pressure of the interests which will emerge in the course of the negotiations and of international powers.

Israeli Needs. Harkabi belives that what Israel needs is a policy which combines both positions—the recognition of the gravity of the Arab challenge inherent in the first view together with the pragmatism and flexibility of the second. In other words, we may finally have to adopt the policy of "limited withdrawal", and it is that which will predominate. A clear refusal to make concessions may be damaging; concessions on secondary matters of borders will facilitate the adoption of a firm stand on the basic question of national survival. Although these concessions will worsen security situation, Israel needs them both for internal purposes—for the sake of national unity, to contradict the middle roaders who may maintain that Israel did not meet the Arabs half-way, and for external purposes—to ensure support and aid.

CENTO and the Baghdad Pact 1995. The Western security interests in Middle East led to the signing of the Baghdad Pact in 1955, which in 1958, got transformed into CENTO. Initially, Britain used to look after the defence of Middle East. However, due to its weakened position after World War II, and because a rise of strong anti-British sentiments as a result of the creation of Israel coupled with the rise of Arab Nationalism and the continued backwardness of the region, the U.S.A. and several Western powers were compelled to take steps for the security of Middle East. The strategic importance of Middle West for the security of Europe forced them to work for creating a security alliance system for this region.

Baghdad Pact. The first attempt of the Western powers, in the form of an anti-Soviet alliances in the Middle East, came in the form of Baghdad pact. It was British sponsored pact, though at first if did not join it. In 1955, this pact was signed between Turkey and Iraq and by it the two agreed to protect their security by joint measures. Later on, Britain, Pakistan and Persia joined this pact. A such this pact came to be a West-led move against Soviet interests in Middle East.

However, this act proved counter productive in so far as it attracted opposition from several Arab countries. Egypt, Syria and Saudi Arabia decided to take a neutral stand. The Anglo-Franch-Jewish attack on Suez in 1956, further made the environment unhealthy for the operation of this pact. The Soviet Union used the situation for building up anti-West feeling in this region and it was in a position to increase its influence over Egypt, Syria and Lebanon.

The CENTO. This increase in Soviet influence in Middle East greatly worried the United States. As a counter move, America stepped up its military and economic aid to some of the countries of the region, but at the same, time stopped giving aid to Egypt, Syria and Jordan. However, the pact received a set back when Iraq, after having undergone a coup, withdrew from the Pact in 1959. Thereafter, it came to be known as CENTO. The Central Treaty Organisation with Ankara as its head quarters.

IMPORTANCE OF MIDDLE EAST OIL

Middle East has been a cause of acute international friction because of its rich oil resources. From 1912 to 1939 the oil resources of the region were mainly exploited by the Anglo-Persian (subsequently Anglo-Iranian) Oil Company. During the war the Soviet-Iranian Oil Company was also formed. and the Iranians government agreed to grant oil concessions to this company in 1946. In view of the deteriorating, economic condition in the country, the monopolistic position of the Anglo-Iranian Company attracted the attention of the nationalists and a movement was directed against the economic domination of foreign capital. The announcement of Truman Doctrine by U.S.A. in 1947 and extension of a military credit of 25 million dollars had prompted the Iranian Government to cancel its agreement with the Soviet Government. In 1950-51 the National Front Government led by Dr. Mossaddeq began to clamour for nationalization of the Anglo-Iranian Oil Company. In this demand the government was supported by the Tudeh Party, this demand the government was supported by the Tudeh party, which contained some communist members also. On April 28, 1951, the Iranian Majlis (the Parliament of Iran) passed a bill nationalizing the Oil Industry. Soon he proceeded to implement the nationalization of the Anglo-Iranian Oil Company. In October all the foreign employees of the A.I.O.C. were withdrawn both from the oilfields and form Abadan refinery. As Britain was opposed to nationalization, she made an appeal to the International Court of Justice. The court directed the government of Iran to maintain *status quo*. The Government of Iran, however, refused to comply with the directions of the Court and withdrew from its membership.

The controversy over the question of nationalization and compensation continued to rage between Britain and Iran till August, 1953. During this period U.S.A. tried to intervene by offering financial aid, which was rejected by Iran. The British efforts to refer the case to Security and the Stokes Mussion also failed to move the Iranian Premier Mossaddeq. But due to lack of technical hands Iran failed to work the oil-fields, which greatly of affected its financial stability.

Although Premier Mossaddeq enjoyed great prestige he could not meet the crisis. The wealthy landowners who governed the country (who had been deprived of their huge royalties) were determined to oust him. Consequently, demonstrations were organised in the streets to denounce Mossaddeq. In August, 1953 the Shah of Iran appointed General Zahedi as Premier, who had emerged as a leader after the military coup. In September, 1953, President Eisenhower of U.S.A. granted 45 million dollars to Iran on the condition that the oil dispute should be settled. In August, 1954, Iran signed an agreement by which an International Consortium consisting of 8 Oil Companies was formed. Forty per cent shares were reserved for the Anglo-Iranian Oil Company. Henceforth, the Consortium was to carry on the production and marketing of Iranian oil on behalf of the Iranian Oil Company in exchange for a royalty amounting to nearly 50 per cent of the profit.

Following sharp fall of prices of the crude oils in the fifties the Petroleum exporting countries formed an organisation, O.P.E.C., to conserve its oil and directed the foreign oil companies to restrict their production. Conscious of the shortage of oil in several parts of the world, the O.P.E.C. countries signed Tehran Agreement with the oil companies in 1971 and increased the price of crudes by 33 cents a barrel. In January, 1972 and March, 1973 further upward revision of price took place.

With the outbreak of Middle East conflagration in October, 1973, the Arab countries started using oil as a weapon for bargaining a settlement of the Middle East problem. Complete oil embargo was declared against the two pro-Israeli powers, United States and Netherlands. The Saudi Arabian Oil Minister openly declared "Oil is one of the most important weapon we are using to achieve victory". Cut was imposed on supplies to other countries, excepting friendly countries.

In spite of these reactions it cannot be denied that oil has been effectively used by the Arab countries to press on various countries to pressurise Israel to come to an agreement with the Arabs.

In recent year, United States and other Western countries developed deep interest in the Middle East primarily because of its rich oil reserves. During the Gulf War of 1991 United States and other western powers took the onus of enforcing the resolution of Security Council primarily because they wanted to retain effective control over this region due to its rich oil reserves.

ISRAEL-ARAB RELATIONS

The Palestine problem continued to elude a solution for a long time after World War I. During World War II, the Jews fully cooperated with the Allies, while the Arabs maintained a more or less neutral attitude. At the end of War, Great Britain announced her intention to get out of Palestine. On April 2, 1947, Britain referred the Palestine question to the United Nations. A session of the General Assembly was called to examine this question. The General Assembly was called to examine this question. The General Assembly as a result of deliberation established a Special Committee on Palestine, consisting of representatives of eleven member States, which after a visit to the Middle East presented a report. The majority report favoured the formation of a Jewish state and an Arab State with Jerusalem under a special international regime. The three were to be linked together by one economic union. The General Assembly of U.N. accepted the plan.

This plan was not acceptable to the Arabs, who wanted a unitary sovereign state with an Arab majority and Jewish minority. As a consequence civil war broke out in Palestine, and a number of British soldiers were killed. As a result of public presssure Great Britain terminated her mandate over Palestine on May 15, 1948. Immediately at Tel Aviv, the Jews proclaimed the establishment of the state of Israel. Dr. Weizmann was elected its Presient and Ben Gurion was named as the Prime Minister of the new State. President Truman of U.S.A. immediately accorded de factors recognition to Israel. The Arab States of Egypt, Syria. Lebanon, Jordan and Iraq declared war against the new state. The Security Council called upon all the parties to cease hostilities and arranged a four-week truce. At the termination of this period of four weeks, the Security Council appealed to parties to prolong the truce. This appeal was accepted by the provisional government of Israel but the Arab States turned it down. As a result fresh hostilities broke out on September 17, the

Mediator and the Chief of the Franch observers Colonel Andre Serot were shot and killed in the Israel sector Jerusalem by 'Jewish irregulars'.

Large scale fighting between Palestine and Egypt continued from October to December, 1948. Ultimately, the Security Council called upon the parties to order a cease-fire and to come to some sort of agreement. Dr. Kalph Bunche, an American Negro was appointed as the new Mediator of U.N.O. As a result of tact and patience of Dr. Bunche, armistic agreements were signed between Israel on the one hand and Egypt, Lebanon and Trans-Jordan on the other. Though Israel was admitted as a full-fledged member of the United Nations in 1949, the attitude of the Arabs has been consistently hostile towards her and continuous frontier incidents, despite the existence of armistic, continued.

Clash of 1956. In 1956 Israel and Egypt once again clashed and Israel emerged victorious. After 1956 clash, an armed force of the U.N. was stationed in the Gaza Strip to prevent any armed hostilities between the two countries. In 1957, U.A.R. (a union of Egypt and Syria) was created. Iraq, another Arab country, withdrew from the Baghdad Pact after the coming into power of General Kassim. But in spite of all this Israel has been able to make lot of progress and strengthen her position mainly with the assistance and support of U.S.A. She has tried to establish friendly relations with the Afro-Asian countries and has been carrying on extensive trade and technical collaboration with them. But the attitude of the Arab countries has remained unchanged. They describe Israel as an instrument of imperialism. They have also not permitted Israel to make use of Suez Canal.

War of June, 1967. The seeds of discord between the Arabs and the Israelis ultimately led to a great conflict in June, 1967. The chief causes which contributed to this conflict were as follows:

1. As a result of Arab-Israel conflicts of the past years about one million Arabs had become refugees and their rehabilitation problem created economic complications for the Arabs.

2. The dispute over Jordan water between the Arab States and Israel increased the tension in the Middle East.
3. The cold war also partly contributed to the hostilities between the two countries. The Arab nationalists could not tolerate Israel, which received patronge from the Western powers.
4. But the immediate cause of the conflict was the border disputes between the Arab States specially Syria and Israel. President Nasser came to the rescue of Syria and asked the U.N. Military Command to withdraw the peace keeping forces from the country's border with Israel. The U.N. Secretary-General U. Thant complied with this request and ordered the withdrawal of U.N.E.F. from Arab-Israel border. Massive military preparations were made by Egypt, Syria, Jordan and Iraq to avenge the defeat of 1956.

U. Thant, Secretary-General of U.N.O. made an appal for restraint during the war but it was completely ignored. Then U.S.S.R. moved a resolution in the Security Council demanding a cease-fire. This resolution was unanimously aproved by the Council and later accepted by U.A.R. and Israel on June 9. However, Israel refused to surrender the gains of June war. She showed her willingness to vacate these areas only on the basis of a permanent peace settlement through direct talks between Israel and Arabs, unhindered by third party. During the war the Arab countries had imposed a ban on the export of oil to Western countries. After the war this ban was continued and thus it caused great revenue loss to these countries.

The War and the U.N. Charter. How far the action of Israel was in keeping with the Charter of United Nations? *(1)* In the first place, the U.N. Charter provided for various methods of peaceful settlement of disputes. Israel did not resort to any of them and struck the first blow on the plea of 'preventive war'. This concept is no doubt country to the U.N. Charter. *(2)* Israel has refused to vacate the territories which legitimately belong to the Arab countries. She wants to bargain from a position of strength. Israel under the Charter cannot have any right over these territories which are the fruits of aggression. *(3)* Territorial disputes cannot be settled or boundaries cannot be adjusted through armed conflicts under the Charter. That can jeopardize the very existence of the World Organization.

However, in fairness to Israel, it may be said that her claim that 'parties must sit across the table to get the matters settled' is fair. Her refusal to return the Arab territories occupied by her is the outcome of a fear of traditional Arab hostility towards Israel.

U.S. Plan of 1970. With a view to reduce hostilities and enhance the prospects of peace in the Middle East, U.S.A. submitted a plan through its Secretary of State Mr. Rogers in March, 1970. This plan aimed at *(i)* encouraging both the sides to adhere to the U.N. cease-fire resolution; *(ii)* calls upon the Arabs and Israelis to reappraise positions which have become road-blocks to peace; *(iii)* help the U.N. Peace Representative launch a process of negotiation among the parties; and *(iv)* seek open talks with the Soviet Union and other major arm suppliers in the hope of reaching an arms limitation agreement. This plan was accepted by Israel as well as U.A.R. As a result the guns were silenced along the confrontation line and the war planes stopped their raids over Suez Canal.

War of October, 1973. As no negotiated settlement of the problem could be found, the Arabs resorted to armed action for the recovery of their areas from Israel is October, 1973. After some initial succcess, the Arabs failed to achieve any substantial gain. While U.S.A. gave extensive arm help to Israel, the Arabs received extensive assistance from U.S.S.R. Ultimately a cease-fire was agreed between the two parties. But the cease-fire did not prove effective.

The two parties reached an agreement through good offices of United States and the two agreed to observe the cease-fire called by the U.N. Security Council. They agreed to hold discussions for return to 22 October positions. In September, 1975, Egypt and Israel reached an interim agreement on Sinai for three years under which Israel agreed to withdraw from the Abu Qudies oilfields. Israel also agreed to withdraw from the eastern end of the Giddi and Mitla passes and the same were to be placed under U.N. forces.

Peace Treaty of 1979. A final peace treaty was concluded by the two in 1979 in the presence of U.S. President Carter at Washington, which was subsequently approved by the Cabinets and Parliaments of two countries. Under the treaty Israel agreed to return to Egypt Sinai desert and Egypt agreed to recognise Israel. Israel also agreed to hand over town of El Arish within two months and pledged to provide more freedom to Palestinians living in Western Gaza. However, the peace treaty did not find approval with the other Arab countries because it did not contain any reference or assurance about Israeli withdrawal from other Arab territories. Despite the opposition of various Arab countries, Egypt pledged to implement is terms. Egyptian leaders held that solution of the Palaestinian problem was vital in the interest of permanent peace in the Middle-East.

As the other Arab states did not like the treaty they protested against it and expelled Egypt from the Arab League for signing the treaty. However, Egypt went ahead with implementation of treaty an insisted on solution of the Palestinian problem in the interest of permanent peace in Middle East.

Following annexation of Golan Heights and West Bank by Israel, fresh tension was generated. Israel's attack on Lebanon further aggravated the situation. The massive Israeli attack on West Beirut which resulted in massacre of large numer of Palaestinians evoked world wide criticism and an international peace-keeping force was sent there for maintenance of law and order.

In January 1983 the two parties to end state of war and establish peace, but this agreement was not well received by most of Arab states. During subsequent months civil-war conditions developed in Lebanon and all efforts to bring about negotiated settlement proved futile. It was only in 1986, at the intervention of Syria that fight ended in Beirut. In May 1991 Syria and Lebanon concluded treaty which called for greater cooperation on security, economic, commercial, cultural and foreign policy issues. Despite protests from Israel Syria and Lebanon demanded withdrawal of Israeli military from Southern Lebanon.

The two parties to the conflict have also conflicting economic interests. The Arabs were opposed to the Jews mainly on economic ground and feared that with their higher degree of education, greater industry etc. They will be able to establish their sway over the Arabs.

And above all, the two parties hold faith in two different religions. While the Arab states have faith in Islam, the Israelis are Zionists.

It can thus be said in conclusion that religious and economic differences between the Arabs and Israel have consistantly strained their relations and involved them in several wars. The things were rendered more serious due to the involvement of the two-super powers in the conflicts.

THE PALESTINIAN PROBLEM

Crisis in West Asia. The geographical and physical features of the area provide an answer to the endemic character of the crises in the West Asia. This area in the context of Arab awakening, Arab-Jewish Conflict and global power struggle cannot help becoming a great problem area in world politics. The great powers whose interests in this area are thereby involved directly or indirectly, are competing for the favour of the new ruling groups or are striving to push them overboard and preserve the *status quo*. So in recent years most of the countries of the world have paid their attention towards it. In fact, the Middle East Crisis, *i.e.*, Arab-Israeli conformation, is a part of an international crisis around the leaders of the two power groups—the United States and the Soviet Union.

Case of Middle East. The core of the Middle East may be said to lie in Palestine. It is situated in the heart of the Middle East. It is bounded on the North by the Republics of Syria and Lebanon, on the West by the Mediterranean and on the South by the Sinai desert of Egypt and Hejaz territory of Saudi Arabia, and on the East is the State of Jordan Valley and the Dead sea. Palestine is roughly 240 miles long and 23 miles wide in the North and about 80 miles write in the South. This area (excluding Trans-Jordan) is 10,429 sq. miles.

History of Palestine. Palestine for centuries has been known as a land of peace and prophets. History, Geography, Economic and power politics have however, combined to turn it into the most inflammable area in the world. It is for the most part a chronicle of successive invasions and conquests.

Jewish Connections. The origins of Jewish connection with Palestine go back to the remote realms in which history is merged with religious tradition. The Bible tells the story of God's command to Abraham to go forth from his native land of Ur, to what came to be known as Palestine, which country he promised to grant to his descedents. According to legend, Abraham had two sons—Ismael and Isaac. Ismael, because of his mother being an Egyptian slave, was forced to leave his father's land and become an exile. The Arabs of to-day trace their descent from him. In his turn, Ismael's brother Isaac became the ancestor of some of the Ismael tribes.

During Second Millennium. In this regard history is able to tell us something. We know generally that during the second millennium B.C. there were periodical incursions of semitic tribes from the Syrian desert into the land lying on the sea coast of Mediterranean. One of these tribes or groups of tribes claims descent from Abraham of Ur and is known as Hebrews or Israltedites. After three generations of living in the land, the Hebrews voluntaily migrated to Egypt. They were later conquered by the Babylonians. Then came Alexander the Great followed by the successive waves of victorious Roman Legions. In 70 A.D. Jerusalem was destroyed by Titus, the Roman conqueror, who also decided to banish most of the Jews from the area. The period between the conquest of Titus and the entry of a newly emerging religion Islam, was perhaps the most difficult time for the Jews.

Arabs and Jews. An important fact to remember is that contrary to popular belief, the-Arabs and Jews have lived together in peace and harmony for hundreds of years. From the Spanish inquisition down to the persecutions to Tsarist Russia, Jews fleeing from Europe found asylum, shelter and tolerance in the Arab and Muslim world. The best example of this peaceful co-existence of the Arabs and Jews was to be found in Palestine itself prior to the emergence of Zionism.

Starting of Tragedy. Briefly speaking, the tragedy started in the late 19th century when under wide-spread Zionism, some settlements of Jews from Poland, Russia and Romania were sought to be established in the Holy land which at that time was a part of Ottoman Empire. It is interesting to note that this wave of Jewish immigration to Palestine look place at the same time when West

European colonialism started to reach out towards the Arab world through the Nile Valley.

Creation of Israel. For the creation of Israel, the manifesto of Bilu 1882 was also significant. In the very beginning some of the Bilu group, *i.e.* a student and youth organization in Russia as well as farm workers in Palestine made their way to Palestine without preliminaries. According to the manifesto of Bilu several resolutions had been adopted with a view to founding a Jewish by Lord Rothschild, the head of the Anglo-Jewish Community. Their idea was to create a Jewish colony in British territory either in Sinai peninsula or in Cyprus. But the Jewish settlement in Cyprus was opposed by the native population. Herzl negotiated with the British Government and obtained from it the offer of Uganda as a territory for Jewish national how Herzl accepted the offer. But due to strategic and imperialistic considerations this idea was finally given up. In 1904, Herzl died but Zionism continued as a powerful movement.

British Game. The British, as usual, were playing a double game. In 1916, the Germans were winning and the British desperately needed the United States help. In return the British promised influential American Jews to secure Palestine for their oppressed brethren in Europe. At the beginning of 1917, while preparing for the seizure of Palestine, the British Government recalled the Zionists claim and decided to enlist their services by accepting the separation of Palestine from the Arab state. On the British Government's instructions, Sir Mark Sykes established contracts with the Zionist leaders in February, 1917. In the summer of the same year, negotiations were resumed. The talks revealed that both sides held identical views and on 2 November, 1917 the British Government issued a declaration on its policy in Palestine, which was published in the form of a letter from Balfour to the Anglo-Jewish banker Rothschild, leader of the Zionist movement.

Balfour's Views. "I have much pleasure in conveying to you, on behalf of His Majesty's Government, the following declaration of sympathy with Jewish Zionist aspirations which have been submitted to, and approved by the cabinet.

"His Majesty's Government view with favour the establishment in Palestine of a national home for the Jewish people, and will use their best endeavours to facilitate the achievement of this object, it being clearly understood that nothing shall be done which may prejudice the civil and religious rights of existing non-Jewish communities in Palestine or the rights and political status enjoyed by Jews in any other country."

The Balfour declaration received the immediate support of the United States Government, which in many ways contributed to the success of the Anglo-Zionist negotiations.

Arab-Turkish Contact. The first Arab-Turkish contacts were made in November 1917. Acting on behalf of Porte, Jemal Pasha despatched his emissary to Aqaba and invited Feisal to Damascus for peace talks. In the summer of 1918, the talks were resumed, but came to nothing because of Turkish insolence in refusing to recognise the Arabs' national demand. It was only in September, 1918 that the Turkish Government accepted the Arabs terms for spearte peace, but by this time it was too late. The Turkish flect was being defeated and the Entente's victory was becoming an accomplished fact. It ended Turkish domination of the Arab land in Asia and it resulted in the British controlling Palestine first through a military and then a civil administration.

Peace Conference. During the Peace Conference Emir Feisal, the son of Husain, the sheriff of Mecca, met various Jewish leaders and signed who in 1921 became King of lraq as a leader of the Arab, included a clause according to which Arab peasants and tenant and farmers' rights were to be protected in the proposed Jewish State.

Mandate. The San Remo Conference decided on 24 April 1920 to assign the Mandate under the League of Nations of Britain. The terms of the Mandate were also discussed with the United States which was not a member of the League but approved the Mandate for Palestine at the Anglo-American convention of December 1924. An agreed text was confirment by the Council of the League of Nations on 24 July 1922 and it came into operation in September 1923.

Colonial Status. Under the Mandate Palestine was ruled like any other British Colony of those days. The administration had instructions that it should work for the eventual establishment of a Jewish State in Palestine. The mandatory authorities, almost from the beginning encouraged tens of thousands of Jewish migrants from Europe to settle in Palestine. Thus by Articles 2,4 and 6 of the Mandate, the League of Nations expressed agreement with the principle of establishing a "national home for the Jewish people in Palestine," sanctioned the immigration of Jews, and recognised the Zionist movement, whose mouth-piece from then on was to be the Jewish agency. Sir Herbert Samuel, member of the prominent British Jewish family but not a Zionist, was appointed first High Commissioner of Plaestine. The Arabs opposed the Mandate. As a result Arab-Jewish riots broke out. Courts of Inquiry were appointed. Before one such court the Zionist Commission said in 1921, "there can be only one national home in Palestine, and a Jewish one, and no equality in partnership between the Jews and the Arabs, but a Jewish preponderance as soon as the number of the race is increased."

Jewish Immigration. The sudden increase in Jewish immigration in 1925 was very largely the result of new restrictive immigration laws, which cut down Jewish immigration to the United States from 50,000 in 1924 to 10,000 in 1925. In September 1929 a British Royal Commission, under the Chairmanship of Sir Walter Shaw was sent to investigate the "Palestine disturbances." The report of the Shaw Commission offered no solution to the problem of the Palestine Mandate.

Wailing Wall Commission. The League of Nations sent its own 'Wailing Wall Commission' to seek solution to the problem of access to the Holy places. In October 1930 British Colonial Secretary Sidney Webb, Lord Pass field, issued a White Paper on Palestine. The White Paper, based on various reports, confirmed the dual obligation of the Mandate to the Jews and the Arabs.

Arab Demand. By 1935, serious trouble was clearly brewing. The Arabs demanded immediate self-Government and a complete stop to Jewish immigration. By the end of April 1936, a general Arab strike had spread throughout Palestine and led to violence between the Arabs and the Jews as well as against Britain. The Arabs fought a guerrilla war against the British Mandate and defied the British armed strength. This critical situation brought separate reaction from the other Arab countries, from the Zionists, and eventually from the British Government, which sent another Royal commission to Palestine under the leadership of Earl Peel.

Peel Commission Report. The report of the Peel Commission recommended the termination of the Mandate and the partition of Palestine

British White Paper. The British White Paper of 1939 was of significant importance in shaping developments in Palestine from 1939 to 1949. Arab Political leaders in Palestine and the other Arab countries of Western Asia differed in their reaction to this new statement of policy by the British Government. Some declared it unacceptable, others protested against it, and only a minority of the Arab political leaders regarded the White Paper as an acceptable compromise. On the whole, however, many of the Arab leaders came to realize how favourable the White Paper was to Palestine Arabs, and eventually the Arabs became reconciled to it. On the contrary, no Zionist could accept this White Paper.

Second World War. The outbreak of second World War presented an unrivalled opportunity to the Zionists for the fulfilment of their objective. Taking advantage of the world-wide sympathy for the Jewish persecution by Hittler in Germany and Eastern Europe, the Zionist lobby got active in Western countries to prepare the ground for the final occupation of Palestine as the so-called Jewish home land. Their first victory came when Mr. Churchill as the Prime Minister allowed in 1940 the formation of Jewish brigade as an integral part of British army in Palestine. The overt objective of the formation of the brigade was to help in the defence of the Middle East against the danger of Nazi onslaught.

Gurion's Visit to U.S. Sometime later during a visit to the United States by David Ben Curion, Chairman of the executive of the Jewish agency, Zionist policy was reformulated. In May, 1942 a conference of American, European and Palestinian Zionists was held at Baltimore in New York. The declaration of the conference has since come to be known as the Baltimore Declaration. Its main demand was that all limits on the Jewish immigration to Palestine be removed and the establishment of a Jewish State should open the doors of Palestine to all the Jews fleeing from Nazi persecution. Therefore, it was at Baltimore conference for the first that the Zionists spelt in precise terms their aim of establishing a Jewish Commonwealth in palestine as an integral part of the democratic world to be erected after the World War II.

Entry of U.S. Diplomacy. The spectacular entry of the United States diplomacy into the Palestine scene was one of the most significant developments at this stage. A United States resolution favouring the Zionist goals was presented and pushed through successfully in both the Houses of Congress. In February 1944 the American Congress declared: "the doors of Palestine shall be opened for free entry of Jews into that country and that there shall be full opportunity for colonization so that the Jewish people may ultimately reconstitute Palestine as a free and democratic Jewish Commonwealth." Thus on 31 August 1945 President Truman addressed an appeal to the British Prime Minister, Clement Attlee, asking for immediate admission of 100,000 Jews into Palestine. The British agreed with President Truman and decided to go ahead with their plans in Palestine. In the spring of 1946 a mixed Anglo-American Commission was sent to Palestine to examine the status of the Jews in former Axis-occupied countries and all related matters.

Report of the Commission. Having completed its task on 20 April, 1946 the committee presented a unanimous report with three major recommendations:

(a) that the Government of Palestine be continued and at present under Mandate pending the execution of a trusteeship agreement under the United Nations;

(b) that the immediate admission into Palestine of 100,000 Jewish immigrants who have been the victims of Nasi and Pascist persecution be allowed; and

(c) that the land transfer limitations be rescinded.

Response. The United State and Great Britain neither accepted nor rejected these recommendations. Britain's position was slowly becoming untenable. Subjected to official American pressure, at odds with the Zionists and with the Arabs and facing growing disorders in its Mandated territory, the British Government decided to take the question of Palestine before the United Nations. On 2 April 1947, British requested the calling of a special session of the General Assembly to consider the problem. The General Assembly, which met between April 28 and May 15, set up a United Nations Special, Committee on Palestine (UNSCOP). The committee composed of eleven States under the presidency of a Swedish delegate, visited Palestine and presented a report to the regular full session of the General Assembly. They were, in fact, two reports. The majority proposed to cut up Palestine into three parts an Arab State, a Jewish State and the city State of Jerualem under an international regime.

GULF WAR AND IMPLICATIONS

The Gulf War, also known as war for the liberation of Kuwait, started on 17 January 1991 and came to an end on 28 February 1991 following defeat of Iraq and liberation of Kuwait. The conflict between Iraq and Kuwait originated on 2 August 1990 when Iraqi forces invaded and occupied Kuwait. Iraq justified this action by arguing that Kuwait was extracting oil from the Iraqi side of the Rumaila oil well and was resorting to over production which had resulted in fall in prices. The other factors which strained the relations between Kuwait and Iraq were that a dispute existed between Kuwait and Iraq were that a dispute existed between the two over the Bubiyan island.

Iraqi action invited world wide condemnation. On 6 August 1990 the UN Security Council imposed economic sanctions against Iraq. The very next day the United States president ordered deployment of American forces in the Gulf. On 29 November 1990 the Security Council adopted yet another resolution directing Iraq to pull out its forces from Kuwait within six weeks. It authorised U.N. members to use all necessary. measures to secure the objective of liberating Kuwait if Iraqi forces did not leave by 15 January 1991. It may be noted that it was for the third time in the life span of the United

Nations that it permitted use of force. Earlier it permitted use of force in 1950 (in Korea) and 1961 (to prevent civil war in Congo.)

As Iraq failed to comply with the directive of the United Nations, the forces of United States and 28 other countries, stated a military offensive on 17 January 1991 to liberate Kuwait. This action was condemned in several quarters on the ground that before resorting to armed action various channels to find out a negotiated settlement had neither been explored nor exhausted.

The war lasted for 42 days. During this period there was bombardment, bursting of missilies and counter-missiles, and infliction of heavy damage in Iraq, Kuwait Saudi Arabia and Israel. The war finally came to an end on 28 February 1991 when Iraq announced acceptance of all the UN resolution (12 in all) and halted its operation. This amounted to virtual surrender.

The war resulted in heavy casulties on the Iraqi side ranging between 85,000 to 100,000 killed or wounded. About 80,000 were taken as prisoners. The allies casualties were rather light. In all 126 soldiers were reported to have been killed in this section, while 56 soldiers were reported missing. Score of them were also taken prisoners.

A notable point about the Gulf War was that an impression went around that the conflict was in reality a personal war between President Bush of United States and President Saddam Hussain of Iraq. In support of this contention it has been said that President Bush was not willing to settle for anything less than Saddam's removal and destruction of Bagdad's immense war-making capability.

CEASE-FIRE

Within hours of the acceptance of UN resolutions by President Saddam Hussain, President Bush announced a halt to six-week old Gulf War. He announced "This war is behind us; Kuwait is liberated. Iraq's army is defeated. Our military objectives are met." However, the economic sanctions imposed agains Iraq and the embargo on arms was continued. On 2 March 1991 the U.N. Security Council adopted a resolution which imposed eight conditions on Iraq the cease-fire to take effect. These eight conditions were rescinding of

Kuwait's annexation, acceptance of war reparation liability, release of foreign nationals, return Kuwait property, ending of provocative actions, meeting of commanders to arrange cease fire modalities, release of prisoners of war and identification of minefields and body-traps.

On 3 April 1991 the UN Security Council adopted US sponsored resolution by 12-1 (with Cuba voting against it) and Yemen and Ecuador abstaining. The resolution stated that Iran must formally accept its current border with Kuwait. It must surrender all material that can be used to make nuclear weapons. It must agree to let a portion of its future oil earnings be used to compensate Kuwait. It should renounce terrorism and accept a ban on import of weapons. In return the resolution offered withdrawal of US forces from Southern Iraq and lifting of much of the trade embargo against Iraq after it accepted the resolution. The other important features of the resolution were lifting of embargo on shipments to Iraq of food and other goods considered necessary to meet the essential civil needs; and creation of a U.N. peace keeping force to monitor the border areas. Iraq was also required to submit to international inspection and control of nuclear material. Accordingly a U.N. peace keeping force (UNIKOM) comprising of about 1500 personnels was stationed on the Iraq-Kuwait border extending 10 kms into Iraq and 5 Kms into Kuwait.

In October 1991 the UN Security Council reviewed the sanctions against Iraq and decided not to lift them despite the plea of Yemen to case these sanctions. It was argued that Iraq had defined the Security Council by detaining United Nations inspectors. It may be noted that the Security Council reviewed the embargo because in terms of resolution 3 April 1991 adopted by the Security Council the embargo has to be reviewed every two months.

How Far War Was Justified? It is admitted at all hands that Iraq's invasion of Kuwait and its annexation was wrong because no country has a right to annex another sovereign state. But critics have also challenged the right of United States to act the way it acted against Iraq to get Kuwait liberated. Obviously, United States was motivated by selfish considerations. One of the main consideration which prompted United States and other western powers to act against Iraq was that they could not tolerate Iraq's access to oil and her ambitions to attain regional pre-eminence. In the past United States itself had violated the sovereignity of other nations viz., Panama, Granada, Nicaragua etc. without caring for the international opinion.

Implications of Gulf War. The Gulf War had far reaching international implications which can be studied under the following heads:

1. ***Decline in Influence of Soviet Union.*** The conduct of Soviet Union during the Gulf War clearly demonstrated that it was not in a position to play an active role. This was probably due to the fact that it was making frantic efforts to gain full membership of the International Monetary Fund (IMF) with a view to restructure its economy. And clash with United States would have proved counter-productive. This surprises may because Soviet Union had been playing an active role in West Asia for the past 35 years.
2. ***Kurdish Problem.*** The war provided a new impetus to the Kurdish problem because United Stated and its allies were able to prevail upon the Security Council to create security zone for the Kurds within Iraq. The Kurds, which number some 25 million inhabit the mountainous area where the borders of Syria, Turkey, Iraq and Iran meet, are mainly migratory people. They are largely Sunnis and their language is closer to Persian. They have not enjoyed any common land or right to self-determination. Following Iraq's defeat in the Gulf War, United Stated Proceeded to establish 'safe havens' for refugees inside northern Iraq and warned Iraq not to hinder humanitarian work.
3. ***New Role of United Nations.*** The Gulf War provided United Nations a rare opportunity play an effective role as peacemaker. The United Nations was pushed to play this role under pressure from United States. This is clear from the fact that instead of utilising the various avenues open to

the UN body to settle the dispute through negotiation, enquiry, mediation or arbitration, it adopted resolution authorizing use of all means for the liberation of Kuwait. After the adoption of this resolution the Security Council was relegated to the background by President Bush, who virtually dictated the terms and assumed the authority of a world policeman.

4. ***New Concern for Security in West Asia.*** After successfully waging a full-scale war in the region and getting Iraq's aggression in Kuwait vacated, United States has been feeling greatly concerned about the security in this region. Though outwardly United States has given the impression that it has no intention to dominate the region and put forth a suggestion that friendly Arab Nations should take a lead in devising an appropriate security framework, in reality United States is keen to dominate this region and would maneouvre its long presence in the Gulf region to prevent autocrates from launching aggression against their weak neighbours. Even the weakened Arab Nations would be expecting greater role for United States in this region because they know it fully well that Washington alone can provide them necessary economic and military aid and help is resolving differences among the West Asian countries.

5. ***Enormous Gains For Israel, Iran and Saudi Arabia.*** The war has immensely benefited countries like Israel, Iran and Saudi Arabia which fought on the side of United States. The havoc caused by the Gulf War on the economies of countries of West Asia encouraged these stated to come to some sort of understanding with Israel and establish diplomatic links with Israel, despite its rejection of Palestinian peace overtures and repression of palestinian Intifada. Iran also emerged with more clout after the Gulf War which has enabled her to embark on an activist foreign policy.

ARAB-ISRAEL CONFLICTS

Third Confrontation. The spectacular Six Days War in June, 1967 smashed the armed forces of United Arab Republic Syria and

Jordan in a display of military power and considerably disturbed the world power in the Middle East.

Syrian Attack. In March 1967, a Syrian force attacked Israeli farmers while they were tilling the land in Tyberious lake region which damaged many Israeli tractors. Immediately following the incident, Israel retalied with vengeance. A bitter battle was waged between Israeli and Syrian air forces and this was the biggest battle after 1956. In the battle both sides suffered heavy losses. The United Nations Peace Mission tried to work out an acceptable cease fire but Syria demanded that Israel not cultivate the demilitarised Zone and Israel was not prepared to concede the demand. Thus, the event once again assumed highly provocative posture.

Nasser's Action. On 7 April 1967, a minor border incident would have developed into a war, if the United Arab Republic had plunged in. In May, 1967 there was evidence of concentration of troops on the Israel-Syria border which made President Nasser act in haste. He made the United Nations Peace Mission (troops) leave United Arab Republic, moved his country's troops along the 117 miles frontier with Israel and closed the Gulf of Aqaba, Israel's only outlet to Red Sea, which resulted in fierce fighting breaking out in June, 1967. At the same time, the Arab League announced that any aggression committed on any Arab Nation by Israel would be considered as an aggression on the whole Arab world. The force of Saudi Arabia began their march through Jordan towards Israeli border and the war broke out all over the region. The United Nations Security Council remained in emergency session to evaluate the situation.

The Planned Attack by Israel. Like the Israeli attacks in the past, this attack too had been carefully pre-planned. On 5 June 1967 full scale Arab-Israeli war had started on four fronts—Gaza, Sinaji, Jordan and Syria.

In the initial hours of the war on June 5, Israeli planes sweeping in low over the Mediterranean, destroyed some 450 Arab air craft most of them on ground. Israeli ground forces swarmed over the Gaza strip and chopped up a 100,000 Egyptian army in the Sinai peninsula in a drive to Suez Canal. In a simultaneous action, the old city of Jerusalem was captured and all Jordanian territory west of Jardan river bordering on Israel was occupied.

Result. As a result of its aggression in June 1967 Israel occupied and still holds large territories of United Arab Republic, Jordan and Syria. The total area of these territories is 60,000 square kilo meter, three times the size of Israel within the borders established by the 1949 armistice agreement and four times that of territory allotted for the Jewish State by the United General Assembly decision of 29 November 1947. Israel thus gained an absolute command of the air from Sinai to Galiee. The worst hit targets in the U.A.R. which were subjected to the first wave of attack were 16 Egyptian airfields extending from the Canal Zone to Cariro area to Luxor and the Red Sea coast. Israel had started an almost simultaneous action on the ground.

Jordanian Front. On the Jordanian front fighting was reported in various areas and Amman and Mafraq airfields were heavily attacked by the Israeli air force the day. In the morning Jordanian troops seized the United Nations building in Jerusalem where Lieutenant General Odd Bull (Chief of Staff of United Nations Truce Supervision Organisation) had his headquarters, but the building was retaken later in the day by an Israeli counter attack

Israel's War-gains. On 6 June, however, Israel had secured complete mastery of the Arab skies and its troops were deep in Sinai. Israelis has also captured Bethleham, Hebron and Jenin in Jordan. By 7 June, most of the United Arab Republic formations having been cut off from the rear were nearly paralysed. On the Jordanian front Jerusalem had fallen, and Particularly the entire West bank was in the Israeli hands. The remnants of United Arab Republic's defence forces in Sinai were systematically mopped up on 7 and 8 June.

Arab Reaction. The Arab reaction to the war was both prompt and united. As expected, the United Arab Republic declared a nation-wide state of emergency followed by Jorden, Syria and Iraq. Other Arab States also came out with fraternal offers ranging from despatch of troops to financial help and facilities for the transit of troops.

The fiercest fighting took place in Jerusalem on the night of 5-6 June. On 6 June the main Egyptian defences in Sinai, held by three Egyptian divisions, were Shattered. At the end of 35 hours of fighting, the gates of Sinai had been opened wide to Israeli armour.

Six Day War. In the Six day war, Soviet Union avoided a direct confrontation with the United States in the Middle East and thus resisted the pressure of Russia's Arab clients to intervene. The war was thus a one sided affair. By the time United Nations arranged cease fire agreements. Israelis had conquered territores four times its own size, killed some 35,000 Arabs and captured thousands more, destroyed between 600 and 700 Soviet-built Egyptian tanks as well as captured hundred tanks and armed personnel carriers. Israel losses of 679 dead and 2,563 wounded were reported by 11 June.

Many thought that in June 1967 Israel had scored some kind of an overall victory. Israeli politicians considered that the Arabs had no alternative but unconditional surrender. They considered the progressive Government in the United Arab Republic and other Arab countries as dead.

Israeli Advance. As the hostilities broke out on 5 June with both sides blaming each other for striking the first blow, on the very first day, some war planes of five Arab nations had been destroyed. Israel too suffered losses but they were not very heavy. On the ground also the Israeli forces made significant advances and captured most of the relevant parts of Sinai peninsula, the West Bank of the Jordan and the West Bank of the Suez Canal. After a week long fighting, one by one, Jordan, the United Arab Republic, Syria and Israel accepted the United Nations cease fire but not before Israel had extended its conquest 15 miles from its Syrian borde. Following this defeat President Nasser tendered his resignation to the people of the United Arab Republic but had to withdraw because of popular appeal.

Skirmishes. Desptie the cease fire in July 1967, there were daily Skirmishes between Egyptian and Israeli forces stationed along the Suez Canal.

Settlement Terms. On 23 July the Persident of the United Arab Republic stressed two basic points for a settlement. *(a)* "Israeli withdrawal from Golan Heights, *(b)* the West Bank of the Jordan river, Jerusalem, Gaza and Sinai, and recognition of the rights of the Palestinian people." Israeli Prime Minister Golda Meir, on the other hand, said on August 4. "Not a single Israeli soldier will be withdrawn from the cease fire fines until a binding agreement is reached. Israel well not return to the from of June 4, 1967." However, the negotiations are still under way.

Aggression Against Arab World. The Arab peoples justly regard the 1967 Israeli aggression aganist the UAR, Syria and Jordan as an aggression against the Arab world as a whole. In defending their right to independence and national dignity, their right to be the masters of their resources and follow the road of social progress, the Arabs are not merely defending their own interests their just struggle is a substantial contribution to the common struggle for complete elimination of colonialism and neocolonialism, for setting up a new, genuinely democratic system of international relations.

Difficult War. This was indeed a difficult war, a war in which the Jewish force retreated before the massive Arab forces. In the Sinai Sector, two Egyptian armies crossed the Canal and advanced up to about 20 kilometres to the East. In the Golan, the Syria armour broke through and penetrated up to almost 20 kilometres in several sectors. Long and difficult hours elapsed until the reserve forces joined the battle and reversed the situation. Israel paid a high price for this checking campaign-hundreds of young fighters fell in battle.

Fourth Confrontation. On 6 October 1973 it was the turn of the Arabs to launch an offensive against the Israelis. By complete surprise and on the most sacred day of the Jewish people—the Day of Atonement—a co-ordinated and combined offensive was launched with the full force of Egypt and Syria. This combined force which included over 2200 tanks on the front, about 2000 artillery guns and more than 1000 fighters was met by the limited regular deployment of the Jewish force.

Israeli Thrust. The main Israeli thrust began on 8 October when reserve units were successfully deployed for a multi-pronged attack, repulsing the Syrian forces which had been both checked and depleted by intensive air attacks, and by the small defensive force on the front at the time. As the Israeli attack progressed the Syrians broke, leaving behind 1,200 tanks—400 of them in perfect working order. Before the cease fire was implemented on 22 October, Israeli forces had conquered an area of 600 square kilometres extending from the foothills of the Hermon in the North, to the Damascus Kuneitra axis. Tel Harra in the south, thus securing base which brought the suburbs of Damascus into Israeli artillery ranged and gave Israel control of the routes through the impassable volcanic Ledga.

U.N. Cease Fire. The United Nations cease fire ending the 17-Day War between Israel and Egypt officially went into effect on Monday, the 23 October 1973 at 10.20 p.m. IST. This was in pursuance of a Security Council resolution worked out by U.S. Secretary of State Henry Kissinger and Soviet Communist Party Chief Brezhnev during the weeked in Moscow.

Resolution. In Addition to a halt in the fighting, the resolution called upon the Arabs and Israelis for an immediate start toward implementation of the 1967 Council Resolution on West Asia and immediate negotiations for a just and durable peace in the Middle East.

The 1967 resolution called for Israeli withdrawal to "secure boundaries" from the Arab territories it occupied in the 1967 war. The Arabs contend this means a withdrawal from all occupied territory, while Israelis made it clear that they intend to hold on to certain areas that they consider necessary to secure boundaries. The respective positions as a result of October 1973 war are evident from the attached political map.

Sadat Reports. Anwar El Sadat reported: "I would not be exaggerating if I said that military history will sand for a long time to study and examine the October 6 military operation. When the Egyptian forces succeeded in crossing the complex Suez Canal obstacle, and in storming the strong Bar-Lev Line, establishing bridgeheads on the eastern bank of the Suez Canal, after having caused the enemy to lose its balance within six hours."

Six hours after the crossing began, there were 80,000 Egyptian soldiers on the eastern bank of the Suez Canal. 15 strongholds were captured on the first within 6 hours. The crossing troops covered 5 kilometres inside Sinai within 2½ hours.

INDO-SRI LANKA RELATIONS

Bilateral Relations. Among the bilateral relationships India has with its neighbours, the domestic factor is the most pronounced in the case of Sri Lanka. The ethnic composition of the island it such that not only does a sizable minority there claim its origin in India (ironically, even the majority is of Indian origin), it also looks upon India as its potential saviour. On its part, India cannot afford to ignore the problems of this minority because of the co-ethnics in the Indian state of Tamil Nadu. Thc Goverment in New Delhi has to take cognizance of the Tamil emotionally-charged chauvinistic concern for the said minority for political reasons of its own. India-Sri Lanka relations thus have been caught in a complex wed of domestic politics from which neither nation is able to extricate itself.

India's Policy. India's policy towards Sri Lanka from the time of their independence to the present, may be divided broadly into two phases. The first phase lasted virtually three decades, from the 1950s through the 1970s when India was primarily concerned with the problem of Indian Tamils. Although the problem was never solved, in the 1980s it was overshadowed by the ethnic conflict between the majority Sinhalas and the minority Sri Lanka Tamils. Since the problem had serious international ramification, more so for India-Sri Lanka relations, India became deeply involved in it. This involvement constituted the second phase of India's Sri Lanka policy. Before we discuss these phases it is necessary to keep in mind the ethnic mosaic of Sri Lankan population.

Sri Lanka's Ethnic Mosaic. Ethnically, the population of Sri Lanka may be divided into six main groups: the Sinhalas, the Sri Lanka Tamils, the Moors, the Indian Tamils; the malays and the Burghers. The Sinhalas, who form the majority (74%), are predominantly Buddhist and speak Sinhalese. The Sri Lanka Tamils (12.5%) descendants of settlers who arrived in the island from southern India about a thousand years ago, are predominantly Hindu and speak Tamil. They are concentrated in the for north of the island, on and near the Jaffna peninsula and along the east coast. The Moors (7.1%) are of Arabic and Indian Muslim descent and live in the eastern provinces. There are also some moor pockets on the west coast and around Kandy. Moors are generally Tamil-speaking but of late there has been a tendency among those living in Sinhalese-speaking aras to identify themselves as Sinhalese-speaking. The Indian Tamils (5.6%) are mostly working class people; they are principally Hindu and speak Tamil. They were originally brought by the British in the nineteenth century from southern India to work on tea and rubber estates. The Malays and Burghers are small minorities who form only 0. 3 per cent each of the Sri Lankan population.

Ethnic Plurality. The ethnic plurality of Sri Lanka might not have been a major problem had the various groups been evenly distributed throughout the island. As it is the majority Sinhalas are actually in minority in 8 out of the 24 districts into which the country is administratively and electorally divided. Of these 8 districts the Sri Lanka Tamils are in absolute majority in 5 and have the largest numerical strength in one.

Physical Segregation. The physical segregation of the ethnic populations, for understandable reasons, aggravates Sri Lanka's integrational problem. The Sri Lanka Tamils are concentrated in the northern and eastern areas and the Sinhalas in the southern western, the two regions being separated by vast tracts of high lands. Except the district of Nuwara Eliya, where the Indian Tamils are in majority, the seven districts where the Sinhalas are in minority are contiguous and situated in northern and eastern parts of the island. It may be noted that is the area which is viewed by the Tamils are their "traditional homeland".

India and the Issue of Indian Tamils. According to the census of 1981, India Tamils were 825,233 in number, constituting 5.6 per cent of the Sri Lankan population. Their presence in the island is a legacy of the colonial period. During the so-called 'coffee era' of 1820-1880 the British encouraged large scale migration of cheap Tamils and other South Indian labourers to work in Sri Lanka's coffee plantations. In the 1880s when the coffee plantations were destroyed by disease, tea gardens emerged as substitutes and the demand for labour increased. Tamil immigration became a family phenomenon; from 10,000 in 1827, the number of Tamil immigrants rose to 603,000 in 1941 and to 758,264 in 1949. By this time the Sinhala-Tamil cleavage had become an important political issue. The conflict of interest between the Sinhalas an the Indian Tamils centred primaily around the policies related to development and redistribution of "crown lands".

India and the Sinhal-Tamils Ethnic Conflict. By the early 1980s when the issue of Indian Tamils seemed to have become virtually stalemated and both India and Sri Lanka appeared to have reconciled themselves to living with an unresolved yet not so critical problem, there was serious deterioration in ethinc relations between the Sinhalas and the Sri Lanka Tamils. The new phasic began with the outbreak of anti-Tamil riots in Colombo in July 1983. The riots drew international attention. An essentially internal problem of Sri Lanka became internationalised with India developing a major stake in its solution. India's involvement in the Tamil problem has had both domestic and external dimensions ever since both countries became independent but in recent years there have been significant changes in the latter making it almost impossible for the Sri Lankan authorities to deal with its ethnic problem purely as an internal affair. The changes in the global strategic environment, an ever-growing militarisation of the Indian Ocean region in particular, have also contributed to this shift. Domestically speaking the undercurrents of Tamil Nadu politics have influenced New Delhi's position *vis-a-vis* Sri Lanka's ethinc policy.

Role of Religion. Unlike the Sinhalese case, religion did not paly a very important role in building Tamil national consciousness. As K.M. de Silva has rightly pointed out; "Buddhist-Hindu rivalry has been much less significant as a point of contention between the Sinhalese and the Tamils than ethnicity and language.

Actually Hinduism in Sri Lanka was never thretened by Buddhism. whatever thereat it had faced was in the social realm because the caste system among Hindus has a religious sanction in addition to the social as with the Sinhalas though untouchability did not exist among the Sinhalas. The vellalas among the Hindu Tamils were the equivalent of the goyigamma among the Sinhalas but unlike the latter who formed a thin upper crust, the vellalas were in substantial number if not in majority among the Hindus. They used the sanctions of Saivtie orthodoxy to maintain their caste privileges at the expense of lower castes, particularly the untouchables. This aspect of Hinduism which was essentially social in its dimension contributed to the Sinhala-Tamil dichotomy particularly as untouchability was non-existent in Sinhalese society.

Tamil Nationalism. While the Hindu religion did not play a significant role in building Tamil nationalistic, consciousness its image of itself in the historic process contributed significantly to the shaping of this consciousness. Broadly speaking, the Tamil nationlistic myths were based on territory, dynasty (the Nallur Kingdom) and language. Over the years, these myths became stylized by the mythology of "the other"—the "Sinhalese bucolic hordes, bent on brutal oppression". A Tamil scholar from Sri Lanka has captured this deep-seated hatred well: "At this point of history, the Tamils do not have a State and cannot perpetuate this myth through official school texts.

Rise of Tamil Separatism. The Systematic encroachment upon their rights made the Tamils restive. In the election of 1956, which saw the replacement of Tamil congress by the Federal Party as the repersentative of Tamil interests, their struggle for autonomy received a major boost. The two main objectives of the party were, one, to achieve autonomy for the Tamils so that their cultural and economic interests were safeguarded, and two, to achieve a unity of Tamil speaking peoples in Sri Lanka so as to increase their political bargaining power. To attract the Indian Tamils and the Tamil speaking Moors the party stressed the "unity of the Tamil-speaking people without distinction of caste, creed or geography". To allay the fears of other Tamil communities that they would be discriminated against in a predominantly Tamil province if and when federalism was introduced in Sri Lanka, the Federal Party even substituted the term "autonomous Tamil State" by "autonomous Tamil States".

Unemployment. Several circumstances, perticularly a growing rate of unemployment, contributed to the restiveness and militancy among Tamil youths. Although unemployment was rampant in Sri Lanka by the late 1960s, it particularly affected the Tamil community because of its almost toal dependence on public service.

TUF Conference. At a conference held in May 1976, the TUF changed its name to Tamil United Liberation front (TULF) thereby declaring its motto of secession. A resolution passed at the conference contained a long list of Tamil grievances and charged that "the Republican Constitution of 1972 had made the Tamils a slave nation ruled by the new colonial masters, the sinhalese, who are using the power they have wrongly usurped to deprive the Tamil nation of its territory, language, citizenship economic life, oppotunities for employment and education thereby destroying all the attributes of nationhood of the Tamil people". The resolution concluded by saying that "the restoration and reconstitution of the Free, Sovereign, Secular, Socialist State of TAMIL EELAM... has become inevitable in order to safeguard the very existence of the Tamil Nation in this country."

Political Organisations of Tamils. The political organisation of the Indian Tamils, the Ceylon Workers Congress, did not endorse the demand for a separate state of Tamil Eelam and withdrew from the TULF. Being relatively backward in education and in their standard of living while being resident in an area not contiguous to the proposed Tamil State, their problems were naturally different than those of the Jaffna Tamils. They were more interested in the question of labour relations and were either seeking Sri Lankan citizenship or preparing to leave for India.

Rise of Tamil Extremism. In the evolution of the tiger movement the years 1977—were of crucial importance. Shortly before the 1977 elections two important elder politicians of Jaffna, namely S.J.V. Chelvanayagam, the founder leader of the Federal Party, and G.G. Ponnambalam, founder of the Tamil Congress, had passed away. They had been a great integrative and moderating force among the Tamils. In their absence the militant groups which were already in the field, and which has made their presence felt in the killing of SLFP mayor of Jaffna, Alfred Duraiyappah, in 1974, were unleashed. Their arrival on the centre-stage of Tamil politics was signalled by the murder of four policemen in Velvettiturai in April 1978. the incident triggered off a confrontation with the government which injected a new and most complex dimension to Sri Lanka's ethnic problem and eventually plunged the country into a virtual civil war. "In retrospect", as Phadnis has said "if the Sinhalese youth insurgency of 1971 was a child of 1958, so was the Tiger Movement of the Tamil youth in the north inasmuch as the impulse for insurgency in the case of both was more or less identical." The Sinhalese educated unemployed youth had revolted against the system in 1971.

The Indian Connection. The ethnic strife in Sri Lanka has recently become the most dominant factor influencing Indo-Sri Lankan relations. In the 1960s when there was an active separatist movement in Tamil Nadu, which found its most militant expression during the anti-Hindi riots, the central government in New Delhi was careful not to meddle with the Tamil problem in Sri Lanka. Any support to the separatist Sri Lankan Tamil Nadu. The main thrust of India's policy towards the questions of Sri Lanka Tamils was that of non-interference. In May 1957, when Jawaharlal Nehru visited Sri Lanka and the Sri Lanka Tamils sought his intervention to set right the wrong done to them by the introduction of Sinhalese as the sole official language, he was careful not to meddle in the country's internal affairs. He expressed concern but said: "We do not think that any official step that we might take will be helpful at all on such matters. He saw the danger of the strong secessionist demand in Tamil Nadu being aggravated if the Sri Lanka Tamils were given support in their demands for self-determination.

Reaction in India. The developments on Sri Lanka's ethnic front have made the Tamil community of India sensitive. Consisting of about 55 million people it is effectively repersented in the national bureaucracy, communication media and the country's academic, intellectual and professional establishments. The voice of the community influences the opinion of the Indian government indirectly which the politics of Tamil Nadu does so directly. In 1977 when racial riot's rocked Sri Lanka there was a wave of protest against atrocities committed against Tamils in that country. The Tamil Nadu

Assembly adopted a unanimous resolution condemning the riots in Sri Lanka and called upon the Government of India to depute a representative of the status of a Cabinet Minister to the island to find out the true state of affairs and have direct talks with the Sri Lankan government "by way of assuaging the feelings of the Tamils there."

AIADMK and DMK Response. Tamil Nadu politics was again rocked in 1981 when racial riots broke out in Sri Lanka in August that year and both the AIADMK and the DMK vied with each other to show their "Tamilism". When young Jaffna Tamils sought refuge in Tamil Nadu to escape from the repression in Jaffna, the leaders of twenty political parties in the state appealed to Indira Gandhi to grant them political asylum.

The July 1983 massacre evoked a dramatic response in Tamil Nadu to Sri Lanka's ethnic conflict. The DMK President, M.Karunanidhi, and the deputy leader of the party in the state assembly, K. Arbazhagan, resigned from the assembly in protest against AIADMK's alleged apathy to Sri Lanka Tamils. The AIADMK government countered this by declaring a week-long mourning in the state and issued a call for a statewide bandh on 2 August 1983. The bandh was supported by all the political parites and by the Centre as well, a clear indication of how the Congress (I) government considered it wise to go along the Tamil mainstream opinion. It was the first time in independent India's history that the Central government officially participated in bandh called by a state government.

Political Clout. It appeared that both AIADMK and DMK used the concern for Sri Lanka Tamils as a handle to strengthen their own political clout. While the DMK leaders took recourse to resignations from assembly memberships, fastings in public places, and so on, the ruling AIADMK tried aggressive rhetoric.

The Foreign Policy Dimensions. Though the ethnic problem of Sri Lanka is essentially an internal problem, or at best concerns Tamil Nadu politics and thereby that of India, it also has an extra-regional dimension. This dimension perhaps more than the domestic, has influenced India's Sri Lanka policy. In fact, both are closely interlinked.

New Delhi reacted sharply, within weeks of the July 1983 massacre, to the reported news of Sri Lanka's intention of seeking assistance from extra-regional powers to preempt Indian intervention. India, it was announced, would not tolerate external intervention in a conflict situation in any South Asian country if it was likely to have any implicit or explicit repercussions aganist Indian interests.

Indian Doctrine. The reassertion of the Indian doctrine evoked sharp reaction from Sri Lanka where it was widely referred to as an Indian threat of intervention. On 7 August 1983, two days before he sent his brother Hector Jayewardene to New Delhi to discuss the ethnic crisis with the Indian leaders, Persident Jayewardene accused India of harbouring and assisting Tamil terrorists. "If India decides to invade us", he said in a interview to the sun (Colombo), "we will fight and may be lose, but with dignity".

The Failure of Indian Peace Keeping Force. The IPKF's virtual failure to liquidate the LTTE certainly created ripples in Indian politics. According to IPKF sources, by July 1988 they had suffered a casualty of 1937 persons—537 dead and 1400 injured. According to the same source, the LTTE lost 1500 boys. In the face of this situation continuing indefinitely, the opposition to the Indian military presence in Sri Lanka become increasingly strident. People had started questioning the efficacy of Indian intelligence. The Times of India echoed the sentiments of many Indians when it called upon Government to "make a discloser of its assessment, past and present, to Parliament and encourage a public debate on how best to tackle the situation in Sri Lanka."

Strategic Divide. The strategic divide that seemed to be in the making was indeed the result of a perceptional gap that existed between India and Sri Lanka over the latter's ethnic tangle. While India saw it primarily as a political problem, which warranted a political solution, the Sri Lankan government considered the problem essentially as a security threat posed by the extremists—"the treacherous internal elements"—who should first be eliminated before the issue could be dealt with politically. Though there was sufficiently valid logic in both the perspectives and the best strategy probably rested in a combination of both, the fast moving developments on all fronts actually widened the gap.

Elections. It was conceivable that If the DMK party won the assembly elections in Tamil Nadu it might not be easy for the Indian government to pursue its policy in Sri Lanka the way it was being done now. The DMK stood by the cause of Sri Lankan Tamils as represented by the LTTE which might mean in the present context withdrawal of IPKF, immediate and permanent merger of Northern and Eastern provinces and more powers to the provincial councils. According to some observers, the LTTE was buying time to see the outcome of Tamil Nadu elections. Contrarily, the Congress party ruling at the centre liked to enter the election fray in Tamil Nadu with a clear record of success in Sri Lanka which essentially mean the overpowering of the LTTE. Either way Indian's Sri Lanka policy was extremely relevant for Tamil Nadu politics.

Sri Lankan Politics. With regard to Sri Lankan politics the provincial council experiment had added a new and complicated dimension to it which was heretofore unknown. The possibility had emerged that the parliament and president could belong to a party different from that ruling the provinces. SLFP parliamentary leader, Anura Bandaranaike, in his interview to the Hindu referred to this problem in no uncertain words. He said that provincial councils had been introduced in Northern and Eastern provinces because of peculiar historical reasons but they should never have been introduced in other areas. With regard to the question of merger of Northern composition of the Eastern provinces, the SLFP leader was emphatic that the demographic composition of the Eastern province was not conducive to its merger with the Northern province.

Wooing India. From the pervailing trends in Sri Lankan politics it was becoming increasing evident that against the background of impending presidential and parliamentary elections both the UNP and the SLFP were trying to woo India without conceding their respective positions on the ethnic issue. For the UNP, the accord did not guarantee a permanent merger without a referendum. For the SLEP, let alone merger certain aspects of the accord itself were negotiable. According to SLFP leader Sirimavo Bandaranaike India had nothing to fear from her government as it would adopt a genuine non-aligned policy. Anura Bandaranaike reiterated the same opinion and said that the exchange of letters between Indian and Sri Lankan governments would not have been necessary had the SLFP been in Power. It showed that India did not have enough trust in Jayewardene's foreign policy. The future image of India in Sri Lanka and the course of Indo-Sri Lankan relations depended on the outcome of Sri Lankan polls, the shape of Tamil Nadu politics in particular and Indian politics in general, and most importantly upon the developments on the IPKF-LTTE battle front. The political indicators were not reassuring.

IPKF. In Sri Lankan politics, the IPKF's protracted involvement had implications for all parties, particularly the UNP and the SLFP. Probably this was the reason that UNP was getting increasingly desperate to see the IPKF fulfil its mission and go home.

Present Position. The LTTE innvolvement in Rajiv Gandhi's murder, even after withdrawal of IPKF worsened the Indo-Sri Lankan relations far a while. But they are normal now at the present juncture. LTTE is still a dominant force despite military operations by the government.

The Tamil tangle in Sri Lanka, remains unresolved.

AFRO-ASIAN RESURGENIC

One of the outstanding events of the mid-twentieth century has been the emergence of Asia and Africa. The countries in these sub-continents emerged from the prison cells of colonial rule and from the obsecurity imposed by the foreign rulers. Between 1945, and 1960, almost one quarter of the world's population won political independence in these two continents. The collapse of colonialism marked the dawn of new era. Commenting on the significance of this development Barraclough says, "Never before in the whole of human history had so revolutionary a reversal occurred with such rapidity. The change in the position of the people of Asia and Africa and in their relations with Europe was the surest sign of the advent of a new era."

But all these states, with the execption of Japan, are suffering from the chronic problems of poverty, unemployment, illiteracy and disease. These problems were mainly the creation of the colonialism which involved the capture of overseas markets for extraction of raw materials and compulsory dumping of manufactured goods. This not only retarded the social and economic progress of the people in Asia and Africa but also deprived them of self-confidence and self-reliance.

Most of the Afro-Asian countries on the eve of their independence were poor, lacked factories of their own, had insufficient roads and railways and poor communications. Majority of the people were illiterate and there were very few institutions of higher learning. Their banking systems were very poor. They exported only raw materials, ores or some stape products. Mostly the exploitation of these sources of export was in the hands of the foreign companies. Mostly the Afro-Asian countries were having mainly agricultural economy.

After their independence most of the Afro-Asian countries embarked on the path of achieving democracy and liberation in the economic and social spheres. Majority of the countries embarked on national economic reconstruction programmes with a view to achieve speedy development of their economics. Though majority of the countries like India, Burma and Sri Lanka in Asia and Guinea, Mali, Congo, Tanzania and the U.A.R. in Africa, have planned their development on socialistic lines, some other countries have stood against socialism. Thus the Asian and African sub-continents are witnessing a contest between socialism and capitalism. Another noteworthy thing is that most of the countries of these two regions are receiving aid from Soviet Union and United States, as well as the various agencies of the U.N.O.

Impact of Afro-Asian Resurgence on International Relations. The emergence of Afro-Asian countries has exercised profound influence on international relations:

1. In the first place it gave death blow to imperialism and racialism. The independence of these countries gave a further stimulus to liberation movements in other parts of the world. The race relations were also transformed into international relations. Earlier the racial problems were concerned as falling within the domestic jurisdiction of the state concerned. However, the Afro-Asian group by raising

it quite frequently at the U.N. elevated it to the status of international problem. This anti-racialist attitude of the Afro-Asian countries inspired the anti-racialist elements in U.S.A. and led to lati-fledged movement.

2. Secondly, emergence of Afro-Asian countries has also strengthened international fraternity are narrowed down the sphere of exploitation. Both in Asia and Africa it gave rise to what is known a Pan-Asian and Pan-African states were held at New Delhi, Cario, Bunding, Accra, Addis Abada etc., where the common problems of these states were discussed and ways were explored to achieve quick development by mutual co-operation.
3. Another noteworthy feature is that in the international sphere most of the Afro-Asian countries are following the policy of peace and co-existence. This policy was an imperative need for them in view of the fact that they want to concentrate their resources for the national reconstruction and development plans. These countries are convinced that involvement in power politics will certainly imply diversion of funds from development projects and will delay their development. This attitude of the Afro-Asian countries has gone a long way in strengthening the forces of peace and stability in the world.
4. In fourth place the awakening of Asian and African countries has strengthened the cause of neutralism in international relations. This concept was first evolved by the Asian countries and India played a leading role in this direction. Later the African countries also adopted this policy of neutralism. It may be noted that there are certain states in these two sub-continents, which are still following either of two blocs. But the number of the non-aligned countries is largest. The policy of non-alignment was also dictated by self-interest. The states of Asia and Africa are so much preoccupied with their national-building and economic development projects that they had of necessity to keep out from bloc politics. As Prof. Robert Good says, the problems

vexing the Super Powers in their contest with one another are of little importance to these states. "Most of the new states do not measure the issue of international politics with cold war calipers."

5. In the fifth place with the independence of Afro-Asian countries there was an influx of new states in international relations, which has greatly complicated it. As Prof. Vernon Mckay says : "This striking increase obviously complicated international relations. It creates not only substantive problems but organizational difficulties for all the foreign offices of the world. It brings forth a large group of untrained and inexperienced diplomats dealing with unfamiliar tasks". In a way, the influx of these new states has added a new source of tension, bargaining and competition in international relations.
6. In the last instance the emergence of the Afro-Asian group in the United Nations has greatly affected the working of this world body. The states of these two regions have placed too much of reliance on U.N. and sought solution of various problems through this forum. Particularly these states have dependend on the U.N. for the social and economic welfare activities. This Special Fund and the various Technical Aid Programmes undertaken by the world body to accelerate the modernization processes of these two states are the examples in sight. These states have strengthened the basis of the U.N.O. by frequently and repeteadly pleading their loyalty to the U.N. Charter and the Universal Declaration of Human Rights. The attitude of the two Super Powers in the United Nations has also been greatly affected by the presence of such a large number of Afro-Asian countries. Both these powers try to win favour of these countries on the various issues because they are considered a vital element in international body. We can hope that the direction and course of U.N. decision on various problems shall be to a great extent determined by the attitude of the Afro-Asian countries.

❑

6

Colonialism and Decolonialism

The classical colonialism *i.e.*, the direct political domination of foreign countries could not withstand the resurgence of nationalism in the subject colonies after the Second World War. As the British Prime Minister, Harold Macmillan once said in Pretoria in 1960, the "Wind of Change" penetrated through the impregnable forts of European Colonial Powers. Thus after the Second World War the Imperial Flags gave way to National Flags and a flood of new nations transformed the political map of the world. This, however, proved a tactical move. The Imperial Powers had developed the subject colonies' economies as subversive of the metropolitan economies. Therefore, the new nations, in spite of their political independence, cannot afford to take independent decision so long they are economically dependent on the ex-metropolitan economies. Their helplessness further increased with the resurgence of cold war among the Super Powers to divide the world into their respective spheres of influence. In that way U.S.A. and U.S.S.R. filled the vacuum created by the withdrawal of European Imperial Powers. The present international position has been such that the chief colonial powers like the U.S.A. and U.S.S.R. have influenced that vital trends of the entire international policy.

The modern complicacies of the world policy have created many difficulties in the path of understanding clearly in shape of new colonialism. These difficulties are discussed in the following order:

(a) This new colonialism has only recently started and, therefore, its various trends could not be finally visualised in the short span of time.

(b) The outer skeleton of this new colonialism has been so developed that its many secrecies cannot be easily visualised and one of its chief characteristics is that the colonial powers of the present age outwardly desist from colonialism and they no more prefer to be called Imperial Powers.

The colonies of Western countries also do not cherish any idea of calling themselves to be Dominions and they instead claim themselves to be free. For example, the satellite states of U.S.S.R. consider themselves to be free states. However, some of the modern events have unveiled certain specialities of the new colonialism. The Soviet Union and its allied states conducted an armed invasion aganist Czechoslovakia in 1968 for it had stopped blindly following the statutes of Russia and began to show its inclination towards making certain amendments in its national policy.

FORMS OF NEW COLONIALISM

1. Political Colonies. All non-self-governing states not being in a position to enjoy their rights of political freedom, can be called political colonies. In most of these cases, the social and economic standard of the people of such colonies is considered to be inferior to that of the people of the ruling state.

2. Economic Dependencies. A nation, economically dependent upon any other foreign state, may not be in a position to conduct its economic affairs independently without the influence of any outside power. The economically backward states sometimes take financial and technical assistance of some rich states although the political and economic institutions of two might differ widely from one another. Under these circumstances the nations economically dependent upon big states are guided by them in their respective economic policies.

The people of economic dependencies, like those of the political colonies, are considered to be inferior to the people of the ruling states in the matters of race and culture. These economic of their produced goods are regulated by them.

3. Satellite States. The satellite states are considered to be completely free states but actually they depend upon some or the other big state from political and economic point of view. They blindly follow the superior power. The Communist states like the Soviet Russia and People's Republic of China have in modern times extended their influence over a number of weak and undeveloped states. They exercise complete authority over all the national industries of their satellite states and for that purpose they also exert their political influence over them. These satellite states are comparatively more effectively controlled by their superior states than the ruling powers of the so called satellite states and economic dependencies:

(i) The first category of satellite states might be subject to the influence of a handful of political leaders of the superior state. The ruling party of the colonial state might through the medium of their influential leaders affect the political and economic affairs of their satellite states whose politicians or political leaders are directly influenced by them.

(ii) The second category of satellite states and economic dependencies are subject to the direct influence of the governments of the ruling state. The ruling state might interfere in their domestic affairs and in case the popular opposition against them becomes conspicuous in their dependencies, the ruling state might take an armed action against them.

(iii) The third kind consists of satellite states that happen to be situated near the big states of the world. They being official of their active foreign policy tend to adopt only such a policy in their external and administrative affairs as might conform to and support the foreign policy of their ruling state.

4. Multinational Corporations. The big powers have also tried to dominate the politics and economics of the developing countries through multi-national corporations. These multinational corporations which operate from a common centre in the imperialist country penetrate in different developing countries and try to merge in themselves certain firms of countries of operation also. As a result the capital in most of the developing countries is getting concentrated in these multi-national corporations, and economies of most of the non-communist countries of the world are being dominated by some three hundred giant international corporations. The multi-national corporations not only play an important role in the export of products from the developing countries but also enjoy monopolies in the exploitation of the resources of the developing countries. The multi-national corporations tend to infringe upon the sovereignty of the third world countries and seek to gain control over their natural resources. They also impose unequal agreements upon them and impede the development of their independent national economies.

It may be observed that the activities of the multi-national corporations are not confined to the economic field alone. Often with the help of the economic power at their disposal they influence the political activities of the developing countries. Through finances to the individual members and political parties they penetrate in political life of these countries and try to control the governmental machinery.

5. Cultural Exploitation. At the cultural level also the imperialist countries have evolved various methods to dominate and control the third world countries. They sell obsolete machines and technology to the third world countries in the name of technology transfer. Generally the imperialist countries have tried to transfer only those industries in the third world countries which they are unable to have in their country or want to avoid in their country *viz.*, industries which consume too much energy; industries which cause pollution of mining and extractive industries which can provide raw materials to the imperialist countries; industries which require large labour force which is available in abundance in third world countries; and industries which require large scale trials for development etc.

COLONIALISM *VS* NEO-COLONIALISM

During World War II, imperialism suffered a setback. Almost all the Imperialist powers had to grant freedom to dependencies and colonies. England freed India in 1947, Ghana in 1957, Malaya in 1957, Somaliland, Cyprus and Nigeria in 1960, Tanganyika and Sierra Leone in 1961, Jamaica, Uganda, Trinidad-Tobago in 1962, Kenya in 1963, Zambia in 1964 and so on. Another great colonial power France freed Morocco, Algeria, Tunisia and colonies on Indian-borders. In the post-World War II period Indonesia got freedom from the Dutch yoke when the Dutch government tried to subjugate Indonesia once again, it was prevented by other independent nations like India and Egypt. In 1949 Indonesia was accorded political recognition.

According to J.A. Hobson, "Colonialism is a natural overflow of nationality; its test is the power of colonists to transplant the civilisation they represent to the new natural and social environment in which they find themselves."

According to E.M. Winslow, "Colonialism is the occupation of virgin territory in which conflict was incidental, or even unnecessary, and subordinate to the desire of Europeans to find a new place to live."

Both Imperialism and Colonialism have common objectives. Both try to impose the power of one nation over the other. Both aim at exploiting the conquered and subject territories for promoting the interests of the imperialist and colonist nations. Both are based on superior-inferior relationship. Colonialism is the modern and economic form of imperialism. Form of colonialism has also undergone a change. 'New Imperialism' and 'New Colonialism' are the modern form of Imperialism and Colonialism, embracing the nations called 'Economic Dependencies and 'Satellites'.

New Imperialism and Neo-Colonialism. Economic imperialism is the form of imperialism in which a country indirectly carries out its directions. Today by giving economic aid to underdeveloped countries, the U.S.A. and the Soviet Union indirectly exercise their influence upon them. By giving 'Dollar' to underdeveloped and small countries.

Neo-Colonialism. 'Neo-Colonialism' is the empire of the 'sphere of influence'. The imperialist power does not easily allow any dependent nation to move out of its sphere of influence. According to Palmer and Perkins, 'Neo-Colonialism is a new and more insidious form of imperialism widely prevalent and particularly pernicious and dangerous." "The president of Ghana Kwame Nkrumah wrote a book entitled "Neo-colonialism". The last state of imperialism." Neo-colonialism seeks to establish economic dominance in place of political and military dominance. In the words of Late President Nasser, "Trade and aid becomes a veil to dominate the resources of nations and to exhast them for the benefit of exploiters." Britain exercised its economic influence over the Arab world by means of oil diplomacy. American dollar imperialism was established over the Western Europe and the newly independent nations of Asia and Africa. After the Second World War, Latin American nations are sovereign states, but their economic life is so completely dependent upon the United States that they are unable to propose any policy to which the United States would object. The East European nations behind the iron curtain are completely under the Soviet control. When Hungary and Czechoslovakia wanted to pursue independent policies, the Soviet Union interfered in their internal affairs by using force. Asia, Africa and many other areas of the world have fallen prey to new form of colonialism, known as Modern colonialism or Neo-colonialism.

Types of Neo-colonialism. A.F.K. Organski has descried three types of colonialism—classical or political colonialism. Economic Dependencies and Satellites. Political colonialism is that form of colonialism in which a territory is under the direct and complete control of a foreign country and whose inhabitants are not granted full political rights. Organski has included in Neo-colonialism the latter two types of colonialism—Economic dependencies and Satellites:

1. ***Economic Dependencies.*** These are politically independent and sovereign nations whose major economic enterprises are controlled by a foreign country. Economic Dependencies are economically underdeveloped nations. Their home economy is not owned and operated by their own government. Even the businessmen of a foreign nation can control the economy of another nation by investing more and more capital in another nation and establishing economic enterprises there. If the major economic enterprises in the nation are funded and controlled by foreigners, the foreign nationals control industry, finance and export import trade, and also industries, mines, commercial houses and banks.

The top managerial and technical personnel are nearly all foreigners, 51% of the national income is earned by foreigners, the nation is an economic dependency.

2. ***Satellites.*** A satellite is formally an independent nation controlled both politically and economically by some powerful foreign power. In communist nations as the major economic enterprises are run by the governments, it is not possible for one nation to control the economy of other without dominating its political institutions. Thus a nation both politically and economically controlled by some foreign power, completely dependent on it without any freedom of action is callled a 'Satellite'. The control exercised by a foreign power over Satellites is much more complete than that exercised over the Economic Dependencies which enjoy more independence than the Satellites. Unlike Satellites, they have the freedom to make a choice between Democracy and Communism, for example changes in Russian governmental policy are reflected almost immediately in the sattellites.

Cultural Imperialism. According to Morgenthanu. "Cultural imperialism is the most subtle and, if it were ever to succeed by itself alone, the most successful of imperialistic policies". It aims at the conquest and control of the minds of men as an instrument for changing the power relations. The state is able to impose its political ideology, which is far more superior to military victory and economic mastery. That end would have already been realised by the persuasiveness of a superior culture and a more attractive political philosophy. This cultural imperialism wing a more complete victory than military victory and economic mastery. The Soviety policy towards Eastern Europe is a classic example of Cultural imperialism. Cultural imperialism prepares ground for military conquest or economic penetration. For example the Communist International works under the directions of Moscow and ensures that the policies pursued by national communist paties were in accord with the foreign policy of the Soviet Union. Thus the control of the Soviet Union on particular nations goes on increasing.

FEATURES OF NEO-COLONIALISM

Traditional and New Forms. Imperialism-colonialism, in its traditional form, stands almost totally liquidated as a result of the rise of strong and successful anti-colonial national liberation movements in the colonies. Almost all the former colonies have emerged as sovereign states in the past five decades or so. However, the process is not yet complete because Imperialism-colonialism, as transformed into neo-colonialism, continues to be operative in international relations. Through subtle indirect methods, the farmer colonial powers are continuing to control the economies and policies of the newly emerged sovereign states of the world. The economic backwardness of these new states has been a source of big strain on their powers, and despite being politically independent these states find themselves dependent upon the rich states which are former imperial and colonial masters, for meeting their economic needs.

Exploitation. The former colonial powers continue to exploit the resources of these states through a number of means, like foreign aid, loans grants, tariffs, monopoly over international trade, exploitative price system, control over international economic institutions and multinational corporations. They have been successful in substituting their political domination by economic domination of the poor state. Such a state of affairs, in which the newly emerged sovereign states, though politically independent, continue to be economically dependent upon the former colonial powers, has come to be characterised as neo-colonialism.

What is Neo-Colonialism? Neo-Colonialism has been defined by a number of statesmen and scholars as a system of continued economic domination of the newly emerged sovereign states by the former colonial powers.

In the words of Kwane Nkrumah. "The essence of neo-colonialism is that the state which is subject to it, is in theory independent and has all the outward trappings of international sovereignty. In reality, its economic system and thus its political policy is directed from outside."

Generally speaking, Neo-Colonialism is a system of continued economic control over the newly emerged sovereign states by former colonial powers. "The mechanism of neo-colonialism results in the continuing economic dependence of former colonies upon their former colonial masters, integration of the former into colonial economic blocs through capital investments, loans aids, unequal change and finances directly controlled by colonial powers."

Reasons for the Emergence of Neo-Colonialism. The transformation of colonialism into neo-colonialism took place in the post-1945 period due to several reasons, which can be discussed as under:

1. ***Weakened Position of European Powers.*** The two world wars within a short duration inflicted very heavy losses upon the imperial powers of Europe. Their weakened position made it difficult for them to maintain their big colonial empires. The rise of strong national liberation movements in the colonies further made it difficult for them to continue their traditional empires. The emergence of decolonialisation and anti-imperialism as the strongest movements of post-war international reations led to the drive towards liquidation of the colonial empires and consequently to the rise of new sovereign states in international relations.
2. ***Rise of Consciousness Against Imperialism.*** The imperial powers found it difficult to justify the continuance of their rule over colonies because of the spread of political consciousness, and the acceptance of the right of self-determination as upheld by the Atlantic Charter and later on by the Charter of the United Nations. Further. the intensification of national liberation movements in several key countries like India, also compelled the imperial powers to grant independence to their colonies and yet keep up the system of economic exploitation of the new states.
3. ***Impact of Cold War Power Politics.*** The cold war that emerged in the post-war period and the subsequent emergence of two rival blocs in international relations, made things worst for the new states. Many of the new

states felt compelled to join either of the two blocs for securing vitally needed economic assistance and military equipment.

4. ***The Need of the Developed States to Maintain hold over Resources of the Poor Countries of the Third World.*** The continued need for raw materials and markets for selling their goods compelled the imperial powers to somehow maintain their economic domination of such states of Asia and Africa as had attained the status of sovereign independent states in the post-45 period. The imperial powers decided to serve their economic interests by new, subtle and indirect economic devices. Having been forced to abandon the old colonial system, they decided to go in for neo-colonialism—the systematised economic domination of their former colonies. The most common device which they adopted for this purpose was to break up "the former large united colonial territories into a number of small non-viable states, which were incapable of independent economic development and had per force to rely upon their former colonial masters for their economic and security needs."

5. ***The Continued Dependence of the New States on Developed States.*** The dependence of the new states upon the former colonial states for selling raw materials as well as for purchansing industrial goods from them. brought into existence Neo-Colonialism. Their traditional economic dependence upon the colonial powers continued even after the attainment of independence. Their increased needs, because of the new objective of promoting the welfare of all its people, further compelled the states to accept the economic control of the former colonial powers.

6. ***The Policies of the USA and the Erstwhile Soviet Union.*** In the era of Cold War (1945-90) both the USA and the erstwhile USSR wanted to expand their respective areas of influence. For this, they decided to exploit the economic needs of the new states. Through such devices as foreign

aid, loans, supply of arms, control over international economy and economic institutions multinational corporations etc., they were successful in creating their economic dependencies and satellites. An economic dependency is a sovereign state whose economic interests are controlled by a rich and powerful developed state. A satellite state is that sovereign state whose economy stands linked up and dependent upon a rich and powerful state. America and other western powers have been using the creation of their economic dependencies and the erstwhile Soviet Union used the creation of its satellite states as a means for operationalising neo-colonialism in international relations.

Methods of Neo-Colonialism. Neo-Colonialism is practised by the rich and powerful state through a number of well settled definite methods. The following methods are usually used by them for exercising control over the neo-colonial states:

1. ***Through Interference in the Internal Politics of New States.*** The subject of political culture has been the hall-mark of the political systems of the newly emerged sovereign states. The former imperial powers have their "Groups", the Elite Groups, which are involved in active struggle for power in these states. By supporting a particular loyal group to the opposition of other groups, the imperial powers are in a position to interfere and influence the policies of the Neo-Colonial States. By supporting puppet regimes and by securing desired military or civilian coups in such states, the imperial powers are in a position to exercise control over the policies of these states. Of course, here the fault lies fundamentally with the newly independent nations themselves. Due to their internal problems and conflict these states are not in a position to secure political stability. The frequent Military *coup d'etats* in these states provide adequate opportunities to the powerful states, particularly the super powers, to assert their power over these states—Congo, Zaire, Nigeria, and the list is indeed

very big have all been victims of frequent coups and counter coups and hence have been ripe objects for the enforcement of neo-colonialism the powerful and developed states.

2. ***Through the Supply of Arms and Weapons.*** The existence of several disputes and the continued tensions of cold war have been big sources of insecurity for the newly emerged sovereign states. The desire for security has been a continuous and big problem for these states. Consequently, these states have been very keen to secure arms and military equipment from the developed and powerful states. Their inability to become self-sufficient in respect of their military needs keeps them dependent upon the powerful states.

3. ***Use of Foreign Aid and Loans.*** The most common and the most forceful means adopted by the Neo-Colonial powers have been foreign aid and loan. The economic backwardness of the new states has been a curse in so far as it has kept these economically dependent upon their former colonial masters and other developed states. The rich and powerful states always use their capacities to give foreign aid and loans as means for influencing a desired change in the economy and policies of the dependent nations. While giving foreign aid or loan, the donour states impose a number of conditions, like agreement for economic co-operation right to secure certain concessions, right to influence certain economic changes as pre-conditions for the grant of aid or loan, lowering of trade barriers in favour of the donour country's goods and capital, laying down the manner of use of funds, forcing the recipient to set up counter funds for buying goods from the donor national etc.

4. ***Role of Foreign Capital.*** The foreign capital invested in the neo-colonial states is meant not so much for the development of the less developed areas, as for the promotion of the interests of the development countries." Foreign aid

is always used as a weapon of foreign policy of the donour nations and is never given without strings. The American PL 480-Food for Peace, aid was given to channelise the American surplus in food production and to make the recipient states dependent upon the USA. For the dependent and lowly developed neo-colonial states of the Third World, the benefit of the foreign aid has been only marginal, it has infact, perpetuated the dependence of the Third World countries on such aid.

5. ***Through the use of Multinational Corporations.*** The most powerful instruments of neo-colonialism are the multinational corporations (MNCs). These MNCs have been formed by rich investors of developed states with a view to control economic and industrial enterprises in all parts of the globe. These are international business organisations operating in many countries and acting for monopolising international capital trade, commerce and production and distribution of goods. Through several monopoly rights and international patents. These MNCs are in a position to secure huge profits for their owners and consequently for the rich states. International firms like IBM. General Motors. GEC, Standard Oil etc, have more powers then most of the sovereign governments. The international profits of Standard Oil are four times larger than its domestic profits with only a third of its assets invested abroad. The MNCs execise a powerful influence over the policies of many Asian, African and Latin American states. Through their strong economic potential and control over the economics of poor and weak states, the MNCs are in a position to exert sufficient influence on the political and economic policies of the these countries.

6. ***Through Control Over International Economic Institutions.*** The international economy of the post-war period is regulated and controlled by a number of international economic institutions like the World Bank, IBRD, IFC, IDA, etc. The rich states have a monopolistic

control over these institutions. When the new states try to get aid and loans from these institutions, the rich nations use their control over them for securing favourable and desired economic policy decision. The conditions imposed on India at the time of securing of the IMF loan bear ample proof of the potential of this method of neo-colonialism. The grant of funds as loans and aids by these international economic institutions, particularly IMF, has been always governed by political considerations as well as by the interests of the rich states which really control these institutions. The demand for a New International Economic order by the Third World is designed to make these institutions really effective international institutions for promoting the interests of all the countries of the World.

7. ***Creating Economic Dependencies.*** Economic Dependencies are lowly developed economically backward states whose economy and key financial enterprises are controlled by a foreign power. The foreign control over the economy of the economic dependency is exercised both by the government and the private investors of the neo-colonial power. For selling its raw-materials and other commodities as well as for the import of vitally essential goods, the economic dependency is fully dependend upon the foreign power. The foreign power controls its imports and exports. The top managerial and technical personnel are all foreigners. Sometimes the neo-colonial power runs the industries and other services for the neo-colonial states and pays a fixed percentage of profits as royalty to the economic dependency.

8. ***By Creating Satellites.*** When the economy and political policy of a poor and backward state is almost completely dependend upon a foreign power, it is called a satellite state. A satellite state enjoys considerably less independence in internal policies than an economic dependency. Satellite states are like autonomous units of the foreign power which controls and regulates the policies and administration

of its statellites. The change in policies of the foreign power always produces corresponding changes in the policies of the Satellite States. These Satellite States are of three types:

1. There are certain satellite states which are controlled by the leaders of the powerful superior state. The policies of the satellites are fully controlled by these leaders.
2. Certain satellite states are under the direct control and influence of the government of the superior state.
3. Finally, certain satellite state are located in so close a proximity of the superior big state that these states deliberately adopt policies which are akin to the policy of the powerful neighbouring state. Such satellites are always keen to avoid the wrath of the superior state.

Soviet Control. The Soviet control over the policies and economies of the Eastern European socialist states during the period 1947-89 was so complete that the latter virtually acted as satellites of the former. The revolts against Soviet hegemony and the rise of strong and successful democratic regimes in the Eastern European States in late 1980s secured an end of the Soviet control over these countries. The final collapse of the Soviet Union (1991) finally ended the era of Centre-Satellite relationship in Eastern Europe.

Colonialism in Disguise. Neo-Colonialism is colonialism in disguise. It is as much bad and harmful system as have been the systems of colonialism and imperialism. The curse of exploitation and backwardness continues to exercise its evil effect upon the newly emerged sovereign states. Under neo-colonialism their position continues to be weak and low. To be politically independent and sovereign state is a matter of pride and status, but to be economically dependent neo-colonialism state is the most harmful and dangerous situation for the states of the Third World. Under Neo-colonialism, the powerful and rich nations are successfully maintaining a subtle and indirect, but very effective control over the policies of the new states. The economic exploitation of the poor and backward states—

"The South" by the rich and powerful states—"The North" continues to be there almost unabated. The fight against imperialism and colonialism is as such not complete. There exists a strong need to fight neo-colonialism. The rich states are determined to keep up their superior position in international relations through a near monopolistic control over international economy and international economic institutions. The Third World states—the new states are equally determined to secure a restructuring of international economy with a view to make it equitable and just. The end of cold war has made the issue of restructuring of international relations. The need is to pool all efforts for securing a new International Economic Order which alone can go a long-way to strike hard at the roots of Neo-colonialism. Dependency theorists have used Centre-Periphery models for explaining the nature of neo-colonial control of the Developed over the Developing countries.

❐

7

Balance of Power

RELEVANCE OF THE CONCEPT

It has been observed that there is inconsistency between the theory of balance of power and its practical application. Now the question arises whether the theory of balance of power has any relevance today. On the one hand, here are scholars who believe that the conditions essential for the successful operation of the balance of power system do not exist today, therefore, the theory of the balance of power cannot operate under the present day conditions. On the other hand, there are scholars who do not question the validity of the theory of the balance of power and hold that it is relevant under the present day conditions. They also hold that the concept of the balance of power is essential for the international society based on power politics. Morgenthau remarks, "The balance of power and policies aiming at its preservation are not only inevitable but are an essential stabilizing factor in a society of sovereign national." According to Organski, the theory of the balance of power has, in fact, become obsolete after the Industrial Revolution and does not work number the present day conditions, Morgenthau observes, "The instability of the international balance of power is due not to the faultiness of the principle but to the particular conditions under which the principle must operate in a society of sovereign nations". It is claimed that the principles of the theory are correct but the altered conditions have prevented the balance from operating correctly. Palmer and Perkins observed that the conditions of the modern world are peculiarly unfavourable to the balance of power system. These unfavourable conditions may be discussed as below:

1. The balance of power worked best in those periods of modern history when in Europe a number of states of

approximately equal strength existed. Later on, when the European balance of power turned into a world balance of power, conditions become less favourable for the suceessful adjustment of balance of power among nations. The impact of new forces like nationalism, industrialism, new methods and techniques of warfare, developments in international organisation and law, growing economic inter-dependence of nations, have greatly affected the nature of contemporary world politics.

2. At the outbreak of the First World War there were 8 Great Powers This number was reduced to 7 at the outbreak of the Second World War. After the Second World War the number was reduced to 3 only—the U.S.A., the Soveit Union and Great Britain. In the post-War period, there was a further decline in the British power. As a result there were left only 2 powers—The U.S.A., and the U.S.S.R. which deserve to be called 'Superpowers'. In former times the balance of power operated by way of coalition among a number of nations. The principal nations, though differing in power, were still of the same order of magnitude. The greater the number of active players, that is, the number of Great Powers, the greater the number of possible combinations that will actually oppose each other. The likely combinations and the role of individual players both would be uncertain.

3. The emergence of bi-polarism after the Second World War has made the balance of power difficult to operate. All the major nations of the World are firmly committed to one camp or another, and no single nation is strong enough to tip the balance between the two Super Powers. As Prof. Morgenthau observes, "The power of the United States and of the Soveit Union in comparison with the power of their actual or prospective allies has become so overwhelming that through their own preponderant weight they determine the balance of power between them. The balance cannot at present be decisively affected by changes

in the alignments of one or the other of their allies. The balance of power has been transformed from a multipolar into a bipolar one." To-day the disparity in power between the Super Powers and other powers is so great that each is stronger than any other power or possible combination of these powers. As a result, the major powers have not only lost their ability to tip the scales but they have almost lost the freedom of movement to switch sides. The preference of the minor powers count for little. The will of the Super Powers, and other circumstances beyond their control, determine their political and military alignments. Gone is the era of ever shifting alliances.

4. The implication of the nuclear weapons have made the traditional assumptions of the balance of power obsolete. The changed character of modern war would shudder even the most rutheless proponents of the balance of power from taking the risk of precipitating a world-wide-struggle to right the balance.
5. The disappearance of the balancer is another factor which has made the system of balance of power in-operative. There is no power to-day to play the role of a balancer which was successfully performed by Britain. Britain no longer holds so decisive a position as to tip the balance. Its role as a balancer has come to an end. A different line of reasoning has been advanced by Prof. Morgenthau that because of the structural changes in th functioning of the balance of power itself, no nation in the place of Britain can play the role of a balancer at present.
6. The growing importance of idelogical consideration has also produced unfavourable condition for the operation of the balance of power. The ideological factor in the world politics has become so potent that it has superseded nationalism. The ideologies are cutting across national boundaries and thus undermining the balance of power concept. Palmer and Parkins remark, "Where the foreign

policy of a state is highly flavoured by ideology, that state is usually not much interested in the balance of power and is poorly equipped to pursue it."

7. The disparities in the power of states are increasing. While the super powers are becoming more and more powerful, the lesser states are becoming weaker. This situation runs counter to the requirements of a working system of balance of power.
8. The growing influence of collective security, international law and international organisation (the United Nations) has also undermined the balance of power concept. Most present day writers believe that law and its enforcement should depend more on moral consensus of nations, public opinion, the United Nations, and collective security than on a mechanism of balance of power.

IS THE BALANCE OF POWER CONCEPT RELEVANT TO-DAY?

Although the concept of the balance of power has lost much of its validity in the present day conditions, its operation is still meaningful. As long as the multi-nation state system exists, balance of power politics will continue to be followed in practice by the nations. So long as the international society is based on power politics, balance of power will remain as a relevant concept. The change brought about in the international society have removed many of the conditions in which the balance of power functioned in the past, but it has not eliminated the reality of power. Since the balance of power is a dervice of the management of power, it will remain relevant till some other device of managing power has not been found out. Quincy Wright hoped that the U.N.O. would take over the function that the balance of power has so far been performing. He observed, "If democracy and human liberty are to survive, the nations that espouse the balance of power must find some other device than the balance of power to give them political security." The balance of power is an important concept in international politics. In its heyday it was a basic feature of the nation—state system. Palmer and Perkins remark, "as long as the nation-state system is the prevailing pattern of international society, balance of power policies will be followed in practice, however soundly they are damned in theory." In its own way balance of power has performed some useful functions: it did sometimes help to preserve the independence of states, and prevent a single nation from becoming all powerful. If it averted some wars, it also led to greater ones. The reason for the remarkable survival of the balance of power is that its effective substitute has not yet been possible. Such a substitute can probably be found out in the effective world organisation, world public opinion and world-wide acceptance of the obligations of international law. But this prospect is very remote. Being more realistic Carl J. Friedrich remarked, that the balance of power "may yet be preferable to the international anarchy which is prevailing at present." However, Palmer and Perkins believe that balance of power will continue to operate, even if super national world organisation is formed. We conclude with the observations of G. H. Snyder that "the idea of balance of power is still the central theoretical concept in international relations."

PRINCIPLE OF BALANCE OF POWER

There is of course a greater need of the maintenance of balance of power in the modern world comparatively more than it was felt in the bygone period. The balance of power is the very back-bone of world peace and in actual practice this very principle guarantees the cause of international security. If all the nations are given a free hand in the field of accumulating as much armed power and wealth as they can, the Third World War might again become a probability in no time. We refer to the balance of power as was enunciated in the Vienna Congress (1815), though it aimed at the protection of the Monarchies against the rising masses against their rulers. That principle envisaged that a particular state or a group of a states might not become so much powerful that might cause a terror to or dare an onslaught upon other states.

This principle of balance of power aimed at checkmating the power of a state or a group of states that may develop into a great danger to the freedom of weaker nations. The balance of power enunciated by Bismarck in 1870s was different from the principle accepted in the Vienna Congress. Actually his concept of balance of power conceived that it is better to be "one of the trio" to govern the world consisting to "five". According to him and in reality the world then was overwhelmed by five major powers *viz.*, Great Britain, Germany, France, Austria and Russia.

Prof. A.F. Pollard is of the opinion that there are several thousand possible meanings of the phrase "the Balance of Power". Prof. Sehleicher points out, "It has so many meanings that it is virtually meaningless. In fact, every writer has given his own colour to it." Schwarzenberger speaks of it as an "equilibrium". Marsn Wright A.J.P. Taylor and Charles Lerche speak of it as a "System". Sidney B. Fay, maintains that the balance of power is just an equilibrium of power among the members of the family of nations as would prevent anyone of them becoming sufficiently strong to enforce its will upon the others. According to Prof. Morgenthau the term balance of power issued in four different senses, *(i)* as a policy aimed at a certain state of affairs; *(ii)* as an actual state of affairs; *(iii)* as an approximately equal distribution of power; *(iv)* as any distribution of power. Prof. Morgenthau says, "Whenever the term is used without qualifications, it refers to an actual state of affairs in which power is distributed among several nations with approximate equality".

The Elements of Balance of Power. There are two main elements of balance of power *viz.*, equalisation of power and direction of power.

(i) ***Equalisation of Power*** implies that various groups of nations must invariably be maintained.

In case a particular group of nations grows in power, it must stabilise at least for a specific period, till the other group who is less powerful, gradually increases the proportions of its power. It can therefore, be said that every power bloc is free to make its efforts of increasing its strength and there would be no chance of collision between the powers of the two or more blocs of nations, provided they remain at equilibrium.

(ii) Direction of Power. Each and every state of the world would like to associate itself with the greatest power. It is not practicable. Therefore all the states with a view to maintaining their own national security on the one hand and world peace on the other should so direct their foreign as well as home policies that the International balance of power might not be disturbed:

(a) England and Germany. England remained a topmost power of the world before the advent of the Second World War. Her observance of the principle of balance of power was criticised thus by an English politician, Sir Eyre Crowe : "So long as England remains faithful to the general principle of the balance of power her interest would not be served by Germany being reduced to the rank of a weak power, as this might easily lead to a Franco-Russian predominance equally, if not more, formidable to the British Empire."

It is said England acted on the opinion of Sir Eyre Crowe and she changed her policy in relation to Germany whose power she had absolutely crushed down in the First World War. When the position of Germany started deteriorating tremendously since 1923, with the result that the "Franco-Russian predominance" appeared to be becoming all the more conspicuous in Europe. England soon reverted to her appeasement policy in relation to Germany. She acted on the basis of the balance of power and thereby tried to improve the condition of Germany.

(b) England and the U.S.A. England remained favourable to Germany till 1933, but in the event of the growing tenacity of Hitlerite dictatorship in Germany England had to change her policy. She again befriended France and tried to come closer to Soviet Russia. Thereupon, Germany in her desperate haste of searching for her own allies, completed her axis power bloc in Europe

and Asia by establishing her alignment with Italy and Japan. Not only that, Hitler gained the sympathies of Stalin also, and a non-aggression pact was duly signed between Germany and Russia. This grievously hurt the continental balance of power in Europe and it could not be recovered until the grave defeat of France and England at the hands of German arms was witnessed by the world. These vanquished powers of West Europe were therefore obliged to call in the United States in the theatre of war, who made up the balance of power.

The Balance of Power Favouring the World Peace. Mr. Harold Nicholson published in 1932 in 'Public Faces' that "the dry and indefinite relationship between suppression and resistance in the samee happens to be the cause of balance of power" and it is needed to rescue the weak nations from the repression of the powerful nations so that they might not be in a position to exploit the freedom of their weak neighbours by use of force. This arrangement was made in order to checkmate the growing discontent and resentment of weak nations of Europe against the exceeding expansion of the powers of Napoleonic France, Hitlerite Germany and the Communist Russia. At the end of the Second World War the Allied powers found that their victory was short living and their alliance only seasonal. Now in place of Germany, Soviet Russia emerged as a great terrorising power to threaten the balance of power in Europe and the world peace. Therefore England and U.S.A. had to reshuffle their policies. Now they decided to lift Germany and Japan whom they had mercilessly crushed in the face of the great war against the expansion of Russian Communism. England, France and the U.S.A. combined to declare free the so called "Trizonia of Germany", so that it was again after the acquisition of its lost power, roused to action against the expansionism of Soviet Russia. The emergence of China in 1949, appeared to be more dangerous than Soviet Russia to world peace and therefore its old enemy—Japan—had to be declared free by the Western Allies. By 1960s, the Communist bloc started dividing itself into two bloc separately led by Soviet Russia and China. At the same time, De-Gaulle's dream of building Western Europe as a self-reliant bloc to dispel the designs of the USA and Soviet Russia to divide the world into a tight bipolar system also realized. As a result another potential group of European States emerged under the aegies of the European Economic Community (EEC). The EEC at the same time started defusing the tense existing with the Soviet bloc. This policy was much more harmful to the USA than the Soviet Union. It compelled the USA to come closer both to the Soviet Union and China. This move envisaged to counter-balance Soviet Union by befriending China and the EEC by befriending to the Soviet Union.

Besides, there exists a power bloc of all the neutral countries of the world whom either of the above two major power blocs have been trying to win over to their side. India is a powerful nation amidst the other neutral countries and has more or less taken the leadership of the third bloc. It is feared that India might not be drifted to collaborate with either of the two militant power blocs which would again disturb the balance of power in the world. However the Western powers as well as India herself view her separation from the two militant power blocs with high expectations of maintaining the balance of power in the world and the preservation of international peace.

DECLINE OF THE PRINCIPLE OF BALANCE OF POWER IN MODERN TIMES

The concept of Balance of Power was very popular during the period from 15th to 18th century, when a number of states of approximately equal strength competed with each other according to the well-established and generally recognized rules. However, with the widening of the sphere of international relations from Europe to World, the concept of 'balance of power' suffered a set back.

Four factors have mainly been responsible for the decline of the concept of Balance of Power in modern times. These factors are as follows:

1. Growing Bi-Polarity. The first set back to the system of balance of power was given by the decline of Britain as a strong power. In view of her weakened position in the present world she is not in a position to play the role of a balance, which is so vital for the working of this system. At present there are two Big Powers—U.S.A and U.S.S.R.—but none of them can hope to play the role of a balancer because both of them are very much involved in the bi-polar politics of cold war. In this regard profs. Palmer and Perkins say: "As it is, neither country is well prepared to play the balance of power game, for the simple reason that the power of either alone is incomparably greater than that of any possible combination of other states". While U.S.A. is unwilling to play the role of a balancer because of her traditional opposition to the principle, the Soviet Union is not interested in regulating the balance of power because it stands in the way of the Communist objectives.

2. Association of Ideology and Balance of Power. The ideology which has cut across the national boundaries and supplanted the ties of nationalism has also undermined the balance of power concept. Though ideology and balance of power concepts are not necessarily antithetical yet, as Proft Palmer and Perkins say, "it is true that where the foreign policy of a state is highly favoured by ideology, that state is usually not much interested in balance of power and is poorly equipped to pursue it."

3. Frightening Implications of Total War. Another factor which discourage any country to play the role of the balancer is the frightening implications of the toal war with the modern destructive weapons. The only independent agency which can serve as a balancer is the United Nations. But its working over all these years has fully demonstrated its incapacity to play a more vigorous role in world politics. No doubt the U.N. can and has played a useful role in mitigating the conflicts and tensions that threaten the peace, but "as an instrument of the nation-state system it lacks the power authority, and status to be an effective regulator or balancer of an international system which still rests more on balance of power considerations than on considerations of genuine collective security or genuine supernationalism."

4. Growing Disparity in Power of States. The growing disparity among the powers of the various states has also upset the balance of power. While the Super Powers are becoming more and more powerful, the smaller states have not been able to increase their position relatively.

Relevance of Balance of Power in Modern Times. The above discussion should not lead us to the conclusion that the concept of Balance of Power has become obsolete though some of the critics hold that the doctrine is incompatible with the present system. For example Quincy Wright says, "If democracy and human liberty are to survive, the nations that expose these principles must find some device other than the balance of power to give them political security...The balance of power as the structure of world politics is incompatible with democracy, with free enterprise, with welfare economy, and with peace."

Explaining the reasons for the survival of the doctrine of balance of powers. Proft. Palmer and Perkins say, "As yet the nations and people of the world have not been willing to create any effective substitute. Such a substitute can probably be found only through world organisation on the supernational level, backed by a world public opinion and a world-wide acceptance of the principles of international law". He further says that, "as long as the nation-state system is prevailing pattern of international society, balance of power policies will be followed in practice, however, roundly they are damned in theory. In all probability they will continue to operate, even if effective-supernational groupings on a regional or world level, are formed."

TYPES OF THE BALANCE OF POWER

There are essentially three types of balance of power, which are as follows:

1. Simple and Complex Balance of Power. *(a)* The changing times of the modern age have multiplied the number of free states with numerous complications of their respective problems and therefore the rise and fall of the balance of power has become a natural course of world politics. The complex balance of power which would be explained here is considered to be a complex one due to the warring position of the two militant nations. But some of the political philosophers have maintained that the simple balance of power entails the radical nationalism of the collaborating powers while the complex balance of power aims at the preservation of peace. The first is simple because it concentrates on the stand point of maintaining the balance of power for the safety of the nationalities of the world. The second is complicated because its approach is hazardous to the maintenance of balance of power as it directly concentrates upon the preservation of peace. *(b)* The two forms of the balance of power are very apt to run concurrently in a given time between the peace loving nations on the one hand and the warring nations on the other. The reason is that hundreds of free nations in the world of whom every one is beset with specially different problems cannot remain pacific for any considerable length of time. However, there are a good number of such states as would like the principle of co-existance in respect of solving their respective problems on the basis of simple Balance of Power. Apart from them some of the nations who live in the turbulent regions of the world, militantly, aim at solving their respective problems by resorting to arms. Wherever the matter of struggle is conspicuous between the two nations and not more, and each of them concentrates upon keeping the Balance of Power in its own favour, their Balance of Power is considered to be simple. Contrary to it, the matter of the struggle for power of political influence becoming conspicuous between more than two nations seeking the course of alignment, makes the Balance of Power complicated enough.

2. The Rigid and the Flexible Balance of Power. The U.S.A. and the U.S.S.R. at maintaining their rigid Balance of Power as their groupism had assumed a state position with hardly and chance of change in their policies in spite of the most catastrophic circumstances. But the position of international politics can never remain homogeneous for a considerable length of time. It is subject to natural and automatically changing circumstances. The changing problems and political outlooks of various States oblige them to break off their existing alignments and seek their alliance with other power blocs afresh. The enemy states turn friendly due to their selfish motives and vice versa.

3. The Local, Regional or the World-Wide Balance of Power. The Balance of Power aiming at checkmating only one power of a particular state is considered to be a local one. In the event of any one nation suddenly growing in its power as a great danger to the freedom of other neighbouring states, but not in a position to brook conflict with any of them, the Balance of Power remains all the more local in its operation. The question of Balance of Power wherever it becomes connected with one or more geographical and political regions, is to be named as regional Balance of Power. The third is the world-wide Balance of Power as is the case with the modern age. By the end of nineteenth century the western powers had confined their struggle for power to the frontiers of the European Continent and it was called the regional Balance of Power. The European rapture has now entered the whole world after the preceding century. The people only talk of the world-wide Balance of Power during the course of the two world wars of the present century but since the conclusion of the later, it became conspicuous in the face of the groupism of the U.S.A. on, the one hand and the U.S.S.R., on the other.

THE POLICIES OF BALANCE OF POWER

It is obligatory for the States of the world that they cling to the augmentation of their powers merely for the sake of their national security. The run in the desperate haste of searching for their friends or allies in the event of their fear from any neighbouring states growing into tremendous powers suddenly. Any state subject to such crucial circumstances when maintains its Balance of Power with its most feared neighbouring state, ultimately breaths an open air. The sphere of alliance is extend by a particular state or a group of states. As soon as it finds itself powerless before the strength of the other states or a group of states. Thus two and even more states might be aligned in a single group or bloc and thereafter other group also endeavours to extend its power by searching out new friends. It then succeeds in balancing its power with its rivalling state or the group of states so that it may be able to meet the challenge or onslaught of its rival or the enemy. Apart from the process of Balancing the power of states or that of the groups of various states, the basis of practical Balances of Power is the diverse policies of the different states of the world. Upto the present times the following policies have been influencing the process of the Balance of Power:

1. The policy of extending the state or bloc influence and control over the weak regions of the world.
2. The policy of appeasement or compensation to the appallingly down trodden states. The provision of compensation or appeasement can be made in terms of arms, political facilities territorial or in some other probable way.
3. The policy of managing mutual security between the member states of a particular power bloc and those of the rival power blocs.
4. The policy of maintaining the *status quo* and resorting even to war for the same, such as the Crimean war which was fought for protecting the Mediterranean waters against the entry of the Soviet Russia.
5. The creation of buffer states or buffer zones as neutral countries. For example, the free and neutral states of Belgium and Luxemburg had been prepared as buffer zones between France and Germany.

THE POSTULATES OF THE SYSTEM OF BALANCE OF POWER

The postulates of the balance of power are liable to be carried out only by the liberal minded yet powerful nations of the world, who indulge not in the hot haste for the acquisition of power but in the pacific struggle for the same. In the words of Professor Nicholas Spykman, "He who plays the Balance of Power, can have no permanent friends. His devotion can be to no specific state but only to balanced power. The ally of today is the enemy of tomorrow and one of the chance of power politics is that it offers no opportunity to grow weary of one's friends."

It can hardly be denied that only the peace-loving countries, in order to preserve their territorial homogeneity and national freedom aim at maintaining the Balance of Power. The chief postulates of the policy and system of Balance of Power are as follows:

1. The position and power of states as well as the international policies are liable to timely and natural changes and therefore with a view to maintaining the world peace and order in the various states, the state policies must be subjected to necessary amendments.

2. The states should also be prepared to make necessary change-over in their system of alignments in order to maintain the Balance of Power.

3. The weakness is a great misery and it encourages the powerful state of attack the weak state. Therefore after the conclusion of war it is unavoidable to notice any country becoming intolerably powerful or weakened.

4. The states should never tend to acquire tremendous power nor should they turn almost weak. At the end of the Second World War the U.S.A., ordered the retreat of her forces—even from those territories where the Red Armies of the U.S.S.R., were all along stationcd and thus the U.S.A., presented an instance of her weakness. This encouraged the U.S.S.R., to despatch her battallions to various regions of the American influence and they created a violent disorder in them. Ultimately the U.S.A., had to take the U.N. help for getting vacated those regions from Soviet occupation. North Korea passed into the influence of Soviet Union and the position of Vietnam also worsened due to the same reason of American slackness. It resulted in the loss of lives of the several thousands of French soldiers.

5. The responsible states should at all hours be prepared for resort to arms against such foreign or internal elements of the states which create discontentment and disorder so that the free and peace loving nations might be protected against terror and onslaught of the power blocs of powerful states.

6. It is quite indispensable that the harmless yet powerful nations should at once go to the rescue of the weak

countries in the face of any armed attack on them by the militant powers. They should eventually come forward to sign mutual peace treaties with the terrorised nations so that the terrorist countries might not be in a position to succeed in their selfish designs against them.

The significance of the Balance of Power is still very much in the sphere of international politics. The ninetenth century remarks of Lord Palmerston in 1848, are here worthy of mention : "England had no perpetual friends, no natural enemies but eternal interest" of preserving the Balance of Power for the sake of continental peace. Contrary to it some of the twentieth century politicians of the rank of the U.S. President Wilson have refuted the importance of Balance of Power in the interest of an organised common peace.

MERITS AND DEMERITS

As a concept in international politics, Balance of Power has been the object of both high praise and strong criticism. Many, like Martin Wright, regard it as "nearly a fundamental law of politics as is possible to find," or as Palmer and Perkins observe, "Balance of Power is a basic principle of international relations." As against this many others strongly criticise it as unreal, inadequate and uncertain system. In the words of Richard Cobden, "The Balance of Power is a chimera. It is not a fallacy, a mistake or an imposture, it is an indescribable, incomprehensible nothing: mere words, conveying to the mind not ideas, but sound." The supporters advance a number of arguments in favour and give example of the 1815-1914 period of history to prove the effectiveness of balance of power as a device of power-management and peace. The critics, however, challenge its underlying assumptions and hold that it is an inadequate, dangerous and risky device of power management which wrongly projects war in the interest of peace.

MERITS OR ARGUMENTS IN FAVOUR OF BALANCE OF POWER

The supporters of balance of power advocate that it is a natural principle of international politics. In the struggle for power among nations it is the consideration for balance or equilibrium that alone can secure peace in the world. Morgenthau and Thompson defend Balance of Power as the maker of international system. "At many stages of history it has helped the nations to successfully prevent a nation from becoming so much powerful as could have made it capable of destroying the freedom of others." Even critics like I.L. Claude accept that it can create and maintain an equilibrium in power relations. It has been praised by its supporters on the following grounds:

(1) **BOP as a Source of Stability in International Relations.** Balance of Power provides stability to international relations. It is a device of effective power management and peace. During the past 400 years it was successful, at most of the times, in preserving peace. In the words of Fredric Geniz, "It has many a times prevented war. War breaks out only when any state assumes excessive power" Commenting upon the main reason that led to the out break of First World War, Clemenceau observed, "First World War was the result of the breakdown of Balance of Power. Had it been maintained, war would definitely have not broken out."

(2) **BOP Suits the Nature of International Relations.** Balance of Power is in tune with the dynamic nature of international relations. It helps continuous adjustments and re-adjustments in relations without any grave risk of war among nations.

(3) **Ensures Multiplicity of States.** Since Balance of Power postulates a balance in power relations of a number of major international actors (7 or 8 or even more), it ensures multiplicity of nations and their active participation in preserving balance in relations *i.e.*, peace.

(4) **Guarantees the Freedom of Small States.** Balance of Power ensures the preservation of small and weak nations. Its rule that no nation is to be completely eliminated favours the continued existence of all states. Each state feels secure about its security in the balance of power system.

(5) **Discourages War.** Balance of Powers discourages war because each state knows that any attempt to become unduly more powerful shall invoke an action by all other states and hence, it keeps its power ambitions under control.

(6) **Checks Imperialism.** Balance of Power checks imperialism in so far as it cleraly rules out the elimination of any small state by any big state.

(7) **A Source of Peace in International Relations.** Finally, Balance of Power is a source of peace and order in international relations. It Supports *status quo* in relations.

On all these grounds the supporters of Balance of Power praise it as the natural and ideal principle of international relations.

CRITICISM OR DEMERITS OF BALANCE OF POWER

The critics of Balance of Power reject the view of its defenders and hold that it is an ambiguous, uncertain, unreal and inadequate principle which cannot preserve international peace and security, particularly in the contemporary stage of international politics. They challenge its fundamental assumptions and question its operationability. They reject thc thesis that peace in the pre-1914 period was preserved due to the operation of Balance of Power principle. The following are the main arguments of the critics of Balance of Power:

(1) **Balance of Power cannot Ensure Peace.** A balance of power does not necessarily bring peace. Even during its hey days, it failed to pervent the domination of small states by the big states. It was not successful in preserving a stable international peace and the security of small states. The history of its operation during 1648-1918 gives a long list of wars that were fought among nations. In fact wars were fought in the name of preservation of Balance of Power. The universal domination by one state was prevented at the price of warfare which from 1648 to 1815 was virtually continuous and which in the 20th century engulfed practically the whole world. The three periods of stability— one starting from 1648, the second from 1815 and the third from Treaty of Versailes (1918), were preceded by

continuous warfare and by the wholesale elimination of small states and were interspersed, starting with the destruction of Poland, by a great number of isolated acts of a similar nature. The tragedy is that all these acts were accomplished in the name of balance of power. In the words of Morgenthau, "Not only did the balance of power fail to protect the independence of Poland, but the very principle of territorial compensation to each member for the territorial aggrandisement of any other member brought about the destruction of the Polish state. The destruction of Poland in the name of balance of power was but the first and most spectacular instance of a series of partitions, annexations, and destruction of independent states which, from 1815 to the present, have all been accomplished of that same principle." Balance of Power cannot really secure peace and freedom of the nations.

(2) **A Mechanical View of Peace.** Balance of Power wrongly takes a mechanical view of world peace as a situation of balance of equilibrium in power relations. Peace does not depend upon the balance in power relations. It depends upon international consciousness and morality. It is not a mechanistic configuration but a human ideal.

(3) **Narrow Basis.** The concept of Balance of Power is based upon a narrow view of international relations. It makes power-relations as the whole of international relations. It gives near total importance to preservation of self and self-interest as the motives of all state actions. It fails to give proper weightage to other ends—social, economic, cultural and moral that provide strong motives to international relations. Balance of Power fails to realise the importance of the economic and psychological aspects of national power and it wrongly concentrates all its attention upon military power as the factor of the national power.

(4) **Nations are not Static Units.** Another point that must be raised about the balance of powes is that nations are not static units. They increase their power through military

aggression, seizure of territory and alliances. They can change their power from within by improving social organisation by industrializing and by mobilizing internal resources.

(5) **Preponderance of One Power can also Secure Peace.** A preponderance of power in the hands of one nation or group of nations does not necessarily threaten world peace or the indepenence of nations. A.F.K. Organski points out. "Periods of balance are periods of warfare and those of preponderance of power are periods of peace." John Herz also offers a similar view. The "imbalance" of power and not "Balance" of power is the preserver of peace. But only a decisive and not a marginal imbalance leads to peace. For, if the imbalance is marginal, both sides may by tempted to precipitate a show down." The unipolarism resulting from the collapse of one super power (USSR) and continuance of the other super power (USA) has not in any way been a disturbing development for International peace and security or power balance.

(6) **Equality of a Number of States a Myth.** Balance of Power presupposes the existence of a number of equally powerful states. In practice no two states have or can have equal power. It involves the conception of equilibrium which is infact disequilibrium and is subject to continuous change.

(7) **Nations are not Free to Break Alliances at Their Will.** The theory of the balance of power can also be criticised on the ground that it wrongly assumes that nations are free to make or break alliances as and when they desire for the main consideration of power. As a matter of fact, this assumption of the balance of power may have been more true in pre-industrial and dynastic Europe, but this assumption does not help either the nineteenth century or the present day world. Since industrialization became wide-spread, shifts of a nation from one nation to another have been very rare. Even wherever they have occurred

they have usually been preceded by far reaching internal changes. As Organski remarks, "Modern nations are tied to each other by subtle, deep and intricate ties that are political, economic and psychological in nature. Their quest for power is but one aspect of a far more fundamental set of relationships." Nations cannot easily change their alliances or treaties only in the interest of a balance of power.

(8) **Uncertainty of Balance of Power.** Morgenthau criticises Balance of Power for its uncertainty unreality and inadequacy. The balance of power is uncertain because its operation depends upon the evaluation of power of the nations. It can be only through such an evaluation that a praticular nation can be judged as more powerful than others and that whether it tends to pose a danger to the balance not. Further more, it is only through an evaluation of power of nations that variations in power can be converted into quantitative units to be transferred from one scale to the other in order to restore balance. However, there exists and there can be no objective standard or system by which the power of the nations can be correctly and effectively evaluated. Under the circumstances every evaluation is bound to be uncertain and hence the balance of power is bound to be characterised by uncertainty. The need to weigh the power of a group of nations *vis-a-vis* the other group or groups further makes the task more uncertain and complicated.

(9) **Inadequacy of Balance of Power.** Balance of Power in itself is an inadequate device of international peace and security. Even if we may accept the contribution of this principle towards the maintenance of peace and security during the classical period of international relations (1648-1914), the question that need an answer is: Was it the balance of power alone that attained these beneficial results or were there some other factors in operation without which the balance of power could not have attained them? The answer is no. It was not balance of power alone

that maintained peace during this period. All writers on international relations agree that these was prevailing an intellectual and moral unity in this period which helped the balance of power to avoid major wars. During this period, there existed a mature consciousness that Europe was one republic having civilisation, culture, law and manners. It was this moral consensus on the basis of which the balance of power could operate successfuly towards the attainment of peace and security. This clearly shows that in itself balance of power is a weak and inadequate device of peace and even of power management.

(10) Unreality of Balance of Power. The uncertainty about the power of nations makes the balance of power system unreal. Since the evaluation of the power of nations is always uncertain, no nation dares to afford dependence upon the balance of power as determined by evaluation of power. Each nation as such tries to have a safe margin for herself. It always keeps a secret about its power and power potential. Since all nations keep safe margin, the balance of power at a particular time is always unreal Balance of Power is as such seldom really operational in practice. It is used more as an ideology and less as a guiding principle or director of international relations.

(11) Balance of Power has Lost Much of Its Relevance in Contemporary Times. Finally, the critics argue that even if we may accept that Balance of Power preserved peace and security during the classical period, we cannot accept that it continues to be a fully relevant principle of international relations in our times. The big structural changes in the international system as well as in the balance of power system have made it almost an obsolete principle. To begin with rise of two super powers; the emergence of Cold war, bi-polarity, polycentrism and nuclear weapons; the stabilisation of the UN and other international agencies; the change in councept of war from simple war to total war; the absence of a holder or balancer the end of Europe's pivotal position in world politics, and the rise of new states and the Non-aligned Movement, together produced a big change in the nature and realities of international relations of post-war period. The net effect of this change made balance of Power much less relevant if not altogether an obsolete system.

BALANCE OF TERROR

The concept and practice of balance of power has been playing a leading role in international politics since time immemorial. However, the balance of power is now considered by most of the people as an obsolete concept. This is mainly due to the fact that various changes in international politics have taken place in modern times. The typical among the changes is the revolution in the field of technology which has advanced to a terrible stage. There has been a great progress in nuclear and thermo-nuclear weapons. Both the blocs, rather various countries of the world, have developed highly sophisticated weapons of war. Among them are atomic, hydrogen and neutron bombs, inter-continental ballastic missiles, supersonic jets and nuclear powered submarines. The development of these weapons has brought about a qualitative change in that balance of power has now been replaced by the balance of terror between the two blocs. Balance of terror means that none dare start a war which may result in total destruction.

Nuclear Weapons have Brought an Age of Overkill. It is, in fact, the total destructiveness of new weapons that has changed the character of international politics in more than one respect. It is because of the total destructiveness of new weapons that Max Lerner characterizes present period as the "age of overkill" and the title he has chosen for one of his books is 'The Age of Overkill'. The expression "over-kill" has been borrowed from John Medars who holds that both the United States and the Soviet Union individully have the capacity to kill every person in the world many times over. Lerner has examined the changing nature of international politics in the light of this capacity of "overkill". He contends that today we live in the age of potential over-kill of power surplus, rather than power scarcity. Power scarcity was the distinguishing mark of the age of classical world politics. Since power scarcity has now been replaced by power surplus of over-kill capacity, the nature of international politics is bound to change.

Balance of Terror Result of Nuclear Weapons. In modern age, the importance of the nuclear factor is greater than anything else. It is the possession of nuclear and thermo-nuclear weapons that creates a terror in the minds of other nations. Only those nations which have nuclear weapons are considered to be a terror. All other nations have fallen in the background. It has reduced even the impact of bipolarity. Bipolarity already seems to be in the process of passing. With the rise of countries like China, West Germany, Japan, India and possibly one or two countrier of Africa, a disintegration of bipolarity into a multicentre system has come into existence. In fact, persons like George Kannan and Wiliam Douglas, former Judge of the United States Supreme Court, believed even in early fifties that a multipolar system was in existence even then, at least potentially, if not actually. If the rise of additional nulear powers takes place, the world may witness the return of the multipolar system which disintegrated as at result of the Second World War.

Nuclear Weapons have Created Balance of Terror in International Politics. The real impact of this argument can be better understood in the light of the fact that it has become a dilemma (problem) to use force in foreign policy as pointed out by Robert Oppenheimr and Hans Morgenthau and lately by A. Appadorai. Briefly stated, the doctrine of dilemma in foreign policy is that new weapons have created a situation in which policy-makers find it a terror to decide whether to use or not to use force in order to safeguard even their national interests. If force is used, it may have risk of an ultimate nuclear war leading to total destruction. If force is not used, a nation may have to suffer what it regards injustice. Further, non-use of force may also be mistaken for weakness.

This dilemma of whether to use or not to use force is beyond doubt a consequence of the development of nuclear weapons. While in the past, nations could go to war to solve an unsolvable problem, they cannot now think of war because of the fear of the total destruction. A number of examples are available in recent history which would show that use of force was avoided only because of the fear of its eventual escalation into general all-out war. Late in 1962, a show-down between the United States and the Soviet Union seemed imminent over Cuba. But the Soviet Union soon withdrew its atomic warheads from the Caribbean Sea because it was told by President Kennedy that if the Soviet Union did not withdraw them, the United States would also use nuclear weapons, which obviously involved the risk of complete destruction.

An example from the Korean question is also relevant here. It will be recalled that the aggression South Korea by North Korea was repelled by the United Nations forces in August-September 1950. In October, the United Nations forces crossed the 38th Parallel, the dividing the between line two Koreas. This was done much against India's advice and in spite of India's warning that crossing of the 38th Parallel might lead to China's entry into the war. As a result of crossing the 38th Parallel, Chinese volunteers joined the forces of North Korea. At this point, General Mac Arthur, the Far East Commander, suggested a blockade of the coast of China by the United Nations and the bombing of the Chinese mainland.

Nuclear Weapons have Posed a Dilemma in International Politics. The sum and substance of the argument is that war, which was the core of international politics before 1945, has lost its primacy among the fundamental elements of the classical system of world politics in the present age of overkill. Thus, war has become an independable and difficult means of international politics. This change in the nature of war has given birth to what Appadorai calls dilemma in foreign policy. This dilemma is rendered more serious and unresolvable on account of the fact though war has become almost a rare phenomenon today, nothing has come up to replace it.

Nuclear Weapons have not Eradicated War. Of course, there are people who take a very optimistic view of the impact of new weapons on international politics. P.M.S. Blackett, for instance believes that the fear of total destruction is so great that nuclear weapons will never be used and that a general war would, therefore, never occur. In other words, an all-out nuclear war is an impossibility.

It is believed by those who endorse Blackett's view that the development of nuclear weapons has abolished total war. Such a contention does not appear sound for two reasons. Firstly, there are some who do not subscribe to the view that a nuclear war would bring about total destruction of mankind. It is interesting to note the following part of a speech of a Chinese leader, Pleng, made on 22nd August, 1956. "America possesses atomic weapons and is threatening us with them. But we are not afraid of atomic warfare. Why? Because China has 600 million people. Even if 200 million people were killed by atomic weapons, 400 million people would still survive. Even if 200 million people were killed, 200 million would still survive. Even if 200 million survived, China would still constitute a big country of the world. Furthermore, these 200 million people will absolutely not surrender, therefore, at the end America will lose the war." Further, in February, 1965, Mao-Tec-Tung told Edgar Snow in an interview that China does not fear war and that even a nuclear war will not lead to total destruction. On the American side also, we find persons like Herman Kahn who argues that the United States can win even a nuclear war and that American civilization can emerge as a victorious civilization. Reports are available to show that scientists and military expert have already been busy for sometime with thinking as to how useful shelters against a nuclear war be built up. All this shows that though war has lost its primacy today, nations are not prepared to rule it out completely from international relationships. They realize the ineffectiveness of war and yet go on with preparation for it. As a matter of fact, one lesaon that the history of development of weapons teaches is that whenever technological innovations take place, they affect the psychology of people about the possibility of war. Thus, prior to the First War the invention of machine-gun and other developments in war-craft seemed to be revolutionary to the extent that Jean Block, a military expert, predicted that new developments in the machinism of war would make war an impracticable operation and that it could be possible only at the risk of suicide. This prediction we know, came out untrue. The point being attempted here is that new weapons have not altogether abolished war, howsoever they might have changed the character of war and howsoever difficult it might have become to use force today.

Balance of Power Now Works as Balance of Terror. It should be clear from what has been said above that the impact of the changed character of war on the nature of international politics, though undoubtedly great, is not total. Let us not presume that total destructiveness of modern weapons or the principle of over-kill has abolished war or will soon abolish war, or that the operation of power in international politics has been eliminated, or that fundamental principles of classical world politics have ceased to count. We cannot ignore the fact that the nation State still continues to function and is likely to continue functioning at least in the forstecable future. The alliance system and the concept of enemy are still kept alive. The balance of power offers signs of its continuation as an ideal means of world equilibrium, even though in the changed form of what Winston Churchill called, "balance of terror". In its essentials, therefore, international politics still has the characteristic of classical world politics except that war has lost its primacy as a readily available means for the settlement of international disputes. That is why Max Lerner talks of only the beginning of the end of classical world politics and not of its end as such. The beginning is clear from the fact that many international problems today—like Kashmir and Palestine—remain unsolved mainly because the use of force has the risk of leading to a nuclear war. These and the like problems could perhaps be solved in the pre-nuclear age by a threat of outbreak of war but the character of a possible nuclear war forbids such a solution to a very large extent. It is difficult to say at the present stage whether the classical system of world politics would come to an end completely.

❑

8

Cold War

The tension and strains that came to develop in the postwar international relations in general and U.S.-U.S.S.R. relations in particular came to be collective characterised as cold war. The end of Second World War was accompanied by the emergence of East-West differences and distrust between the two, which created a situation in which each side tried to isolate the other by promoting alliances and counter alliances. The situation came to be characterised as a cold war between the USA and the USSR *i.e.*, between the West and the East.

Cold War denotes the existence of strained and tense relations between two rival competitors in international relations. In the post-war period the term cold war came to be used for describing the highly strained relations which came to be gradually developed between the Soviet Union and the United States.

The term cold war was for the first time used by Bernard Baruch, an American statesmen, but was popularised by Prof. Lippman. He used it for describing the tense situation which had come to develop between the U.S.A. and the U.S.S.R. The spirit of co-operation and understanding that characterised the war-time relations between the Soviet Union and the Western powers began to evaporate gradually after the war and mutual distrust and suspicion began to resurface. In the post-war years, on many issues and in almost all situations, the USSR and the Western powers found themselves standing on opposite sides. The ideological differences and opposite views on social and economic policies further made their opposite stands more rigid and deep. Consequently, there came to develop a situation in which each side started working for the isolation and weakening of the other. Through propaganda and psychological warfare each side started making attempts at winning friends and consolidating its power through the conclusion of such security alliances as were directed against the other. Wartime tensions, and strains came to be developed in the relations between the USSR and the USA. No bullet was fired and no blood was shed and yet tensions, risks and strains were kept up. Proxy wars were fought in different regions of the world but the two super powers always avoided a direct military clash.

DEFINITIONS OF COLD WAR

Cold War can be defined as a state of intensive unhealthy competition—political, economic and ideological—which falls short of an armed conflict between the states. As a concept in international relations, it denotes a states of constant conflict, strains, tensions and strife maintained and perpetuated by political and psychological warfare but without a direct war between the opposing sides.

Analysing the meaning and nature of Cold War Joseph Frankel has observed. "The cold war may be regarded as a sparring match between the two giant states, a succession of moves and of counter moves." "Cold war embraces all phenomena pertaining to the conflict between the communism and the democratic ideologies as well as their protagonists, the Soviet Union and the United States, and the two blocs led by these super powers; nuclear deterrence is an important strategic aspect of the situation. As the term most aptly expresses, it is neither peace nor war, a conflict which cannot be easily ended by mutual compromise and accommodation or by the use of force, as conflicts were traditionally settled in the past."

End of War Time Co-operation and Beginning of Cold War. The war time co-operation between the Soviet Union and the Western powers could not prove to be enduring relationship. In fact, towards the closing years of the War, the Western powers had begun to express their strong disapproval of the growing influence of Communism in international relations and also of the key role that the USSR started playing in promoting the cause of socialist revolutions in other states. It was regarded as a policy really designed for strengthening Soviet role in world politics. The Western powers were greatly disturbed by the growing power and influence of the Soviet Union and over its violation of several agreements which had been reached at the Yalta and Postdam conferences. The Soviet pressures on Turkey, Greece, Iran and several Eastern European nations. were strongly resented to and opposed by the Western power. The East-Wast differences over the issue of peace settlements with the defeated nations, further increased the gap between Russia and the Western powers. By 1946, the Western powers felt that they had no other option but to check the growing communist menace in World Politics.

Likewise, during the course of War itself and in the two years after the end of this war the USSR felt that Western powers were out to create such conditions as were designed to make it difficult for it to pursue the goals of its national interest. It got highly annoyed with the Western powers because of the deliberate delay that they made in opening a second front against Germany—a delay which, according to the Soviets was designed to help Germany in inflicting losses upon them. Moreover, the Western power eagerness to develop relations with fascist Italy, to create West Germany, and to keep atomic secrets from the Soviet Union were interpreted as moves designed to keep the Soviet Union weak. The USSR consequently, felt greatly annoyed with the Western powers and regarded the extension of Soviet influence and power in international relations as the only effective way of meeting the Western threat to communism.

CAUSES OF THE ORIGIN OF COLD WAR

The following reasons are given for the cold war which started between nations of the above two militant power blocs. These blocs began contesting for their success politically and economically with a view to domination all the other countries of the world.

1. Mutual Distrust During War. The Western countries on the one hand and the Soviet bloc on the other, during the course of the Great War, emphasized their mutual distrust the Western power had no doubt sided with the Soviet Russia in facing the Nazi attack against Moscow but their friendship could not continue after the end of the War. The Russian Communists had, as at the very start of their

Bolshevik Revolution in 1917, once again renewed their attitude of distrust and contempt against the Western powers. So also the western powers could not forget the Soviet determination of eliminating the capitalist hold from the countries of the world, of propagating the scope of Russian Communist upsurge all over the world.

2. War Strategy of Western Countries Aimed at Containment of Russia Even During War. The Soviet Russia had in 1942 proposed to the Western powers to open a second front for fighting against the Nazis in Europe. But England and France did not accede to it. They came forward with their counter resolution of utilizing the U.S. and British forces which were soon to March towards the North of Balkan Peninsula after defeating the Nazis there. The international delay made by the Western allies in opening the Western front on the Balitic against Germany largely proved to the Soviet Russia that the Western allies were keeping themselves in utmost alertness to check the expansion of Soviet Union in the Eastern part of Europe.

3. Efforts at Enlarging Areas of Influence. Soon after the Second World War, both the Soviet Union and the Wertern countries began to make efforts at enlarging their areas of influence. The Western allies on the one hand and the Soviet Union on the other, started their most effective endeavours of winning over to their own side the chief political parties of the various countries, who had since been engaged in their National Revolutions for emancipation from foreign domination. The Western allies began supporting fascists of Italy to put an end to the Communist influence in their country. The chief opponent of German domination, Yugoslavia's Marshal Tito, was not believed by Churchill as he had passed into the Communist influence. England, therefore declared to reinstate the abdicated ruler of Yugoslavia.

Besides all these, the Polish measures resulted in the penalty in cold blood of the thousand anti-communist Polish people conducted by the red army sent by Stalin. It had also meted out the most barbarous treatment to the other eleven thousand anti-Communist persons who had been kidnapped to unknown places by the nomadic soldiers of red army. An Anglo-Soviet agreement was, therefore, signed in 1944, which recognised that the region of Soviet influence was to be protected and maintained by the red army, and the area of Soviet influence was to be limited to Bulgaria and Rumaina. Greece had to remain under the protection and influence of only the Western powers while the Western powers and the Soviet Russia had to maintain security, peace and order in Hungary and Yougoslavia under their joint guardianship. This agreement however, could prove of no avail for the making up of the distrustful and strained relations between the Western allies and the Soviet Russia.

4. Secret of Atomic Weapons Disclosed by America to England but not to Soviet Union. The last but the most important reason for gradual aggravation of cold war between the Western powers and the Soviet bloc was that America gave the secret of atomic weapons to Great Britain and not to the Soviet Union. The confidential understanding between England and the United States came to the notice of Marshal Stalin as late as July 24, 1945 when Truman declared to the world that the United States thought it worthwhile to disclose the secret of producing atomic weapons to no other country except England, the test of atom bomb made over Hiroshima brought an end to the remaining friendship and sympathy between the Soviet Russia and the Western powers. England, France and the United States were proud enough to believe that they could maintain the balance of power in their own favour and keep peace all over the world without the least contribution of the Soviet Russia to it.

The Soviet Union discovered at last that the chief of the Western powers, now the U.S.A., was very much inclined to isolate and weaken Russian position in the sphere of world affairs. Therefore, it paid its immediate attention towards its scientifie progress. It was on October 4, 1947 that it made an experiment of sending a Sputnik in space in order to make a detailed enquiry into the important affairs and concrete circumstances of the various countries of the world. This was the first experiment of its kind which the great powers had upto that time made in respect of their aeronautic study in which Russia now excelled even United States and England.

All these reasons considerably widened the gulf of political differences between Soviet Russia and Wertern allies. The result of that was apparent in the growing jealousy and strained relations of the two power blocs. Their differences became conspicuous in the various international conferences and foreign policies of the States of the world. The allies which had taken up arms against Hitler in the preceding War now arrayed themselves into two camps rival to each other. U.S.A., Great Britain and France got into one camp to oppose the U.S.S.R. they carried on propaganda against each other through through the medium of newspapers, magazines and radio programmes. The world now stood divided between the two armed and militant power-blocs, one of which was called the Anglo-American Bloc or that of the Free World and Capitalistic Democracy, populartly known as the Western Camp while the other came to be known by the term Soviet or Communist Democratic camp or the Eastern Camp.

Political Events Leading to Cold War. The following most important political events were witnessed by the world upto the present period since the end of Great War in 1945.

1. ***Expanison of Soviet Russia in East Europe.*** Winston Churchill of England wanted to curb, even during the course of the Great War, the expanistionist designs of the USSR. In the month of may in 1945 he again desired that the United States forces should by all means hasten to occupy the largest possible portion of the defeated Germany so that it may not be taken over by the Communist forces. However, the same happened when the USSR occupied the Eastern part of Germany after the close of the War.

   Russian occupation of Germany was facilitated by the absence of the Western forces from the scene as the US forces were eager to return to their home-land. The swift expansion of Soviet powers in East Europe now alarmed the entire Western world beyond measure. This gave birth to the rise of a new strong and resistant organisation of Wester allies against the Moscovite power.

2. ***Role of Russian in Greek Civil War.*** The fourth event causing the out-break of the said cold war was the

provocation of Greek Civil War, when the Greek Communist guerillas were integrated and effectively supported by the various countries of Eastern bloc—Alania, Bulgaria and Yugoslavia—to overthrow their existent non-Communist Government of the country. The Soviet Union at the same time exerted its utmost pressure upon gaining its supremacy over the Turkoman State, and the Bosphorous and Dardanelles. Therefore, the problem of the Middle East had become all the more serious and extremely dangerous to the interests of the Western nations of whom the United States had to concentrate upon the need of extending sufficient armed and economic help to the backward and poor nations of the Middle East by executing the Marshall Plan which in turn became one of the causes of the increasing hostility of the Soviet Union against the Capitalist countries of the West.

3. ***Declaration of Anti-Communist Policy by Churchill.*** Sir Winston Churchill in 1946 formulated his anti-Communist policy in his timely and eloquent speech at Foulton. The U.S. President, Truman supported the British stand against the Communist Expansionism in 1947 and afterwards. The U.N. Chambers and the various international Conferences turned to be an arena of hostile resentment of the countries belonging to the above two armed camps against each other. Even on the eve of the first session of the Security Council, the Soviet representative levelled the most coercive criticism against the Western attitude on the point of establishing world-peace. The other meetings of U.N. General Assmebly and the Security Council proved since then to be spectale of hot contestation, charges and counter charges of the nations of the West against those of the Soviet bloc. At the very oustset of the U.N. meetings when majority of the Western countries guided most of their resolutions on international peace and security the Soviet bloc was confined to the strength of only the five votes at the disposal of Soviet Russia.

4. ***Inconsistent Russian Demands at the London Council of Foreign Ministers.*** The second event of the cold war between the Western powers and the Communist Russia was the London Council of Foreign Ministers. Molotov, the Soviet Foreign Minister, put forth certain inconsistent demands. He, it is said, in spite of his eagerness to establish a lasting peace put forth certain resolutions which instead of earnestly solving the peace problems misentangled other issues.
5. ***Formation of Cominform by Russia Against American Marshall Plan.*** As a matter of sharp contrasting reply to the Marshall Plan envisaged by the U.S. Government, the Soviet Russia envisaged on March 25, 1947 the "Cominform—Communist Bureau" of nine Communist States. In the event of Benelaux Treaty and Berlin Blockade the cold war between the U.S.A. and U.S.S.R. and their allies aggravated beyond measure. Again, their differences became much more serious at the point of the Austrian and German Peace Treaties to be concluded at the end to the Great War. The question of unifying east Germany with West Germany was still trembling in the balance of indecision and suspicion due to the growing differences of the above two opposite power blocs.
6. ***Refusal of Soviet Russia to Call Back her Forces From Iran.*** The third event taking place as a cause of the cold war was the flat refusal of the Soviet Union to retreat her forces from Iran even at the end of the Great War when the allied powers had readily agreed to withdraw their armed forces from those regions of the world which had earlier been exposed to the Nazi aggression. This created a strong suspicion among the Western nations against the expansioinst desings of Soviet Russia in Europe and Asia.

THE BASIS OF COLD WAR

The cold war was based on a number of assumptions. First, it assumed that the real threat to the world peace was posed by the military strength of Soviet Union. It may be noted that Soviet Union's military strength was virtually destroyed during World War II. This assumption gave rise to the policy of strength which was responsible for the development of military theory of cold war on the basis of atom bomb, hydrogen bomb and clear warfare. Secondly, it assumed the ineviability of conflict between the socialist and capitalist States, which prompted the states of both the blocs to keep themselves in condition of constant preparedness for a final show down. It assumed that no co-operation was possible between states with different social systems. It was on account of this feeling the Western powers equated all socialist movements which subversive movements. This explains the American interventions from Greece and Turkey in 1947 to Vitenam. It assumed that the struggle between West and East was a struggle between freedom and tyranny.

CAUSES OF COLD WAR

The main factors which contributed to the rise of cold war were as follows:

In the first place, Soviet Union tried to increase its influence in Eastern Europe in violation of the terms of Yalta Agreement. Thus Soviet Union established Lablin Government in Poland in violation of her commitment that the exiled Polish government at London and the Soviet influenced Lublin government would be duly represented in the future government of Poland. It also tried to liquidate the democratic parties and non-communist population of Poland.

In the Balkans also Soviet Union tried to establish communist government despite an understanding with Britain regarding their spheres of influence in the Balkans. All this aroused the suspicion of the Western powers and they decided to check further expansion of Soviet influence. Secondly, Soviet Union refused to with draw its forces from Iran and instigated a rebellion in Northern Ireland. Soviet Union also compelled Iran to sign a treaty on 4 April, 1946 which recognised Soviet interest over oil resources of North Ireland for 25 years. This was in complete contrast to the policy adopted by Britain and

USA which withdrew their forces from Iran as per terms of agreement of 1942. The question of presence of Soviet forces in Iran was raised in the UN and ultimately Soviet Union was made to withdraw its forces from Iran. This policy of Soviet Union greatly contributed to sharpening of tension with Western powers.

Thirdly, Russia extended support to the Communist to pull down legally consituted government in Greece which soon engulfed the country in a civil war. This was greatly resented by Britain and USA and they extended every possible assistance to save the democratic government.

Fourthly, Soviet Union brought undue presure on Turkey to modify the Straits Convention and demanded certain territories. As Turkey refused to oblige, Soviet Union began to forment trouble in Turkey. Thereupon USA came to the rescue of Turkey the growing communist threat in Greece and Turkey led to the enunciation of Truman doctrine by USA which pledged support to people who were resisting attempted subjugation by armed minorites or by outside pressures.

Fifthly, the attitude adopted by Soviet Union towards Germany also greatly contributed to cold war. Soviet Union, unmindful of its commitments in the Potsdam Agreement and London Protocol, tried to put unnecessary burden and pressure on the German region under its occupation. It also deprived the people of Germany under Soviet zone of their fundamental political freedom. All this was greatly resented by America and other Western powers.

Sixthly, refusal of United States and other Western powers to accord recognition to the governments of Bulgaria and Rumania also generated tension between the two blocs. The plea of the Western powers that they had refused to extend recognition to these countries on the ground that they lacked popular representation, could not satisfy the Russians.

Seventhly, frequent use of veto powers by Soviet Union during the initial years of the working of United Nations was also responsible for generating tension between Soviet Union and America. It convinced the Americans that the Soviet Union and America. It flouting all their plans. On the other hand, the Soviet Union complained that since United States had manipulated majority in the Security Council, it had no other choice but to make frequent use of its veto power. This sense of distrust towards each other greatly contributed to cold war.

Eighthly, the unnecessary obstacles put by Soviet Union in the way of conclusion of peace treaties also raised a good deal of suspicion in the minds of the American people about the ultimate intentions of Soviet Union.

Ninthly, bitter criticism of the capitalist system and vociferous propaganda against United States also contributed to the tension between the two countries. Soviet Union stepped up its activities in United States and even tried to smuggle out some of the confidential and secret documents. This compelled United States to adopt stiff attitude towards Soviet Union.

Tenthly, the unnecessary delay by the Western powers in opening the second front during the Second World War, and the consequential losses suffered by Soviet Union, made her suspicious about the true designs of the Western powers. The inadequate aid given by the western powers of the Soviet Union during the war also raised doubts in the minds of Russian leaders about true intentions of their Western allies. This suspicion was further heightened due to the attempt on the part of America and England to keep their programme of atom bomb secret Soviet Union and other East European countries.

Finally, the abroupt suspension of the land-lease aid by United States to Soviet Union, soon after the surrender of Germany, convined the Soviet leaders that the Western powers were jealous of their progress.

All the above factors contributed to the growth of cold war.

Phases of Cold War. The cold wars passed through a number of phases. The first phase lasted from 1946 to 1949. During this period it was held that if strong pressure could be organized, the ked regime in Soviet Union would collapse like a house of cards. This feeling arose because America was having monopoly of Atom Bomb and Russia was in very weak condition. Therefore, it was held that U.S.A. due to her superiority in military could determine the history of world and influence the internal affaris of Soviet Union. The policy of containing Soviet Union could not be implemented because the Allies of America were not yet fully armed for such a war and the memories of Second World War were still fresh in their mind, which prevented them from resorting to war.

During this phase America resorted to direct military intervention through Truman Doctrine of March, 1947 and economic integration of the West European Powers by Marshall Plan of June, 1947. U.S.A. during this period followed the policy of intervention and defender of *status quo*. This phase was also marked by anti-commiunist feeling, which U.S.A. tried to implant throughout the world. This phase of cold war ended with the conclusion of North Atlantic Treaty on April 4, 1949. This treaty was a sort of new Anit-Comintern Pact and was openly directed against the Soviet Union. These activites of U.S.A. naturally provoked Soviet Union to take necessary measures for self-defence.

The second Phase lasted from 1949 to 1953. During this period U.S.A. continued her policy of military and economic assistance against Soviet Union. During this period U.S.A. concluded security treaty with Australia and New Zealand (ANZUS) and Peace Treaty with Japan (1951). This period also witnessed the Korean War which was a major confrontation between U.S.A. and U.S.S.R. The United States intensified her anti-communist propaganda and spent millions of dollars for the purpose. She also invested huge amounts to carry out subversive activities in the socialist countries. This provoked natural reaction from Soviet Union which exploded the atom bomb and broke-down the American monopoly.

The Third phase of cold war listed from 1953 to 1957. During this phase U.S.A. continued her policy of military and economic offensive. She orgainsed the South East Asia Treaty Organization (S.E.A.T.O.) and the Middle East Defence Organization (M.E.D.O.).

These two treaties became new defence links with N.A.T.O. America also made a serious effort to perpetuate American domination in the Middle East by extending the Truman Doctrine to this area. U.S.A. also established a number of military bases around Soviet territory and concluded defence treaties with 43 states. It was also during this period that U.S.A. involved herself in Vietnam, which turned out to be a grim climax of the cold war.

During this phase Soviet Union also increased her influence. She sponsored WARSAW Treaty with East European powers as a counter-measure to N.A.T.O. She concluded defence treaties with 12 states and foiled the American attempt to promote counter-revolution in Hungary. This period also witnessed the permanency of the Postdam partition of Germany. The subsequent establishment of two German States allied to the two blocs was also the outcome of cold war during this period.

The phase also saw simultaneous explosion of hydrogen bombs by U.S.A. and Soviet Union. During this period a dialogue between the two countries was opened which forecast that the next phase of international relations would be marked by a spirit of negotiation and not mutual threats of extermination.

The fourth phase lasted from 1957 to 1962. It saw two extreme trends. On the one hand, the principles of peaceful co-existence were asserted and on the other hand, it saw the most dangerous tence prevailed. The two countries exchanged cultural and political delegates. The heads of governments of two countires paid visits to each other. The agreement for Paris Summit clearly demonstrated that the cold war attitude had ended. But this spirit was sabotaged by the U-2 incident.

The damage done by the U-2 incident was partly repaired by the General Assembly Summit of 1960 and the Vietnam meeting of Khrushchev and President Kennedy in 1961. But the Cuban crists literally brought the two countries to the verge of war. Howerver, the situation was finally saved by an agreement between Khrushchev and Kennedy by which Soviet Union agreed to withdraw the missile base in exchange for the American guarantee never to invade Cuba.

The fifth phase started from 1962 and is marked by a deep appreciation of the futility of nuclear war strategy. This phase saw the conclusion of "Partial Test Ban Treaty" of 1963. By the Geneva Hot-Line Agreement of 1963 the two countries were closely linked. The Non-Proliferation Treaty of 1968 could also be concluded due to the understanding of the two powers. However, even during this period the problems of Germany and Vietnam stood in the way of full co-operation between the two countries.

A process of detente between the two major powers started in 1959 when Khrushchev advocated the policy of peaceful co-existence. In pursuance of this policy he visited Washington and met President Eisenhower. On this occasion he also addressed the General Assembly of the United Nations and proposed that within four years all the States should completely disarm themselves.

Another important step in the direction of easing the cold war was the Three Power Partial Nuclear Test Ban Treaty formally signed on 5 August, 1963. This treaty porvided for a limited ban on all nuclear tests in the atmosphere including territorial waters or high seas. On The recommendations of the General Assembly United States, Soviet Union and Great Britain adopted the Nuclear Non-Proliferation Treaty. Under this treaty the nuclear powers agreed not to transfer their nuclear weapons or control over them to any non-nuclear power or the provide assistance in producing those weapons.

The cold war assumed new dimension in the wake of Sion-Soviet rift in early sixties. This cold war between Soviet Union and China brought about a thaw in the traditional cold war between Soviet Union and United States. In the wake of American bombing of North Vietnam, the Arab-Israel conflict of 1967 and the Soviet military intervention in Czechoslovakia in 1968, the cold war assumed more serious shape. During the Berlin crisis of 1969 there was a possibility of direct confrontation between the two super-powers. However by 1970 the tension somewhat subsided and the two super powers agreed not to use force against each other. Soviet Union concluded a treaty with West Germany under which it agreed to have diplomatic relations with West Germany and not to use force against it. This helped in reducing tension in Europe. In August, 1971 as a result of agreement over Berlin between U.S.A., Britain, USSR and France the tension further subsided. The agreements between North Korea and South Korea and East Germany which were signed on 4 July, 1972 and 8 November, 1972 respectively also contributed to the reduction of tension between the two super-powers.

In the field of arms limitations also significant progress was made.

In 1973 Brezhnev, the Chief of the Communist Party of USSR, paid a return visit to Washington and Summit talks were held. In these talks the two parties agreed to work for lasting world peace and to end the nuclear arms race. This summit talk resulted in the conclusion of four agreements between the two countries. These agreements related to cooperation in the field of research in agriculture, transportaion, and expansion of cultural and scientific exchanges between the two countries. The two countries also committed themselves to negotiate a treaty for mutual reduction of nuclear weapons, and co-operation in nuclear power research. The two countries also undertook to avoid nuclear war not only between then but also with the third state. The leaders of the two countries asserted that a lasting peace in Europe was the paramount goal of their policy and pledged to work for the success of the Conference on European Security scheduled to be held at Helsinki in July, 1973.

The Change in leadership in USA, following Persident Nixon's resignation in the wake of Watergate scandal, did not mark any change. The new American President Ford continued efforts for reduction of nuclear weapons and concluded and agreement with Brezhanev for limiting strategic offensive weapons for the next ten years. The two leasers also attended the Summit Conference on Security and Cooperation in Europe held at Helsinki in July, 1975 and an atmosphere of complete detente between the two supers powers prevailed. In July, 1975 the two super powers participated in the joint Apollo-Soyuz space mission, which was an important indication of the cordial relations.

But despite the detente, there were many points of conflict between the two powers and they thired to check each other's influence. For example, America favoured military buid-up in Iran with a view to maintain their influence in the Middle East, and to check the growing influence of the Soviet Union. The establishment of Diego Garcia military base was aimed at counter-checking the Soviet presence in the Indian ocean area. The Soviet Scheme of Asian Collective Secrutiy was also aimed at replacing the American influence in the South-East Asia as well as to contain China. In Bangla Desh also the two powers supported the opposite parties. While Soviet Union supported the cause of the people of East Bengal and rendered every possible help to India to deal with the Refugee problem, the United States extended full support to Pakistan. In the war between Egypt and Israel in 1973 once again they supported the rivel parties-Soviet Union sided with Egypt while USA backed Israel.

As the duration of the treaty in the limitation of strategic offensive arms concluded between USA and USSR in 1972, drew closer, they commenced negotiations for a fresh agreement and concluded SALT-II in June, 1975 under which both the super powers agreed to limit the expansion of clear weapons. They also pledged to work for reduction of strategic arms in order to achieve the goal of complete disamament. However, subsequently the US Senate refused to ratify the treaty and it could not come into force.

The cold war which somewhat subsided during the early seventies got once again reactivated following Soviet intervention in Afghanistan in 1979. The western powers were so bitter about it that they decided to boycott Olympic Games held at Moscow in July, 1980. In the subsequents years also the two super powers adopted critical attitude towards their opponents. This new phase of cold war was described as a 'new cold war' or 'second cold war'. It differed from the earlier cold war in many respects. Firstly, unlike the earlier cold war, this war was mainly confined to two super powers. Secondly, in the new cold war the two super powers were involved in nuclear armament race and as such was more threatening. Thirdly, the element of ideology which was a dominant feature of the earlier cold war, was conspiciously absent this time.

IMPACT OF COLD WAR

1. The cold war gave rise to permanent types of alliances which were concluded much in advance of war. N.A.T.O.,

S.E.A.T.O., C.E.N.T.O. and the Warsaw Pact were all formed in the wake of cold war this alignment system covered most countries of the world. Thus cold war led to alignment system even during the peace times and constant efforts were made to strengthen these alliances. However, the newly independent states of Asia and Africa tried to avoid alignment with either of the two groups.

2. Cold war stood in the way of achieveing the objective of one world. The mutual rivalry reduced the U.N.O. to the states of a simple forum of world opinion. The cold war prevented some of the states form becoming members of the world body. The denial of representation to people's China in the Security Council for a long time was mainly due to this Cold war.
3. Cold war adversely affected the economic development of the country by diverting human labour an resources to the manufacture of destruction weapons.
4. Cold war resulted in mad race for armaments. States of both the blocs spent huge amounts to equip themselves with latest weapons. This not only led to diversion of money which could have more profitably been utilised for improving the lot of the people. It also led to both the camps arming themselves to the teeth. Under the circumstances even local quarrel or misunderstanding could lead to a nuclears war.
5. The cold war and the consequent competition among Great Powers resulted in more freedom of action for the small and middle powers. Each group tried to win them over. The influencc which the Afro-Asian countries were able to exert in the U.N. cold war.

EMERGENCE OF COLD WAR

The war time co-operation and alliances between USSR and the Western Powers were born out of exigencies of time paιticularly the need to defeat the common enemy. Between 1917 to 1942, the relations between USSR and Western powers were far from being co-operative and cordial. The coming of Socialist Revolution in Russian in 1917, was strongly disliked by the democratic West. The consolidation of socialism in USSR was regarded as a dangerous development as it was regarded the biggest threat to capitalism and democracy. The Western appeasment of Germany during the inter-war years was motivated by the desire to make Germany a counterpoise to the USSR. Under the circumstances, during 1917-39 period, the Soviet Union continued to follow a self-imposed aloofness in international relations. This aloofness was designed to consolidate internally the gains of the socialist revolution. The Non-Aggression pact with Germany was designed for the purpose. When the Second World War broke out, the Soviet Union decided to remain aloof from "the imperialist war—the war among the imperialists."

End of Wartime Co-operation Between East and West. The War produced a unique alliance between the USSR and the Western Powers and it led to the development of co-operative relations between the former enemies—the communists and the anti-communists. The post 1942 period of the War witnessed a number of conferences like the Yalta Conference, the Potsdam Conference etc., in which the USSR and the Western powers participated to co-ordinate and pool their efforts for securing the defeat of the Axis powers. These conferences produced a number of agreed decisions which made it possible for the Allies to defeat the Axis. The decision to establish a new international organisation—the UNO, further gave rise to the optimism that Soviet-Western co-operation shall continue to characterise the post-war international relations. However, this was not to be. Behind their co-operative efforts during the war, the Soviet Union and the Western powers kept up nourishing their differences and apprehensions about each other. The Western powers always kept on fearing the growing power of the Soviet Union-the communist menace in international relations. Several Soviet decisions during war, and more particularly the Soviet attempts to export socialist systems to Eastern European countries made the Western powers apprehensive about Soviet intentions in international relations.

Causes of the Cold War. The causes of cold war between Communist East and Democratic West (The Anglo-American Bloc) can be conveniently studied in two parts:

(a) The Western complaints against the East or the Anglo-American grievances against Russia.

(b) The Eastern complaints against the West or the Soviet grievances against USA, UK and France.

(A) THE WESTERN GRIEVANCES AGAINST THE EAST

A-I. General Grievances

1. ***Western Fear of Growing Soviet Power in World Politics.*** The Western or the Anglo-American nations were dissatisfied with several Soviet decisions during the course of Second World War. They were further alarmed by the fast growing power of the USSR. Since the coming of October 1917 Socialist Revolution, the Western powers were fearing the possible repercussions of this even upon the course of international relations, and upon the political systems of other nations. The growing strength of the Soviet Union, and the exhibition of Soviet power in the Second World War made the Western powers more apprehensive about the growing communist menace in international relations. The secret security pact that the USSR and Germany concluded on 1939, and the Soviet refusal to join the war against Nazi Germany made the western powers very fearful of the Soviet role in world politics. The suspicions about Soviet motives in international relations made the Western democracies Highly apprehensive of the role of the Soviet Union. The War time co-operation was accepted by them as a necessary evil and hence after the war, it was quite natural for them to work for containing the growing power of the Soviet Union.

2. ***The Ideological Conflict—Communism Vs. Capitalism.*** The communist thesis of the inevitability of conflict between socialism and capitalism, and the final triumph of socialism also made the democratic states highly apprehensive about the growing strength of Soviet Union and her policy of exporting socialism to other countries. The differences between the Soviet Union and the Western democracies

were the direct product of contradicting ideologies of communism and capitalism. Most of the early disputes between the two were also due to the diametrically opposed ideological stands of the two groups. The ideology of communism advocated that the liquidation of capitalism was the final end of socialist revolution and for achieving this end a push to historical evolution *i.e.*, a revolution by the workers, was the natural and ideal means. Such a negative view of capitalism was strongly opposed to the ideology of liberal democracy or capitalism. The capitalist countries regarded communism as degraded materialism which involved the destruction of human values of liberty and prosperity. The communist view of capitalism was regarded by the Western powers as the biggest hindrance to peace and peaceful co-existence in international relations.

3. ***Western Fears of Growing Socialist Movement.*** After the coming of Socialist Revolution in the Soviet Russia, labour movements became very popular and powerful in almost all the states of Europe. The emergence of socialist parties in various states of Europe and elsewhere greatly alarmed the capitalist states. They felt that socialist movements were really subversive movements as these were guided by the ideology that class interests were stronger than national interests and that workers of the world had no country of their own. The support that these socialist movements in various countries received from the Soviet Union made the capitalist States annoyed with the USSR. They believed that the USSR was trying to spread subversion in other countries and hence felt justified in undertaking measures designed at limiting the spread of socialist movements and their mentor—the Soviet Union. The decision of the Soviet Union to join the Second World War was considered more as a decision guided by the self-interest of protecting her security and less by the desire to really co-operate with the Western countries. During war, the western countries accepted Soviet participation as a necessity created by the exigencies of the situation.

A-II Specific Western Grievances Against USSR

Besides the above three factors which made the Western Powers generally dissatisfied with the Soviet Union role in international relations, there were several specific Soviet policy decisions which made these powers annoyed with the Soviet Union. The specific Western complaints against the Soviet Union were as under:

1. ***USSR was Guilty of Violating Yalta Agreements.*** It was felt by the western powers that the USSR was guilty of violating the agreements reached at the Yalta Conference.

   The following Soviet decisions were quoted as proof in support of such charge:

   (i) *Soviet Interferences in Poland.* The Soviet role in establishing Lubinon Government in Poland violated the commitments to transfer power to a duly elected Government of Poland.

   (ii) *Soviet Help to Chinese Communists.* The USSR used its control over Manchuria for helping the communist forces of Mao and refused to help the nationalist army of China to operate against the communist forces. This was again a source of big dissatisfaction with the Soviet role in the War.

   (iii) *Arrest of Polish Leaders.* The arrest of democratic leaders of Poland and the refusal to permit the entry of the U.S. and British observers into Poland.

   (iv) *Conversion of Eastern Europe to Communism.* The Sovietisation of Eastern Europe by securing the establishment of pro-Soviet regimes in Hungary, Bulgaria, Rumania and Czechoslovakia. At yalta, the western powers had almost accepted the Soviet influence over Eastern and Central Europe, but it was agreed that after the peace settlement, democratic institutions would be established in the liberated states. The conversion of Balkans soicalism was regarded as a violation by the USSR of the Yalta and Balkan agreements.

(v) *The Soviet Reluctance to Join War Against Japan.* The Soviet unwillingness to join war against Japan and its hesitation in allowing Allied troops to use Siberian airfields were considered unfriendly acts and the Western powers were quick to criticise Soviet Union for its unhelpful and harmful attitude.

2. ***Soviet Refusal to Withdraw its Forces from Northern Iran.*** By an agreement of 1942, the Soviet Union and the Western powers had agreed to withdraw their foces from Iran within six months of the surrender of Germany. As agreed, after the war, America and Britain promptly withdrew their armies from Iran and they expected that the USSR would soon follow suit. However, the Soviet Union was not quite willing to withdraw its forces from Northern Iran. It instigated a rebellion Iran and forced the latter to sign a treaty with the Soviet Union and recoginse Soviet interests over the oil resources of Northern Iran for a period of 25 years. This was totally opposed to the East-West agreement and hence was strongly opposed by the Western powers.

3. ***Soviet Attempts to Tame Turkey.*** After the War, the Soviet Union put pressure on Turkey and demanded the cession of some Turkish territories to the USSR. In particular, it wanted to establish a military base at Bospherus. These demands were opposed by Turkey and the Western powers. U.S.A. came forward to support Turkey in a big way. U.S. President Truman enunciated the famous Truman Doctrine in which he promised "all help to all such countries who were struggling to safeguard their right to have a government of their choice." He followed this up by promising huge economic and military help to both Greece and Turkey. The Soviet attempts at pressurising Turkey made the Western countries realise the danger of communist expansionism and they felt compelled to follow a policy of "containment of communism."

4. ***Soviet Pressures on Greece.*** The attempts made by the Soviet Union and its camp followers to secure the establishment of liftist and pro-communist or communist goverments in Greece and Turkey were also strongly opposed by the western powers. When after the outbreak of civil war in Greece and as a result of war between Greek forces and communist guerillas, the Soviet Union started giving support to the communists of Greece, the Western powers, particularly the U.S.A. came forward to provide help to Greece Government Civil war in Greece indirectly brought the USSR and the U.S.A. into a situation of conflict and this development gave a big set-back to the East-West relations.

5. ***Soviet Pressures on Germany.*** The Western powers were strongly of the view that the Soviet Union was deliberately violating the war-time agreements regarding the nature scope of Allied control over Germany. Soviet policies in East Germany, which was under Soviet control, were considered to be violative of Postdam agreements. The following proofs were offered in support of this charge.

   (a) *Transportation of German Machinery.* The Soviet decision to transport heavy industrial machinery from East Germany to the USSR as a part of repatriation.

   (b) *Imprisonment to German Leaders.* The Imprisonment and exiling of German leaders and people.

   (c) *Separation of East Germany.* The Soviet decision to separate of East Germany from West Germany.

   (d) *Non-acceptance of a Single Economic Zone.* The Soviet refusal to recognise Germeny as a single economic zone.

   (e) *Soviet Hegemony Over Germany.* The Soviet decision to make Oder-Niese line as the border between Poland and Germany. The Soviet acquiescene in transferring some areas of Germany to Poland.

(f) *Soviet Control Over German Socialist Party.* The forcible assimilation of German Socialist Party with the Communist Party.

All these Soviet decisions were strongly objected to by the Western powers.

6. ***Frequent Use of Soviet Veto in the UN Security Council.*** The Western powers were greatly disturbed by the frequent use of veto power by the Soviet Union. The veto power, believed the Western powers, was being used by the Soviet Union simply for opposing the Western policies and for preventing the Security Council from acting effectively in the direction of preserving international peace and security.

7. ***The Differences Over Berlin.*** The nature of the Berlin occupation by U.S.S.R., U.S.A., U.K. and France also acted as a big irritant in post-war East-West relations. The Soviet control over East Berlin and the roads leading into Berlin, and the Anglo-American-French control over the West Berlin, made Berlin a big home of contention between Russia and the Western powers. The western attempt to introduce a new currency in their occupation area in Berlin gave rise to strong opposition from Soviet Union. The tension became very high when the Soviet Union enforced a blocade of Berlin in June 1948, and this was matched by the Western decision to airlift the supplies to West Berlin. Both the USSR and the Western powers reached almost at dead end in respect of their respective Berlin policies and this increased the already growing cold war tensions between the East and West.

8. ***Communist Activities in U.S.A. and Canada.*** The post-war years witnessed a spurt in communist activities in the U.S.A. and Canada. It came to be widely believed by the people of these two countries that the USSR was behind the increased anti-American and anit-democracy propaganda which was being carried out in various parts of the globe, and particularly in U.S.A. and Canada. The belief that the

Soviet Union was engaged in wide-spread espionage activities in Europe and in the American continent, gave further strenght to mutual distrust that had come to develop between the East and the West during the 1944-47 period.

9. ***Differences Over Peace Treaties.*** The Western powers were greatly annoyed with the Soviet attempts to secure most favourable conditions during the course of discussions on the peace treaties with the defeated nations. For example, while discussing the peace treaty with Italy, serious differences cropped up between the Soviet Union and the Westen powers on the question of Italy-Yugoslav frontier, Trieste, and over the issue of reparation. The differences that cropped up at the London Conference and other conferences gave a big jolt to the East-West relations.

(B) SOVIET GRIEVANCES AGAINST THE WEST

B-I. General Grievances

(i) **Soviet Displeasure Over Several Western Policies.** The Western powers had several grievances against the Soviet Union, likewise the latter too had several specific complaints against the former. The Soviet Union was greatly disturbed and annoyed with several policies and actions of Western powers which it felt were designed to limit its power and rold in international relations. Initially, the Western attempts to encourage a counter revolution in Socialist Russia were strongly disapproved and objected to by the Soviet leadership. Later on, the Western policy of appeasing Hitler's Germany was interpreted by the Soviet leadership as the Western strategy to build Germany and Italy as a counterpoise to communism. They believed that the Western powers were encouraging Hitler to embark upon a policy of expansionism towards it. It concluded a non-aggression security pact with Germany only for checking such a possibility. Its decision to remain aloof during war between Germany and the Western powers was also guided by such a thinking.

B-II. Specific Grievances

(i) Soviet Apprehensions of Western Intentions. During the war several Western decision were interpreted by the Soviet Union as decisions which were planned with a double motive; to defeat the Axis powers and the Weaken the Soviet Union. Such decisions were strongly opposed and criticised by the Soviet leaders and these were responsible for forcing the Soviet Union to pursue goals which were opposed to the interests of the Western powers.

The following Western decisions and policies were strongly criticised by the Soviet Union as attempts of the enemies of communism, and therefore of the Soviet people:

1. The Delay in the Opening of Second Front against Germany. When the German forces were rapidly advancing into the Soviet Union, Stalin believed that there was an urgent need to immediately open a second front against Germany. This alone, felt Stalin, could stem the advance of German forces into the USSR and thereby reduce the pressure upon Soviet security. As against such a Soviet view, both Churchill and Roosevelt maintained that it was not possible them to immediately open a second front against Germany as that required a long and full preparation. Later on, the Western powers agreed to open the second front but in doing so they decided to operate from the Central European side and not from the western side, as advocated by Russia. The delay in the opening of second front as well as the western decision to choose a different area for operations against Germany, greatly disturbed the USSR.

2. Inadequate Western Aid to the Soviet Union. Soviet Union Was greatly disturbed both by the delay and the inadequacy of Western aid during the course of war. She felt that since she was bearing heavy losses due to the big German assault on her, it was the duty of the western powers to provide adequate help enabling her to withstand and meet the pressure of German attack. However, to her dismay, the Western powers come out to provide only 4 per cent of the requirements of Russia and that too only in a delayed manner.

3. The American Secrecy Over the Atom Bomb. The American decision to maintain secrecy over her atomic capability and in respect of the decision to drop atom bombs over Japan without taking the Soviets into confidence greatly irked the Soviet Union. It felt that as war ally it was its right to have access to all war technology and use of weapons, but the Americans felt otherwise. Despite its decision to share the atomic secret with Britain and Canada, America decided to keep it a secret from the USSR. Stalin considered it as a great betrayal which demonstrated lack of Western trust and confidence in the Soviet friendship and cooperation. He felt greatly alarmed at the American monopoly over the atomic secret and considered it a threat to Soviet interests.

4. Western Relations with Fascist Italy. Soviet Union was the view that the rise of Fascism in Italy was backed by the capitalists as they considered it as an effective bulwark against communism. The Western leniency in conducting the peace settlement with Italy and the eagerness shown by USA, UK and France in developing relations with Fascist Italy made the Soviet Union more convinced that the enemies of communism were out to limit the role of Soviet Union in world politics.

5. Abrupt End of Lend-Lease Agreement. The American decision to terminate the 'aid' that it was giving to the Soviet Union under the Lend-Lease Agreement was strongly disliked by the Soviet leaders. Already the USSR was dissatisfied with the meagre aid that it got from the Western powers, and this American decision which came immediately after the surrender of Germany, added fuel to the Fire. The Western opposition to the Seviet demand for huge reparations from defeated nations further acted as an irritant in the East-West relations.

6. Anti-Soviet Propaganda by Western Press and Leadership. Despite the fact that since 1942, the Soviet Union had been acting as a war ally of the Allies, the Western Press and leadership always kept up their propaganda against communism and Soviet policies. As a war-ally, the Soviet Union expected that Western powers shall refrian from pursuing anti-communist propaganda trade against USSR. However, the Western press showed no sign of relenting from its professed and active anti communist role. It kept on talking of the grave threat that coummunist menace was posing to the free world and that the Soviets were out to transfer the world into a communist world. The USSR feft greatly annoyed with such Western tirades against conmunistm and its policies.

All these factors made the Soviet Union greatly dissatisfied with the Western powers. It felt itself psychologically and emotionally withdrawn from the Western leaders and their policies. In order to strengthen its position as a socialist power, the USSR decided to secure a ring of communist states in Eastern Europe. The success that it secured in this venture further increased the growing differences with the Western powers. In the process, the USSR found herself engulfed in a cold war with its "former allies."

Thus, the Cold War that came to develop in the post-war years of international relations had its roots in a number of factors. The mutual complaints and grievances of East and West created an environment of distrust and disharmony between the USSR and the Western-powers. The end of the Second World War can be termed as inglorious in so far as it gave rise to Cold War between the USSR and the Western-powers. Several unfortunate war-time decisions and postwar developments led the World to live, even after end of the War, on the brink of a Third World War and in an environment infested with risks, tension and strains, *i.e.*, the Cold War.

PHASES OF COLD WAR

The history of cold war in international relations between 1945-70 can be analysed in its several phases. For the sake of convenience we can adopt the following divisions.

(A) The Preparatory Stage of Cold War (1945-47)

(B) The First Round of Cold War (1947-53)

(C) The Second Round of Cold War (1953-63)

(D) Third Round of Cold War (1963-70)

(A) THE PREPARATORY STAGE OF COLD WAR (1945-47)

1. Churchill's Fulton Speech. In his famous Fulton Speech—(the Iron Curtain speech March 1946) British P.M. Churchill epitomised such a thinking. He observed: "A shadow has fallen upon the scenes so lately lighted by the Allied victory. Nobody knows what the Soviet Russia and its communist international organisation intends to do in the immediate future. From Stettin in the Baltic to Trieste in the Adriatic, an iron curtain has descended across the continent." He further predicted that "post-war struggle against 'the Soviet barbarianism' is inevitable and that the only language that the USSR understands is the language of force". Such a view was also shared by many Americans, particularly those holding high positions in the U.S. State Department.

2. Growing Fear of Soviet Expansionism. Such a western thinking got strengthened when the Soviet Union undertook the expansion of her influence in Eastern Europe and decided to pressurise Turkey, Greece and Iran in favour of her power in world politics. The conflict that surfaced at the London Conference of Foreign Ministers also gave air to the view that the Soviet Union was out to expand that communism constituted the biggest threat to the free world.

3. End or U.S. Isolationism. As an immediate measure, U.S.A. decided to end her policy of isolationalism and in its place to work for filling the powers vacuum in Europe and elsewhere.

4. Conflicting Ideologies. The conflict between the ideologies of Democracy and Communism, or Freeland and Marx-land or Freedom and Tyranny, once again came to dominate the minds and speeches of Western statesmen.

5. Mutual Fear and Distrust. During 1945-47, both the Soviet Union and the Western powers became increasingly critical of each other. The conflict over several issues revived the mutual distrusts and fears which had been kept back during the War years. Consequently, the Western powers once again became supicious of the communist menace as mani-fested in the rise of Soviet power in world politics and the Soviet Union became determined fight capitalism.

6. The Truman Doctrine. The Truman Doctrine of March 1947, heralded this change in U.S. Foreign Policy. This doctrine affirmed that "It must be the policy of the United States to support free people who are resisting attempted subjugation by armed minorities or outside pressures." It was further stated that international peace would be endangered in case of the establishment of communist dictatorship over the free peoples of the world and consequently, the security of the American continent would be threatened as well. The Truman Doctrine was, as such, designed to check the growing Soviet power and role in international relations. Its object was to contain communism and check the Soviet attempts at expansionism in Balkans and the Middle East. As a practical step, President Truman asked the U.S. Congress to sanction 400 million dollars for helping Greece and Turkey who were struggling to maintain their freedom and democratic systems. The U.S. Congress accorded sanction to his demand and thus opened the era of U.S. involvement in international relations.

7. Marshall Plan. In 1947, the European Recovery Programme under the Marshall Plan was sponsored by the United States as a major measure to help the socio-economic reconstruction of war-torn Europe. In reality, it was an attempt to win over the European states and keep them away from communism. The underlying aim of Marshall Plan was to save Europe from communism. It was also designed to increase the U.S. influence over Europe as a means to contain the growing Soviet influence in Eastern Europe. Technically all countries were invited to join the Marshall Plan but in reality it was formulated for helping the non-communist states.

8. Soviet Reaction and Counter-Moves. The Soviet Union felt greatly disturbed by the Truman Doctrine and Marshall Plan, as these were viewed as measures designed both for spreading U.S. hegemony in Europe as well as for isolating the Soviet Union and other Socialist Countries. Since 1917, when the Western troops in Soviet Russia tried to secure a counter revolution against Bolshevic Revolution the Socialist leadership had been highly suspicious of Western intentions. Between 1917-41 the Soviet policy was governed by the goal of building a strong national power base for meeting the possible threat of capitalism to the socialist system. Western appeasement of Germany greatly annoyed Russia as it felt that this was governed by the sole motive of producing a war between Nazi-Germany and Socialist USSR. Its decision to conclude a secret non-aggression pact with Germany was motivated by the desire to foil such a Western move.

However, in 1941, when Germany attacked USSR, the latter had no option but to join hands with the Allies. During 1941-45, the Soviet Union co-operated with the western powers for powers for defeating Germany. However, such a co-operation did not lead her to believe that the Western powers were really prepared to coexist with communist USSR. Consequently, the Soviet leadership decided to use its success in Second World War as a basis for pursuing an increase of its influence in Europe, and the successful conversion of several Eastern European nations definitely emboldened such a thinking. The emergence of conflict with the Western powers over the issue of peace treaties, future of Germany, Berlin problem, etc., made it realise further the need to increase its influence in world politics. The U.S. attempts to use its monopoly power-status as the sole possessor of Atomic Bombs and as the richest country in the world were viewed with alarm by the Soviet Union. The Truman Doctrine and Marshall Plan further convinced it that Western powers as led by the U.S.A., were out to isolate the Soviet Union in the international system. Consequently,the Soviet leaders decided to counter the Western moves by the following two moves:

1. **Sovietisation of Eastern Europe.** The USSR decided to boycott the Marshall Plan as well as to influence the other socialist states to Europe to remain away from the U.S. hegemonious programme.
2. **COMECON Vs. Marshall Plan.** As a counter move, the Soviet Union initiated the Molotoy Plan and established the Council of Mutual Economic Assistance. COMECON, for helping the economic consolidation of socialist countries. In September 1948, Communist Information Bureau (Cominform) was established for co-ordinating the policies of Communist Parties on the international front. The enforcement of Marshall Plan by U.S.A. & the COMECON by U.S.S.R. came to be the events which heralded the era of cold war in international relations or at least between the USA and the USSR.

Resulting Fears, Distrust and Tensions. The period between 1941-47, was as such a period in which mutual mistrust and fear between the USSR and the Western powers increased to a very large extent. Each side became prepared for attempting to isolate, challenge and weaken the other. It was a preparation stage because both sides undertook several policy decisions which were designed to produce a stiff competition and race for domination. The ideal of international peace and security, as had been solemnly affirmed by both the sides, was forgotten or deliberately ignored in favour of psychological and political warfare motivated by the selfish desire of each of the two super powers—USA and USSR to establish their own domination over the international system of the post-war period.

(B) THE FIRST ROUND OF COLD WAR (1947-53)

In the first round of Cold War *i.e.*, from 1947 to 1953 (Death to Stalin) both the U.S.A. and the U.S.S.R., tried hard to consolidate their influences over Europe. Consequently, Europe, more particularly, Germany came to be the major centre of the Cold War. The issue of atomic weapons, Disarmament, Peace Treaties with Germany, Japan and Austria, Berlin problem and Korean War provided the environment within which the U.S.A. and the U.S.S.R. tried to extend their respective holds over international relations.

1. Berlin Issue and Cold War. In 1948, the Cold war between the USSR and the Western powers got manifested in the from of Berlin Blockade by the former. With a view to check Western economic intervention in Berlin which resulted from the decision to introduce a new deflated currency in the western zone and Berlin city, He USSR decided to introduce it own economic reforms immediately and as part of such an exercise decided to apply the new East Zone currency and goods to Berlin. It enforced a blockade of Berlin which produced a strong western reaction in the form of Berlin Airlift. This led to the development of a real crisis which produced a stalemate when the USSR refused to lift the blockade and the U.S.A. refused to abandon the airlift. The former insisted that the West should evacuate Berlin, and the latter announced its determination to remain in Berlin until the Germany was reunited. Such opposed stands made the conferences over Berlin big failures.

The attempt made by the U.N. too proved to be a failure because of the veto power potentials of the U.S.A. and the U.S.S.R. It was in May 1948, that the U. S.S.R. agreed to lift the block, but it was too late to produce good result.

2. Rise of Communist China and Cold War. In 1949, the rise of Mao's Communist Party to power in China gave a big boost to Soviet influence in world politics and it produced a reaction in the form of U.S. commitment to follow containment of communism more vigorously.

3. Organisation of NATO and Division of Germany. The immediate fall out of such policies came in the from of the establishment of NATO on 4 April, 1949 by the U.S.A. and her allies and the subsequent establishment or Federal Republic of Germany on 21 September, 1949.

4. Germany as the Centre of Cold War. In respect of Germany, the U.S.S.R. came to adopt a policy which was strongly opposed by the Western powers. The division of Germany into Federal Republic of Germany and German Democratic Rupublic was affected in the process of attempts made by U.S.S.R. and the Western powers to maintain their powers in their respective occupation zones. The politics of Marshall Plan Vs. COMECON kept Europe in the midst of a cold war between U.S.A. and U.S.S.R. Orgainsed American propaganda and political warfare led to the formation of Cominform by the USSR as a counter measure.

5. Termination of War in Korea, but Continuance of Cold War. However, despite armistice, the American and Soviet troops continued to remain stationed in both the Koreas and cold war hostility continued to be there The U.S.A. stepped up its propaganda war against communism and Soviet Union intensified its drive for popularising communism. The Soviet success it solving the mystery of the Atom greatly enhanced its influence and she became involved in the nuclear armament race with the U.S.A. This development further increased the intensity of cold war. It made the efforts for disarmament a big failure. The U.N. found itself helpless in the presence of cold war between the two super powers.

6. Korean Crisis and Cold War. In 1950, the Korean war provided the ground for the pursuance of cold war politics in Far East. The situation created by the North Korean aggression against South Korea provided U.S.A. and the Western powers with an opportunity to attempt containment of communism by helping democratic South Korea against communist North Korea. In the Korean war, North Korea was supported by the U.S.S.R. and Communist China, where as South Korea was supported by U.S.A. and other western countries. American success in making the U.N. Security Council agree upon the need to enforce collective security system in Korean war was strongly opposed by the Soviet Union. The differences between U.S.A. and U.S.S.R. over the issue of peace in Korea sharply divided the U.N. Security Council and consequently, it failed to perform its responsibility of preserving international peace and security against aggression.

7. Issue of Peace Treaty with Japan and Cold War. Besides the above important developments of cold war during 1947-53 period, the issuc of peace treaty with Japan also demonstrated that both the U.S.A. and the U.S.S.R. were committed to pursue cold war in their relations. The U.S. decision to summon the San Franscisco Conference in September 1951, for considering and approving the draft of peace treaty with Japan was strongly opposed by the U.S.S.R. However, Soviet opposition did not deter America to conclude the treaty. It followed this up by concluding a defence treaty with Japan and thereby got the right to station its troops in Japan.

Thus, during 1947-53, the U.S.S.R. and the Western powers followed a cold war in their relations. The cold war kept the international relations highly strained and tense.

(C) SECOND ROUND OF COLD WAR (1953-63)

The history of the second round of cold war can also be, in the main, described as cold war between the U.S.A. and the U.S.S.R. during the Eisenhower-era in U.S. politics and Khrushchev-era in Soviet politics. In 1952 U.S. Presidential elections. Eisenhower got elected. He and his Secretary of State, John Foster Dulles were committed to follow "Containment of Communism" and 'Massive

Retaliation' as principles of U.S. foreign policy. In the Soviet Union, the death of Stalin in 1953, brought a change in top leadership but there too, Molotov kept up this commitment to spread communism and to check the forces of capitalistic imperialism. In mid fifties, Soviet Premier Khrushchev came out with his call for peaceful co-existence between East and West and initiated several bold moves for securing reapproachment with U.S.A. However, he found himself involved in the Cuban missile crisis which brought the cold war to the brink of a hot war in 1962.

During 1963-70, a see-saw game emerged between the U.S.A. and the U.S.S.R. in which on the one hand both the countries entered into several meaningful contracts and agreements but on the other hand kept engaged in pursuing cold war in Middle East, Vietnam, Berlin and other parts of the Globe The cold war between the two super powers adversely affected the functioning of United Nations. The history of cold war during 1953-70 can be analysed as under.

1. SEATO and Warsaw Pact. During this phase of cold war, the U.S.A. continued her policy of military and economic offensive. On the pattern of NATO, it organised the SEATO and MEDO. These organisations were meant to check the spread of communism into South East Asia, and Middle East. As a counter action to such American moves, the U.S.S.R. on 4th May, 1955 was successful in organising a communist defence pact—the Warsaw Pact involving Eastern European socialist states. It was designed to "resist the attacks of the imperialists and capitalists." This led to the organisation and consolidation of Soviet Bloc or the Socialist Bloc against the American Bloc or the Democratic Bloc. The international system came to be vertically divided into two parts: the Soviet Bloc and the American Bloc, with cold war in between. The development of Bipolarity in international power relations further increased the intensity of cold war.

2. Nuclear Arms Race and Cold War. Further the emergence of Nuclear armament race between U.S.A. and U.S.S.R. followed by the space race further made the cold war more grave. The overkill capacity developed by each of the two super powers created a highly dangerous situation in which talks for disarmament and arms control were held but without success. In September 1953, U.S.S.R. rejected a no war pact proposal made by the Western bloc. In March 1954, the West rejected the Soviet wish to join NATO.

3. Civil War in Indo-China and Cold War. During this phase the cold war made its appearance in Indo-China. By 1954, the war between the Ho Chin Minh forces and the French forces had reached a critical stage. Ho Chin Minh's forces were backed by the U.S.S.R. and Communist China, and France was strongly backed by the U.S.A. France wanted to get rid of her involvement and therefore advocated a peaceful solution. Likewise, Soviet Union and China also wanted to avoid increasing U.S. involvement in Indo-China and hence expressed their willingness for a peaceful settlement of Indo-China problem. It was under these circumstances that Geneva Agreement on Indo-China was affected in 1954. Vietnam got partitioned with North Vietnam under the Communists and South Vietnam under the Democrats. However, within 24 hours of the singing of the Geneva Agreement the war broke out between communist guerillas and South Vietnamese forces. In order to check the spread of communism, the U.S.A. started giving huge aid to South Vietnam, and of subsequently got directly involved in the Vietnam war. After this development, the U.S.S.R. and China started giving huge military and economic aid to North Vietnam and thus, the war in Indo-China got inseparably joined up with the cold war between U.S.A. & U.S.S.R. The war got intensified in the sixties as U.S.A. became thoroughly involved in this war U.S. policy in Vietnam war governed by the thinking that Communist victory in Vietnam would endanger the prestige of U.S.A. in S.E.A. and would encourage the spread of communism to Cambodia, Laos, Thailand and Burma. The growing power of North Vietnam and the Vietcong forces compelled the U.S.A. to resort to heavy bombardment of Vietnamese positions—a decision which was thoroughly opposed by the non-aligned and several other countries including France. However, U.S.A., in complete disregard of international public opinion, maintained the bombardment of North Vietnam positions. Soviet Union, China and other communist countries strongly opposed the

American involvement in Vietnam war and therefore came out to give full support to North Vietnam. During 1953-70 period, Vietnam continued to be a source of tension and strains in U.S.—U.S.S.R. relations. The cold war between them prevented a settlement of Vietnamese problem.

4. Eisenhower Doctrine and Cold War. However, in June 1957, Eienhower Principles, under which the U.S. Congress authorised the President to send U.S. armed forces to any place for checking the danger of Communism, gave a new intensity to the Cold War. During the last two years of tenure of President Eisenhower, heightened cold war continued to characterise the relations between the U.S.A. and the U.S.S.R., Germany, Berlin, Indo-China, Korea, Japan and Middle East continued to be the major centres of cold war.

5. Khrushchev's Visit to USA—a Hope for Peace. In 1957-58 Soviet Premier Khrushchev came out openly in support of peaceful co-existence between East and West. He expressed strong desire to renounce war and to get engaged in peaceful co-operative international intercourse. He expressed his readiness to visit the U.S.A. and meet President Eisenhower for sorting out U.S.—Soviet differences. This appeared as a welcome change, particularly when the U.S.A. decided to extend an invitation to Khrushchev. From 15 to 28 September, 1959, Soviet Premier Khrushchev paid a visit to Washington and conducted meaningful talks with President Eirenhower. Khrushchev's visit successfully made the international environment develop a healthy look.

6. Hungarian Crisis and Cold War. In 1956, the Soviet intervention in Hungary was strongly opposed by the Western countries. But the former exhibited its ability to keep the iron curtain tight over the Eastern European states.

7. Suez Crisis and Cold War. During the Suez Canal War of 1956, U.S.A. and U.S.S.R. found themselves engaged in unintentional co-operation. The Anglo-French-Jewish invasion of Egypt for maintaining a forcible occupation of Suez was strongly disliked by the U.S.A., as it held that it would force Egypt and other Muslism countries of Middle East to accept Soviet aid and be under Soviet influence. Hence, the U.S.A. wanted an early end to this invasion. Likewise, the U.S.S.R., found in the Suez Canal crisis an opportunity to increase its influence in the Middle East by siding with Egypt. It, therefore, gave call for the end of the invasion of Egypt and followed this up immediately by holding the threat to use atomic weapons in case Britain, France and Israel failed to terminate the war.

8. U-2 Incident, and Renewal of Cold War. Unfortunately, however, just a few days before the Summit, the U-2 incident of 1 May, 1960, took place and spoiled the entire environment that had been developing since 1957 U-2 was a U.S. Spy plane which was shot down by the Soviet forces. The U.S.S.R. felt greatly annoyed with the U.S.A. and wanted a U.S. apology and assurance to end the such spy missions over the Soviet Union. The U.S.A. was not prepared to accept the Soviet demand, and hence the U-2 incident once again made the U.S—U.S.S.R. relations highly tense and strained.

9. Berlin Wall Crisis 1961 and Cold War. In 1960, John F. Kenndy was elected as thc President of the U.S.A. and he continued to be so till 22 November 1963. Initially, an attempt was made to repair the damage that had been done to the U.S.—U.S.S.R. relations by the U-2 incident. However, little meaningful progress could result from such efforts. On the contrary, the Berlin wall crisis of 1961 and the Cuban Missile crisis of 1962 brought the two countires to the verge of a full hot war. In August 1961, the construction of a wall by the Soviet Union for separating the Soviet sectors from the Western sectors of Berlin city, was strongly opposed by the U.S.A. Both the U.S.A. and the U.S.S.R. moved their tanks to the frontiers and war appeared to be a distinct possibility.

10. Failure of Paris Summit and Cold War. The Paris Summit was held on 16th May, 1960, under the shadow of the U-2 incident. Despite an earlier assurance that U-2 incident shall not be raised at the Paris Summit, Khrushehev demanded an American apology over the incident, and as a mark of protest refused to shake hands with President Eisenhower. Under the circumstances, the Paris Summit failed to reach any decision, and cold war continued to be the natural form of U.S.—U.S.S.R. relations.

11. Cold War Towards Hot War—Cuban Missiles Crisis 1962. However, it was in October 1992, that a really big crisis—the Cuban Missile crisis, came to be developed between the two super powers and brought them to the threshold of a war. The Soviet decision to establish a missile base in Cuba was strongly opposed by the Americans. When the Soviet missile carrying ships were on their way to Cuba, America, in order to prevent their entry into Cuba ordered the blockade or strict "Quarantine" of all military equipment bound for Cuba. The American goverment declared that it would regard any missile launched from Cuba against any nation in the Western Hemisphere as an attack by the Soviet Union on the United States requiring a full retaliatory response. On 23 October 1962, the U.S.A. decided to take all necessary steps for ending the Soviet threat to peace and security of the American continent. On 24 October 1962, the U.S. Blocade of Cuban ports became effective. The war between U.S. and U.S.S.R. became a distinct possibility. U.N. Secretary General, Mr. U. Thant tried to prevail upon U.S.A. to suspend the blocade and also asked the Soviet Union to halt Shipments to Cuba, but failed to break the dead lock. Soviet Union demanded the withdrawal of U.S. rockets from Turkey as a precondition for stopping installation of Soviet missiles in Cuba. This demand was rejected by U.S.A.

(D) THIRD ROUND OF COLD WAR (1963-70)

Unfortunately, however, this was not destined to be so. In the post-63 period of their relations both the U.S.A. and the U.S.S.R. kept up playing a see-saw game. At times they behaved as mature states working for the peaceful conduct to mutual relations while at other times they kept on conducting their relations in a spirit of cold war. Between 1963-70, Vietnam, South Asia, Middle East, U.N.O. , and Berlin experienced the continuance of cold war, but at the same time there took place exchange of visits, summit meetings, signing of Non-Proliferation Treaty in 1968 and several other positive developments.

1. Indo-Pak War and Cold War. In 1964, President Johnson's decision to increase the strength of U.S. military operations in Vietnam, invoked strong Soviet opposition. In 1965, the Indo-Pak war came and both U.S.A. and U.S.S.R. took opposite stands. The Soviet role as mediator between India and Pakistan at Tashkent Conference greatly irked U.S.A.

2. Change of Leadership in USA and USSR and Cold War. In November 1963, President Kennedy was assassinated and Mr. L.B. Johnson became the U.S., President. In October 1964, Khrushchev was ousted from power in Moscow and in his place Brezhnev and Kosygin emerged as the two powerful Soviet leaders.

3. 1967 Arab-Israel War and Cold War. In 1967. Arab-Israel war, the Soviet Union came out openly and strongly against the pro-Israeli policies of Western powers. The U.S.S.R. used the war to voice consolidation with the Arabs and thereby to increase her influence in Middle East. Once again the competition for strengthening their respective holds in Middle East increased the intensity of cold war between U.S.A. and U.S.S.R.

4. An Attempt to Reduce Tensions—The Classbrough Summit. Kosygin and Johnson met in a summit at classbrough from 23 June to 26 June 1967 and exchanged views on Vietnam and Middle East. The summit was held under the shadow of the growing nuclear capability of China who had successfully exploded a hydrogen bomb in 1967. This summit helped the two countries to understand better the problems of their mutual relations and the key international issues and problems. The signing of Non-Proliferation Treaty (1968) further helped the process of securing more contacts between the U.S.A. and U.S.S.R. The U.S decision to suspend the bombing of Vietnam further made the environment less tense.

5. The Thinking Towards Detente. Thus, during 1953-1970 the world continued to live with the tensions and strains created by the cold war between East and West in general and the U.S.S.R. and U.S.A. in particular. The only good thing that resulted from the U.S.—Soviet relations during this period was that there appeared a welcome positive view in favour of the desire to end or atleast lessen the gravity and intensity of cold war and to develop mutual contacts and co-operation. Several factors helped in the emergence of such a decision. The Cuban Missile crisis made the two super powers highly conscious of the dangers of unbriddled and unlimited cold war. The rise and subsequent strength of Non-aligned Movement, the weakened positions of both the American and Soviet Blocs, the emergence of China and France as big military powers, the rise of Japan and West Germany as great economic powers. The economic integration and resultant big improvement in the power status of Western Europe, the awakening of Asia, Africa and Latin America etc., produced several important changes in the international system which forced the two super powers to think in terms of a detente.

6. 1969 Berlin Crisis and Cold War. In March 1969, Berlin again became the source of cold war tensions and strains in Soviet-American relations. The decision of the West German Government to hold the election of FRG Chancellor in West Berlin was strongly opposed by the U.S.S.R. and the Government of G.D.R. on the ground that such a step was designed to show that Berlin was a part of West Germany and as such was opposed to the Potsdam Agreement. The persistence of the FRG in pursuing the election led to the enforcement of Berlin Blocade by G.D.R. The FRG then airlifted the members of the electoral college into West Berlin and got the election conducted there. The peaceful conduct of election paved the way for the diffusion of the crisis.

OBJECTIVES OF COLD WAR

Theories regarding objective of Cold War are as follows:

1. ***Defence and Deterence.*** Theories the medium of cold war a country tries to protect itself from the deceptive and misleading propaganda of the opponent and it is by the same methods that it can deter the activities of its opponent.
2. ***Protection of Ideology.*** The capitalistic, communist and democratic countries initiate cold wars among themselves in order to protect their own ideologies and also to refute the views of the other philosophies. One of the main reason behind the cold war that continues between America and Russia is the protection the their respective ideologies.
3. ***Contradiction of the Opposing Government.*** In a cold war, the opposing government is constantly opposed and

contradicted. Even its creditable activities are presented in a bad light all its dirty linen is washed in public, in the eyes of the entire world. Sometimes, what is done is that a national of the opposing country is persuaded to come over, and then through the medium of newspapers and radio he is made to criticise his own government and country. When this individual recounts the injustices heaped by his government on his own people, then it is natural that his words should appeal to his people. In this manner the objectives of the people who initiated the cold war are achieved.

4. ***Helping a Friendly Government.*** Once a government that favour the propagandists has been established, then the propagandists turn their propaganda and cold war against those who oppose this government. The aim behind this activity is to ensure the continued existence of the friendly government, since this ultimately benefits mutual trade, etc.

5. ***Persuading the Public.*** In its psychological form, the cold war is a means to persuade the public to accept one's own ideals. Through it efforts are made to make the general public accept the ideals of the propagandist and forget the ideals of the opponent.

6. ***For Attainment of Specific Objectives.*** In much the same manner a cold war is sometimes intended to influence some government or nation or some political party in such a manner that it will be induced to make some political or economic concessions, in the from of trade monopoly in that particular country is forced and even covered in accepting economic, military or technical assistance. It is only natural of the cold war that it will turn against its enemies.

THEORY OF THREE COLD WARS

The cold wars, the modern versions of the old fashioned wars, are caused by the same factors that caused the wars in the old days.

In other words, the objectives for which wars were fought in the ancient times no longer necessitiate those extreme measure for their achievement in the present context. Today, it is the cold war that achieves those same objects. Why did this change occur? There are some very definite cause why change did take place. They are as follows:

1. Modern War is More Expensive. In the mdoern era of science, a war is an expensive affair because it is fought on land, in air as well as in water, and it further involves the entire population of the country, not only its army. In the ancient days, the armies fought with each other, while the people continued their leisurely ways, unaffected by the clash. In a situation of war in the modern time the entire economic organisation of the country is forced to bear a very heavy burden which cannot be borne a very long time. And irrespective of whether the country wins or losses in the war, its economic organisation is completely disrupted and even shattered. The result is a fall in the standard of living and greater poverty. At the same time, the number of crimes in the country also increases. In this way and because of the serious shock that it suffers, the economy is incapable of achieving the same level of prosperity for a very long time.

2. War Threatens to Annihilate the Entire Human Race. In the olden days, the wars were capable of wreaking only limited destruction in terms of individuals killed, and this number included only those directly involved in it. But modern warfare is capable of devastating the entire human resources of the national engaged in it, and it is even possible for one war to wipe the entire human race off the face of the earth. Since the discovery of atomic and nuclear energy and the invention of atomic weapons the entire human race is threatened by prospects of annihilation in the event of a war. Any war in which these media of mass destruction are employed will spell automatic disaster for humanity. And it is not only the present existing brand of humans that are threatened by destruction in this way but also all the forthcoming generations. Some scientists hold the belief that is an atomic and nuclear war takes place, not a sign of life will be left on this earth. Hence, modern warfare is fatal not only to those who are participating in it but also for those who are indifferent to this show of hostility and have nothing to do with it one way or the other.

3. Improvement in the Techniques of Psychological Warfare. In the modern world any number of new techniques and methods of psychological warfare have been invented through the medium of which people situated over a large area can be effectively influenced. These techniques of psychological warfare are also available to all the nations, and hence in the modern world, armed conflict has been replaced by psychological war, or what it known as a 'war of nerves'.

4. War does not Bring Victory of Principles. As has been indicated at various stages earlier, one of the main aim of cold war is the propagation of one's own idelogy and the refutation of the other's principles. This end cannot be achieved through the medium of war. Arms cannot spread principles and idelogies because they are not things that can be forced on people. It is for the people to adopt them. Hence, for this the most appropriate means is propaganda and not arms.

5. Victory Through Resistance. James Forrestal has written, "The surest way to avoid war is to make it clear to any possible group of enemies that the risk of engaging us are too great to make it worthwhile," In this way victory over nations can also be achieved through contradicting war and robbing them of their self-confidence. Once good example of this method of avoiding war is continued testing of atomic weapons that is being indulged in at the moment by a number of nations. America, Britain, Russia and some other leading nations almost momentously advertise their programmes, for the testing of atomic weapons so that the enemies should beware of their powers and should desist from any aggressive activity. Another method of contradicting and avoiding warfare is to enter into a mutual defence treaty.

Theory Regarding the Process of Cold War. The process of cold war is of psychological nature. In the book, Sociological Aspects of Psychological Warfare R. Sorenssion has written, "The means of psychological warfare are its weapons, words and deeds are its ammunition, with the added consideration that words and circumstances under with they are conveyed often are viewed as deeds *per se* in the target system." In this way, in the cold war, words are used in many numerous ways which serve the purpose of propaganda, motive, threat, example, assurance etc., as and when the circumstances warrant a particular use. The department most intimately related to and involved in the cold war is that of foreign affairs. In some few countries some individual and private organizations also participate in this activity and sometimes such activity is lavishly financed by the capitalist class of society.

Means of Using Words in Cold War. As has been indicated earlier, the main weapons and means of the cold war are the words. These words are put to use through the following media:

1. Broadcasting and relaying through radio or television.
2. Posters and paper cartons that are dropped from aeroplanes or balloons or are set through post.
3. Over and invisible or unapparent diplomatic moves.
4. Declarations made by government officials in the midst of the public or in press conferences or from the government benches in the parliament or in debates.
5. Protest notes that are sent to the government that is hostile.
6. Debates in organisations of a international nature such as the United Nations Organisation.

Theory and Methods of Psychological Warfare. The following methods are adopted in psychological warfare:

1. ***Exhibition.*** Efforts are made to frighten and to overawe the other countries by exhibiting power and strength through atomic tests and soldier rallies and other comparable methods. One nation tries to intimidate the other.
2. ***Assistance.*** Another method of controlling other nations is to render to them economic, medicial, political, technical, military or other help. In this way they are brought under the influence of the one who is rendering resistance and

they are at the same time persuaded to contradict its enemies.

3. ***Diplomatic Relations.*** Pressure is brought to bear on different countries by breaking off or resuming diplomaic relations with them.
4. ***Cultural and Commercial Mixing or Cooperation.*** Now-a-days, another method that is adopted for increasing one's own sphere of influence is through sending cultural delegations of authors and painters and other artists to other countries and reciprocating by inviting similar delegations from them. Similarly, youth festivals and commercial fairs are organised and delegations from different nations are invited. This meeting and exchange strengthens the bond between some people while it also serves to frighten other people.
5. ***Laws Relating to the Return of Emigrants.*** By means of these laws some people are prevented from returning to their country while other people are granted permission to return.
6. ***Discriminatory Activity in Trade.*** Attempts are made to intimidate or influence other nations by boycotting the good produced by them and put in the world market. The other aspect of this is controlling or influencing a nation through giving it bounties in the form of relaxation of the trade agreement or rendering it assistance.
7. ***Control on Communication with other Countries.*** The means of communication are extensively utilised in any cold war. Hence, commnication with foreign countries is subject to rigourous control and supervision. Newspapers and other magazines are strictly censroed. People who operate illegal transmitters are severely punished and emigration and immigration is controlled and subjected to many difficult conditions.
8. ***Establishment of Political Parties in other Countries.*** Sometimes even political parties are created in other

countries in order to oust the existing government from power of to conduct campaigns of propaganda against it. If this is not feasible then the help of some political party is secured. The communist countries encourage communist parties in non-communist countries and in this way promote cold war.

The foregoing description of the techniques of cold war or psychological war is not an exhaustive account of these techniques. Almost unceasing and incessant efforts are directed towards this and new experiments are made and new techinques are being evolved everywhere. Although apparently a cold war does not potentially possess all the dangers inherent in an armed conflict, yet it is quite as dangerous as the latter and its consequences can be as violent as that of the latter. And the truth of the matter is that it can sometimes prove even more destructive than armed conflict since it can pollute the thinking of an entire nation while in an armed conflict only the soldiers are killed. Cold wars promote conditions of tension which continue over long periods. This leads to a disturbance and disruption of normal system and organisation of a country and it also endanger international peace. And because of the very subtlety of the techniques of cold war they are even more difficult to control and counteract than the methods of an ordinary war, but nevertheless, it is quite as important to control them as it is destructive to the human race.

ROLE OF USA

Soon after World War II the world was engulfed by cold war—an era on neither peace nor war. The origin of cold war can be traced back to the war period when the two major partners of estern and Eastern blocs fought together against the common Axis danger. But their mutual relations were guided by mutual distrust and jealously. This distrust assumed the shape of a rivarly after World War II over the questions of Germany and Japan.

The cold war was based on a number of assumptions. First, it assumes that the real to the world peace was posed by the military strength of Soviet Union. It may be noted that Soviet Union's military strength was virtually destroyed during World II. This assumption gave rise to the policy of strength which was responsible for the development of military theory of cold war on the basis of atom bomb, hydrogen bomb and nuclear warfare. Secondly, it asumes the inevitability of conflict between the socialist and capitalist states, which prompted the states of both the blocs of keep themselves in condition of constant preparedness for a final show down.

(1) It assumes that no co-operation is possible between states with different social systems.

(2) It is based on the assumption of Western powers to equate all socialist movements as subversive movements. That explains the American intervention from Greece and Turkey in 1947 to Vietnam.

(3) It assumes that the struggle between West and East is a struggle between freedom and tyranny.

Phases of Cold War. The Cold war passed through a number of phases. The first phase lasted from 1946 to 49. During this period it was held that if strong pressure could be organized the Red regime in Soviet Union would collapse like a house of cards. This feeling arose because America was having monopoly of Atom bomb and Russia was in very condition. Therefore, it was held that U.S.A. due to her military superiority could determine the history of world and influence the internal affairs of Soviet Union. This policy of 'containing' Soviet Union could not be implemented because the Allies of American were not yet fully armed for such a war and the memories of Second World War were still fresh in their mind which prevented them form resorting to war.

During this phase America resorted to direct military intervention through Truman Doctrine of March 1947 and economic intergration of the Wast European Powers by Marshall Plan of June 1947. U.S.A. during this period followed the policy of intervention and defender of *status quo*. This phase was also marked by anti-communist feeling, which U.S.A. tried to implant through-out the world. This phase of cold war ended with the conclusion of North Atlantic Treaty on April 4, 1949. This treaty was sort of new anti Comintern Pact and was openly directed against the Soviet Union.

The Second Phase lasted from 1949 to 1953. During this peroid U.S.A. continued her policy of military and economic assistance against Soviet Union. During this period U.S.A. concluded security treaty with Australia and New Zealand (ANZUS) and Peace Treaty with Japan (1951). This period also Witnessed the Korean War which was a major confrontation between U.S.A. and U.S.S.R. The United States intensified her anti-Communist propaganda and spent millions of dollars for the purpose. She also invested huge amounts to carry out subversive activities in the Socialist countries.

The third phase of cold war lasted from 1953 to 1957. During this phase U.S.A. continued her Policy of military and economic offensive. She organised the South East Asia Treaty Organisation (SEATO) and the Middle East Defence Organisation (MEDO). These two treaties became new defence links with NATO. America also made a serious effort to perpetuate American domination in the Middle East by extending the Truman Doctrine to this area.U.S.A. also established a number of military bases around Soviet territory and concluded defence treaties with 43 states. It was also during this period that U.S.A. involved herself in Vietnam, which turned out to be a grim climax of the cold war.

During this face Soviet Union also increased her influence. She sponsored Warsaw Treaty with East European powers as a counter measure to NATO. She concluded defence treaties with 12 states and foiled the American attempt to promote counter-revolution in Hungary. This period also witnessed the peramnency of the Postdam partition of Germany.

The fourth phase lasted from 1957 to 1962. It saw two exterme trends. On the one hand the principles of peaceful co-existence were asserted and on the other hand it saw the most dangerous Cuban missile crisis. During the initial years the spirit of co-existence prevailed. The two countries exchanged cultural and political delegates. The heads of governments of two countries paid visits to each other. The agreement for Paris Summit clearly demonstrated that the cold war attitude had ended. But this spirit was sabotaged by the U-2 incident.

The damage done by the U-2 incident was partly repaired by the General Assembly Summit of 1960 and the Vietnam meeting of Khrushchev and President Kennedy in 1961. But the Cuban crisis literally brought the two countries to the verge of war.

The fifth and the last phase started form 1962 and is marked by a deep appreciation of the futility of nuclear strategy. This phase saw the conclusion of 'Partial Test Ban Treaty' the 1963. By Geneva Hot Line Agreement of 1963 the two countries were closely linked. The Non-Proliferation Treaty of 1968 could also be concluded due to the understanding of the two powers. However, even during this period the problems of Germany and Vietnam stood in the way of full-co-operation between the two countries, Emergance of Willy Brandt in West Germany lessened the tension and he launched the policy of "Ostopolitik', which sought improvement to relations with the East. Nixon, Former President of U.S.A. also brought an end to Vietnam War and thus paved the way for further co-operation among the rival blocs.

IMPACT OF COLD WAR

(1) Cold War has stood in the way of achieving the objective of one world. The mutual rivalry has reduced the U.N.O. to the status of a simple form of world opinion. The cold war has prevented some of the states from becoming member of the world body. The deanial of representation to people's China in the Security Council for such a long time was mainly due to his Cold War.

(2) Cold War has resulted in mad race for armaments. States of both the blocs have been spending huge amounts to equip themselves with latest weapons. This has not only led to diversion of money which could have more profitably been utilised for improving the lot of the people. It has also led to both the camps being armed to the teeth. Any local quarrel of misunderstanding can lead to a nuclear war.

(3) Cold war has adversely affected the economic development of the country by diverting human labour and resources to the manufacture of destructive weapons.

(4) The cold war has given rise to permanent types of alliances which are concluded much in advance of war, NATO, SEATO, CENTO, and the Warsaw Pact were all forment in the wake of cold war. This aligments system covers most countries of the world. Thus cold war has led to alignment system even during the peace times and constant-efforts are made to strengthen them. However, in recent times there is a general tendency on the part of the newly independent states of Asia and Africa to avoid alignment with either of the two groups.

(5) The cold war and the consequent competition among Great Powers has resulted in more freedom of action for the small and middle powers. Each group tries to win them over. The influence which the Afro-Asian countries are able to exert in the U.N. is well known.

❒

9

End of Cold War

After having kept the world involved in the politics of confrontation and conflict 1945-90, with the exception of 1970-79, the Cold War got a final burial in late 1980s. After 1987, the U.S.A. and the U.S.S.R. got engaged in a maturer and continuous detente. Through it, the two were successful in harmonising their relations and in ushering into an era of peaceful co-existence and co-operation. Perestroika and Glasnost in the U.S.S.R. and their impact upon the countries of Eastern Europe produced big liberal changes in the political systems of Poland, Czechoslovakia, Hungary, Romania, Bulgaria, and East Germany. These changes brought these states very near to the Western European states. A new era of co-operation among European states had its emergence. West Germany and East Germany got united into Germany. Berlin Wall, the symbol and physical manifestation of Cold War in Europe got demolished. Superpower involvement in regional conflicts got reduced. The U.S.S.R. pulled out of Afghanistan. The U.S.A. became now more objective in approach towards Afghanistan. The U.S.S.R. began adopting a maturer policy towards socialist states. Several local wars came to an end. No nation tried to fish out of the troubled waters in Sri Lanka. Both the U.S.A. and the U.S.S.R. adopted a positive and maturer position over the Kashmir issue between India and Pakistan. The thinking in favour of Cold War, alliance politics, arms race, nuclear deterrence, balance of terror and aggressive power-politics got replaced by a commitment to detente, peace, security, development peaceful methods of conflict resolution, increased co-operation for protecting the environment, disarmament and arms control and the principles of the U.N. The Cold War-politics got replaced by relations in favour of peace, prosperity and development. Gorbachev

Phenomenon in international relations—Perestroika and Glasnost in international relations, played a key role in ending the era of Cold War.

Disintegration of the U.S.S.R. and the Final End of Cold War. The big change that came into the international system under the impact of the Socialist Revolutions, in Soviet Russia in 1917 again underwent a big change in the last months of 1991 when the Soviet Union got collapsed and disintegrated. The U.S.S.R. which continued to be a super-power during 1945-91failed to maintain itself as a single integrated state due to internal political and economic pressures. It failed to adapt itself with the changes that began coming under the concepts of Perestroika and Glasnost. After 1988 the Soviet Federation started developing cracks and the central leadership failed to control the situation. Initally the three Baltic States—Estonia, Latvia and Lithuania—secured their independence from the U.S.S.R. Later on other republics also, one after the other, started declaring, their independence. The central leadership became helpless. In August, 1991 there was an attempted coup in Moscow against Mikhail Gorbachev's leadership. This coup failed, but the U.S.S.R. also failed to preserve its identity as a single state. In November, 1991 all the republics declared their independence. Nine of them joined hands to form a Commonwealth of Independent State (CIS)—a loose. Organisation of sovereign republics of former U.S.S.R. Russia came to be recognised as the successor state of the U.S.S.R. Finally on 31st December, 1991, the U.S.S.R. faded into history. The collapse of the U.S.S.R. gave a final burial to the cold war. Russia being a weak economic power and begin a state faced with internal political turmoil was incapable of pursuing a Cold War or confrontationist policy *vis-a-vis* the U.S.A. and the West. Its dependence on the U.S.A. and other developed and rich countries of the West for securing foreign aid compelled a low-profile and pro-west orientation in world politics. Its decision to side with the U.S.A. and the West got reflected in several decisions of the U.N. Security Council regarding Angola Cambodia, Somalia, Israel, Palestine, Iraq, Bosnia Herzegovina, Libiya and on several other issues. The new detente of post-1987 years also influenced it to abandon the idea of Cold War. The help that the U.S.A. and other developed countries started giving it also encouraged Russia to keep the cold war buried alongwith the U.S.S.R. and the Berlin Wall.

Thus, the collapse of the U.S.S.R. completed the process of the end of Cold War in international relations.

The end of cold war in international relations stands reflected in the following features of the international relations of this last decade of the 20th century:

(1) A new faith in peace, peaceful co-existence and co-operation for development among the members of the international community.

(2) End of cold war mechanism like Warsaw Pact. NATO continues, but it has lost much of its relevance.

(3) Increased peace-keeping role of the United Nations.

(4) Increased ability of the U.N. Security Council to take timely and effective collective security decisions and actions.

(5) Increased global commitment for the preservation and protection of the human rights of all the people.

(6) Universal efforts towards the protection of environment.

(7) Universal acceptance of the principles of democracy, decentralisation, depolarisation, denuclearation and development.

(8) End of conflict in several parts of the world. Germany is now one Nation; the two Koreas are trying to be one; China and Taiwan have reached several agreements (April 1993); Cambodia is heading for peace; Afghanistan crisis is getting diluted; Arab-Israel talks are in progress; democratisations of politics and end of apartheid has been taking place in the South Africa; U.N. peace keeping operations are successfully taking place in several (13) parts of the world, fuller European integration is on the cards; several countries of the world are trying to force regional co-operation for development; peace is returning to Angola, Cyprus, Somalia, Ethopia and other trouble torn countries; and the world is

now gearing to enter the 21st century in an environment free from many tensions and strains.

(9) Good progress towards arms control and disarmament is reflected in INF, START-I, START-II and chemical weapon treaties.

All these features indicate the end of cold war in international relations. Now the world community is keen to direct its efforts towards the securing of an end of a neo-colonialism and under-development in the world. Cold War has ended yet complete peace, harmony, development and peaceful co-existance is yet to be secured in the years to come. This must be the international agenda for the 21st century, which is just a few years away.

PROCESS OF DECLINE THE COLD WAR

The International relations commencing from 1970 were marked by a detente between U.S.A. and U.S.S.R. Several important developments helped the process of decline of cold war and the emergence of detente. A conscious attempt was made by the two super powers to reduce areas of tension, of stem the further escalation of cold war and to attempt the development of friendly co-operation and collaboration in their bilateral relations. This development came to be popularly named as Detente. During the 1970s, on the one hand several key issues and problems of post-war international relations were peacefully resolved and on the other hand a approachment between the U.S.A. and China got under way. Unfortunately, however, these developments were accompanied by increased Sino-Soviet conflict and a mutual cold war.

The process of decline of cold war and the consequent emergence of detente in international relations can be reviewed through an account of the following helpful and positive developments between 1970-79.

(1) Moscow-Bonn Agreement 1970. On 12 August 1970, Moscow-Bonn agreement was signed by Kosygin and Willy Brandt whereby both sides accepted *status quo* in respect of Germany and concluded a mutual non-aggression, non-use of force agreement. This Agreement went a big way to reduce cold war tensions in

Germany and paved the way for a rapproachment between West Germany and East Germany.

(2) Berlin Agreement 1971. After the Moscow-Bonn Agreement, the West German Chancellor initiated measures for resolving the Berlin problem. After prolonged negotiations, on 3 September 1971, U.S.A., U.S.S.R., Britain and France signed a 4-powers agreement on Berlin. By this agreement it was decided to maintain the *status quo* but at the same time permit be people of W. Berlin to go to East Berlin and German Democratic Republic. This agreement led to a considerable reduction in tension over the Berlin issue.

(3) Korea-Agreement 1972. By an agreement of 4 July 1972, both North Korea and South Korea agreed to work for normalising their relations and desist from undertaking any such action as may lead to weakness of any one of them.This agreement was followed by another agreement in 1973 whereby both the countries agreed to promote mutual co-operation in various spheres of relations.

(4) East Germany-West Germany Agreement 1972. On 8 November 1972, an agreement was signed between East Germany (GDR) and West Germany (FRG), whereby both agreed to recognise each other and to work for the promotion of mutual co-operation in various spheres of their relations. Both affirmed a commitment to renounce the use of force for the settlement of German problem. This agreement virtually ended the old era of cold war in Germany. In the 28th session of U.N. General Assembly both the states, FRG and GDR participated as two sovereign states.

(5) Helsinki Conference (1973) and Helsinki Agreement 1975. The Helsinki Conference on European Security was held from 3 to 5 July 1973 and the European nations, both communist and non-communists expressed with one voice the need to increase their mutual contacts and co-operation in international relations. It was agreed that no nation should try to resort to force for securing the desired goals of national interest. On 1 August 1975, Heads of 35 states of Europe and America entered into the Helsinki Agreement, which laid down a code of conduct for orderly and peacctul conduct of their relations. 33 out of 34 European states (*i.e.*, the whole of Europe except Albania) alongwith the U.S.A. and Canada agreed to work for the promotion of mutual co-operation without any consideration for the communist or non-communist nature of the political systems of the states. Mutual respect for sovereignty, sovereign rights, territorial integrity of each state, non-use of force of threat or use of force, peaceful settlement of disputes, non-interference and non-interventions in the internal affairs of a state, promotion of co-operation and trust among the states of Europe etc., were the key principles which were to be followed by the signatory states. This agreement indeed had the potential to end the era of cold war in Europe. Both U.S.A. and U.S.S.R. formally affirmed their commitment to follow the Helsinki Agreement. After 1975, the Helsinki spirit of goodwill and co-operation became the basis for the development of peaceful and co-operative relations among the European states.

(6) End of War in Cambodia (Kampuchea) 1975. In April 1975, the end of war in Cambodia as a result of the victory of the Sihanouk forces ended the civil war in Cambodia (Kampuchea). It ended another centre of cold war in Indo-China.

(7) End of the Vietnam War 1975. On 30 April 1975, the war in Vietnam came to an end. It resulted into the unification of Vietnam. The end of war in Vietnam greatly helped the process of decline of cold war, as since mid-sixties Vietnam had been proving to be a major center of cold war in international relations.

(8) U.S.—China Rapproachment. The emergence of Sino-U.S. detente in 1971, further helped the international community to come out of the era of cold war. It paved the way for China's entry into the United Nations, and eliminated an anachronism in international relations of post-war period. However, the emergence of increased conflict between China and the U.S.S.R. considerably reduced the possible advantages that could have been secured as a result of Chinese rehabilitation in the international system.

(9) Third European Security Conference 1977. The third European security conference was held in June 1977 at Balgrade and an attempt was made to strengthen the Helsinki spirit.

(10) Camp David Accord Between Egypt and Israel 1979. The conclusion of Camp David Accord between Egypt and Israel, on 26 March 1979, was another significant development which took place as a result of the efforts made by the U.S. President, Mr. Carter. It was a sort of treaty between Egypt and Israel and was designed to reduce the conflict in the Middle East.

(11) American-Soviet Detente. A very welcome development of 1970-79 years was the emergence of a full detente between the two super powers. The mutual contacts between the leaders of the two countries in the post-1962 period helped the emergence of U.S.-U.S.S.R. detente (conscious attempts to lessen hostile relations and to worked for the promotion of collaboration and co-operations in mutual relations). In May 1972, the U.S. President Nixon visited the U.S.S.R. and signed two important agreements—The Treaty on the Limitation of Anti-Ballistic Missile Systems and the Interim Agreement on certain measures with respect to the Limitation of Strategic Offensive Arms (SALT-I). In June 1973, the Soviet Communist Party Chief, Brezhnev paid a return visit to Washington. During his visit four agreements were signed with a view to increase their mutual co-operation in spheres of research in agriculture, transportation and oceanography and expansion of cultural and scientific exchanges. Both Nixon and Brezhnev agreed to avoid nuclear war and to hold immediate and urgent consultations at any time whenever there appeared a risk of Nuclear war. Both the countries agreed to co-operate in the forth-coming Helsinki Conference.

In 1974, President Ford and Brezhnev met at Vladivostok and agreed on "the essentials of a new accord limiting strategic offensive weapons for, the next 10 years." They kept up their contacts and held bilateral talks at the time of 1975 Helsinki Conference. In 1975, the space-handshake between the U.S. and Soviet astronauts clearly reflected the progress made by detente between the two super powers. On 15 June 1979, the two countries concluded the SALT-II Agreement.

Thus, during 1971-79 period several bold and positive developments took place in the mutual relations on two super powers.

The development of friendly co-operation against cold war characterised their relations. Such a detente between the U.S. and the U.S.S.R. led to the decline of cold war in international relations. Unfortunately, however, detente could not continue for a long time and towards the end of 1979, the cold war reappeared on the international scene. The Soviet intervention in Afghanistan on 27 December, 1979 came as the first and big manifestation of the re-emergence of cold war. Since then the spirit of detente strated a decline and forces of cold war again began overshadowing the international relations of 1980s.

CIRCUMSTANCES TO END OF THE COLD WAR

Cold War, an era of neither peace nor war, which was a dominant feature of international relations in the post World War II period finally came to an end towards the close of 1980's and early 1990's. Earlier also in the 1970's the cold war somewhat cooled down and the two super powers agreed to work for lasting world peace and end of nuclear arms race. The two super powers concluded a number of agreements for cooperation in the field of research in agriculture, transportation and expansion of cultural and scientific exchanges between the two. The leaders of the two major countries time and again asserted that a lasting peace was a paramount goal of their policy and pledged to work. In fact the atmosphere of cold war was replaced by conditions of detente between the two super powers. This spirit of co-operation manifested itself in 1975 when the two participated in the joint Apollo-Soyuz space mission. However, during this period certain points of conflict continued to cause some sort of tension in their relations.

The cold war which had subsided during early 1970's was reactivated following Soviet intervention in Afghanistan in 1979. The Western powers were so bitter that they decided to boycott the Olympic Games held in Moscow in July 1980. In the subsequent years also the two super powers adopted critical attitude towards their opponents. This situation came to be described as 'Second Cold War'. This 'second cold war' differed from the earlier cold war in several respects. Firstly, unlike the earlier cold war, this war was mainly confined to the two super powers and the other satellite states were not involved in it. Secondly, in this cold war, the two super powers were involved in nuclear armament race and as such it war more threatening than the earlier cold war. Thirdly, the element of ideology, which was a dominant feature of the earlier cold war, was conspiciously absent in the new cold war.

Cooling of Second Cold War. After some time the leaders of two super powers realised that war must be avoided at all costs in view of the serious consequences of nuclear war. Therefore they persisted with efforts to reduce tension and come to some sort of understanding. They held a number of meetings where efforts were made to come to some sort of agreement on nuclear disarmament. However, these efforts proved fruitless. But one important thing which was noted in these parleys that the leaders realised the importance and desirability of regular and intensified dialogue. A serious bid in this regard was made at the Reykjavik meeting in October 1986 where effort was made to come to some sort of understanding on INF, strategic weapons, etc., but no success could be achieved because Soviet Union insisted on an over-all package, including an agreement on SDI.

In 1987 fresh talks were held at Geneva where proposals regarding elimination of INF missiles in Europe, and elimination of all ballastic missiles (land based or submarine based) within ten years were considered. This time also no agreement could be reached. A break-through in this regard was made towards the close of 1987 when at the Washington Summit the leaders of two countries reached an understanding on intermediate range of missiles. This was a clear indication that the two super powers were keen to eliminate nuclear weapons as far as possible. In the Moscow Summit of 1988 the two super powers exchanged documents on ratification of INF Treaty and pledged to strive for Treaty on Strategic Arms Reduction (START). A little later Soviet Union proceeded to announce unilateral reduction of Soviet troops and armaments in Europe and indicated intention to have closer relations with the western world. This attitude of Soviet Union indicated that by this time it had probably come to realise that preservation of any kind of closed societies was hardly possible because the world economy had become a single organism in which no state, whatever its social system or economic status, could develop outside it. This realisation on the part of Soviet Union greatly contributed to reduction of tension between two super powers and cooling of the second cold war.

A change in the attitude of the two super powers was clearly visible during the subsequent years. They showed greater spirit of accommodation on various international issues and tried to remove the existing irritants in their mutual relations. This was made possible due to several Summit meetings between the two super powers. It is true that all the Summit meetings did not produce the desired results, but it cannot be denied that they greatly contribute to the reduction of cold war. These summit meetings also paved way for greater economic and cultural cooperations between the two super powers. The leaders of two countries also showed greater understanding on various international issues which had strained their relations in the past. Thus they showed complete understanding on the questions of unification of Germany and the Gulf War. This clearly indicated that the second cold war was gradually coming to an end.

Several factors contributed to this change. In the first place, the two super powers realised that in view of their parity of nuclear weapons, none of the two powers could win the war. On the contrary nuclear war would cause irreparable loss to both. Secondly, they realised that the enormous amount being spent on the maintenance of military basis was greatly straining their economies and it would be desirable to curb this future expenditure. Thirdly, the leaders of two super powers realised that the proxy wars in which they were involved in the past *viz.* wars in Vietnam, Angola and Afghanistan, had proved futile and caused serious financial burdens on them. This had resulted in diversion of limited resources to these activities and hampered the progress of the people of their countries. Hence, they thought it desirable to avoid this useless expenditure.

Formal End of Cold War. Though the process of easing cold war had been going on for the past few years, it was only in mid 1990 that the cold war formally came to an end, at the London Summit of the NATO leaders. They asserted that the Atlanitc community must reach out to the nations of the East which were our adversaries in the Cold War and extend the hand of friendship. It asserted that nuclear arms should be used only as a last resort. The NATO leaders also decided to invite Soviet President Gorbachev to address special meeting of NATO at Brussels. The NATO leaders pledged to begin withdrawal of 1470 nuclear tipped artillery shells based mainly in West Germany, as soon as Soviet Union pulled out its troops from Central and Eastern Europe. Thus, at the London Summit of NATO leaders there was a clear change in the attitude of NATO from war-making to peace-searching.

The declaration of London was welcomed by Soviet Union which responded with equal warmth. Thus the second cold war formally came to end in 1990.

IMPACT OF INTERNATIONAL RELATIONS

The end of cold war was a turning point in the domain of international relations and is bound to exercise profound influence on the future course of international relations. Some of the important implications of this can be summarised as follows:

1. Firstly, it would put an end to all sorts of military alliances and hence forth there would be no justifications for the building up of stocks of various types of weapons. This implies that a new kind of world, free from military alliance, if likely to emerge in future.
2. Secondly, the enormous amounts which would be saved as a result of stoppage of arms race between the former adversities, would lead to enormous funds which could be used for the betterment of people all over the world.
3. Thirdly, the role of the non-aligned movement is also likely to undergo a change in the new context. As is well known, non-aligned movement made its appearance, chiefly to the existence of two rival power blocs. The disappearance of these blocs has, according to some scholars, rendered the non-aligned movement inoperative. However, this is not correct. The non-aligned nations can still play an important

role in protecting and promoting the interests of the underdeveloped countries of the world.

4. Fourthly, the end of cold war is likely to go a long way in promoting understanding among various waring groups in Vietnam, Cambodia, Korea etc and likely to promote greater co-operations among them.
5. Fifthly, the end of cold war is bound to exercise profound effect on Soviet policy towards third world countries. So far Soviet Union had projected as the big champion of the cause of third world countries at the various international forums. It also extended them every possible military and economic assistance to counter the growing influence of its adversaries. In the changed context this will no more be needed. Hence, Soviet assistance and support to the third world countries is bound to decline. Even the miserable condition of the Soviet economy is bound to influence the Soviet decision in the same direction.
6. Finally, cold war is bound to have deep impact on the foreign policies of countries like India and Pakistan. While India will have to look for closer relations with United States and other western powers (due to disintegration of Soviet Union), it is also bound to effect Pakistan's foreign policy. The United States and her allies are no more likely to go out of way to support Pakistan on various issues, which they did earlier because they found in Pakistan a convenient tool which could be used against Soviet Union. This in turn is likely to result in decling in the economic and military assistance to Pakistan from United States. Furthermore, it is bound to provide a new thrust to Indo-Pakistan relations. The two countries shall not be able to play Soviet Union and United States against each other to promote their national interests. Hence, they shall have to conduct their relations on the basis of relations of situation.

END OF THE SECOND COLD WAR AND ITS IMPACT

The End of the Second Cold War. After having kept the world involved in the politics of confrontation and conflict during

1945-90, with the exception of 1970-79, the cold war got a final burial in late 1980s. After 1987, the U.S.A. and the U.S.S.R. got engaged in a maturer and continuous detente. Through it the two were successful in harmonising their relations and ushering an era of peaceful co-existence and cooperation. Perestroika and Glasnost in the U.S.S.R. and their impact upon the countries of Eastern Europe produced big liberalising changes in the political systems of Poland, Czechoslovakia, Hungary, Romania, Bulgaria and East Germany. These changes brought these states very near to the Western European states. A new era of cooperation among European states had its emergence. West Germany and East Germany got united into Germany. Berlin Wall, the symbol and physical manifestation of cold war in Europe got demolished. Superpower involvement in regional conflicts got reduced. The U.S.S.R. pulled out of Afghanistan. The U.S.A.. became now more objective in its approach towards Afghanistan. The U.S.S.R. began adopting a maturer policy towards socialist states. Several local wars came to an end. No nation tired to fish out of the troubled waters in Sri Lanka. Both the U.S.A. and the U.S.S.R. adopted a positive and maturer position over the Kashmir issue between India and Pakistan. The thinking in favour of cold war, alliance politics, arms race, nuclear deterrence, balance of terror and aggressive power-politics, got replaced by a commitment to detente, peace, security, development, peaceful methods of conflict resolution increased Cooperation for protecting the environment, disarmament and arms control and the principles of the U.N.

Disintegration of the U.S.S.R. and the Final End of Cold War. The big change that came into the international system under the impact of the Socialist Revolution in Soviet Russia in 1917 again underwent a big change in the last months of 1991 when the Soviet Union got collapsed and disintegrated. The U.S.S.R. which continued to be a super power during 1945-91 failed to maintain itself as a single integrated state due to internal political and economic pressures. It failed to adapt itself with the changes that began coming under the concepts of Perestrokia and Glasnost. After 1988, the Soviet Federation started developing cracks and the central leadership failed to control the situation. Initially the three Baltic State—Estonia, Latvia and

Lithuania-secured their independences from the U.S.S.R. Later on other Republics also, alone the other, started declaring their independence. The central leadership became helpless. In August 1991, there was an attempted coup in Moscow against Mikhail Gorbachev's leadership. This coup failed, but the U.S.S.R. also failed to preserve its identity as a single state. In Novemeber, 1991, all the Republics declared their independences. Nine of them joined hands to form a Commonwealth of Independent State (CIS)—a loose organisation of sovereign Republics of the erstwhile U.S.S.R. Russia came to be recognised as the successor state of the U.S.S.R. Finally on 31st December, 1991, the U.S.S.R. faded into history. The collapse of the U.S.S.R. gave a final burial to the cold war. Russia being a weak economic power and being a state faced with internal political turmoil was incapable of pursuing a Cold War or confrontationist policy *vis-a-vis* the U.S.A. and the West. Its dependence on the U.S.A. and other developed and rich countries of the West for securing foreign aid compelled it to follow a low-profile and pro-West orientation in world politics. Its decision to side with the U.S.A. and the West got reflected in several decisions of the U.N. Security Council regarding Angola. Cambodia, Somalia, Israel, Palestine, Iraq, Bosnia, Herzegovina, Libiya and on several others. The new detente to post-1987 years also influenced it to abandon the idea of Cold War. The help that the U.S.A. and other developed countries started giving it also encourage Russia to keep the Cold War buried along with the U.S.S.R. and the the Berlin Wall.

Thus, the collapse of the U.S.S.R. completed the process of the end of Cold War in international relations.

Features of International Relations. The end of Cold War in international relations stands reflected in the following features of the international relations of this last decade of the 20th century:

1. A new faith in peace, peaceful co-existence and cooperation for development among the members of the international community.
2. End of Cold War mechanism like Warsaw Pact. NATO continues, but despite expansion it has lost much of its relevance.

3. Increased global commitment for the preservation and protection of the human rights of all the people.
4. Increased peace-keeping rolc of the United Nations.
5. Universal acceptance of the principles of democracy, decentralisation, depolarisation, denuclearisation and development.
6. Increased ability of the U.N. Security Council to take timely and effective collective security decisions and actions.
7. Universal efforts towards the protection of environment.
8. End of conflict in several parts of the world. Germany is now one nation; the two Koreas are trying to be one; China and Taiwan have reached several agreements (April 1993); Cambodia is heading for peace; Afghanistan crisis is getting diluted: Arab-Israel talks are in progress, democratisation of politics and end of apartheid have been taking place in South Africa; the U.N. peace keeping operations are successfully taking place in several (15) parts of the world, fuller European integration is on the cards; several countries of the world are trying to forge regional cooperation for development; peace is returning to Angola, Cyprus, Somalia.
9. Good progess towards arms control and disarmament is relfected in INF, START-I START-II. chemical weapons abolition treaty, indefinite extension of NPT and signing of CTBT. Many states like India, however, do not accept CTBT as a real step towards Arms Control because it ignores the core issue of nuclear disarmament.
10. Ethnic Civil War in Bosnia has come to an end and the Bosnian Muslims, Serbs and the peace-keepers were in a position to celebrate the new year day 1996 peacefully. The peace process continued to work slowly but steadily.
11. Angolan Peace Accord of November, 1994 gave further strength to the cause of world peace.
12. The world today has been witnessing a steady action towards more fruitful march for securing economic

development through regional economic co-operation and increased international economic diplomacy.

Impact. Globalisation, Sustainable development Democratisation, Protection of Environment and assuring the enjoyment of Human Rights and Freedom for all the inhabitants of our planetary mother Earth now stand accepted as universal objectives.

All these features indicate the end of Cold War and the emergence of the era of peaceful coexistence and co-operation among the people living in various parts of the world in international relations. Now the world community is keen to direct its efforts towards the securing of an bed of a neo-colonialism and under-development in the world. Cold War has ended but complete peace, harmony, development and peaceful co-existence is yet to be secured in the years to come. NPT has been extended indefinitely but a plan for global nuclear disarmament is yet to be formed and agreed upon. China continues to test its nuclear devices as Pakistan continues to keep up its nuclear plan. India has refused to sign the discriminatory NPT and CTBT and demands an agreement for Global Nuclear Disarmament. The logic "Do not develop nuclear weapons. Destroy the existing stockpile of nuclear weapons and enforce strict arms control measures," constitute a good package for peace. It is, however, yet to be accepted by all, particularly by the Nuclear Nations.

❐

10

Nuclear Weapons and Disarmament

Nuclear Weapons and War. The invention of nuclear weapons has heralded a new era in the field of ·international relations. These weapons have different quantitative and qualitative attributes than the conventional weapons on the nature of international system. This does not mean that the weapons preceding thermo-nuclear weapons have lost the validity to-day, they are still in vogue and are used to deal with limited provocations. But it should not obscure the fact that since a line of demarcation cannot be drawn between the conventional and nuclear weapons a state while using the conventional weapons to deal with limited provocations, may be compelled to use nuclear weapons under the stress of many factors. Hence, the use of conventional weapons may be valid to the non-nuclear powers only. The nuclear powers, in case of armed involvement cannot observe scrupulously the rules of the games—using of the conventional weapons. In the words of Morgenthau, "I think a revolution has occurred, perhaps the first true revolution in foreign policy since the beginning of history, through the introduction of nuclear weapons into the arsenal of warfare [In the Past] a statesman cold [and did] ask himself whether he could achieve what he sought for his nation by peaceful diplomatic means or whether he had to resort to war....the statesman in the prenuclear age was in the position of a gambler who is willing to risk a certain fraction of his material and human resources. If he wins, his risk is justified by victory; if he loses, he has not lost everything. His losses, in other words, are bearable. This national relationship between violence as a means of foreign policy and the ends of foreign policy has been destroyed by the possibility of all out nuclear war."

The thermo-nuclear weapons have tremendous destructive capacity. The atom bombs which were dropped on Hiroshima and Nagasaki at the close of Word War II are only a miniature of the bombs developed by the Soviet Union and the U.S.A. to-day. In 1961 the Soviet Union tested a bomb rated at 61 megatons (61,000,000 tons of T.N.T.). These super powers, have huge stock piles of these weapns. It is asserted that nuclear stock piles contains the equivalent to ten tons of T.N.T. for every human being on earth and they are continuing to grow. With the development of nuclear weapons, the thermo-nuclear powers evolved an accurate long range missile delivery system capable of destroying any given target at the fastest speed across the continent. Speed and accuracy of the I.C.B.Ms is so overwhelming that it has reduced the conventional warning systems to the vanishing point. Any crisis that confronts the nuclear powers in an armed struggle will leave no time to the statesmen to repent and retrace their steps.

LIMITED NUCLEAR WARS

Some scholars feel that only all out nuclear war is catastrophic to the humanity. If the nuclear weapons with prescribed and limited destructive power and used for limited political ends they can replace the conventional weapons and will leave sufficient scope for diplomacy to function. The limited nuclear war is best defence against massive land armies by permitting substitution of technology for manpower. There is no doubt that the limited nuclear war would provide credibility to land armies and would deter the limited aggression but there is very likelyhood that once the atomic barriers breached it would be impossible for the combatants to agree on new limits. Once the war breaks out the nations will use the weapons of 'overkill capacity' to impose an early victory or simply out of suspicion that the adversary may retaliate with all its might.

Nuclear Weapons as Deterrent. The importance of nuclear weapons lies in their deterrence. "Deterrence by which decision makers can prevent certain action by potential adversaries by threatening military retaliation can be considered as one aspect of intergroup influence." Deterrence, being a psychological phenomenon, presupposes certain conditions. It must be communicated in a convincing way to the potential adversary so that the decision makers do not brushoff the impending threat terming it as a hoax. Their knowledge about the weapons must not be based on guesswork.

Nuclear Weapons and Cold War. On 6th and 9th August 1945, the U.S.A. dropped two atom bombs on two Japanese cities to warn and deter the Soviet Union against its further advances in Europe and Far East than to compel Japan for early surrender. This incidence has been of serious magnitude and of far reaching consequences. It established that only the thermo-nuclear power can claim the world leadership and that no agreement can be valid unless the consent of the nuclear power is forthcoming. The regional arrangements in Europe, Latin America and Asia, in this era, clearly manifest the American influence and its big brotherly attitude in almost all world issue. Thus, the break through in thermo-nuclear technology provided the U.S.A. preponderance over all international political issues. The decision makers in Washington exploited this novel situation and implemented their policy of 'containment of communism'. The threat of retaliation in case of Communist uprising in any part of the world became more credible and the Soviet expansion was significantly checked. However, the U.S. monopoly was soon challenged and the Soviet Union established itself as a super power having equally destructive nuclear weapons in its arsenal. Under these circumstances, international politics became entirely different from the period of pre-nuclear age.

The ideological differences, the accusations and counter accusations of war time comradeship and the U.S.A.'s efforts to alienate the Soviet Union from the free world heralded an epoch of tension, mistrust and mutual hostility generally termed as 'Cold War'. In this era diplomacy and war, the traditional means of diplomacy relegated into background and propaganda and ideology became the popular methods to denigrate the rivals and woo the allies. The nuclear weapons, thus, are being used as a threat of massive retaliation and the statesman's foremost task has become to convey the convincing credibility of his nuclear threat to his opponent.

The impase evident with respect to the settlement of outstanding issues of 'Cold War' such as divided Germany is precisely due to the limits imposed by nuclear weapons on the statesmen. They remain reluctant and avoid the use of force in support of their diplomatic demands. The super powers, in such issues, endeavour to maintain *status quo* and allow the netural factors to operate. The active involvement of super powers in any of the issue creates a precarious situation as the super power can not dictate its terms to a population confident of rival super power's nuclear deterrence. And at home too, the public opinion quite fresh about the nightmares of the past war, does not support the decision makers. An effective pressure in the form of demands is brought on the political system to shun the misadventures. The Veitnam episode to the U.S.A. and the Afghanistan entanglement to the U.S.S.R. explain this contention.

Nuclear Weapons and Alliances. The third instrument of state craft whose efficiency is not questioned by some as a result of modern technology is the alliance. In pre-nuclear age, states threatened by a third state or group of states agreed to support one another in the event of war so that the *status quo* was maintained and the interests of the smaller states were not jeopardised. But in thermo-nuclear age; the support to a state threatened by a nuclear power may mean complete and irrevocable destruction. As a result of grave risk involved in coming to the aid of the threatened state the belief is generally expressed on peace through universal deterrence. The existing military alliances in different part of the world are vaxed with this phenomenon and have become inoperative to great extent. The development of long range ballistic missiles have created a crisis of confidence among the members of an alliance. Due to the speed and destructive power of these weapons the uniformed national policies and centralised and unified command and control become essential pre-requisites for the useful functioning of the alliances. This tells too much on the resources of the alliance partner and there is every likelihood that their political systems may not bear the pressure of these extra societal factors. The stress may ultimately force the alliance partner to abandon such pervasive institutions. The stress and strains in NATO are quite evident and partners like France, desirous to pursue their independent national policies have started expressing doubts about the efficacy of such alliances. Charles de Gaulle suggested the idea of an international deterrence as an alternative of military alliances as he felt that the structural changes if introduced to make the alliances effective they will certainly erode the basic assumptions underlying the state sovereignty.

The Nuclear Weapons and Balance of Power. The nuclear weapons have destroyed the traditional instruments which were basic to the operations of balance of power system. The seventeenth century intellectuals envisaged the concept of international system as a framework for analysis and diplomatic actions. They found that there was a tendency among the states to align and part whenever a potential rival emerged and threatened implicitly or explicitly their national interests. The fundamental purpose of the system was to ensure the survival of the system of which they were the part. In was the basic for rational calculation in the formulation of policy and a means for negotiation and settlement of disputes. It succeeded in its purpose of restraining the behaviour of the states and preserving the independence of the majority of the smaller states. But the invention of the nuclear weapons have made the system of balance of power obsolete. Balance of power, in classical age operated with a number of tools. Alliances, conquest, occupation and distribution and division of colonies were some of them. As has been already explained, the alliances now no longer are as effectively operative as they were in 19th century.

Nuclear Weapons and the Third World. The nuclear weapons have brought one more significant change in international politics. It is now no longer an exclusive domain of the European powers. The scene has shifted to Asia and Africa. The new nations with different social economic systems and with European interactions have transformed the nature of international politics. In the classical age the measuring rod for big power status was the over all development of a nation including the war machinery but now a nation posseing the nuclear weapons and sophisticated delivery system may be termed as big power irrespective of its economic development. This new demension has created an urge among nations to amass huge stockpiles of nuclear weapons even at the cost of basic industrial and agricultural development. Their yearning for the thermo-nuclear energy is so passionate that they become oblivious of super power's encroachments in their domestic policies. This development is a matter of grave concern as these states, lacking the political maturity and stable democratic institution may precipitate a crisis of catastrophic consequences. The checks imposed by the nuclear powers on the acquisition of nuclear technology and inadequate are ineffective. The mutual hostility and distrust of the states have encouraged the clandestine channels to operate for the smuggling of the instruments and technical know how. The number of nuclear powers is steadily increasing and threat of a thermo-nuclear conflict is becoming more real. The existence of a number of terrorist organisations, their fanatic mission and absence of strict security check on the nuclear technology and weapons are some of the development which hold the fate of humanity ransom.

Nuclear Weapons and the U.N.O. Some scholars feel that the U.N.O. can function as an institutional constraint on the use of nuclear weapons. This contention may be partly true but the U.N. structure is not adaptive to discharge the functions of a super sovereign state and naturally its decisions depend heavily on the whims of constituents. The U.N. has a significant role to play in the context of thermo-nuclear conflicts inspite of its inherent weaknesses. It has dealt successfully with some crises which otherwise would have engulfed the world in nuclear war. Where in the past an international organisation had no role to play in the event of big power involvements it is now developing into an institution of peace. Collective-security and disarmament are its ideals and the concern for human rights it shows through its different agencies have always universal implications.

Nuclear Weapons and the Disarmament. Nuclear weapons have initiated a mad race for armament. Billions and trillions of dollars are being spent on dangerous experiments at the cost of basic civic amenities to taxpayer. The story is more tragic in the third world. The majority of nations live below the line of poverty while their governments are ruthlessly engaged in stock piling the instruments of devastation. For example, during 1960's Jordan devoted over 21 per cent of its gross national product to military purposes Libya, Saudi Arabia and Laos devoted nearly 10 per cent of their G.N.P. to military spending. In order to put an end to the wanton arms race and to generate confidence among the smaller nations disarmament has become more than necessary. Attempts to control and abolish the use of force are as old as war itself. In the Hague conference of 1899, Washington conference of 1922 and Kellog Briand Pact of 1938 the use of force for promotion of national interests was condemned. A moratorium was imposed on the manufacture and use of certain category of weapons. Since World War II, inspite of considerable activity on questions of disarmament there have been no significant results. However, the nuclear powers have observed self imposed limits on the use of nuclear weapons. During the Korean crisis President Truman firmly rejected to use tactical nuclear weapons against the Communists and the Soviet leaders too stopped their personnel from disrupting the American supply lines to Japan to localise the crisis. The super powers have also taken certain other self imposed measures for arms control. They include *(i)* efforts to prevent the proliferation of nuclear weapons, *(ii)* moratovia on nuclear tests, and *(iii)* restraint in deployment of certain types of weapons. These are only the meagre results and disarmament still remains an idea to be discussed in international forums and lacks support of nations due to a number of causes.

The weapons are still most comprehensible instruments for threats. Whenever the states feel that some incompatible demands are being forced on them and there is no centralised agency to check the onslaughts of the strong adversaries they are left with only alternative for successful resistance through the threat to retaliate. In other words the arms are not only used for creating better bargaining positions but also for resisting a potential adversary and irrevocable damages. The decision makers generally do not have a fair idea about the military capabilities of adversaries and potential neighbours. They credulously succumb to the newspaper reports about the military might of the rivals and double up their efforts to stock pile arms. The ideological differences and the fear of being caught unawares in crisis situations have again send the whole edifice of disarmament in jeopardy. A further obstacle to arms conrol agreements is proliferation of nuclear weapons.

What has been the consequence of modern technology for international politics? One answer would appear to be that atomic weaponry and rockets have indeed had a significiant impact on the nature and instruments of statecraft. This aspect we have explained in preceding paragraphs. These changes are not fundamental and be giving changes on the other hand, the threat of thermo-nuclear weapons gives the nations, for the first time in history, a strong overriding common sense to avoid wars. We will explain this argument in the following paragraphs.

The atoms bombs and hydrogen bombs have revolutionised the international relationships. These thermo-nuclear weapons have been called the great equalizers. In the words of Sulzberger, "The day is bound to come when not only super powers and Great Powers but also smaller nations will have access to atomic weapons and will regard them as conventional. The international balance has already altered as weak countries with large deposits of fissionable material have assumed new importance. It will alter again when little lands possess arms capable of blowing up the world. For the atom bomb will then become, among nations, the equalizer that the six shooter was in the days of our own wild west," with the advent of atomic age has emerged that real equility of all states with the long established belief of sovereign equality of nations. Under these circumstances the dormant traditional state crafts like conventional wars, alliances, diplomacy, and pursuasion and rewards have revived. The decision makers know that the use of atomic weapons for defence purposes would leave nothing to defend and hence recourse to peaceful methods for the promotion of national interests should be emphasised.

Atomic fission and fusion generates incalculable mass of energy. This energy can be cultivated for destructive and constructive purposes. The scientific researches have shown that atomic engergy can used for peaceful purposes.

Atoms for Peace. On August 6 1995, a United Nations's sponsored International Conference on the Peaceful Uses of Atomic

Energy opened in Geneva. These were the exhilirating moments as the scientists from the 'Iron Curtain' countries also participated. For a decade, the purpose of scientific researches had been to develop dangerous weapons but at Geneva the scientists exchanged the views to explore the possibilities of using the atomic energy for human betterment. William L. Laurence wrote, "Nuclear energy offers the greatest promise in history to increase greatly the world's food supply, to prolcng life, to congues discase, and in general, to create a better life for the world's millions every where." The scientific researches have made it possible to generate electricity by atomic reactors. Man made radioactive elements open virtually limit less vistas as the most powerful agents for the treatment of disease, and a search light into the living labyrinth of many of natures most vital processes. The traditional sources of energy Petroleum and Coal are limited and their reserves will deplete with the present rate of consumption, atomic energy is the only hope to replace these sources in future.

ROLE OF NUCLEAR WEAPONS

Nuclear weapons were rightly described by Kore Jaspers as the "new facts of International life" which had produced a big chance in the international system of post-1945 period. These produced widespread, deep and big changes in the nature of power structure, war and even in the speculative thinking of man. In the words of Edmund Stillman and William Pfaff, "The atomic credibility is all pervasive. It affects strategic thinking, diplomacy, and even speculative thought on the future condition of mankind." Indeed the coming of nuclear weapons induced the philosophers to describe the age as the nuclear age in which man found himself on the one hand possessing adequate means for adequate development of the whole world and on the other hand, living with a serious threat of total destruction by a future nuclear war. In the nuclear age, balance of power in international relations got replaced by balance of terror. Preservation of international peace and security came to be the first priority but at the same time this came to be most problematic and precarious issue when nuclear powers came to develop the "Overall Capacity". Whereas the non-nuclear nations became virtually defenceless; statesmen of nuclear nations found it difficult to estimate their own capability to use power in international relations; and humankind found itself living in a MAD situation which till recently defied all attempts at disarmament and arms control. However, after INF Treaty, START-I, START-II, agreement regarding the ban on chemical weapons, the USA and Russian decisions to stop the production of mobile missiles have signalled the emergence of a process of controlling the MAD situation.

Analysing the impact of the nuclear weapons in international relations just after 10, years of American use of atom bombs on Hiroshima and Nagasaki, C.I. Sulzberger wrote: "Within one post-Hiroshima decade the entire world power relationship has altered. The failure to achieve satisfactory peace settlements with the major defeated nations, the growing split between the communist and non-communist worlds, the rise of sensitive new nations afflicted with bitter memories and unstable economies and government, the rise of the pressures of nationalism and of the resolution of rising expectations, and other developments created more than enough crucial issues and problems to test the capacities of statesmen and institutions. The advent of the nuclear age has made the era of transition infinitely more trying, for unprecedented power had emerged at a time of unprecedented political moral and spiritual crisit." Indeed the nuclear weapons materially affected the course of post-war international relations.

The impact of nuclear weapons on international relations can be analysed as under:

1. Impact on International Power Structure. The emergence of nuclear weapons had a big impact on the international power structure of the post-war years. Initially, the U.S. monopoly over the atomic weapons definitely made it the most powerful nation in the world. Later on, when the USSR was also successeful in breaking the atom and in securing nuclear weapons, it led to the emergence and strengthening of bipolarity in international relations. With the extension of the nuclear club, as a result of the entry of Britain, France and China, the bipolar power structure got transformed into a multipolar structure. Nuclear weapons acted as a determinant of the power status of the two rival actions in the era of Cold War. Later on, these played a role in the emergence of bi-multipolarism in international relations.

2. Defencelessness of the Non-Nuclear States. As against the overkill capacity of the nuclear powers, the non-nuclear powers came to live in a state of "defencelessness". The later found themselves quite helpless in securing their interests *vis-a-vis* the nuclear powers. They found it difficult to protect their people from the nuclear threat posed by the nuclear powers. They had no means to confront the threat of total destruction and nuclear blackmail that the nuclear nations posed or could, at any time, pose to their security an other interests Defencelessness of the non-nuclear nations and overkill capacity of the nuclear nations are the two important realities of contemporary international relations.

3. Change in the Concept of War. The emergence nuclear weapons changed the character of war from a simple war, which used to be fought at the frontiers, into a total war involving the while territory of the belligerents as a battle-field. It virtually eliminated the gap between military personnels and the civilians, or between the combatants and non-combatants. A modern war is bound to be a nuclear war and a nuclear war is destined to be a totally destructive war after which there will be no victor and no vanquished beacuse all would get destroyed and became one in the form of a uniform grave of humanity. The change in the concept of war from simple war to total war gave rise to a situation in which no state could hope to use the traditionally accepted laws of war as specified by International law. The whole concept of the Laws of war appeared to have become redundant in the era of total war. Moreover, the nuclear weapons, conpled with highly advanced computer technology have now made a modern war a machine war in which the role of soldiers appears to have become much less than what it was in the pre-nuclear age. The change in the concept of war from simple war to total war *i.e.*, a nuclear war has been a factor responsible for a decline in the role of nation state.

4. Cold War and Nuclear Weapons. During the era of cold war the nuclear factor acted as a determinant of US-USSR relations. It became a factor of conflict between these two countries. During the Second World War, the refusal of the USA to share the atomic secret with the Soviet Union made the latter immensely annoyed with the former. Later on, the Soviet decision to break US monopoly over the atomic secret became a factor in the cold war that emerged in international relations. The emergence of nuclear armament race between the two power blocs greatly intensified the cold war in 1950s and continued to be a major factor in the era of cold war (1945-50).

5. Overkill Capacity of the Nuclear Powers. While power Scarcity was the hall-mark of the era of classical international system, power-surplus came to be the distinguishing characteristic of the post-war international system. For the first time in the history of international relations, the nuclear nations came to acquire the overkill capacity, *i.e.*, the capacity to destroy the entire world several times. Each of the two super powers (1945-90) had a large amount of overkill capacity and this made each a super global actor capable of achieving its interests in world politics even in complete disregard to the opinion and wishes of other states. Both the super powers successfully used intervention as means of imposing their wishes on small nations.

6. Difficulty in the Exercise of Power. While on the one hand, the nuclear age has made available to the nuclear powers a power, surplus, on the other hand it has made it difficult for them to actually exercise power in international relations. The transformation of the conventional military power into nuclear military power has proved to be a source of limitation. After the first use of two atomic bombs in 1945, there has been no further use of nuclear weapons in actual practice. It has made it difficult for the policy makers to regard the use of nuclear weapons as a practical possibility. The strong public opinion both domestic and world, against nuclear weapons and the highly dangerous possibility of an escalation of a limited war into a full totally destructive nuclear war prevent them to regard the use of nuclear power a possibility in actual practice. USA failed to use nuclear weapons in Vietnam and had to withdraw from this area. Likewise despite being a super power with huge overkill capacity, the (erstwhile) USSR failed to achieve its desired objective a Afghanistan.

Indeed, the emergance of nuclear weapons has confused the statesmen. They have the means but they do not kown whether they can actually use them or not.

7. A New Basis of State Power. In the pre-nuclear age, geography, population, natural resources and industrial capacity constituted the major elements of the national power of a states. In the nuclear age, nuclear techonology, nuclear energy and nuclear weapons have come to be the most important factors of national power. Today, even a small state, by acquiring nuclear technology and weapons can become a formidable power in international relations. It can become over powerful and thereby pose a serious threat to its competitors or opponents. Pakistan is tyring to go nuclear with such an end in view.

8. Balance of Terror in International Relations. The development of highly destructive nuclear weapons and other weapons of mass destruction in the post-1945 era was responsible for creating a balance of terror of in international relations. The fear of total destruction including the destruction of the agg-essor state which may try to violate global peace, however indirectly helped mankind to avoid a new global war. The fear generated by the nuclear weapons resulted into a precarious balance of terror in international relations. Explaining the concept of balance of terror, A.F.K. Organski observed, "The balance of terror or mutual deterrence means simply a situation where two (or more) opposing nations are sufficiently frightened of one-another that neither is willing to risk any action that would provoke a military attand by the other." In the age of balance of terror, the nuclear nations fear each other so much that each of them has now become anxious to avoid war. The nuclear powers find themselves in a situation which has come to be popularly by characterised as MAD situation Mutually terror, necessitating mutual restraints in the exercise of power. This has foreed them to be moderate in power conflict. According to Abba Eban, "This complex net work of mutual restraints serves not only to moderate super power-conflict but also to preserve their own predominant position in the world system." Indirectly and in a negative way, the balance of terror, as created by nuclear weapons, has tended to support world peace. It has compelled the statesmen to aviod war and keep the crises limited. The balance of terror has, become responsible for giving rise to the possibility of accidental and machine failure wars. In the process, it has however become instrumental in preserving peace under a shadow of war-a peace characterised by strains, tensions, risks and possibility of an accidental all destructive nuclear war.

9. Nuclear Weapons have Strengthened Status Quo in International Relations. Nuclear weapons have made it difficult for a nation to upset the status quo by resorting to war or aggression. In the past, the revision of the borders of the states through the use of force was a common feature and was frequently used or settling the border dispute. In the nuclear age, the nations fear war and aggression as it can lead to a total war. During 1945-90 the two super powers always tried to maintain a particular *status quo*. Attempts to upset the *status quo* mere met with little or no success in the era of cold war and nuclear balance of terror.

10. Nuclear Weapons and Diplomacy. The difficulty in the use of nuclear weapons has tended to reduce the importance of threat of war in the exercise of diplomatic negotiations. Diplomacy often uses threat of use of force as a means securing the desired objectives of the foreign that it represents. However, the virtual unusable character of power backed by nuclear weapons has tended to reduce the credibility of a threat to use force as part of diplomatic exercise. Diplomacy now finds it difficult to use the threat of war (total war) as a means for securing its objectives.

11. As a Principle of International Relations Balance of Power has Suffered a Breakdown. The classical international system was characterised by balance of power. Several powerful European states maintained a certain balance in their power relations and whenever any nation tried to upset the balance by aggression or by accumulating a disproportionately large power for itself, the other nations or another nation took remedial measures, including the use of force or war, for reducing the power of such a state and for resorting the balance of power. Thuoughout 1815-914 period, balance of power acted as the arbiter of international relations. In the nuclear age, the emergence of nuclear powers with other states enjoying inferior power positions, it bacame very difficult, almost impossible for the balance of power to get operationalised in international relations. No preponderance of power could be created against the USA and other nuclear powers. Even a super power cannot create a balance of power against other through the use of force or war because such a step can lead to its own destruction.

12. A New Peace in International Relations. The existence of nuclear weapons in international relations undoubtedly gave a new meaning to the concept of peace. Previously, peace was regarded as a positive condition of mutual goodwill, friendship and co-operation. It used to be regarded as an ideal condition of mutual relationships free from fear, mistrust and tensions. As against this, peace in the nuclear age came to be "a peace in the shadow of terror." It came to be a negative peace –peace imposed by technology. It because peace in the form of a balance of terror. It came to be a peace of preparedness for a total war, a tense peace and a peace characterised by fear, inequalities, risks and distrust. Survival of the human civilisation formed the basic objective of contemporary era of peace. It has, as Prof. Harakabi specifies, three main features.

(1) It is rooted in mutual interests of nations which are governed by the desire for survival.

(2) It prevents war without resolving the conflicts and without eardicating the sources of conflicts and tensions; and

(3) It is place of mutual tolerance. It is not brethren dwelling in harmony but enemies living together despite their mutual distrust and for lack of an alternative".

13. Impact on Disarmament. The impact of nuclear weapons on the objective of disarmament and arms control has been paradoxical—both helpful and unhelpful at the same time. The emergence of a big arms race *i.e.*, race for nuclear and other weapons of mass destruction, has compelled the humankind to think and work more the favour of preserving international peace and security. It has given strength to the demand for disarmament and arms control as the possible means for securing this objective. It has compelled the states to work for securing disarmament and arms control. However, on the other hand, the emergence of these weapons and arms race has made the negotiations for disarmament and arms control highly complex, confusing and problematic. The issue of disarmament has come to be the problem of disarmament in international relations. The problem of fixing the ratio, the issue of fixing the standard for allocation of military strength to various nations and the issue of securing liquidation of huge stockpiles of nuclear weapons have together made disarmament and arms control a difficult exercise in actual practice. The problem of nuclear disarmament and arms control has come to be a pandora's box that continues to defy a solution. However, in recent years, after 1987 the dangerous potentiality of nuclear armament race has been realised by the nuclear power. The have been now keen to accept nuclear arms control measures. INF (1987) Start-I (1991), Start II (1993) and chemical weapons treaty 1993, all reflect the new consciousness in favour of arms control, arms reduction and arms limitation. France and China have now signed NPT

14. Impact on the Concept of Nation-State and National Sovereign. Finally, the nuclear age has produced a big change in the concepts of Nation state and State sovereignty in respect of the functions of a sovereign nation state. Traditionally, a state has been a sovereign institution responsible for the exercise of supreme power over all its people and places with a view to provide protection from internal anarchy or disorders and external aggression or war. Its justification as the custodian of supreme power stands based upon its ability to provide security to its citizens. In the nuclear age however, the nation state finds itself incapable of defending its people against a possible nuclear war. Many scholars, like Prof Herz., are of the opinion that, "The nuclear weapons together with other factors have made the nation state and its sovereignty obsolete and under the pressure of development it is destined to disappear from the world scene." While we do not subscribe to such an extreme view, we do admit that the nuclear age has defintely limited the ability of the state to act for the protection of the secuirty of its citizens.

NUCLEAR BAN TREATY

Non-proliferation Nuclear Treaty. This Treaty was signed at Moscow, the capital of Soviet Russia, on August 5, 1963 but it came into force on October 10, 1963. So far a hundred countries of the world have signed this treaty. The government of the United States of America, the United Kingdom of Great Britain and Northern Ireland, and the Union of Soviet Socialist Republics were "Original parties". They proclaimed as their principal aim the speediest possible achievement of an agreement on general and complete disarmament under strict international control in accordance with the objectives of the United Nations which would put an end to the armament race, eliminate the incentive to the production and testing of all kinds of weapons, including nuclear weapons.

Seeking to achieve the discontinuance of all test explosions of nuclear weapons for all time these nations determined to continue negotiations to this end:

1. Each of the Parties to this Treaty undertakes further more to refrain from causing, encouraging, or in any way participating in, the carrying out of any nuclear weapon test explosion, or any other nuclear explosion, anywhere which could take place in any of the environments described, or have the effect referred to, in paragraph of this article.
2. Each of the parties of this Treaty undertakes to prohibit, to prevent, and not to carry out any nuclear weapons test explosion, or any other unclear explosion, at any place under its jurisdiction or control.
   (a) In the atmosphere: beyond its limits, including outer space: or under water, including territorial waters or high seas; or
   (b) In any other environment if such explosion causes radioactive debris to be present outside the territorial limits of the state under whose jurisdiction or control such an explosion is conducted. It is understood in this connection that the provisions of this sub-paragraph

are without prejudice to the conclusion of a treaty resulting in the permanent banning of nuclear test explosions, including all such explosions underground, the conclusion of which, as the parties have stated in the Preamble to this Treaty, they seek to achive.

3. Any party may propose amendments to this Treaty. The text of any proposed amendment shall be submitted to the Depositary Governments which shall circulate it to all Parties to this Treaty. Therefore, if requested to do so by one-third or more of the Parties, the Depositary Governments shall convene a conference to which shall invite all the Parties, to consider such amendment.
4. Any amendment to this Treaty must be approved by a majority of the votes of all the Parties to this Treaty, including the votes of all of the Original Parties. The amendment shall enter into force for all Parties upon the deposit of instruments of ratification by a majority of all parties including the instruments of ratification of all of the Original parties.

MEMBERSHIP

1. This treaty shall be open to all states for signature.
2. This treaty shall be subject to ratification by signatory states. Instrument of ratification and instruments of accession shall be deposited with the Governments of the Original Parties—the United States of America, the United Kingdom of Great Britain and Northern Ireland, and the Union of Soviet socialist Republics—which are designated (as the Depositary Governments).
3. For states whose instruments of ratification or accession are deposited subsequent to the entry into force of this Treaty, it shall enter into force on the date of the deposit of their instruments of ratification of accession.
4. This treaty shall enter into force after its ratification by all the Original Parties and the deposit of their instruments of ratification.

5. The Depositary Governments shall promptly inform all signatory and acceding states of the date of each signature, the date of deposit of each instrument of ratification of accession to this Treaty, the date of its entry into force, and the date of any requests for conferences or other notices.
6. This treaty shall be registered by the Depositary Government pursuant to Article 102 of the Chapter of the United Nations.

Duration. This Treaty shall be of unlimited duration.

Each party shall in exercising its national sovereignty have the right to withdraw from the Treaty if it decides that extraordinary events, related to the subject matter of this Treaty, have jeopardized the supreme interests of its country. It shall give notice of such withdrawal to all other Parties to the Treaty three months in advance.

PEACEFUL USES

(i) All parties to the treaty; affirmed the principle that the benefits of peaceful applications of nuclear technology, including any technological by-products which may be derived by nuclear-weapon states from the development of nuclear explosive devices, should be available for peaceful purposes to all parties to the treaty, whether nuclear weapon or non-nuclear weapon states.

(ii) Convinced that in furtherance of this principle, all parties to this treaty are entitled to participate in the fullest possible exchange of scientific information to contribute alone or in co-operation with other states to the further development of the applications of atomic energy for peaceful purposes.

(iii) Declaring their intention that potential benefits from any peaceful applications of nuclear explosions should be available through appropriate international procedures to non-nuclear-weapons state party to this treaty on a non-discriminatory basis and that the charge to such parties for the explosive devices used should be as low as possible and exclude any charge for research and development.

(iv) Declaring their intention to achieve at the earliest possible date the cessation of the nuclear arms race, urging the co-operation of all states in the attainment of this objective.

(v) Desiring to further the easing of international tension and the strengthening of trust between states in order to facilitate the cessation of the manufacture of nuclear weapons the liquidation of all their existing stockpiles and the elimination from delivery pursuant to a treaty on general and complete disarmament under strict and effective international control.

Nothing in this treaty affects the right of any group of states to conclude regional treaties in order to assure the total absence of nuclear weapons in their respective territories.

All parties to the treaty have agreed as follows:

1. Each nuclear weapons state party to this treaty undertakes not to transfer to any recipient whatsoever nuclear weapons or other nuclear explosive devices or control over such weapons or explosive devices directly or indirectly; and not in any way to assist, encourage or induce any non-nuclear weapon state to manufacture or otherwise acquire nuclear weapons or other nuclear explosive devices or control over such weapons or explosive devices.
2. Each non-nuclear weapons state party to this treaty undertakes not to receive the transfer from any power whatsoever of nuclear weapons or other nuclear explosive devices or of control over such weapons explosive devices, directly; or indirectly, not manufacture or otherwise acquire nuclear weapons or other nuclear explosive devices; and not to seek or receive any assistance in the manufacture of nuclear weapons or other nuclear explosive devices.

INTERNATIONAL CONTROL

1. Nothing in this treaty shall be interpreted as affecting the in alienable right of all the parties to the treaty to develop research, production and use of nuclear energy for peaceful purposes without discrimination as well as the right of the parties to participate in the fullest possible exchange of information for, and to contribute alone

or in co-operation with other states to the further development of the application of nuclear energy for peaceful purposes.

2. (a) Any party to this treaty may propose amendment to this treaty. The text of any proposed amendment shall be submitted to the depository government which shall circulate it to all parties to the treaty. Thereupon, if requested to do so by one third or more of the parties to the treaty, the depository governments shall convene a conference, to which they shall invite all the parties to the treaty to consider such an amendment.

(b) Any amendment to this treaty must be approved by a majority of the votes of all the parties to the treaty, including the voters of all nuclear-weapons states, party to this treaty, and all other parties which on the debate the amendment is circulated, are members of the Board of Government of the International Atomic Energy Agency.

3. Five years after the entry into force of this treaty a conference of parties to the treaty shall be held in Geneva, Switzerland, in order to review the operation of this treaty with a view to assuring that the purposes and povisions of the treaty are being realized.

4. This treaty shall be open to all states for signature. Any state which does not sign the treaty before its entry into force in accordance with Paragraph C of this article may accede to it any time.

5. This treaty shall be subject to ratification by signatory states. Instruments of ratification and instruments of accession shall be deposited with the government of..., which are hereby designated the depositary governments.

6. This treaty shall enter into force after its ratification by all nuclear-weapon states signatory to this treaty, and ... other states signatory to this treaty, and the deposit of their instrument of ratification for the purpose of this treaty; a nuclear weapons state is one which has manufactured and exploded a nuclear weapon or other nuclear explosive device prior to January 1, 1967.

7. The states whose instruments of ratification of accession are deposited subsequent to the entry into force of this treaty, it shall

enter into force on the date of the deposit of their instruments of ratification of accession.

8. The depositary governments shall promptly inform all signatory and acceding states of the date of each signature, the date of deposit of each instrument of ratification or accession, the date of the entry into force of this treaty, and date of receipt of any request for convening a conference or other notices.

9. This treaty shall be registered by the depository governments pursuant to Article 102 of the Charter of the United Nations.

10. This treaty shall be of unlimited duration.

Each party shall, in exercising its national sovereignty, have the right to withdraw from the treaty if it decides that extra-ordinary, events related to the subject-matter of this treaty, have jeopardized the supreme interests of its country. It shall give notice of such withdrawal to all other parties to treaty and to United Nations Security Council three months in advance. Such notice shall include a statement of the extraordinary events it regards as having jeopardized its supreme interests.

11. This treaty, the English, Russian, French, Spanish and Chinese texts of which are equally authentic, shall be deposited in the archives of the depositary governments. Duly certified copies of this treaty shall be transmitted by the depositary governments to the governments of the signatory and acceding states.

THE PROSPECT OF NUCLEAR PROLIFERATION

The likelihood is that additional states will acquire nuclear, weapons writes Prof. Osgood, and the probable consequences of their doing so present problems of analysis far beyond technological prediction of strictly miliary considerations. Thus it is clear that the next political incentive or disincentives for a state to build nuclear weapons has been as important in determining the number of nuclear powers as the technological and economic capacity of states, since several nuclear states Canada, West Germany, Japan, Italy, India and Sweden-have at least as great a capability to acquire nuclear weapons as China.

In the next ten to fifteen years, says Prof. Osgood the spread of plutonium production for civilian energy will probable enable at least 2 dozen more states to build nuclear weapons with limited delivery capabilities if they should decide to make the effort, if all these states should rush into nuclear production as fast.

Instinctively, the United States and the Soviet Union oppose the spread of nuclear weapons, not only because they do not want competition, but also because they have become very sensitive to the dangers of nuclear and do not want the problem of keeping these dangers under control complicated by the addition of other fingers on nuclear triggers. When faced with specific nuclear candidates in specific political situations, however, their general opposition to additional nuclear force may be overruled by calculations of the relative advantages and disadvantages of discouraging nuclear acquisition, passively accepting it, or even assisting it.

Securing genuine guarantees to non-nuclear states through the United Nations would be of no use because the Security Council cannot be expected to apply conventional force against a major aggressor. Among the major international competitors there are no common interests, requiring the use of force that can be relied upon to take precedence over special national interests. Following the first Chinese atomic explosion, he announced in a national address on October 18, 1964, "The nations that do not seek national nuclear weapons, can be sure that if they our strong support against some threat of nuclear black-mail then they will have it".

NUCLEAR DETERRENCE

Balance of Terror and Nuclear Deterrence are almost interchangeable terms in the dictionary of International Politics. The coming of nuclear weapons had provided to be a blessing in disguise in so far as it has acted as a deterrent against use of force, aggression or war as means for securing the desired gaols of national interest. "That a resort to war or aggression can lead to a full scale totally destructive war" has acted as a deterrent in international relations. However, this has not checked the production of nuclear weapons and the nuclear nations particularly the U.S.A., have been going ahead with the production of more deadly weapons of mass distruction. The USA even after abandoning its Star War programme in March 1993, has been keeping intact its nuclear superiority in international relations. INF, Start-I Start-II have still left a big stockpile of nuclear weapons with the USA and Russia. Both have been keeping intact their single nuclear warhead missiles. Both have resurrected their right to transform the multi-war-head nuclear missiles systems into simple warhead missile systems. The nuclear and strategic arms race has given rise to a situation which involves a sort of terror. The over-kill capacities of the nuclear powers and their ability to destroy each other have forced them to maintain a balance in their power relations. This balance is different from the traditional balance of power. It is balance or terror in which they are not prepared to risk a war. As such Nuclear Deterrene and Balance of Terror are so intimately related concepts that both can be described without any reservation, as the two sides of same coin. Both can, be used interchangeable.

What is Balance of Terror? In the words of AKF Organski, "The balance of terror or mutual deterrence means simply where two (or more) opposing nations are sufficiently frieghtened of one another, that neither is willing to risk any action that would provoke a military attack by the other. Mutual deterrence is said to be caused by the fact that each side possesses nuclear weapons in sufficient quantity to implicit unacceptable damage upon the other even after having observed surprise attack. Therefore, no aggressor can hope to escape punishment. It is the fear of nuclear punishment that acts as a deterrence."

Explaining the concept of deterrence, Schleicher has observed, Arms are wanted to deter war and to wage war if the deterrent fails. Although the use of the term deterrence has been especially prominent in the nuclear age, the concept is an old one. In essence, it means that a state which could otherwise attack, is restrained from doing so because it believes that the gains would not be worth the cost.

The stress on deterrence has been the direct outgrowth of the potential destructiveness of modern armaments. It is popularly called nuclear or strategic deterrence and it is a condition in which a nation has the means to attack and destroy the opponent but in actual practice does not attempt such a move as it fears its own destruction in the process. Fear of destruction at the hands of the adversary acts as a deterrent. Such a situation in international relations of contemporary era has helped the prevention of breach of peace. However, in the process there has come to be developed a balance of terror in which peace is neither positive nor really productive of harmonious and co-operative relations among nations. It is a peace in the shadow of terror. It is a negative peace, peace imposed by technology and fear. It is the peace of preparedness for war, a hostile peace, a peace characterised by nerve straining armament race, a peace in the environment of terror, mass destruction, death and violence. The concept of balance of terror does not mean a total balance or even a balance of nuclear weapons. It means a balance of fear generated by the possession of nuclear and other weapons of mass destruction with some of the states. It involves two key concepts:

(a) ***Deterrence.*** When the abilities of two nations are roughly equal and each is equipped with the ability to present certain threat and actions from other with equivalent or greater threat, the situation can be described as a strategic balance or deterrence. It is the ability to deter aggression by matching the power of the opponents through the possession of matching weapons and armament systems. Deterrence, in order to be effective, covers both the "first-strike power" and the "Second-strike capacity", the latter is considered even more important than the first.

(b) ***Unacceptable Damage.*** The second key concept in balance of terror is the concept of unacceptable damage. It refers to casualities and physical destruction to an extent that a government will not willingly risk the suffering of such a damage.

In this era of Balance of Terror peace is preserved precariously through dependence upon nuclear weapons as a deterrent to war. This makes the present era an era of tension, strains and mistrust in which the survival of human civilisation has come to be highly problematic. The existence of weapons of total destruction and the over-kill capacities of the two super powers have forced the human kind to concentrate upon the need for survival over and above all other needs. It is basically an era of non-war and not really of peace, security and development.

BALANCE OF TERROR AND BALANCE OF POWER

For a clear understanding of the nature of the balance of terror that prevails in contemporary international relations, it is worthwhile to examine its similarities and dissimilarities with the traditional concept of balance of power. AFK Organski has pointed out the following similarities and dissimilarities between the two:

Similarities

1. Both the nations are always involved in seeking to maximise their power.
2. Both interpret peace in terms of a balance of power or terror which is reached through conscious attempts.
3. Both specify that the vital interests of nations are in danger when the balance is upset.
4. Both the theories involve the acceptance of such national policies which are in reality dangerous and risky. Both accept military power as a means for maintaining the balance.

Dissimilarities

1. Balance of power accepts resort to war as a means, balance of terror accepts only the threat of war or threat of nuclear weapons as a means for securing the balance.
2. Alliances are used as tools in balance of power. However, these do not effect the balance of terror because no alliance can create a preponderance of power against the super powers.
3. Balance of power accepts armament race as a natural phenomenon, balance of terror seeks to limit or maintain a particular low level in armament race.

Thus, both balance of power and balance of terror have several similarities as well as dissimilarities. In the post war-era of international relations balance of power became alomsot obsolete, and balance of terror began acting as a device of maintaining peace. But it had a doubtful validity both in the the sphere of maintenance of peace and the regulation of the behaviour of states. With fear as its main background factor, balance of terror failed to perform the function of peace-keeping. Fortunately now, the mankind has fully realised the dangers of balance of terror. The end of cold war, the death of Warsaw Pact, the demolition of Berlin wall, the unification of Germany, the disintegration of the USSR and the emergence of Russia as its successor state with a commitment to work for disarmament and arms control, the emergence of CIS, the improvement in US-Russian, US-China and Russia-China relations, the emergence of process of close economic co-operation between East and West, and the successful conclusion of several arms control measures particularly the INF Treaty, Start-I, Start-II and Chemical Weapons Treaty, have all combined to give rise to a positive qualitative change in contemporary international relations. Now peaceful co-existence, peaceful conflict-resolution and co-operation for development through democratisation, liberalisation, denuclearisation, demilitarisation and development are the popular lines upon which post-cold war relation are being sought to be developed. The Balance of Terror has suffered a decline. But for securing its final end all the nations would have to unite their energies and efforts They should not allow unipolarism to dominate the world.

All the nations now realise that nuclear disarmament and arms control can go a long way in help the process of ending the state of fear and distrust that come to develop in their relations. Nuclear weapons as deterrents have been doing more damage than help to the cause of healthy international relations. These have been keeping the world on the brink of a nuclear holocaust. The need to replace balance of terror among with a balance of confidence and goodwill and peaceful co-existence nations has now been fully realised. The need of the hour is to keep up and invigorate the process. Nuclear weapon-states should accept and follow nuclear disarmament and states which have potential to produce nuclear weapons should refrain from doing so. World public opinion now strongly demands and favours this view. Disarmament, especially nuclear disarmament and not the preservation of nuclear deterrents can be the only right step towards the creation of a world environment really conducive to peaceful co-existence in international relations. The new environment of this last decade of the 20th century gives rise to the hope that the concept of balance of terror would finally and fully get replaced by an environment of mutal goodwill and confidence.

DISARMAMENT AFTER SECOND WORLD WAR

The Terrible Situation After Second World War. The debacle of the Second World War and the heavy toll of life of men and their property shocked the mankind. The plight of mass destruction of humanity continued by it for 6 long years could find no parallel in the world history. It is even more terrible that the greed of power has so much stimulated the devilish tendency of some groups of men that they do not shirk from making war propaganda and are directing all of their energies and resources to the unceasing production of highly distructive weapons of war. It is unequivocally appalling that soon after the end of the Second World War, Soviet Russia, China and the Western powers started making preparations at an unusually greater speed. The world thus having been divided into militant Eastern and Western power blocs became subject to an incessant cold war. The Hundred Megaton Bombs already produced by them are more destructive than even the Atomic and Hydrogen bombs.

The modern scientists are now engaged in making experiments for the production of extremely dangerous gases, bacteriological weapons and radio-active rays etc., would take only a few minutes to turn the planet of earth into a heap of ashes.

The group of states formed before the advent of the Second World War in an atmosphere of distrust, suspicion, spite and rivalry have given place to such militant, avaricious and yielding power blocs as are subject to even more violent, repugnant and silently revengeful presisting hatred and jealousy Therefore it is evident that the growth of jealousy, hatred and vengeance between the states at the end of the

Second World War has made the problem of disarmament more complicated and inconsistent with the need of peace, security and order in the world.

The U.N.O. which was born out of the ashes of the League of Nations, can hardly remain untouched by the inborn recrudescence of the latter. It resumed the task of disarmament from the place where it had been abandoned by the League of Nations. The U.N. Charter has banned the armaments for the maintenance of peace and security in the world.

1. Atomic Energy Commission. The dropping of Atom bomb made the U.N. devote it first attention of this problem. Consequently, the General Assembly adopted a resolution by which provision was made for the establishment of a Commission on Atomic Energy. The Commission was expected to make fruitful suggestion for the control of atomic energy for peaceful purposes and effective safeguards by way of inspection to protect the violations and evasions on the part of the states. The Commission recommended in its report that an effective system of international control of atomic energy be established. Soviet Union, however pleaded for the outlawing of the production and use of atomic weapons. It wanted destruction of all strocks of atomic weapons within a period of three months. Therefore Russia rejected the idea of all controls.

On November 4, 1948, the General Assembly rejected the U.S.S.R. proposal regarding a draft convention on the prohibition of atomic weapons and establishment of effective international control over atomic energy. However, no progress could be made in the direction of disarmament because of the attitude of U.S.A. and U.S.S.R. Whereas U.S.A. was unwilling to give up the possession of bombs already in its custody and stops production of new one's without the guarantee of an international inspection. U.S.S.R. on the other hand opposed the plan of international inspection on the ground that it violated the sovereignty of the states. Therefore, the Atomic Energy Commission suspended its work for an indefinite period till the sponsoring powers were able to arrive at some agreement.

2. Commission for Conventional Armaments. The Commission was set up by the Security Council in February, 1947, in persuance of the General Assembly resolution of 14 December, 1946. The Commission which was expected to consider the principles governing the regulation and reduction of national armaments consisted of all the members of the Security Council. It was expected to submit its proposals to the Council within three months. It was also expected to suggest effective safeguards.

Soon differences cropped up between U.S.A. and U.S.S.R. and they submitted two different proposals. Therefore, the Commission decided to set up a Working Committee to formulate the principles which should serve as the basis for the establishment of a system for the regulation and reduction of armaments and armed forces. On 12 August, 1948, the Commission adopted a resolution which insisted that:

1. A system for the regulation of reduction of armaments should be set up. It suggested that states having substantial military sources must be included in the system.
2. The resolution specified that the conditions essential for the creation of such confidence and security would include establishment of an adequate system of agreements under Art. 43 of the Charter establishment of international control of atomic energy; and conclusion of peace settlement with Japan and Germany.
3. A system of regulation and reduction of armament. This implied that the armaments and armed forces should be reduced to the extent they were indispensable for the maintenance of international peace and security.
4. It emphasised the need of creating an atmosphere of international confidence and security because it was convinced that the measures for reduction and regulation of armaments could succeed only after necessary confidence had been created.
5. Effective enforcement action in case of violation.
6. Adequate safeguards most be provided.

The Soviet Union strongly opposed the resolution and insisted that atomic weapons should not be excluded from its purview. When the issue came up for discussion in the Assembly, the Soviet Union persisted with her stand. Soviet Union also proposed establishment of a body for the supervision of reduction of armaments and prohibition of atomic weapons. This proposal did not find favour with the Western powers. Ultimately, the Assembly adopted a resolution urging to Commission for Conventional Armaments to continue its work and to formulate proposale for the receipt, checking and publication by international organ of control all information (to be supplied by member states) with regard to their conventional armaments.

3. Disarmament Commission. The failure of the two Commissions convinced U.S.A. that fresh efforts were needed to solve the problem. Accordingly, in October, 1950 and again in November, 1951, President Truman of U.S.A. make a suggestion of the U.N. General Assembly to merge the work of the Atomic Energy Commission and the Conventional Armaments Commission. Consequently, on January 11, 1952, General Assembly asked for the merger of two commissions into a single Commission known as Disarmament Commission. The Commission consisted of 11 members of the Security Council as well as Canada. This Commission worked under the Security Council and laid before it a number of proposals like *(i)* inventory and verification *(ii)* calculation of limits and reductions for all armed forces and all armaments. *(iii)* determination of armaments programme through negotiations among states, *(iv)* agreement upon disarmament etc. The Commission also discussed various projects for armament limitations such as Nuclear weapons, conventional weapons budgetary expenditure for armament, inspections and controls etc.

4. Atoms for Peace (1953). In December, 1954, President Eisenhower of U.S.A. proposed 'Atoms for Peace Plan'. The Plan aimed at peaceful uses of atomic energy. It urged those powers which possessed atomic energy, to contribute the same of the Atomic Energy Commission under the U.N. The Commission was expected to use these materials for promoting the cause of international peace and security.

5. The Geneva Summit, 1955. In july, 1955 a Summit meeting of the leaders of U.S.A., U.S.S.R., United Kingdom and France was held at Geneva to hold discussion on various international problems. These leaders also discussed the problem of disarmament. One of thc most imortant proposal which was mooted out was the Open Skies plan of President Eisenhower. Under the plan U.S.A. and U.S.S.R. were expected to exchange military information which could be verified by mutual aerial reconnaissance. Russia did not approve of the plan and insisted on the acceptance of the Soviet poposals for the reduction of armaments. The main reasons advanced by Soviet Union for not accepting the plan was that the U.N. may not be able to carry out inspection of concealed nuclear weapons.

6. Anglo-French Plan 1954. In June 1954, France and United Kingdom submitted a fresh plan regarding disarmament before the General Assembly. Under this plan disarmament was to be effected through three phases. During the first phase the military expenditure and man power were to be frozen at specific levels and a control organ was to be established. During the second phase the control program was to became fully operative. During this phase expenditure on conventional weapons and maintenance of military was to be reduced by one half and further manufacture of nuclear weapons was to be prohibited.

7. Plan of 1957. In March, 1957, the U.S. representative informed the General Assembly about the willingness of his country to effect reduction in armaments subject to adequate inspection. He proposed a plan suggesting *(a)* checking of trend of larger stockpiles of nuclear weapons with a view to reduce nuclear threat; *(b)* provision against surprise attack; *(c)* enconomy in expenditure on armaments and utilisation of money for improving the standard of the people; *(d)* reduction of political tension among nations and settlement of important political issues; *(e)* research in outer space for scientific and peaceful purposes. The plan also proposed establishment of inspection posts at strategic points to keep a watch over disarmament. These supervision posts were to work under the direction of Security Council and hence subject to 'veto'.

8. Ten Nations Disarmament Conference. In 1960 a Ten Nations Disarmament Conference was held at Geneva. This conference was attended by five members of each bloc. The Western bloc was represented by U.S.A. U.K., Canada, France and Italy and the communist bloc (Soviet bloc) was represented by Soviet Union, Yogoslavia, Poland, Romania, Bulgaria. Both the groups made many proposals to ban the nuclear weapons, the destroy rockets and to reduce military man-power.

9. Nuclear Test Ban. Simultaneously efforts were made to secure an agreement regarding Nuclear Test Ban. A Conference was held at Geneva from October, 1958 to April 1961 in which U.S.S.R., U.S.A. and Great Britain participated. The Conference agreed that all tests in the earth's atmosphere, in outer space, in ocean and underground should be stopped. The treaty was to be enforced by a world-wide detective system operated by a single neutral administrator and an international staff. However, in April, 1961, Soviet Union demanded replacement of the single impartial administrator by a three member Commission (Troika) consisting of one member from the Western bloc, one from Soviet bloc and one from neutral nations.

10. Eighteen Nations Disarmament Conference. In 1962 another conference was held at Geneva which was attended by 17 national, prominent among them being U.S.A., U.K., was Canada, Italy, U.S.S.R. Romania, Bulgaria Poland, Czechoslovakia, Brazil, India, U.A.R., Sweden, Nigeria etc. It may be noted that although the Conference is known a Eighteen Nations Conference actually only seventeen nations participated in it (France boycotted it from the very beginning). At the Conference, United States proposed a cut of 30% in nuclear delivery vehicle and major conventional armaments in the first stage to be carried out in three years. A ban was to be imposed on the production of nuclear weapons. U.S.S.R. proposed general and complete disarmament with effective international control to be reached in four years in three stages beginning with the destruction of all means of delivery of nuclear weapons and the simultaneous elimination of all foreign bases.

11. Johnson's Seven Point Plan, 1966. This plan was suggested by Lyndon Johnson, President of U.S.A. and called for a treaty to halt the spread of nuclear weapons to non-nuclear countries, demanded international safeguards over peaceful nuclear activities, called for strengthening of international security organisation and establishment of a system of inspection. The plan also proposed freeze on 'offensive and defensive' strategic weapons and missiles designed to carry nuclear weapons. And in the last place its suggestion to the nations to limit competition among themselves for costly weapons often sought for reasons of illusory prestige.

12. Test Ban Treaty, 1963. In August, 1963 a Test Ban Treaty was signed between U.K., U.S.A. and U.S.S.R., which marked an important step forward in the direction of disarmament. The treaty prohibited all those nuclear tests which could be scientifically detected. The treaty was for an unlimited period and was open to all states for signatures. It•may be noted that the treaty prohibited ony those tests which could be scientifically detected. It established no control posts, no on-spot inspections and no international bodies. It did no reduce the nuclear stockpiles. France and China refused to sign the treaty and continued their nuclear tests. These two countries were willing to sign the Test Ban Treaty only if U.S.A. and U.S.S.R were willing to destroy their nuclear stokpiles.

13. Non-proliferation Treaty, 1968. In 1968 of a draft the Non-proliferation Treaty was prepared by the U.N. on the basis submitted by the 17-Nations Disarmament Committee. The draft represented the ideas and proposals which had emerged out of the negotiations of many states desiring to achieve an effective halt to further spread of nuclear weapons. The treaty imposed an obligation on the nuclear as well as non-nuclear states, to rule out any possibllity of further spread of nuclear weapons. This treaty was signed by large number of states and the hopes of the world were for the time being pinned on this treaty. However, the treaty suffered from a number of defects. It left the issue of control and inspection unsolved. Similarly, though the non-nuclear powers surrendered their right to develop their own nuclear deterrent, the nuclear protection assured to them could not be fully relied upon, as it as to be given on the basis of political considerations.

14. Strategic Arms Limitations Talks (SALT 1969). After a long Disarmament Conference at Geneva in 1969, U.S.A. and U.S.S.R. decided to meet at Helsinki to decide about the strategic arms limitations. These talks different from the former disarmament conference in as much as it involved only two super-powers, who aimed at maintaining the present state of nuclear stability. The talks were useful in the sense that they made an effort to restrain and stop the fierce competition between the two powers to put in more and more sophisticated weapons. The talks continued at Vienna.

In 1972, U.S.A. and Soviet Union concluded the Strategic Arms Limitation Treaty after prolonged negotiations lasting over four years. It is said that before the conclusion of this treaty the representatives of the two countries held as many as 127 plenary meetings. This Treaty made an effort to curb the race in nuclear arms between the two powers. In fact the treaty consisted of two separate agreements—Treaty on the Limitation of Anti-Ballistic Missile System and the Interim Agreement on Certain Measures with respect to the Limitation of the Strategic Offensive Arms. While the former was of an unlimited duration, the second treaty was concluded for a period of five years. It shall be desirable to know about the details of these two treaties.

The Anti-Ballistic Missle Systems Treaty permitted the two super powers to have only two sites for the ballistic missile defences—one for the protection of their national capital area and the other for the protection of the field of ICBMs. It also specified the details regarding the dimensions of the two ABM systems. While one of the system was not to have more than 100 ABM launchers and 100 ABM interceptor missiles, the national area complex was not to have more than six ABM radar complexes, each with a diameter not exceeding 3 kilometres. The two powers also agreed not to develop, test or deploy ABM systems or components which were sea-based, air-based, space-based or mobile land-based. The testing and development of automatic, semi-automatic or other similar systems for rapid re-loading of ABM launchers were also prohibited.

The Interim Agreement with regard to the limitation of Strategic Offensive Arms was a very complex one. It covered both land-based

ICBMs sub-marine launched ballistic missiles. The number of ICBMs for Soviet Union and America was fixed as 1618 and 1054 respectively *viz.*, as per their actual strength as on 1 July, 1972. This agreement allowed the two powers to undertake modernisation and replacement of Strategic Offensive Arms, but the numerical limits stipulated in the agreement were to be scrupulously adhered to.

Accord on Limitation of Nuclear Arms, 1973. In 1973 Soviet Union and U.S.A. concluded an agreement for checking armament. Under the agreement the two powers agreed to permanently limit nuclear weapons by the end of 1974. They also agreed on adequate verification measures. In fact this agreement made an effort to control nuclear fission as well research on fundamental properties of physical matter.

Pact of 1974. In Soviet Union concluded a pact with U.S.A. for ten years. Under this pact the two countries agreed to limit the offensive nuclear weapons and to stop all underground tests of more than 150 milo-tons. They agreed to permit the observers of each other to inspect the sites to ensure that two countries were faithfully complying with the terms of the agreement. However, subsequently, no agreement could be reached on this issue as the two sides failed to convince their military establishments of the benefits of exercising restraint.

Conference of Security and Co-operation in Europe. In August, 1975, U.K. U.S.A. and Soviet Union along with a large number of other European States concluded the Final Act at Helsinki with a view to strengthen world peace. Under this Act the signatory states agreed to refrain from threat or use of force against any state. They agreed to exchange observes to help promote contacts and mutual understanding. The signatory states also agreed to notify their major military movements with a view to build the confidence.

Convention on Prohibition of Military or other Hostile Uses of Environmental Modification Techniques. In May, 1977 a convention was signed at Geneva with a view to halt arms race and bring about complete disarmament under strict and effective international control. By December, 1977 over 44 states has signed this convention. Under this convention the signatory states realising that the use of environmental modification techniques for peaceful purposes could improve the international relations, agreed not to engage in military or other hostile use of environmental modification techniques having widespread and long lasting effects.

Salt-II (1979). In 1979 Soviet Union and United States signed the Salt-II treaty to limit the strategic offensive weapons. However, the American Senate refused to ratify the treaty and the treaty could not be enforced. The disturbed conditions created by Soviet intervention in Afghanistan gave a further set back to the provisions of the treaty. However, in actual practice United States continued to adhere to the terms of Salt-II till May, 1986 when President Reagan announced that United States was no bound to observe the terms of Salt-II.

Agreement on Moon and other Celestial Bodies. In 1979 an agreement was reached which prohibited any threat or use of force or any other hostile acts on the moon as well as use of moon and other celestial bodies for such purposes.

Measures by U.N. General Assembly. In 1981, U.N. General Assembly took initiative to check nuclear weapons, chemical weapons and to promote disarmament. It proposed as international convention on non-use of nuclear weapons and invited practical suggestions for prevention of nuclear war. It also called on states to refrain from action which could impede negotiations for prohibiting chemical weapons. It suggested that a world disarmament campaign should be launched to promote disarmament. However, these suggestions of the U.N. General Assembly did not meet with any success on account of mutual cold war and accusations of aggreesiveness.

Four Continents Peace Initiative. In May, 1984 six leaders from four continents—Africa, Asia, Europe and Latin America suggested a plan for prevention of nuclear catastrophe and called upon the five nuclear weapon powers to halt all testing, production and deployment of nuclear weapons and substantial reductions in nulcear forces.

Six Nations Summit (1985). A six nations summit, attended by Argentina, Greece, Sweden. Mexico. Tanzania and India, was held at New Delhi in January 1985, which appealed to the nuclear weapon powers to halt and reverse the nuclear arms race and also to halt testing of all kinds of nuclear weapons. It also emphasised the neeed of strengthening of UN system and diversion of expenditure from arms to development.

Geneva Talks 1985. In January, 1985 foreign minister of United States and Soviet Union held talks at Geneva but much progress could not be made since Soviet Union tried to link control of offensive missiles with the termination of Star Wars Programme by United States. However, United States refused to link the two. Despite these difference the two powers succeeded in breaking the ice and pledged to work for effective agreements aimed at preventing arms race in space and terminating it on earth.

Reykjvik Meeting (1986). This was another step in the direction of disarmament. In this meeting between President Reagan and Mikhail Gorbachev several bilateral matters realting to arms control and they reached an agreement on INF and Reduction in Strategic Offensive weapons. However, difference appeared between thee two over Strategic Defence Initiative Programme (SDI).

INF Treaty (1987). At the Washington summit held in December 1987, Reagan and Gorbachev signed Intermediate Range Nuclear Force (INF) Treaty. The treaty provided for the Climination of land-based missiles having a range of 500 kms to 5000 kms and the launchers on which these missiles were mounted, within three years. It also provided for the elimination of the short-range missiles within next 18 months. The two parties also undertook to inform each other of the type of missiles and the place where these were being destroyed.

Third Special Session of UN Assembly on Disarmament. The disarmament issue was also taken up at the Third Special Session of UN General Assembly on Disarmament held in June 1988. The session looked into the progress in the implementation of the decisions taken in the first two special UN session on disarmament held in 1978 and 1982. The session, however, could not achieve any positive results due to adamant attitude of United States on the question of shedding armaments and making commitments regarding nuclear weapons.

Strategic and Reduction Talks (1989). In June 1989 after a gap of seven months. US and Soveit Union held negotiations at Geneva on the reduction of long-range nuclear forces. However, in view of sharp differences between the two powers on various issues, no agreement on strategic arms reduction could be concluded.

US Announces Cut on Chemical Weapons. On 25 September 1989, President Bush proposed a treaty suggesting elimination of chemical weapons from the surface of earth within 10 year indicated readiness to destroy 98 per cent of its chemical stockpiles in 8 years provided Soviet Union agreed to do so. Soviet leadership also responded positive. This was a significant development.

Washington Summit (1990). At the Washington Summit meeting held in May-June 1990 between President Bush and President Gorbachev further progress was made in the direction of disarmament. They concluded agreements on neclear, chemical and conventional weapons. They also reached an agreement on the principles which were to govern the srategic Arms Reduction Treaty (Start) to be negotiated later. Further the two leaders reiterated their commitment to complete the negotiations on the conventional force reductions in Europe before the end of the year.

Treaty Between NATO and Warsaw Pact Countries. In November 1990, the heads of states and government of NATO and Warsaw Pact countries signed a treaty whereby they agreed to drastically reduce their conventional arsenals or the first time since World War II. According to the critics this treaty marked a formal end of cold war which had characterised relations among the states of this region.

Treaty on Cut in Conventional Arms. In September 1990, President Bush, President Gorbachev and leaders of other European countries signed a treaty which sought to cut conventional force in Europe. Under the treaty each alliance was allowed a maximum of 20,000 tanks, 30,000 armoured perosonnel carriers, 20,000 artillery pieces, 6800 aircraft and 2000 helicopters in four zones.

START (1991). In July 1991 President Bush and President Gorbachev signed the Strategic Arms Reduction Treaty (START), whereby they agreed to effect reduction to equal levels in defined strategic offensive arms over a period of seven years from the date the treaty came into force. The treaty provided for a complex verification procedure. The two powers also agreed to set up a joint commission on verification and inspection. The treaty was to be valid for 15 years, unless superseded earlier by a subsequent agreement. It can be extended by five years period at a time thereafter with the consent of both the parties.

Unilateral Disarmament by United States. In September, 1991, United States announced unilateral disarmament and declared its intention to take nuclear tactical weapon out of Europe to reduce the possibility of accidental war. President Bush also ordered removal of all nuclear weapons from surface ships and bomb carried on aircraft carriers. He urged the Soviet Union to match the nuclear arms cut. The proposal evoked favourable response from Gorbachev and he announced that Soviet Union would eliminate nuclear artillery and nuclear warheads from tactical rockets; remove nuclear weapons from ships and submarines and take other steps. He proposed that both the super powers should mutually develop an antimissile protection system.

U.N.'s Role as a Forum of Disarmament. The United Nations has played a three-fold role in the disarmament negotiation. In the first place, it has taken the initiative in starting negotiations and has been primarily responsible for keeping them going. Second, it has established procedures of consultation which the concerned States have been brought together to exchange and discuss porposals. Third, it has made disarmament the business of all states, enabling the smaller and less powerful states to become so well informed about the problem that it has been able to exert an increasing influence on the actual working of the negotiations.

PROBLEMS OF DISARMAMENT

The representatives of the Allied and Associated powers who met at Paris to conclude peace traties also examined the problem of disarmament. The statesmen felt that an abiding peace was possible only if general disarmament was introduced. Consequently, a serious beginning in the direction of disarmament was made by the Treaty of Versailles, when it disarmed the defeated powers of World War I. While disarming these powers it was made clear that these powers were disarmed not with a view to render it impossible for them to resume military aggression but "as the first step towards the general reduction and limitation of armaments which is one of the most fruitful preventives of war and which it will be one of the first duties of the League of Nations to promote."

Therefore, when the League of Nations was established in 1920, one of its first task was to secure an agreement on the general disarmament. The Covenant had made the job of the 'League easy by incorporating a provision by which "willingness to accept arms regulations" was made a condition of League membership [Art. 1 (2)].

The Covenant also provided that League of Nations "shall formulate plans for such reduction for the consideration and action of the several governments." The plans to be thus prepared by the League were to be subject to reconsideration and revision every ten years. For the discharge of this duty the League set up a Permanent Advisory Committee to formulate a programme for reduction of arms. But as the Committee was mainly composed of military representatives, it failed to make a beginning in the direction of disarmament.

1. Temporary Mixed Commission (1920-1924). In 1920 the Assembly of the League, considering that disarmament was not merely a technical problem, urged the Council to create a new Commission. In 1921 it created a Temporary Mixed Commission (TMC). This Commission was a larger body than the Permanent Advisory Committee. The majority of the members of the Commission were civilians. The Commission during its tenure made four important efforts for disarmament:

(i) Firstly, It made an effort to fix the land forces of the countries according to their national needs. This proposal was, however, rejected.

(ii) Secondly, it prepared the Draft Treaty of Mutual Assistance for international aid to victims of aggression. This treaty recommended arms reduction within two years and made an indirect effort to institute 'collective security' as a basis for the reduction of armaments.

(iii) Thirdly, it tried to extend the principles of the Washington Conference of 1922 to the non-signatory powers. This treaty made an effort to limit the naval armaments of the great naval powers of the world. This too failed.

(iv) Fourthly, the Commission produced the Geneva Protocol of 1924, which was an indirect approach to the problem of disarmament. This Protocol proposed to extend the area of compulsory arbitration and imposed sanctions against aggressor states. It thus created an atmosphere of security in which disarmament projects could be hopefully undertaken.

Thus the Commission failed to achieve any conspicuous success in the field of disarmament.

2. Preparatory Commission. The next important step taken by the League in the direction of Disarmament was the establishment of the Preparatory Commission for a Disarmament Conference in 1925. The Commission was entrusted with the responsibility of preparing a provisional draft treaty dealing with all the principal questions relating to disarmament.

3. Geneva Conference, 1932. For the consideration of the 'Draft Convention on Reduction and Limitation of Armaments' submitted by the Preparatory Commission for the Disarmament Conference, the League convened conference at Geneva in February,1932. Sixty-one states including five non-members of League participated in the Conference. After two years of deliberation, in spite of vast differences among certain members, the Conference reached general agreement regarding prohibition of certain weapons such as bombs dropped from aeroplanes or balloons, incendiary and bacteria weapons. chemicals etc.

In the meantime, the international situation took a turn which greatly jeopardised the efforts at disarmament. In 1931, Japan attacked Manchuria. The worldwide economic crisis in some countries added to the general feeling of insecurity. On December 18, 1933, Germany in a memorandum pointed out that while she was genuinely discharging the disarmament obligations embodied in the treaty of Versailles, the other heavily-armed states either had no intention of disarming or did not feel in a position to do so and that it these states did not undertake not to exceed the present level of their armaments, Germany would also not abide by her obligations. The emergence of Hitler and his determination to rid his country from the severity of the peace terms, made disarmament rather impossible. In October, 1933, Germany withdrew from the Disarmament Conference. With her withdrawal the great effort for international disarmament practically came to an end.

In May, 1934, the Disarmament Conference again assembled. This time a deadlock took place between Russia and France on one hand and England, Italy and U.S.A. on the other. While Russia and France put emphasis on security, England, Italy and U.S.A. attached more importance to disarmament. On June 11, 1934, the conference was adjourned sine die and never met again.

DISARMAMENT OUTSIDE THE LEAGUE

While the League was busy making efforts at disarmament some states were making efforts in this regard outside the League also. The chief efforts made in this regard were as follows:

1. Washington Conference, 1921-22. Of all the attempts at disarmament made outside the League, the Washington Conference in 1921-22 was the most important. After long deliberations a treaty was signed between Great Britain. U.S.A., France, Japan and Italy. This treaty is popularly known as the Five Power Treaty. By this treaty the naval strength of the signatory states was fixed at 25,000 for U.S.A. and Britain each; 31,500 for Japan and 175,000 each for France and Italy. No agreement could, however, be reached regarding Cruisers, Submarines destroyers and Aircraft.

2. London Naval Treaty, 1930. The differences between Britain and U.S.A. were resolved by the London Naval Treaty.

Though originally the conference was attended by the representatives of U.S.A., Japan, France, Italy and Britain, ultimately the treaty was signed only by U.S.A., Britain and Japan. France and Italy refused to sign it. The Treaty of London also could not achieve much in the matters of naval disarmament. The real purpose of the treaty was completely foiled when the three singatory states extorted the right to reservation for themselves.

3. Geneva Conference, 1927. As the Washington Conference failed to achieve much success, President Coolidge of U.S.A. convened a Second Naval Conference at Geneva in 1927. As France and Italy did not approve the idea of this Conference, it was attended by three powers (England, Japan and U.S.A.). Soon violent differences developed between U.S.A. and England over the issue of cruisers, and the Conference ended without accomplishing anything.

4. London Naval Conference, 1935-36. Another effort at limiting the naval armaments was made at the London Naval Conference of 1935-36. The Conference met at a time when international conditions were quite unfavourable. Japan had committed aggression against Manchuria, Germany had remilitarised Rhineland in violation of the Treaty of Versailles.

The treaty provided neither for reduction nor for quantitative limitation of naval armaments. No limitation remained on the number of the battleships, aircraft-carriers, cruises destroyers and marines which the signatories might build.

5. Anglo-German Naval Agreement, 1935. In June, 1935, Britain concluded an agreement with Germany by which she conceded a right to Germany to increase her battleships to 35 per cent of the British naval power and to build ships of various types. England concluded this treaty with Germany mainly to protect her interests against the possible German aggression.

During the subsequent years no important attempt at disarmament was made.

Thus by the beginning of 1937, as Schuman has put it, "All treaties imposing quantitative restrictions on the three Great Naval Powers were at end. Britain and Germany had agreed (June 18,

1935) that the German navy should be 35 per cent as large as the British. Anglo-Soviet negotiations for a naval pact came to nothing." U.S.A. proceeded to strengthen the fortifications of its basis in Western Pacific. England announced plans for construction of 2,38,000 tons of new battleships, U.S.A. and Japan followed suit. Germany armed herself for the day of glory and her neighbours armed desperately in self-defence.

CAUSES OF FAILURE

It may be observed that although efforts were made within and the outside League of Nations to effect disarmament, much progress could not be achieved. Some of the important factors which contributed to this failure were as follows:

1. Selfish Attitude of Powers. Almost all the states were interested in strengthening their position rather than in reducing the weapons. For example, France wanted that effective security arrangements must precede disarmament. She wanted a firm commitment from U.S.A. and Great Britain regarding the defence of European frontiers. Similarly, Japan wanted parity in naval armaments with other naval powers at the London Naval Conference and when her demand was not met, she withdrew from the Conference. Again, she resorted to armed attack of Manchuria in violation of her international obligations. Germany under Hitler, was also very keen to wipe out the humiliation piled on her by the Treaty of Versailles. To undo the harm done by the Versailles Treaty, she resorted armament at the earliest available opportunity. She pleaded for arms equality with other leading powers and when it was deined to her, she left the Disarmament Conference in 1933.

2. Differences Among Members of Disarmament Commission. Difference of opinion among the members of the Disarmament Commission on various issues also created complication. This difference particularly existed between England, France, U.S.A. and Germany. While France argued that it was dangerous for the people to lay down arms until the total police power of the world was sufficient to guarantee the safety of the individual countries. She pleaded 'demonstrate security and disarmament will follow'. Britain on the other hand took the stand that the presence of great armaments makes the nations feel insecure. By reducing the armaments their confidence will increase. This impasse was the chief cause of inaction and led to the failure of the Draft Treaty of Mutual Assistance and the Geneva Protocol. Similarly, differences existed between and attitude of Germany and france. While France insisted on 'superiority in armaments over Germany' on the ground of security, Germany demanded equality in respect of armaments demanded restoration to her original position.

3. Difficulty in Distinguishing Between Aggressive and Non-aggressive Weapons. Another obstacle in the way of disarmament was difficulty in arriving at an accepted distinction between aggressive (offensive) and defensive (non-aggressive) weapons. While England considered submarine as an aggressive arm, most of the other states considered it a defensive weapon, because it was the mainstay of the naval defence.

4. Failure of the League to Deal Effectively. The failure of the League to deal effectively with states like Japan, Italy, Germany etc., who resorted to arms in violation of their obligations under the Covenant of the League, proved another stumbling block in the way of achieving disarmament. This failure on the part of the League convinced other members that they could not put much reliance on the international body and they must raise their own forces to meet any unforeseen eventuality effectively.

5. Failure to Give Effect to Psychological Factors. Another cause for the failure of disarmament was that the statesmen focussed their attention solely on reduction of armaments and war equipments. They paid no attention to the economic, psychological and political conditions prevailing in various countries, on which the success of disarmament problem largely rested. The actual reduction of arms should have been preceded by psychological disarmament. In the presence of mental distrust and suspicion, fear and hatred everywhere, disarmament could not be possible.

The above discussion leads us to the conclusion that in spite of the best efforts of the League of Nations and some of the members outside the League, the problem of disarmament could not be solved.

FAILURE OF EFFORTS AT DISARMAMENT

The representatives of the Allied and Associated powers who met at Paris to conclude peace treaties also examined the problem of disarmament. The statesmen felt that an abiding peace was possible only if General disarmament was introduced. Consequently, a serious beginning in the direction of disarmament was made by the Treaty of Versailles, when it disarmed the defeated powers of World-War I While disarmed the defeated powers its was made clear that these powers were disarmed not with a view to render it impossible for them to resume military aggression but "as the first step towards the general reduction and limitation of armaments, which is one of the most fruitful preventives of war and which it will be one of the first duties of the League of Nations to promote." Article 8 of the Versailles Treaty pleaded for reduction of national armaments to the lowest point consistent with national safety and the enforcement by common action of international obligation.

Therefore, when the League of Nations was established in 1920 one of its first take was to secure an aggreement on the general disarmament. The Movemant had made the job of the League easy by incorporating a provision by which "willingness to accept arms regulations" was made a condition of League membership Art. 1 (2). Under the Covenant the members were also expected to "accept such obligations as many be prescribed by the League in regard to its military, naval and air forces and armaments."

The Covenant also provided that the League Council shall formulate plans for such reduction for the consideration and action of the several governments. The plans to be thus prepared by the Council were to be subject to reconsideration and revision every ten years. For the discharge of this duty the League Council set up a Permanent Advisory Committee to formulate a programme for reduction of arms. But as the Committee was mainly composed of military representatives, it failed to make beginning in the direction of disarmament.

Temporary Mixed Commission (1920-1924). In 1920 the Assembly of the League, considering that disarmament was not merely a technical problem, urged the Council to create a new

Commission. In 1921 the Council created a Temporary Mixed Commission (TMC) This Commission was larger body than the Permanent Advisory Committee. The majority of the members of this Committee. The majority of the members of this Commission were civilians. The Commission during its tenure made four important efforts for disarmament.

(1) First, it made an effort to fix the land forces of the countries according to their national need. This proposal was, however, rejected.

(2) Secondly, it tried to etxend the principles of the Washington Conference of 1922 to the non-signatory powers. This treaty made an effort to limit the naval armaments of the great naval powers of the world. This too failed.

(3) Thirdly, it prepared the Draft Treaty of Mutual Assistance for international aid to victims of aggression. This treaty recommended arms reduction within two years and made an indirect effort to institute 'collective security' as a basis for the reduction of armaments. This treaty was also rejected by certain Great Powers.

(4) Fourthly, the Commission produced the Geneva Protocol of 1924, which was an indirect approach to the problem of disarmament. This protocol proposed to extent the area of compulsory arbitration and imposed sanctions against aggressor states. It thus created an atmosphere of security in which disarmament projects could be hopefully undertaken. This too was rejected.

Thus the Commission failed to achieve any conspicious success in the field of disarmament.

Preparatory Commission. The next important step taken by the League in the direction of Disarmament was the establishment of the preparatory Commission for a Disarmament Conference in 1925. The Commission was entrust with responsibility of preparing a provisional draft treaty dealing with all the principal questions relating to disarmament. After a hard work of six years the Commission completed the draft treaty.

Geneva Conference—1932. For The considerations of the 'Draft Convention on Reduction and Limitation of Armaments' submitted by the Preparatory Commission for the Disarmament Conference, the League convened a conference at Geneva in February, 1932. Sixty-one states, including five non-members of League, participated in the Conference. After two years of deliberation, in spite of vast differences among certain members, the Conference reached general agreement regarding prohibition of certain weapons such as bombs dropped from aeroplanes or baloons, incendiary and bacterial weapons, chemical, etc. The other points of agreement included the necessity of arms limitation, international supervision of arms business and publicity of arms budget.

In the mean time the international situation took a turn which greatly jeopardised the efforts at disarmament. In 1931, Japan attacked Manchuria to the complete unconcern of the British and American governments. The world-wide economic crisis in some countries added to the general feeling of insecurity. On December 18,1933 Germany in a Memorandum pointed out that while she was genuinely discharging the disarmament obligations embodied in the Treaty of Versailles, the other heavily-armed States either had no intention of disarming or did not feel in a position to do so, and that if these states did not undertake not to exceed the present level of their armaments. Germany would also not abide by her obligations. The emergence of Hitler and his determination to rid his country from the severity of the peace terms, made disarmament rather impossible. In October 1933, Germany withdrew from the Disarmament Conference.

In May 1934 the Disarmament Conference again assembled. This time a deadlock took place between Russia and France on one hand and England. Italy and U.S.A. on the other.While Russia and France put emphasis on security, England, Italy and U.S.A. attached more importance to disarmament on June 11, 1934, the conference was adjourned sine die and never met again.

Thus all the attempts at resolving disarmament problem throgh the League utterly failed.

Disarmament Outside the League. While the League was busy making efforts at disarmament some states were making efforts in this regard outside the League also. The Chief efforts made in this regard were as follows:

Washington Conference 1921-22. Of all the attempts at disarmament made outside the League, the Washington Conference of 1921-22 was the most important. After long deliberations treaty was ultimately signed between Great Britain, U.S.A., France, Japan and Itally. This treaty is popularly known as the Five Power Treaty. By this treaty the naval strength of the signatory states was flexed at 5.25,000 for U.S.A., and Britain each, 31,500 for Japan and 175,000 for France and Italy. No Agreement could, however, be reached regarding Cruisers, Submarines, destroyers and Aircrafts. By another treaty between these five powers, the use of poisonous gas in warfare was outlawed and restrictions were imposed on the use of submarines. This treaty, however, remained unratified.

Though the Washington Conference failed to achieve much due to French opposition. Further no plan of naval disarmament alone could achieve success in the field of world disarmament without an overall plan of reducing the land air armaments.

Geneva Conference 1927. As the Washington Conference failed to achieve much success, President Coolidge of U.S.A. convened a Second Naval Conference in Geneva in 1927. As France and Italy did not approve the idea of this Conference, it was attended by three powers (England Japan and U.S.A.). Soon violent differences developed between U.S.A. and England over the issue of cruisers, and the Conference failed.

London Naval Treaty 1930. The differences between Britain and U.S.A. were resolved by this treaty. Though originally the conference was attended by the representative of U.S.A. Japan, France, Italy and Britain, ultimately the treaty was signed only by U.S.A., Britain, and Japan. France Italy refused to sign it. The Treaty of London also could not achieve in the matters of naval disarmament. The real purpose of the treaty was completely failed when the three signatory states extorted the right to reservation for themselves. The Conference also agreed that in case of any deterioration in situation any participant to this Conference would have the right to re-armament. In this clause lay the germs of the failure of this Conference.

London Navel Conference 1935-36. Another effor at limiting the naval armaments was made at the London Navel Conference of 1935-36. The Conference met at a time when international conditions were quite unfavourable. Japan had committed aggression upon Manchuria, Germany had remilitarised Rhineland in violation of the Treaty of Versailles. In view of the mounting tension in the sphere of international politics the Conference was bound to fail as it did.

The treaty provided neither for reduction nor for quantitative limitation of naval armaments. No limitation remained on the number of bettleships, aircraft-carriers, cruisers, destroyers and marines which the signatories might build. The signatories, however, agreed to exchange information regarding the future building programmes.

Anglo-German Naval Agreement 1935. In 1935 (June) Britain concluded an agreement with Germany by which she conceded a right to Germany to increase her battleships to 35 per cent of the British naval power and to build ships of various types. England concluded this treaty with Germany mainly to protect her interests against the possible German aggression.

During the subsequent years no important attempt at disarmament was made.

Thus by the beginning of 1937, as Schuman has put it "all treaties imposing quantitative restrictions on the three Great Naval Powers were at end. Britain and Germany had agreed (June 18, 1935) that the German navy should be 35 per cent as large as the British. Anglo-Soviet negotiations for a naval pact came to nothing". U.S.A. proceeded to strengthen the fortifications of its basis in Western Pacific. England announced plans for construction of 2,38,000 tons of new battleships. U.S.A. and Japan followed suit. Germany armed herself for the day of glory and her neighbours armed desperately in self-defence.

Causes for Failure. (1) It may be oberved that although efforts were made by the League of Nations as well as outside the League to effect disarmament much progress could not be achieved due to the attitude of different states. Almost all the states were interested in strengthening their position rather that in reducing the weapons. For example, France wanted that effective security arrangements must precede disarmament. She wanted a firm commitment from U.S.A. and Great Britain regarding the defence of European frontiers. Similarly, Japan wanted parity in naval armaments with other naval powers at the London Naval Conference and when her demand was not met, she withdrew from the Conference. Again, she resorted to armed attack of Manchuria in violation of her international obligations. Germany under Hitler, was also very keen to wipe out the humiliation piled on her by the Treaty of Versailes. To undo the harm done by the Versailles Treaty she resorted to armament at the earliest available opportunity. They pleaded for arms equality with other leading power and when it was denied to her, she left the Disarmament Conference in 1933. Likewise the Fascist regime of Italy and the Communist regime of U.S.S.R. were more interested in promoting their national interests and strengthening respective position in the world than reducing the tension through disarmament.

(2) The failure of the League to deal effectively with states like Japan, Italy, Germany, etc., who resorted to arms in violation of their obligations under the Covenant of the 'League' proved another stumbling block in the way of achieving disarmament. This failure on the part of the League convinced other members that they could not put much reliance on the international body and they must raise their own forces to meet any unforseen eventuality effectively.

This desire particularly became strong after Germany embarked on the path of re-armament.

(3) Difference of opinion among the members of the Disarmament Conference on various issues also created complications. This difference re-particularly existed between England, France, U.S.A. and Germany.While France argued that it was dangerous for the people to lay down arms until the total police power of the world was sufficient to guarante the safety of the individual countries. She pleaded 'demonstrate security and disarmament will follow'. Britain on the other hand took the stand that the presence of great armaments makes the nations feel insecure. By reducing the arrangements their confidence will increase. This impasse was the chief cause of

inaction and led to the failure of the Draft Treaty of Mutual Assistance and the Geneva Protocol. Similarly, differences existed between the attitude of Germany and France. While France insited on 'superiority in armaments over Germany' on the Gound of security, Germany demanded equality in respect of armaments and demanded restoration of her original position. These differences contributed greatly to the failure of efforts at disarmament.

(4) Another difficulty in the way of disarmament was the difficulty in arriving at an accepted distinction between aggressive (offensive) and defensive (non-agressive) weapons. While England considered submarine as an aggressive arm. Most of the other states considered it defensive weapon, because it was the mainstay of the naval defence.

(5) Another cause for the failure of disarmament was that the statesmen focussed their attention solely on the reduction of armaments and war equipments. They paid no attention the economic, psychological and political conditions prevailing in various countries on which the success of disarmament problem largely rested. The actual reduction of arms should have been preceded by psychological disarmament. In the presence of mutual distrust and suspicion, fear and hatred everywhere, no disarmament could be possible.

The above discussion leads us to the conclusion that in spite of the best efforts of the League of Nations and some of the members outside the League, the problem of disarmament could not be solved. The chief obstacle in achieving effective results was the sense of insecurity prevailing among different nations of the world.

❐

11

Non-Alignment and Economic Development

The term 'non-alignment' is usually used to describe the foreign policies of nations which have not allied themselves with either of the two blocs—Communist and Western—which appeared on the international arena after the Second World War. This policy was first adopted by countries like India, Burma, Ceylon and Indonesia and became so popular in the course of time that most of the Afro-Asian countries which gained independence of subsequent years also became adherents of this policy. It is noteworthy that most the countries who adopted non-alignment as their policy were economically and militarily so weak that it would have been in their national to join either of the two blocs and obtained necessary assistace in the solution of their problems. This would have undeniably led to curtailment of their freedom. But these states preferred to retain independence of action and decided to keep out of power blocs. The consideration of playing more active role in the shaping of their policies in the international sphere also prompted them to adopt this policy.

In may be noted that the term non-alignment is quite different from neutrality, which has a relavance only during times of war. A non-aligned country can take a clear stand on the various international issues. Jawaharlal Nehru, who was one of the chief architect of the policy of non-alignment said, "By aligning ourselves with one power you surrender your opinion, give up the policy you would normally pursue because samebody else wants you to pursue another poilcy. I do not think that it would be right policy for us to adopt. If we did align ourselves we would only fall between two stools. We will neither be following the policy based on our ideals inherited from our past or the one indicated by our present not will be able easily to adopt ourselves to the new policy consequent on such alignment." In simple words, the policy of non-alignment is based on the principle of detachment from military blocs and faith in the solution of the international disputes through mutual co-operation. On the other hand, the policy of neutrality has relevance only during the times of war. A country claiming to be neutral has no positive opinion on the issues which divide the two blocs. According to scholars, the policy of non-alignment like any other foreign policy tries to promote the national interest of the concerned country. But this does not in any way take away from the sinificance of this policy.

Causes for the Rise of Non-Alignment. The following factors have been responsible for the growth of non-alignment in the post-World War II period:

1. The emergence of a large number of independent countries in Asia and Africa and the prevalence of a strong feeling of nationalism in these countries was one of the major factors for the rise of non-alignment. These newly emerged states were keen to preserve their independence and looked with suspicion all acts which posed a threat to their independence. Further, they were keen to have freedom of action both with regard to domestic affaris and the international issues.
2. Secondly, the presence of a strong anti-colonial feeling also contributed to the rise of non-alignment. These countries still remembered how they were dragged into the Second World War by the imperialist power without consulting them. After the war, they were keen to avoid entangling themselves in the cold war. They feared that by alignment themselves with either of the two blocs they would run the risk of becoming their satellites and be subjected to 'neo-colonialism'. They fully realised that they were not strong enough to successfully resist the interference of the concerned power.
3. Thirdly, most of the newly emerged Asian and African countries were economically backward and wanted to

devote their full attention to the improvement of the lot of their citizens through quick industrialisation and larger production. They were convinced that this could be possible only if they kept off from the international entanglements and devoted undivided attention to their domestic problems. It has been contended by cretain scholars that the Asian and African countries by adopting policy of non-alignment were able to blackmail both the powers and accepted aid and gift from both. However, the non-aligned countries argue that they accepted the foreign aid without political strings. This point was best brought out by Pandit Jawaharlal Nehru when he said. "There have been times when one word from us would have brought us many of the good things of life. We preferred not to give that word—not a few individuals but millions in this country. If at any time help from abroad depends upon a variation, howsoever slight in our policy, we shall relinquish that help completely and prefer starvation and privation to taking such help; and, I think the world knows it well now." Similar sentiments were also expressed by leaders of ther non-aligned countries.

Rights and Obligations on Non-Alignment. Though the policy of non-alignment does not enjoy any legal basis and is mainly dependent on conventions, the adoption of this policy imposes certain rights and obligations on the countries adopting this policy. These obligations are as under:

First, the non-aligned countries are not expected to be indifferent on issues involving the major powers. On the other hand, they are expected to take a positive stand on such issues in accordance with their judgement. It is a matter of common knowledge that the non-aligned countries took a positive stand on issues like Korean War, dispute over Formosa, Vietnamese war etc. In this sense a non-aligned state differs from a neutral state which is expected to observe strict neutrality in disputes involving two powers. In other words, unlike neutrality, which comes into operation only during the times of war, the principle of non-alignment represents the attitudes of nations during peace times. However, when the war breaks out non-aligned states are expected to take a definite stand, because it is not possible to continue the policy of non-alignment.

Secondly, is the duty of non-aligned countries to be impartial on the international issues. Whatever stand they take on these issues should be justified on the basis of facts and reasoning.

Thirdly, the non-aligned countries must avoid conclusion of strategic agreements with other powers regarding the use of their territory. If a non-aligned country accords such a concession to one power, the doctrine of non-alignment automatically comes to an end. Similarly, the non-aligned countries are not expected to observe any discrimination in accepting financial and technical assistance from the powers. In other words if aid is offered by the two powers on identical terms, they must not accept it from one and decline the same from the other. However, if the terms are not identical they may accept the aid from the power which offers more favourable terms.

Fourthly, the non-aligned countries need not be free from ideology. They may favour a pariticular ideology and may even propagate it, to the detriment of the opposite ideology. This does not effect their non-aligned charter in any way.

It is thus evident that non-aligned countries have certain obligations, which are certainly more difficult than the obligations imposed on a neutral country. A neutral country stands outside the power blocs and the various powers do not make any effort to secure its support. On the other hand, the non-aligned state takes an active part in international affairs and the various powers try to win its support and sympathy.

NON-ALIGNMENT POLICY AND PRINCIPLES

The world was divided into two blocs after the Second World War. One bloc was headed by United States of America whereas the second bloc was led by the defunct Soviet Union. Serious cold war took place between these two blocs for various reasons. Most of the countries of Asia and Europe got entangled in this groupism and joined either of the two blocs. After Independence, Pt. Nehru, the architect of India's foreign policy adopted non-alignment as its base. He clearly pointed out that India, because of its manifold international problems couldn't afford to snap its relations with either of the two blocs rather it needed assistance from both the Blocs. A country with newly attained freedom couldn't interfere in international affairs. So the policy of non-alignment was highly useful for the interest of India. In the words of George Liska, "A posture more than a policy made significant by the unique configuration of the post Second World War Politics non-alignment provided India with influence even power to pursue its major national objective in the international arena."

As India was to play a dominant role as preserver of peace, she thought it desirable to keep away from both the Blocs. This point was made by Nehru as under: "If by any chance we align ourselves definitely with one power group we may perhaps from one point of view, do some good but I have not the shadow of a doubt that from a larger point of view, not only of India but of world-peace will do harm. Because then be lose that tremendous vantage ground that we have of using such influence as we possess and that influence is going to grow from year to year in the cause of world peace. I feel that India can play a big part, and may be an effective part, in helping in the avoidance of war.

India's foreign policy is based mainly on non-alignment. Following are the implications derived from the policy of non-alignment:

1. Firstly, India will remain independent by not joining any group. It won't join even an organisation formed by the different countries of the world. On 4th Sept., 1947 Pt. Nehru, in Constituent Assembly said, "We propose, as far as possible, to keep away from the power politics of groups aligned against one another, which have led in the past to two World Wars and which may again lead to disasters on an even vast scale."

2. The policy of non-alignment is an independent policy. A nation by adopting it can evade subordination of any group, and can easily form its opinion about any problem after its through analysis.
3. Non-alignment is a policy of peacefulness—In Congress convention, held at Jaipur in 1948, it was stated, "the permanent feature of India's foreign policy should be to have friendly and co-operative relations with all the nations so that it may remain aloof from those agreements which divide the world into two opposed Blocs and endanger world-peace."
4. Non-alignment doesn't mean neutrality in international affairs. Pt. Nehru made it clear that non-alignment doesn't stand for remaining neutral to international problems. In 1949, while addressing American Congress, Pt. Nehru said, "When the freedom would be threatened and justice would be in peril, when the security of a State would be jeopardized, we connot remain indifferent and we well not remain indifferent, our policy is not one of indifference. Our policy is that there should be active efforts for world-peace and it should be given a firm foundation."
5. India's policy of non-alignment is a positive one. India wants to abridge the gap between Eastern and Western ideology. According to Pt. Nehru, "India's policy of non-alignment doesn't mean to follow a middle path. It is a positive as well as creative policy which aims at achieving some objective and the elimination of hartred and enmity between other countries."

CAUSES OF ADOPTING POLICY OF NON-ALIGNMENT

India adopted the policy of non-alignment after serious consideration. The causes for its adoption were as follows:

1. Firstly, India after getting freedom from imperialistic exploitation faced the problem of economic reconstruction which could be accomplished in a peaceful atmosphere. So India preferred not to join any group to aviod tension.

2. Secondly, India adopted the policy of non-alignment as Indians were ambitious to enjoy freedom in every sphere. Freedom was an invaluable possession for them. To join any of the two blocs meant to lose this hard-won freedom. India was fully aware of its right to pariticipate in world politics but it had to forego it by joining the power Bloc. Once a member of Parliament proposed to give up the policy of non-alignment. In reply to it Pt. Nehru said that to join any power Bloc meant to accept other's point of view at the expence of individual views to win favour, with regard to a particular question. India couldn't tolerate this situation and so adopted the policy of non-alignment.
3. The policy of non-alignment was followed to elevate India's prestige. If India gives its decisions pertaining to international problems in a neutral way, both the power Blocs would respect its idelogy and the tension, at the international level will lessen.
4. India adopted the policy of non-alignment to seek succour from both the groups. India infact, enjoyed the privilege.
5. The policy of non-alignment is favoured on historical basis also. This history of India bears a testimony to the fact that it has always followed peaceful policies and never aspired for expansion. Thus the policy of non-alignment is a political expression of India's traditional philosophy and ideals. As Nehru said in Lok sabha on 9th December, 1958 that the policy of non-alignment is "inherent in the past thinking of India, inherent in the whole mental outlook of India, inherent in the conditioning of the Indian mind during our struggle for freedom and inherent in the circumstances of the case today."

ROLE OF INDIA IN N.A.M.

Non-alignment is the most important feature of India's foreign policy. No country has been so completely and universally identified with the concept of non-alignment as India has been ever since its independence. It was India who provided initial stability and direction to the non-aligned movement. The first Prime Minister of India Pandit Jawahar Lal Nehru played a very key role in the emergence and development of the concept of non-alignment. There are some persons who believe that it was Pt. Nehru who first suggested the phrase of non-alignment in his radio speech of Sept. 7, 1946. At Belgrade, where the first NAM summit meeting was held in 1961, Nehru sought to emphasize that the developing countries must be united into the NAM so that "Era of classical colonialism" remain dead and gone for ever. NAM is an aggregation of states from all continents of the world. NAM represents essentially the struggling million impoverished, illiterate, and afflicted with centuries of neglect and exploitation by colonial powers. So far ten summit meetings of the Non-aligned countries have been held and India has played crucial and significant role in keeping the NAM relevant to the need of the times. The main thurst of the NAM consists of opposition to colonialism and racialism, support for the national liberation movements, economic development of under developed countries, removal of global poverty, solution of third world debt problems, global peace, protection of the rights and sovereignty of the small countries etc. In all the non-aligned summits India always remained in the forefront to raise these issues. The 7th Non-aligned summit was held in New Delhi in 1983. For the next three years India was chosen Chairman of the non-aligned movement. There is no exaggeration in saying that without India NAM may not remain intact.

ECONOMIC IMPERIALISM

The leading states of the modern world have built their big economic empires. They have adopted the tendency since the end of the Second World War. The industrial states in their pursuit of economic progress and self-sufficiency have therefore tended to build their economic empires for the realisation of their industrial needs. A sharp competition for the exploitation of national resources to their utmost is witnessed between the states of the world. This competition has bound certain independent nations in the chains of economic dependence. These economic dependencies may be classified into three distinct categories as under:

(a) First category consists of those states which have been nominally declared free, yet they are still bound with their ruling states in respect of their social and economic affairs.

(b) The second category of the economic dependencies (for example Pakistan) is of those who have duly attained their political and economic independence from their ruling states, but now due to their attempt for economic progress, have passed into the influence of new, rich and powerful states.

(c) The third category of such dependent states is of certain politically awakened states who in their competition for the acquisition of more and more power have turned into economic dependencies of big and powerful states.

A great number of economic dependencies which come in the first category have no doubt been declared free by their respective ruling states. Yet they still act on their instance and direction. After attainment of their freedom they cannot afford to discontinue political and economic relations with their old ruling states. But as soon as they grow rich, they tend to disconnect their usual realtionship with their old ruling state. Not only that they are inclined towards becoming the satellite states of even more powerful and rich states of the world. For example, Indonesia on being declared free by the Dutch Government it accepted the supremacy of China. Now it has started showing signs of its acceptance of Dollar Diplomacy practised by the U.S.A. It has been accepting economic help from India also. Had India been economically self-sufficient state it would have been in a position to keep the neighbouring states under its economic influence.

In the same way most of the Central European states like Poland, Hungary, Bulgaria, Czechoslovakia and Romania have passed into the Soviet influence in order to safeguard their respective security and economic interests with the help of the Soviet Union. However, they have consequently come under Soviet influence. A number of Afro-Asian nations have been tending to conduct their economic and military affaris with the help of the United States. U.S.A. is the richest country of the world and it has turned to be the most powerful economic magnet in its relation to all other countries of the world. The capitalist power and the economic prosperity of U.S.A. has ever since been attracting various countries of the world, with the exclusion of certain strictly communist countries to come into its economic influence.

In most of the cases it has been seen that the states on becoming free, tend to disconnect their political relations with the ruling state and establish fresh political and economic relations with another powerful state. At the end of the Second World War, all those spheres of military of economic control, which had been evacuated by England, France or Holland were taken over by the U.S.A. Even the Japanese colonies were not spared of the U.S. influence. Middle Eastern states too which had earlier been politically influenced by England and France were in due course brought under the influence of U.S.A. Dollar diplomacy.

The Soviet Government has now started to follow the foot-prints of U.S.A. in most of the backward countries of the world so as to win them over to its side. The Soviet Union is trying to gain the favour of Afro-Asian nations against U.S.A. The active foreign policy of Communist China which has made South and South East Asia as its target. The policy of economic control over the South East Asian countries followed by China had led to the creation of serious animosities at the Northern and North Eastern borders of India in the name of Sino-Indian border dispute.

It is, however, to be borne in mind that most of the economic institutions of any country are generally controlled by its own nationals. They conduct agriculture, retail trade and industry and exploit the natural resources of their country while its major industries, exports and imports and industrial and agricultural outputs all are controlled by the foreign states. The foreigners exploit their mineral resources and control their trade centres and banks. Not only that they remain in charge of the chief managerial and technical posts in the industries.

The economic or political control by the radical countries over the developing regions of the world can easily be under-stood, but in case of the liberal and democratic nations this cannot be so easily perceived. Their control at even the border lines of such poor and weak countries cannot be easilly detected. Sometimes the self-sufficient and powerful states allow the foreign enterprises to invest their capital in their countries, but under those circumstances their economic self-sufficiency can in no way be stabilised.

Further, these nations have developed Multi-National Corporations *i.e.*, investors of different countries create a Joint Stock Company, float the concern and undertake enterprises in the developed as well as developing countries. The presence of Mulit-National Corporations in a developing country does not make it an economic dependence of one State. But this form is worst. Independent studies have oberved that the presence of Mulit-National Corporations always keep the political stability of the dependent nation in dock. People are the most sufferer of their exploitation and still they cannot launch a movement against them like the national liberation movements of the 1940's since the dominant economic power is invisible.

The Use of Force. The state government of any economic depencency is only outwardly a free and sovereign government. It is conducted by the powerful elements of the country, but in most cases it has been seen that the foreign nationals controlling the economic system of any country actually control nearly all departments of administration. This foreign control becomes much more distinct when most of the income of the national Government of any economic dependency is attained by it through those resources, which are controlled by foreign states on the basis of royalty. Such an instance may be found in Saudi Arabia. Sometimes, the foreign states endeavour to establish their indirect control upon the weak and semi-developed states. They win the favour of the national leaders of such a state by pleasing them with bribes. In some cases semi-social relations are established between the political leaders of two different states of whom one happens of be very rich and resourceful while the other is generally a poor and semi-developed state. Their mutual relations also affect the conduct of their governments in relations to one another. The managers and proprietors of the industries of weak and backward nations generally happen to be close friends of the foreign enterprisers.

The economic dependencies may not be directly governed by the foreign states. The foreign states, mostly Western States do not perfer to directly extend their holds upon the administrative machinery of any national state. Contrary to it, countries of Eastern bloc mostly endeavour to recklessly influence the national governments of a weak or a poor state, without any consideration of the world opinion. Once succeding in their selfish attempt of influencing the other weak countries, the states of the Eastern bloc do not leave any loophole for them to extirpate themselves from their impact. If any state of the Eastern bloc endeavours to affect some necessary amendments in its national policy, the remaining states of bloc with the Soviet Union at their leadership make an armed invasion against it.

The Policy of Western States in Relations to the other Weak, and Poor States, has been Found to be Mostly Liberal. They after investing their capital in the foreign states aim only at their economic gains. The foreigners trading with the so called economic dependencies do not take into consideration the weapons of foreign policies utilized by them, their contestations in the U.N. and their support or opposition to the other states. Even then the Western states actively influencing the administration of their economic dependencies always fear that they might not pass into the hands of Communist nations. The U.S.A. has attracted a good number of backward and poor states of the world to its own leadership on the basis of extending necessary economic, technical and armed help as a result of which the U.S. capitalism has been much successful in extending the sphere of its economic and military influence upon the weak and semi-developed states more then any other nation of the world.

The Benefits of Indirect Control. The indirect control upon the economically dominated state is of a great benefit to the dominating power. Most of the present economic dependencies had previously been politically dominated colonies of some or the other powerful state. The Imperial Power cared most to safeguard their colonial assets and their political and economic control over them. Therefore, the subject people were brutally treated since imperialism did not understand the language of equality. But in indirect form the economic domination compels the foreign capitalists not to untowardly suppress the popular will in exploiting the national resources of a weak and undeveloped country. The foreign capitalists therefore carefully manage to keep satisfied the labour class of their economically exploited state. The foreign powers keeping into consideration the safeguard of their own interest generally abstain from doing any harm to the national interests of their economic dependencies. Thus the nationals of the economic dependency cannot be in a position to spread hatred and jealousy against its controlling foreign power.

The foreign Government is generally not held responsible for the actions of its citizens carrying on their economic enterprises on the soil of their economic dependency. Truly enough the foreign elements present unlawful gratifications to the national state authorities of the economic dependency, evoke terror there and indulge in many sorts of untoward action but the control of the poor state by their mother state being of indirect nature they cannot be legally held responsible by their own Government.

Disadvantages of Indirect Control. (1) In the absence of direct control on the economic dependency the foreign Government is not able to easily satisfy its will on an alien soil. Although dominated by the foriegn state in many respects the national Government of an economic dependency can very easily execute its will against the foreign interest of its superior power, without being effectively checked by the concerning foreign state Government. At the time of general elections in any economically dominated weak state the foreign Government can secretly side with the anit-national elements through the medium of its own countrymen who have settled in the said economic dependency. The foreign state cannot openly carry on any propaganda in its own favour or in the favour of its supported candidate at such occassions in the economic dependencies for the national government can under such circumstances instigate the countrymen to rise in severe revolt against those foreign elements and thus it can very well harm the foreign interests in its country, where upon no armed action can be taken against it by the said foreign power.

(2) The states of America and Europe are guided by a singular feeling of superiority against the people of their economic dependencies and this creates a strong tension between the two states. These imperialist feelings are found in the European attitude since long. The Europeans do not even bear to see the spread of any civilization other than that of their own. The European industrialists and traders when they see that in spite of their investment of large capitals on the industries functioning in their economic dependencies and satellite states the labourers do not work satisfactorily and do not care for their implied interests, they become all the more aggrieved and try to exploit their labourers and other national resources in the most obdurate and appropriate manner.

Partnership of the Foreign States in the Exploitation and Economic Profits. The relations of a foreign state with its economic dependency can rarely be strained due to its indirect control over it while the Imperialist State is very liable to provoke the discontent and hatred of the people of their politically dominated colonies. The foreign control upon the economic dependencies is generally very little and therefore the foreign state is not so much defamed as happens in case of any Imperial power. The European states do not make use of barbarous methods in exploiting the resources of their economic dependencies in spite of their feelings of supremacy the foreign power can less exploit the resources of the foreign dependence than they can do to those of their politically dominated colonies. The people of economic dependencies gain sufficiently by the national interests of their superior state for example the royalties, rents, taxes, profits and wages earned by a foreign state in her satellite States and economic dependencies fetch a considerable money income to them. The economic profit cannot be availed of by the political colonies of any Imperial states. It is also true that only the higher classes of the economic dependencies gain by that economic system controlled by the foreign state while the standard of living of the ordinary people is not raised by such economic systems.

Political colonialism and the new economic colonialism are not inconsistent in their effect. The states having political colonies can maintain also their economic dependencies. But the democratic minded people of U.S.A. are a great opponent of the political colonialism while they support the maintenance of economic dependencies. Even then there are political colonies and economic dependencies under the U.S. control. The people of U.S.A. had been engaged in their economic reconstruction and progress of their industries at the time when the European states were busy with their effective efforts of increasing their colonial assets. The U.S. Government felt an acute need of contracting with the foreign markets entered into the theatre of world affaris when the old Imperialist powers had become tried of and fed up with their colonial pursuits. England and France, the two top ranking Imperil powers, had been dominating the world till First World War. Their power was broken by war. They could no more remain in a position of maintaining large armies and controlled their overseas colonies. Henceforth U.S.A. started championing the cause of their political freedom on the basis of self-determination. This mobilised the world opinion in favour of U.S.A. and various nations began to internationally respect the U.S.A. as their saviour.

The U.S.S.R. is far behind U.S.A. in her economic resources. As a result the economic dependencies of U.S.A. are ever increasing, as compared to the dependencies of U.S.S.R. On of the causes of the supreme power of U.S.A. in the sphere of world affairs is its economic self-sufficiency and the fruitful consequences of its dollar diplomacy.

FOREIGN AID

Role of Foreign Aid. Foreign aid implies the economic, material goods, technical assistance that a donor nation, usually a developed nation gives to the poor, backward and needy nations—the recipients. In the words of Morgenthau. "Foreign aid implies the transfer of money, goods and services from one nation (donor) to another (recipient). It is a system of economic assistance to the poor and lowly developed nations by the rich and developed nations." Even developing countries like India have to give some economic and technical aid to such small countries as are less developed than India. In fact, foreign aid has come to be an important instrument of national policy in the contemporary era of international politics. Since 1945, it has been used as a means for protecting the goals of national interest. It was a major instrument of cold war policies and was used by both the USA and the erstwhile USSR for maintaining and increasing their spheres of influence. It was regarded as a valuable method of keeping the allies, winning new friends and pursuing effectively the goals of national interest. Even after the end of cold war the role of foreign aid as an instrument of foreign policy has not only been sustained but also increased.

A. **Traditional Use of Foreign Aid.** As as instrument of national policy, foreign aid is not a new instrument. It has been used by the states for centuries. However, in the past it was used by states for humanitarian purposes and involved the giving of material and economic assistance to such friendly states as suffered natural calamities like earthquakes, famines, outbreak of epidemics etc. At times, it was also used as means for securing immediate political advantage in a given situation. In the eighteenth century, it was used as the means for offer in bribes and pensions to such foreign ministers and diplomats who performed certain valuable services to the donor nation. In the 18th and 19th centuries: Britain used foreign aid as a means to raise her armies and for securing material supplies from her colonies and dependencies.

B. **The Contemporary Use of Foreign Aid.** In the post-war years, foreign aid came to be used as an instrument of national policies of the rich and powerful nations, paritcularly of the two super powers—the USA and the USSR. They used it as a means to win friends, and for expanding their spheres of influence. Initially, they concentrated upon Europe, but later on, after the emergence of new sovereign state in Asia and Africa—the states which were really poor and backward and needed economic assistance for their stability and development encouraged them to use foreign aid as a means for securing the support, co-operation and alliance of these new states. Since1950's foreign aid has come to be a regular economic instrument of national policy. It has come to be an important factor of foreign policy of every state. A rich and powerful states uses it as an instrument for keeping and increasing its influence over the other states, and a poor and backward state formulates its foreign policy with an eye on the need and possibility of foreign aid. The changed international system of the post-cold war and the post-USSR years has witnessed an increasing use of foreign aid as an instrument of foreign policies of the USA and other western powers. Russia and the Eastern European (formerly socialist) states today find themselves dependent upon foreign aid from the USA and other countries like, Japan, Germany, France, Britain and Italy. The G-7, in April 1993, promised a foreign aid of 43 billion dollars to Russia. It was designed to keep up the democratic and liberalisation process that had started taking shape since 1985. The role of foreign aid has registered a big increase in recent times. Foreign aid has been one of the key factors which has influenced the adoption of non-alignment as the principle of foreign policy. The need to secure aid from both the Western and Eastern states influenced the decision of many states to be non-aligned.

Reasons for the Increased Role of Foreign Aid. The following are the major factors which have strengthened the role of foreign aid as a instrument in post-war international relations:

1. ***Shortages Created by Two World Wars.*** Two World Wars within a short period inflicted a huge loss upon all the states, particularly the European states. After the end of the Second World War, one of the biggest problems faced by Europe was the problem of economic reconstruction. The European states found it difficult to develop without foreign assistance. This set the stage for the grant of economic aid to these states by the two super powers. Initially, the USA came forward to offer economic aid to "free states" of Europe under the Marshall Plan and the European Recovery Programme. Later on, the (erstwhile) Soviet Union followed suit and started giving, since 1953, economic aid to East-

European nations which had come forward to adopt the socialist system. By mid-1950s both the super powers has started using foreign aid as an instrument for promoting their respective ideas and interests in international relations. This development opened a new era in the use of foreign aid as an instrument of national policy. The recent changes in the international system—collapse of the USSR and the rise of democratic and economically dependent regimes in the former socialist states, have brought into operation a wider system of foreign aid in international relations.

2. ***Emergence of Cold War and Alliances.*** After the end of the Second World War, the emergence of cold war between the USA and the USSR led to the orgainsation of alliances and counter alliances in international relations. These two developments gave a new strength to foreign aid as an instrument of International Relations. It came to be regarded as a key instrument for keeping up the alliances and for securing new members into the alliances. It was used by the two powers as a means for demonstrating the success of their respective systems—the USA used it to impress upon others the huge gains of liberal democratic capitalistic system and the USSR to demonstrate the rapid gains that can be secured under a socialist system.

3. ***The Emergence of New States.*** The emergence of a large number of sovereign independent but poor and backward states in world politics became also responsible for strengthening the role of foreign aid as an instrument of the foreign policies of the rich states. These new states happened to be, and continue to be so, lowly developed states and hence were and continue to be dependent upon the rich and developed states for economic and technical assistance. This fact encouraged the rich states to use foreign aid as a means for influencing the policies of these states. This made the giving and taking of foreign aid a regular and continuous feature of international relations of post-war period.

4. ***Increased Global Interdependence.*** No state, however developed, is or can be self-sufficient in respect of all its needs. It has to depend upon others for getting as well as for selling several important commodities and goods. The rich and developed states are dependent upon the poor state for getting raw-materials and several other commodities. Likewise, the poor and backward states or lowly developed states (LDCs) are dependent upon the rich and developed states for getting essential goods and technological knowhow or expertise and industrial machinery. The LDCs are often not in a position to pay in cash or kind to the rich states for purchasing the vitally needed goods. The rich states find it essential to strengthen the purchasing power of the LDCs for selling their goods. For this purpose, they find it imperative to provide the LDCs with economic aid or loans. However, at the same time, they always attempt to influence the policies of the aid-receiving nation. This factor has greatly increased role at of foreign aid in international relations of our times.
5. ***New Aspirations.*** The tranformation of states from police state to a welfare state has given rise to new aspirations for socio-economic development and higher standards of living of its people. This has tremendously increased the multifarious needs of the state, and for satisfying these states, particularly every developing state needs foreign aid or help.

KINDS OF FOREIGN AID

Foreign Aid that donor nations give to recipients can be economic aid or even the grant of low interest long-term or short-term loans. It can be general prupose aid given to the recipient country for use in accordance with her own wishes and needs. This type of aid is quite rarely given. Mostly, foreign aid is given for specific purpose and for use in a specific way. In this case the donor nation can give aid for a particular project or for the purchase of a certain goods or machinery from the donor nation. Foreign aid can also be in the form of interest-free loan or low-interest loan or low interest long-term or short-term loan that is to be utilised by the recipient state for the purchase of specified goods the donor nation. Further, the aid can be bilateral or multilateral. Bilateral aid is negotiated directly between the donor and the recepient, while the multilateral aid is regulated through aid consortium or through international groups and institutions like the Colombo Plan, the IBRD, the UNCTED, IMF, etc. The emergence of economic groups G-7, G-15, G-24, ECO, ASEAN, SAARC, OPEC and others have further influenced the role of foreign aid in contemporary international relations.

Morgenthau has classified aid into six kinds. The classification has been made by him on the basis of the purpose and nature of aid that the donor gives to the recipient. The following are these six categories of foreign aid:

1. **Humanitarian Aid.** Humanitarian aid is the aid given by a nation to those countries which fall victim to natural calamities like accidents, floods, famines and epidemics. It is humanitarian aid and has no political purpose. This aid is given by the government as well as by the voluntary social-organisations working in various states. International Institutions, like the Red Cross, also provide humanitarian aid.
2. **Subsistence Aid.** The aid given by rich and developed state to such poor and backward states which are not in a position to satisfy essential needs of their people is called subsistence aid. Its aim is to prevent the breakdown of a state because of its economic and industrial backwardness and poverty. It is also given to strengthen the purchasing power of the backward and lowly developed countries with a view to keep their existence in world politics as well as to make them capable of pruchasing goods and services from the donor nation. Subsistence aid has a humanitarian outlook but in reality it is politically motivated.
3. **Bribes and Pensions.** It is a 19th century form of foreign aid. Under this system, the donor state gives reward or bribe or a pension to foreign ministers or diplomats of

other states for the services rendered by them. It is a sort of price paid for their service to the cause of the national interest of the donor nation. The payment of hush-money or pay-offs or push-money or retainer or recruiting the citizens of other states as paid workers or agents or serving the interest of the donor nation are the modern forms of bribe and corruption. Strictly speaking, these cannot be regarded as kinds of foreign aid.

4. **Military Aid.** Since security continues to be the most vital part of the national interest of each nation, the desire for strengthening the military power of the nation is a strong motivating factor in international relations. Most of the new states find it essential to import to get as military aid—weapons and military hardware, from the developed nations. It was the factor which compelled many nations to become members of military alliances of the two super powers. Of course, the system of giving military aid for securing a desired objective has been traditional technique practised by nation, particularly European nations, since very ancient times, yet its use as a major instrument of national policy became highly popular and quite effective after the end of the Second World War. It was accepted by the two super powers as the major means for strengthening their respective alliances, and in the process for strengthening their respective positions in international relations of the cold war period. Pakistan joined SEATO for getting huge quantities of military aid that the US, as the leader of the alliance, was offering to her alliance partners. The USA offered military aid to most of the newly emerging states for winning their support, friendship and co-operation.

5. **Military Sales as Aid.** Military aid covers not only the giving of military weapons and other hardware which the donor gives to the recipient free of cost, but also the sale of military goods at lower rates and the grant of a loan for the purchase of such goods from the donor nation. Even the decision to sell the weapons guns, tanks, aircraft, ships

etc., is used as a lever to exercise some influence on the policies of the recipients. A denial of sale of military goods desired by a needy nation from a powerful surplus state is meant to influence the policies of that nation or at least to pressurise that nation towards a change in her policies. Generally, a country receiving aid is expected to use the aid in accordance with the terms agreed upon and very often in a manner compatible with the interest of the donor. The recipient of the military aid is expected to grant some concessions to the donor. Military aid is, almost always, "aid with certain strings". It is used for making the recipient dependent upon the donor.

6. **Prestige Aid.** It is the aid given by the donor for maintaining its prestige, or for increasing the status of the recipient in international relations. The donor undertakes certain projects in the developing countries for exhibiting its resources and ability to other nations. Even at the cost of economic loss, the donor tries to complete such projects as are considered to be prestigeous. Prestige is regarded as a source of power and hence prestige aid is considered as an instrument of national policy. It is also given for securing certain political advantages for the donor nation *vis-a-vis* its competitions in international relations. It is used as a means for influencing the people of the recipient state in favour of the policies of the donor. It helps the recipient nation to get benefits of the projects undertaken by the donor state and the donor nation to demonstrate its goodwill and co-operation for the people of recipient nations.

7. **Economic Aid or Aid for Economic Development.** The existence of a large number of lowly developed countries with nearly 70% of population and mere 30% resources alongwith the presence of a small group of highly developed nations with 70% resources with 30% of world population, has been a soruce of economic imbalance in international relations. The lowly developed countries are such countries as have won their political independence after having

suffered for centuries under the yoke of imperialism. These are economically and technologically backward and poor nations which find themselves dependent upon the developed nations. The developed nations are mostly former imperial powers who have attained a very high degree of technological advancement and are highly rich states. They have a near monopolistic control over international economy and are maintaining neo-economistic economic control over the new sovereign states—the poor.

Necessity. The lowly developed nations find it essential to get foreign economic aid or for economic development from the rich states. This is a vital necessity for the satisfaction of the primary needs of their people. The rich nations also feel the need of helping the lowly developed nations on humanitarian gounds as well as for maintaining their existence in international relations and for keeping them as the largest consumers of good manufactured in the factories of the developed states. Consequently, the rich nations provide economic aid to the lowly developed.

Forms of Economic Aid. The following are the major forms of such an economic aid:

(i) ***Loans.*** Even loans come under the category of economic aid. Loans are advanced by a rich nation for helping the recipient to tide over a balance of payment problem or to use it for the completion of a particular specific project or for importing goods from the donor nation. This loan can be interest-free loan, or low-interest loan, or long-term loan or short-term loan. While advancing the loan the donor country can accommodate the interests of recipient country by agreeing to certain conditions which are desired by the recipient.

(ii) ***Technological Aid.*** When a developed country transfers technical know-how in respect of certain scientific or industrial spheres to a developing country, it is called Technical Aid. The developed country can lend the services of its scientists, academicians, technologists economists,

military engineers, doctors and other trained personnels to the developing country. These experts advise and help the recipient country in various spheres and on various projects. The U.S. Peace Corps Volunteers rendered valuable services to different countries in various fields. However, very often the donor state attempts to use its personnels for carrying out propaganda and espionage in the recipient country.

(iii) ***Aid or Grants.*** The transfer of interest-free non-returnable capital from the donor to the recipient is called economic aid. It can be either general grant or aid, that is, the aid which the recipient can use in accordance with its own wishes and needs, or the project aid or specific purpose aid, that is, the aid for a specified purpose or project which the recipient country has to undertake.

SOCIO-ECONOMIC FIELDS

The United Nations was established not merely to ensure international peace and security. It is equally concerned with the promotion of conditions under which genuine peace would be possible. Article 1(3) of the UN Charter clearly states that the purpose of the UNO also includes achievement of "international co-operation in solving international problems of an economic, social, cultural or humanitarian character" as well as "encouraging respect for human rights and for fundamental freedoms for all without distinction as to race, sex, language or religion".

For the achievement of these objectives the UN is assisted by the Economic and Social Council, the Council's Commissions and specialised agencies, the Trusteeship Council and the Secretariat. For the purpose of convenience the activities of the UNO in the social and economic sphere may be studied under the following headings:

1. Social Achievement. The Department of Social Affairs of the UN Secretariat, ECOSOC and a number of the specialised agencies look after the social development. They make efforts to improve the living conditions, housing town and country planning, community development, family, youth and children welfare, rehabilitation of the handicapped population, migration as well as the refugee questions.

UNO has tried to improve the health condition of the people throughout the world through WHO. It provides advisory and public health services to member countries. It has given major assistance to many countries in the fight against malaria, tuberculosis, poliomylitis, venereal diseasses, influenza, small-pox, leprosy, yaws and other communicable diseases. For example, when in 1947 cholera epidemic broke out in Egypt, the UNO took the necessary steps, in collaboration with other states, to prevent the spreading of epidemic beyond Egypt. The UNO has also given assistance to many countries in establishing an efficient national health administration. It has also imparted education to the people on health matter through training programmes, seminars, conferences, etc.

UN has tried to establish control over narcotic drugs and set up a Commission on Narcotic Drugs for this pupose. Though the Commission is primarily concerned with the implementation of the various conventions adopted in this regard, it also advises regarding the changes need in the existing machinery. It also advises the individual governments regarding the machinery they should evolve to control the supplies of narcotic drugs more effectively. It keeps control over the production of narcotic drugs through various agencies to prevent its misuse. As the entire success in this direction is dependent on the willing co-operation of the member states, the UN has not been able to achieve much success in this regard.

UNO through its International Refugee Organisation has done a commendable job in assisting 1.6 million persons to resettle during the period from July 1, 1947 to January 1, 1952. Though the main activities of the UNO in this regard were confined to Europe, especially in Germany, it looked after refugess in other parts of the world also. In Palestine the refugee problem created by the conflict between the Jews and Arabs over Palestine, UNO did a remarkable job through United Relief for Palestine Refuges established by the General Assembly in November, 1948. During the Arab-Israeli war of 1967 the refugee problem again cropped up which was solved with the assistance of the UNO.

UNO has also done a remarkable job in the direction of providing food, clothing and medical aid for needy children in the war devastated countries through U.N.I.C.E.F. The funds for these activities were provided by voluntary contributions of money, goods and services from governments, private organisations and individuals. With the passage of time the activities of the U.N.O. in this regard went on assuming greater proportions and in 1964 the U.N.I.C.E.F. approved programmes totalling 836 million to help children in 112 countries. It also undertook new service in the field of family and child welfare, education and vocational training, etc.

The UNO has also devoted great attention to the promotion of universal respect for human rights and fundamental freedoms without any distinction of race, sex, language or religion. Its first achievement in this direction was the adoption of Universal Declaration of Human Rights. This declaration aimed at providing a common standard of right to be achieved all over the world. UNO also adopted the convention on Genocide in December, 1948 though it came into force after it was ratified by 23 States in January, 1951. According to the convention the following constitute genocide : *(i)* Killing members of a group because of their group affliation; *(ii)* causing bodily or mental harm to group members; *(iii)* deliberately inflicting physical destruction; *(iv)* imposing measures to prevent births within the group; and forcibly transferring children from one group to another.

The ratifying states agreed to implement the convention and permit extradition of persons formally accused of genocide.

UNO has also devoted attention to the improvement of status of women throughout the world. To secure equal status for women the UNO set up a Commission on the status of women. It tried to secure better protection for women under national laws, extension of national educational opportunities for women, equal pay for equal public service, and their increased partcipation with the work of Government. The UNO has also taken steps for the suppersion of traffic in women. It has laid down rules for provision of facilities to pregnant mothers, as well as passed numerous resolutions regarding nationality of women.

UNO has also devoted attention to the protection of the interest of minorities. It has constantly pleaded for 'self-determination in non self-governing territories' and severely condmened religion and social persuasion and discrimination. It particularly adopted strong attitude twoards racial discrimination in South Africa. In 1962, the General Assembly of the U.N.O. established a special committee on apartheid (racial discrimination). This committee has kept a continuing watch on the developments in South Africa and has recommended strong measures against the South African Government.

Taking freedom of information as a fundamental human right and a touchstone of all other freedom, the UNO has attached great importance to the freedom of information and press. The General Assembly passed a resolution affirming the need of freedom of information and press and asserted that "Understanding and co-operation among nations are impossible without an alert and sound world opinion, which in turn, is wholly dependent upon freedom of information". For the implementation of this resolution the Economic and Social Council set up a Sub-Committee on Freedom of Information. The Sub-Committee convened a Conference at Geneva in 1948 which adopted a number of resolutions and draft conventions. Some of these resolutions and conventions were ultimaltely incorporated in the Convention on the International Transmission of News and Right of Correction adopted by the General Assembly in 1949. However, due to contradictory stands of the two rival powers, the UN could not make much progress in this direction.

The UN has also felt concerned with the right of self-determination of the people. In 1962, the General Assembly set up a Commission on Human Rights to make recommendations regarding the steps necessary to develop international respect for the rights of people to self-determination. The Commission submitted two proposals. The first insisted on the right of the people and nations, to permanent sovereignty over their natural wealth and resources. The second suggested the establishment of a commission to study any situation arising out of denial of right of self-determination to the people of any area. These resolutions did not find favour with the Economic and Social Council because the colonial members of the UN insisted on applying the principle of self-determination to the people of the satellite states of the Communist bloc. As a result, much progress could not be made.

2. Economic Achievements. The UN has realised the need to a more organised international cooperation in the economic and financial field to achieve the objective of promoting "higher standards of living, full employment and conditions of economic and social progress and development". It made efforts to reduce trade barriers through multilateral negotiations under the auspices of the General Agreement on Tariffs and G.A.T.T. though much progress could not be achieve in this regard due to the attitude of the developed countries. It organised two International Conferences in 1964 and 1968 through which effort was made to secure the interests and needs of the developing countries.

UN has been giving technical assistance to the under-developed countries for economic development. Huge funds are allocated by the General Assembly to the Secretary General for this purpose every year. Further funds for the purpose are voluntarily contributed to the United National in November, 1965. These funds are made available for activities in the field of agriculture, health service, resources survyes, technical education and training institute, and applied research in the developing countries.

The International Bank and it affiliate the International Development Association (I.D.A.) on behalf of the UN advance substantial loans at market rate for economic development. The UN also invests in productive private enterprises in association with private investors in developing countries through the International Finance Corporation (I.F.C.).

The UN has greatly helped in making studies on Finance and related problems. It has published reports on methods of increasing domestic savings, relative prices of exports and imports in under-developed countries, conditions governing private investment in certain countries, formulation and execution of development projects, the effects of price fluctuations and the rise in raw material prices upon underdeveloped countries. Another important measure was the Report on "Measures for the Economic Development of Under-developed Countries" which analysed the capital requirements for increasing national income and also recommended the creation of an International Development Authority in the UN with power to make grants to underdeveloped countries.

The United Nations has devoted lot of attention to the problem of food shortage. This aspect is looked after by the FAO (Food and Agricultural Organisation). It helped the member states by focussing their attention on the gravity of the crises. It supplies them essential statistical and technical information, organises conferences and helps them in a number of ways. It was an instruments in the drafting of the International Wheat Agreement which is adhered to by majority of the countries. In 1961, U.N. established the World Food Programme to 'explore the possibilities of stimulating economic and social development through aid in the form of food'.

F.A.O. has played a remarkable role in tackling problems like animal and plant disease control, storage of grains, conservation and prevention of soil erosion. U.N.O. has also paid attention to the production of fishery, distribution of food, fertilizers and agricultural machinery.

In the field of communication U.N.O. through the Transport and Communication Commission has devoted particular attention to problem like co-ordination of sea and air safety activities, simplifications of passport and frontier formalities, improvement of road and motor traffic regulations. The U.N. through the International Telecommunication Union has tried to secure agreement regarding regulations for the transmission of international telegraph and telephone communication as well as allocation of radio wavelength frequencies.

Another field which has received lot of attention from U.N.O. pertains to the labour conditions. The I.L.O. has drafted scores of conventions and recommendations regarding employment, conditions of employment, vocational training, industrial health and safety, freedom of association, industrial relations, etc. The I.L.O. also sends commissions of inquiry on request to look into specific problems.

In addition to the above functions there are numerous other economic and social fields where the United Nations has done a commendable job. It is not possible to enumerate all the achievements of the United Nations in these two spheres.

ECONOMIC NEEDS

As a matter of fact the greater part of International politics is concerned with the political economy of the nations. Now only that, the modern political system have been merely serving the complementary part in the smooth working of the economic systems of various nations of the world. For it would never be denied that economy is the very salt of human life, otherwise it cannot be protected against the rigours of nature which are so prevalent in the entire lively existence. Politics cannot separately move on unless it is driving on the vehicle of economy or the economic position of a particular nation or a group of men. The international relations of various States of the world appear to the political at surface soul and the moving vitality, however, originate from the foundation of economic systems of the nations of the world.

The economic status and economic conditions of the State needs a thorough understanding to make a right analysis of the current International politics. In the medieval age money or the matter was not counted so much as it is valued in the present century. The money and the capital began to raise their utility and status in the present economic world since the end of the 18th century. The growth of industrial revolution in England since the closing period of the 18th century was one of the the causes of the extending significance of money, economic and the economic position of every state in the world. Even then the Nineteenth century gave a lesser importance to the economic factor that what the present Twentieth Century had been practically doing. Now the States have come on the forefront of proving themselves as the champions progress of the nations. The State liability is primarly concerned with the annihilation of unemployment as a great social evil, the rise of the general demands of the people of a particular position has set on giving a definite direction to the economic policies of the countries of the world. The States would have to incur a great expenditure on the protection of the political interests and safeguard of the collective interests of the society while they all happend to be vitally economic to the core.

The Economic Needs Being the Basic Demands of the Countries. The countries of the world, whether Capitalists, Communist or the Fascists, have similar economic needs. They are basic and primary in their nature and therefore they deeply influence the shaping of international relations. The state demands can more or less be fulfilled with the help of other states of the world. They are their basic needs and comprise their demands of food meterials and mineral goods and to some extent the raw goods as well. The historic Industrial Revolution has turned the face of all the nations to the modern urge of industrialisation in order to attain self-sufficiency which is a vital factor of national prosperity. The instance of USA is conspicuous is no far as it is self-sufficient in its mineral resources, yet it has to import at leat seventy raw minerals for the fulfilment of its industrial rather than the economic needs. It is to be inferred here that more than ninety per cent of the activities of the present-day world are economic activities.

The countries engaged in the occupation of industries having insufficient agriculturable land, and a large population to fee, would have to look towards other nations who grow enough food. They would invariably be obliged to import food materials from abroad. England, Switzerland and most of the European countries as also some Asian countries like India. China and Japan are not self-sufficient in foodstuffs and therefore, they have to import foodgrains from other countries. Argentina, Australia, Denmark are the instances of those nations who grow enough food but for industrial goods they depend on countries like USA and England. Similarly the industrial countries need race materials for their industries and markets for the products. It makes the nations dependent on each other. Besides electricity it is one of the greatest power resources which is universally needed by all the nations and some states import this power resource from its neighbouring state who is profound in it. Some countries import petroleum and coal from other countries. Water as a power resource had also exceeded in its importance and it is a problem before the countries like Egypt, Kenya and Ethopia as to whether they do not singly usurp all the water of the Nile river. The Brahmaputra flows on the borders of India and Bangladesh. The rivers of Punjab have their fall in the Pakistani territory yet they flow there from the Indian soil. Thus the economic dependence is also generated out of natrual resources.

The Economic Need Fulfilled by the States in Two Ways. The States of the world fulfil their economic needs in two ways:

(1) First by political domination *i.e.*, imperial policy; and *(2)* Second by agreement to get the necessary goods from other States. Some traditions have thus developed in the form of international law which has become an operative factor of international politics.

The political domination through armed invasion has always some economic background in the root. England was economically poor in the 16th century when Spain and Portugal had sufficiently grown in their economic power through their overseas trade. It is happend that England was entangled against Span and she defeated the latter with the help of Sea robbers like Drake and Ralleagh. England thus victorious became the queen of the sea and then she made an extraordinary progress in her trade and industry. Thereafter large industries were established in England and she sought various fields of supplying her necessary raw goods and absorbing the British Supply of Industrial goods as ready markets. In order to increase its colonial status she began to acquire foreign land abundant in raw goods and ready markets. England captured foriegn territories and thus built a big Empire. Similar policy was pursued by other European countries. By the end of the 19th century England and France had made good fortunes by establishing big Empires. Germany too rose into a powerful nation by the end of Nineteenth century and Kaiser Wiliam Second organised the Grand German Army to satisfy her ambition of establishing a great Empire in the world by foreign victories.

Prior to the Second World War Japan and Italy were friends of England but they turned quite inimical to her in the face of the Great World War, due to economic reasons. Japan has the same strategic position in the Asian continent as that of England in Europe. Japan defeated China in 1896 and Russia in 1905 in her formidable attempt of foreign conquests as she craved to become a great imperial power like England or France. Therefore she gradually occupied Korea and Manchuria. In the same way Italy too undertook an invasion of Ethopia to build her empire.

The construction of Suez Canal as a great international waterway some time after, attracted England also to have atleast some hold on this easy means of communication to Asia. The shares of the Suiz Canal Company were bought by Lord Disraeli from the Khadiev Pasha of Egypt in 1875. Since then England established her economic and political hold on Egyptian Government under the pretext of safeguarding the secuirty of Suez Canal. England on the other hand chocked Russia from entering the Mediterranean waters with the same end in view.

The USA became the master of all Latin America by turning out the various European powers from there. She is profoundly rich in her mineral, agricultural and Industrial resources although she had to confine herself to strict Isolation policy in the Seventeenth and the Eighteenth centuries. Afterwards she extended her economic and trade relations first with England and then with other countries of Europe. She began to advance loans to them. She built the Panama Canal in order to encourage her trade with Latin America. She wanted to keep her position secure in the Atlantic and Pacific from the entry of other powers and in the event of England's defeat in the begining of the First World War she sided with her and defeated Germany; otherwise she feared that her position at Sea and the trade routes could not remain secure due to the weakening of naval power of England. In the Second World War the USA and USSR set upon taking their place in the world affairs.

The conclusion of the Second World War encouraged various Communist countries to dominate the world. This could be achieved only with the liquidation of western hold on the economies of developing country. Threatened by this strategy the USA and other European countries powered million of dollars in wooing the developing countries and isolate the Communist bloc. The Soviet Union deprived of her access to warm Sea, has been trying for the last hundred and fifty years to make her safe entry in the warm waters. Yet England and America have all the more been engaged in checking her access to the Sea. Thus it is clear that behind all the political activities of the various states is hidden their inborn design of making their economic systems a huge succeess.

The Inter-State Dependence and Rivalry. No country on earth is self sufficient and every state stands in need on the help of other nations. The nations therefore establish their trade relations with other countries. The economic rivalries of various countries increase the world tension and inter-state hostilities in the international politics.

(a) ***Influence of Prospering States on other States.*** The stability of trade in any country is established by certain agreements which a country has with other nations. If in some of the important countries there happen to be unemployment and economic depression, then it would in due course affect all the countries of the World. The countries producing only one thing as a source of its foreign trade are very much affected by economic depression. For example, most of the Middle Eastern countries produce only petroleum. Bolivia produces tin and Chile can export copper and therefore they would have to depend on many countries in the sphere of international trade and results of economic breakdown prove very much fatal to their economic systems. The total output of USA had diminished by one per cent in 1953 and it decreased the British export trade to the extent of 5 per cent. All the member-countries of the North Atlantic Treaty Organisation underwent a loss of 30 percent, in their export trade in 1948-49 when the economic position of the USA became a little weak. England supplied enough industrial goods to Germany and at the end of the First World War when Germany met her doom, the economic breakdown of the country affected the trade position of England; and therefore she was obliged to improve the economic condition of Germany. It is evident that the unemployment and economic breakdown of a country result in the breakdown of the economies of other countries also. Thus, the economies have now become inter-dependent. Therefore every country likes to be self sufficient to avoid grave consequences of the economic breakdown in other countries. The problem of raising the standard of living of the countrymen and that of eliminating the evils of unemployment is the primary liability of the State Government, otherwise it is feared that country might thus become exposed to either a foreign invasion or the inner discontentment and revolution.

(b) ***Economic Rivalry.*** Before the Second World War all the European countries rivalled against each other and Japan got the most economic advantages from China. This rivalry was one of the causes to bring Japan on the side of the Axis led by Germany. Thus the economic rivalry have been causing international tension.

Therefore after the Second World War all the countries decided to take up such policies as would make themselves sufficient and economically well. The case of the Soviet Union is an illustration. The economic resources and the entire economic system has been nationalised and the foreign influence has altogether been eliminated from Soviet Union. The USSR has been making great strides in the progress of her industry by exploiting to the utmost all her economic resources, with the result that she has attained her object of self-sufficiency almost in all respects. The Soviet Communism has become invincible in its force of making the USSR a most predominant power of the World to save the backward countries from the Soviet influence the USA has been following the policy of bargain in the US Communist rivalry and they take economic assistance from either of them and try to improve their economic condition.

ECONOMIC AND SOCIAL COUNCIL

The Economic and Social Council is one of the six principal organs of the United Nations. It operates under the authority of the General Assembly. Article 55 of the Charter enjoins on the United

Nations to create conditions of stability and well-being which are necessary for peaceful and friendly relations among nations based on respect for the principles of equal rights and self-determination of the people by promoting:

(a) higher standards of living, full employment, and conditions of economic and social progress and development;

(b) solutions of international economic, social, health and related problems; and in international cultural and educational co-operation; and

(c) universal respect, for, and observance of, human rights and fundamental freedoms to all without distinction as to race, sex, language or religion.

Composition. The Economic and Social Council at present consists of 27 members (originally eighteen) of the United Nations elected by the General Assembly for a term of three years. One-third of the members of the Economic and Social Council are replaced every year. A retiring member is eligible for immediate re-election. Each member of the Council has one representative. No criteria have been laid down to guide the General Assembly in electing members to the Economic and Social Council. However, in actual practice an attempt is made to represent a variety of social, economic, cultural and geographical interests. The countries of chief industrial importance are usually assured a place on the Council. The Council can invite any member of the United Nations to participate, without vote, in its deliberations on any matter of concern to that member (Art. 69).

The Council performs these functions, through studies and reports, discussions and recommendations and co-ordination.

1. Studies and Reports. Article 62 (1) of the Charter lays down that, "The Economic and Social Council may make or initiate studies and reports with respect to international economic, social, cultural, educational, health and related matters..."

The Economic and Social Council has made studies regarding the problems of refugees, the world shortage of housing, the reconstruction of devastated areas and the economic status of women.

2. Discussion and Recommendations. The Economic and Social Council makes recommendations to the General Assembly, the member of the United Nations and specialised agencies with regard to international economic, social, cultural, educational, health and related matters [Art. 62 (1). It can also make recommendations for the purpose of promoting respects for and observances of human rights and fundamental freedoms for all [Art. 62 (2)]. It must be observed that the recommendations of the Council are not binding on the members.

3. Drafting of Conventions. The Economic and Social Council has also the power to prepare draft conventions for submission to the General Assembly with respect to matters falling within its competence. A draft convention furnishes the text of a proposed agreement and has proved to be a very useful device for reaching international agreements. Convention of the prevention and punishment of the crime of Genocide and the Draft Protocol relating to the Status of Stateless Persons are examples of this type of conventions.

4. Convening of Conferences. The Economic and Social Council can convene international conferences both on its own initiative as well as upon instructions from the General Assembly. Usually the Council calls only inter-governmental conferences on matters other than those falling within the domestic jurisdiction of the states. Sometimes even non-governmental conferences can also be called *viz.*, World Population Conference of 1954; U.N. Scientific Conference on the Conservation and utilisation of Resources, 1949. It can also call conferences of regional character on variety of topics such as heatlh, trade, transport, employment, refugees and stateless persons.

5. Co-ordination of the Work of Specialised Agencies. One of the most important functions of the Economic and Social Council is the co-ordination on the work of specialised agencies of the United Nations. By specialised agencies is meant the international organisations created by inter-government agreement and having 'wide international reponsibilities. At present the following specialised agencies work under the broad supervision of the Economic and Social Council:

1. International Labour Organisation (I.L.O.)
2. Food and Agricultrual Organisation (F.A.O.)
3. International Civil Aviation Organisation (I.C.A.O.)
4. United Nations Educational, Scientific and Cultrual Organisation (U.N.E.S.C.O.)
5. International Bank for Re-construction and Development (The Bank) (I. B. R. D.)
6. International Telecommunication Union (I.T.U.)
7. World Meterological Organisation (W.M.O.)
8. International Monetary Fund (I.M.F.)
9. World Health Organisation (W.H.O.)
10. International Finance Corporation (I.F.C.).
11. Inter-Governmental Maritime Consultative Organisation (I.M.C.O.)
12. Universal Postal Union (U.P.U.)
13. International Refugee Organisation (I.R.O.) a non-permanent specialised agency.

Each of these specialised agencies of the United Nations has its own constitution, sphere of action, budget and saff in accordance with the principle of functional organisation. Although each of these agencies has a separate and distinct identity, they are not completely autonomous and unrelated to each other. They have been brought into relationship with the United Nations by means of agreement negotiated by the Economic and Social Council and approved by the General Assembly. This co-ordination of various agencies is essential because their various activities are not mutually exclusive but involve a considerable degree of overlapping and concern for different phases of essentially the same problems.

6. Relations With Non-Governmental International Organisations. The Economic and Social Council also maintains close relations with non-govermental organisations like the International Federation of Agricultural Producers, the International Chamber of Commerce etc. These non-government organisations can be broadly classified in two categories. Category 'A' includes those orgainsations which have a basic interest in most of the activitives of the Council and are closely linked with the economic and social life of the area which they represent. They can submit items for inclusion in the provisional agenda of the Council. They can also send obervers to all the public meetings of the Council. Category 'B' includes organizations which have a special competence but are specifically concerned only with some of the fields of activities covered by the Council.

The Economic and Social Council (E.C.O.S.O.C.) has been criticised for an apparent lack of concrete achievement, for delays in considering important problems, and for the interminable debates that take place at each of its sessions on questions which often seemed merely procedural, relatively inconsequential or largely political in character.

PROVISIONS OF U.N. CHARTER

The U.N. Charter accepts the concept of regional arrangements for securing regional peace, security and co-operation. Initially, when discussions were being held over the issue of the nature and organisation of the proposed international organisation, many scholars expressed doubts about the utility of regional arrangement as devices of peace and security. They feared that regional arrangements and alliances would be counter productive in so far as these would encourage competition and conflict among nations. Some other scholars, while accepting the concept of "regional arrangement" wanted that it should be made obligatory that every regional arrangement should take enforcement action only under authorisation from the security council of the new international organisations. Many countries, particularly belonging to the American states and Arab League, opposed the above views and advocated the necessity and desirability of providing for regional arrangements along with the multipurpose international organisation.

PROVISIONS OF U.N. CHARTER REGARDING REGIONAL ARRANGEMENTS

In 1945, it was mainly under the pressure exerted by American, States. France, Arab League, former U.S.S.R. and several other countries that Regional Arrangements were recognised by the U.N. Charter. Chaper VIII of the U.N. Charter stands fully devoted to Regional Arrangements Article 52 of the Charter clearly states; "Nothing in the present charter precludes the existence of regional arrangements or agencies of dealing with such matters relating to the maintenance of international peace and security as are appropriate for regional action, provided that such arrangements or agencies and their activities are consistent with the Purpose and Principles of the United Nations." This article further accepts the principles that members of regional arrangements shall try to achieve pacific settlement of local disputes through such regional arrangements.

However, these provisions do not constitute any limitation on the power of the Security Council regarding the Settlement of disputes among states. Clarify the relation between the peace keeping roles of the Security Council and the regional arrangements. "The Security Council shall, where appropriate, utilise such regional arrangements or agencies of enforcement action under its authority. But no enforcement action shall be taken under regional arrangements or by regional agencies without the authorisation of the Security Council, with the exception of measures against any enemy state— "The Security Council, at all times, be kept fully informed of activities undertaken or in contemplation under regional arrangements or by regional agencies for the maintenance of international peace and security."

ROLE OF REGIONAL ARRANGEMENTS

The U.N. Charter recognises regional arrangements as devices of regional peace and security. However, the Charter no where defines regional arrangements or agencies. "It leaves the whole question of their character and purposes, and of their exact relations with the United Nations," write Palemer and Perkins, "very much up in the air".

(i) **Regional Arrangements and Working of the United Nations.** The inability of the United Nations to act as an effective peace keeping agency at international level has encouraged many states to join regional arrangments. The non-communist states in particular have been encouraged to join the western alliances because of the ineffectiveness of the United Nations. However, this in turn has furhter weakened the United Nations. As Carlos Romulo of Philippines has observed. "The U.N. is dying because member states are more and more taking the great political issues outside the framework of the organisation." Although Art. 103 of the U.N. Charter states that in the even of conflict between the obligations of the members of the United Nations under the present Charter and their obligations under any other international agreement, their obligations under the present Charter shall prevail, "yet in actual practice the members of regional security arrangments have often ignored the wishes of the United Nations in favour of the decades of their regional arrangements."

(ii) **Regional Arrangements as Instruments of International Peace or Cold War.** The supporters of regional arrangements insist that these devices are wholly consistent with the United Nations Charter and that these are necessary steps in regional or collective self-defence. The Charter specifically recognises the right of nations to take action of this sort until and unless the United Nations is able to assert itself effectively in the maintenance of peace. As against such a defence of the regional arrangement, the critics hold that these involve the danger of increasing international rivalry. "There is real danger that they will develop into military alliances against some country or countries (As happened in 1950s and 60s), that they will provoke counter measures—that they will increase international tensions and thereby accentuate the very evils they are presumably designed to prevent." In the words of Leland M. Goodrich "It must be clearly recognised, however, that the world organisation is not being strengthened by the multiplication and tightening of these regional security arrangements." In the post-war era of international relations, the regional security arrangements have been largely the instruments of cold war.

(iii) Negative Role of Regional Military Arrangements. Further, the bipolar politics and cold war situtation had given strength to regionalism over and above the United Nations and the spirit of internationalism that it manifests. Regionalism often paralysed the U.N. In the words of Edger S. Furnies, "In the name of regional arrangements, the U.N. has been palced in a position of inferiority, so that now the link between the regional arrangement and the world organisation exists at the practical pleasure of the former." The regional security arrangements have failed to help the United Nations in performing the function of maintaining international peace and security. However, non-security regional arrangements have in many cases helped the process of promoting international economic and cultural development. The need is to weaken or, ideally to elimanate the military or security oriented regional arrangements. The followers of Non-alignment accept and advocate this view. However, the supporters of regional arrangement continue to maintain that regionalism is fully compatible with internationalism, and that in the contemporary international system both regional arrangements and international organisation can coexist on side by side and work for securing international peace and security. Such a view is held by John C. Stoessinger. He writes: "The record support neither the building bloc theory of regionalism nor the opposite contention that regional arrangements are antithetical to the principles of the U.N. Charter Rather the evidence shows that frequently the U.N. has been a second line of defence for regionalism and that some times regional arrangments have served as back stops for the world organisation. Certainly there is ample room for both types of political order building on the international scene." This view appears partial and unobjective to the supporters of Non-alignment and they are in majority. Security oriented regionalism is definitely a harmful practice. Regional security arrangements like

NATO, SEATO, Warsaw Pact etc. have been sources of militarian and tensions and not of peace, security and stability. Warsaw Pact is now dead but NATO continues. However, the emergence of several Regional Functional assocations like ECM, ASEAN, SAARC, etc., has been a source of strength for the promotion of international co-operation, colloboration and development.

COLLECTIVE SECURITY

Collective security is a modern device of power management at international level which it is believed, can lead to an effective preservation of international peace and security. In the words of Schleicher, "Collective Security has at times been viewed as the supporting pillar of the edifice of peace. When it was incorporated in the Charter of the United Nations, Collective Security was described as the best hope for world peace that provides the teeth to the United Nations for halting aggression against peace." Its purpose was stated to be: "To prevent the outbreak of war, or failing that, to protect the intended victim."

Collective security has been designed as a deterrent against all possible aggressions in so far as it lays down that the collective power of the nations shall be used to repell aggressions against any state. The principle that 'aggression against any one member of the international community shall be viewed as an aggression against international peace and security and hence, shall be met with by the collective efforts of all the nations' is the central principle of the concept of collective security. Over the years it has been developed and advocated as a concept of peace, which seeks to protect peace against war or aggression or even threat of war or aggression.

"Few, terms." write Palmer and Perkins, "are more popular in Western World than collective security, and few are used in such vague and diverse ways". Many writers regard it as a hypothetical proposition involving a large number of "if and buts," Charles B. Marshall has observed, "Collective Security is a generalised notion of all nations banding together in undertaking a vague obligation to perform unspecified actions in response to hypothetical events bought on by some unidentifiable state." The concept of collective security appears to be simple and almost self-explanatory but in reality it is a highly complex concept which defies a universally acceptable conceptualisation because it involves several hypothetical, vague and illusive assumptions.

Collective Security has been defined differently by different scholars:

1. Schliecher also observes, "In essence, collective security is an arrangement among states in which all promise, in the event any member of the system engages in certain prohibited acts (war and aggression) against another member, to come to latter's assistance." He omits altogether the forces and factors at work within the State. He also does not take into account the factors and conditions which lead nations to behave collectively. He also ignores how national interests affect the behaviour of State. This is serious omission from the point of view of the completeness of the system.
2. The theory fails to give the exact number of international system. It is not clear whether all the nations form one international system or they form several participating systems. We also hear of the Communist System. Latin American System and so on. Our approach is likely to be affected by our own views in this regard.

Kaplan is not the only scholar who has done work on systems theory. There are others like Charles McClelland, Stanley Hoffmann, Kenneth Boulding and Harold Guetzkow who have emphasised the significance of the system approach. If Kaplan is associated more than anybody else with the systems theory, it is mainly because Kaplan has made a full attempt at a rigorous, systematic and highly abstract thinking on the subject whereas others have mostly studied it by criticizing Kaplan. More and more system attempts are now being made to study international politics in terms of international systems. This is proof enough if it is at all requried about the place of this theory in International Politics.

ROLE OF FOREIGN AID

1. Use of Economic Aid as a Means of Control of the Rich Over the Poor Countries. The purpose of foreign aid, is to maintain and promote more the interests of the donor and less the interests of the recipient. It is always used as a political tool or lever by the donor nations for securing the objectives of their policies. The super powers have used it, and are still using it for foreign alliances, increasing their spheres of influence and maintaining their controlling positions in international relations. With the possibly exception of humanitarian aid, all other varieties of foreign aid are used by the donors as means for securing their interests in world politics by favourable influencing, or even pressurising the policies of the poor nations. Foreign aid is an economic instrument with a political purpose. The purpose is to perpetuate the existing control of the rich countries over international relations through perpetuation of their control over international economy. What rich nations are presently giving as foreign aid is far less then what they continue to receive in the form of their control over the economies and policies of the poor countries. It is being used to feed the markets of the poor countries with surplus goods manufactured in the factories of the developed countries.

2. Practical Effect of Foreign Aid. Foreign aid is an instrument of Neó-colonialism. When we analyse the real effect of foreign aid that the rich have given to the poor, we find that it has failed to provide for the economic developement of the under-developed. The under-developed countries continue to live in an era of neo-colonialism. Foreign aid has failed to help these countries in achieving development. It has in no way helped any reduction in the gap between the rich and the poor. On the contrary, it has led to an increased gap between the rich and the poor countries. The chief motive of the foreign aid has been political and ideological and not economic. By this device two two super powers were successful in forging alliances by influencing a number of developing countries in favour of accepting membership of alliances as a way for securing security and economic aid. It has been used by the rich nations to keep the poor countries at their respective subsistence level and hence to perpetuate their dependence upon the rich.

3. Economic Aid as an Instrument of Increasing One's Influence. The economic aid given by the donor to the recipient is apparently designed to help the recipient country's economic development. In actual practice, however, it is always used as a means for influencing the policies of the recipient in such a way as can promote the interest of the donor. It is a glorified version of bribe and reward given by the donor to the recipient for gains or the possible gains which are likely to accrue to the donor nation as a result of its influence over the policies of the recipients. Often it is used as a means for making the recipients dependent upon the donor. The donor often makes it certain that the recipient should keep on living with the economic aid. Economic aid rarely helps the recipient to be economically developed. It keeps her dependent upon the donor. The quantum of foreign aid given by the donor is always far less than the needs of the recipient. The practice of giving specific purpose, project aid futher checks the recipients from using aid for its real economic development. General aid or simple economic aid without any condition is almost never given to the recipient.

4. The Political Use of Foreign Aid. Foreign aid is being used for three political purposes: *(1)* for influencing the economies and policies of the poor countries: *(2)* for influencing the poor countries to join alliances like NATO, SEATO and otheres, to enter into peace and friendship treaties with the rich and powerful countries, and *(3)* for influncing desired changes in the foreign affaris and policies of the poor countires. Its economic purpose has been limited to the perpetuation of the neo-colonial control of the rich over the economies and policies of the poor countries.

In the contermporary international system of this last decade of the 20th century, several developments—end of cold war, collapse of the USSR, rise of several independent sovereign republics in the territory of the erstwhile USSR and their economic needs, the economic needs of Russia and the former socialist states of Eastern Europe which have now adopted market economy, privatisation, decentralisation, and liberalism, have all tended to invigorate the role of foreign aid in international relations. Politics of foreign aid has come to be key dimension of international politics. Foreign aid is being given on the consideration for maintaining a particular regime in power or is not given for securing the fall of a particular regime. G-7 agreed to provide foreign aid worth 43 billion dollars to Russia with a view to help Boris Yeltsin to remain in power in Russia as well as to keep him committed to the programme of economic liberalisation.

Foriegn Aid, as such has always acted as an instrument of neo-colonialism. Foreign aid has always been given as aid with strings. Its quantum has been for less than the actual requirements of the poor countries. It has failed o provide any significant help to the poor countries in their struggle towards economic development. It has also not fully served the political interests of the rich states. The USA has been the biggest foreign aid given to the under-developed and yet the US policies have been the object of strong criticism by most of the aid receiving countries.

The poor countries have already rejected foreign aid as a neo-colonialist instrument which has failed to provide a really helpful gain to their economic development programmes. They want aid free from strings. They want liberal general development aid and not the 'foreign aid' that the rich have been giving to them. It is held by them that by giving just 0.7 of the international income as foreign aid free from neo-colonial control, the developed countries can help the development of most of the developing counries of the world. Their major concern is to secure a restructuring of international economic order in such a way as can provide to them a fairer and equitable share in international economy. Foreign Aid stands strong criticised as an economic weapon of the rich for maintaining their interests *vis-a-vis* the interests of the poor. On the whole foreign aid to the developing nations by the developed nations or from international agencies has made the developing countries more and more dependent and has led to increased inequalities. It has in no way meaningfully helped the poor nations to overcome their economic exploitation by the rich. In actual practice, foreign aid has acted like an agent of Neo-colonialism and not as a helping hand of the developed extended to the under-developed. Developing countries realise fully the exploitive nature of foreign aid being given by the developed countries but they find themselves helpless in the face of non-availability of an alternative instrument. Infact now they fear the possibility of diversion of Western foreign aid from the Third World countries to the former socialist stats of Europe and Russia. A denial or reduction of foreign aid to them can further slow the process of their socio-economic development. thus the existing situation can further increase the neo-colonial control over their policies and economies.

ROLE OF MULTINATIONAL CORPORATIONS

The rise of several powerful transnational profit-making economic organisation—popularity called the multinational or transnational corporations, has been a phenomenal development of the post-war international relations. Investments by individuals of one country in the economics system of another country is not new. However, since World War II, the volume of direct investment abroad through multinational corporations has been staggeringly big. This development has given rise to a new process of inter-nationalisation of production and monopolisation of wealth.

I. What is a Multinational Corporation. A multinational corporation is defined differently by different scholars.

In the words of Huntington, "a distinctive characteristics of the transnational organisation is broader than national perspective with respect to the pursuit of highly specialised objectives through a central optimising strategy across national boundaries."

Raymond Vernon regards a Multinational enterprise as a cluster of corporations of diverse nationalities joined together by ties of common management strategy.

Mennis and Sanvant write that Multinational Corporations are "companies that control production facility in two or more countries." The point of convergence in these definitions is, as Kegley and Wittof observe that "an MNC is regarded as a business enterprise, organised in one society with activies abroad growing out of direct investement (as opposed to portfolio investment through shareholding). Typically these are hierarchically organised and centrally directed.

II. Nature of MNCs. Louis T. Wells refers to MNCs as multinational business enterprises and describes these as transnational actors. These move large amounts of resources cross international boundaries, some (rather most) of them have organisations that centralise decision-making process so that these resources can be used to fulfil objectives that may be at variance with those of a particular country in which a subsidiary is located. These firms have at their disposal many tools for frustrating governmental policies, but the policies they frustrate may be of those of the host government or those of the home government.

Increasing Number of MNCs. The impact of this development can be guessed by the estimate that by the year 2000 half or more of all industrial production in the world will be accounted for accounted for by a relatively handful of MNCs. In 1977 *i.e.*, 21 years ago, Robert L. Heilbroner observed, "the growth rate of IBM (an MNC) at home and abroad for the past decade has been sufficiently great, so if it continues uninterrupted for another generation, IBM will be the largest single economic entity in the world, including the entities of national states." Another study shows that the number of foreign subsdiaries of 187 U.S. based MNCs grew from just over 2000 in 1950 to nearly 8000 in 1967, roughly a fourfold increase in less than two decade. In the USA, the number for firms with foreign officials in other countries was 2713 in 1979. The World Bank Atlas it its 1979 edition listed 100 top economic entities (billion-dollar or more firms and nations) in the world, out of these 41 happened to be Multinational Corporations, with General Motors and Exxon outranking all but 22 nation states. Among the top fifty entities, multinationals accounted for only 9, but in the next-fifty, 32 happened to be multinationals. Nearly 30,400 business firms, based in nineteen First World nations, have at least on foreign affiliate in one or more host countries. The United States, Britain and Germany have control over half of these corporations. The United States alone accounts for more than a quarter. Although the growth of trans-national corporations is a global phenomenon, the major part of all trans-national business is located in the developed areas of North America, Western Europe and Japan.

Analysis of MNC Network. When we analyse the MNC network that has come to spread all over the globe, we find that it is dominated by the United States. In 1976, 54% of all 411 industrial firms (with at least 1 billion sales) were Amercian, Japan and Britain, with 12% and 10% respectively were second and third. Among the leading firms were the giants of American firms—Exxon, General Motors, Ford Motors, Texaco, Mobil, Standard Oil of California, Gulf Oil, IBM, General Electric and International Telephone and Telegraph. In 1977, Bank America of Corporation and Citicorp were the two largest camps in the world. Japan accounted for 12 of the 50 largest banks. The trend has been continuing. In between them the US, Japan, Germany and Britain share nearly 90% of the transnational business and profits.

Spread of Activity. The spread of their activity and the potency of their economic potential are important reasons," write Kegley Jr. and R. Witkopf, "Why MNCs have commanded (and are commanding still greater) attention". The attention has been comparatively greater on the part of the Third World countries, since MNCs are generally more important in developing nations' overall GNP and in their most advanced economics sectors. Furthermore, the Third World countries regard MNCs as agencies of neo-colonial control of the developed countries over them. Though MNCs are non-Governmental private, profit-making economic enterprises, these indirectly strengthen the control of their home countries over the economies and policies of the developing countries.

III. Role/Impact of MNCs. The role of MNCs can be analysed in two parts: the MNC's impact on the Host Nations and impact on the Home Nations.

A. Impact of MNCs on Host Nations. Multinational corportions have been important transmission belts for movements of goods, diffusion of technology and managerial know-how across national boundaries.

The MNCs and their supporters believe that these have produced the movement of capital and prduction from the First World to the Third World, and it has been a big gain for the latter. *(1)* The MNCs satisfy the foreign investment needs of the developing nations. *(2)* These pay higher wages, keep more honest records, pay more taxes, and provide more managerial knowhow and training than do local domestic industries. *(3)* MNCs usually provide better social services for their workers, and certainly provide fancy career opportunities.

Execessive Costs. The Third World nations, however, find the costs associated with the MNCs usually excessive. "The capital, jobs and other benefits they bring to developing economies are recognised, but the terms on which these benefits come are seen as unfair and exploitary and as robbing the new nations of their resources." The flow of technology to Third World Countries through the MNCs makes the former dependent. North gets the chance to impede local development. It limits, if not kills, local initiative and really retards the process of industrialisation, economic development and self-reliance.

Fees and Charges. The fees that MNCs chrage for transferring technology, giving know-how and granting licences is exhorbitant and constitute a big strain on the economies of the host countries. The "transfer" pricing mechanism is another device used by multinationals that can effectively increase MNC's profits while minimising their tax burdens. The raw, semi processed, or finished materials produced by a parent's subsidiaries located in different countries are in effect traded among the subsidiaries. Since the same company is sitting on both sides of the transaction, the sale or "transfer" prices of these import-export transactions can be manipulated so as to benefit the parent firm. "The net effect of all this is", write Kegley and Wittkops, "increased capital flow from the South to the North.

Effects. While analysing the ill effects of the activities of the MNCs on the developing states, Joan Edelman Spero has observerd: "Multinational corporations often create highly developed enclaves which do not contribute to the development of the larger economy. These enclaves use capital-intensive technology which employ few local citizens; acquire supplies from abroad, not locally; use transfer prices and technological agreements to avoid taxes and send earnings back home. In welfare terms the benefits of the enclave accrue to the home country and to a small part of the host population allied with the corporation."

The Third World countries fully subscribe to this view and hold MNCs responsible for increasing and aggravating their dependence upon the First World.

B. *Impact of MNCs on the Home Countries.* The role of MNCs *vis-a-vis* their home countries is again a matter of concern. Undoubtedly these help their parent countries to secure economic gains yet the costs are quite high in terms of the upsets they often produce in their economies, and production and employment markets. Critics of MNCs charge that these shift productive facilities abroad for avoiding demands of powerful labour unions for higher wages. The practice of moving from industrially advanced countries to industrially backward countries, where labour is cheap and labour unions are weak, is the cause of structural unemployment in the home countries, because capital is more mobile than labour. Often the MNCs are, because of their economic power, in a position to influence the policies of the host countries in their favour.

Deprivation of Home Countries. The MNCs, because of their abilities to transfer capital, goods and technology to various parts of the globe, can avoid the measures adopted by their home governments for making the domestic economies healthy and strong. For example, tightened credit policy of the home country can be avoided by the MNCs by sending the Multinational enterprize to other rich countries. The MNCs can aggravate the balance of payments problems in the home countries by withholding remissions of profits from overseas. These can avoid an increased cost of local labour by shifting production overseas. As the profit of an MNC grows, it becomes less and less amanable to the control of the home country. It can, by subtle economic and management moves negate the results of tragets expected by the home country. Thus, MNCs can be a source of trouble even for their home countries. Their ability to operate as powerful non-state high profit making enterprises can be a source of trouble or their home countries.

ARGUMENTS FOR AND AGAINST MNCs

Role of MNCs. The growth of multinational corporations as powerful non-state economic actors, playing a key role in international relations, particularly economic relations, has been phenomenal. Their emergence has played a key role in making Low Politics more dominant than High Politics. On the one hand, MNCs have emerged as sources of transfer of capital, industry, technology and know-how from the developed First World to the developing Third World. On the other hand these have made the Third World countries more and more dependent upon the developed countries to develop with their help and experties, on the other side these have tended to be a source of neo-colonial control over their economies and policies. Even for the countries of their origin (home) the MNCs on the one side, have been instruments of profit and health for their economies, on the other side these have exhibited the tendency to remain free from the control of the government of the state as well as to become a source of unemployment. All this has made the multinational corporations the object of support and opposition, optimism and pessimism and praise and denuciation. Let us examine both the arguments for and against them for assessing correctly their role as well as examining the methods of control over them.

A. ***Arguments in Favour of MNCs.*** The supporters of MNCs, the optimists, advance the following arguments, as presented by Couloumbis and Wolfe, in support of the good and active role of the multinational corporations:

   1. *Products*. Multinational Corporations have the ability to produce more and better products at lower prices

thereby satisfying the progressively rising global demands for these products.

2. *Capacity.* Multinational Corporations as huge economic combines have the capacity, know-how and wisdom to treat the world as a single economic unit and to combine the factors of production for maximum efficiency and productivity.
3. *Modernisation.* The MNCs are powerful agents of world modernisation, especially among the less developed countries. They are sources of flow of goods, technology, know-how and capital from the developed to the developing world.
4. *Inter-dependence.* MNCs have proved agents of increasing international inter-dependence, which in turn, has been compelling integration of the world into an international community consicous of and committed to internationalism.
5. *Advancement.* In their host countries, MNCs create new jobs, introduce advanced technologies and train local citizens in the art and science of modern management.
6. *Anti War.* The supporters of MNCs further argue, as Wolfe observe, "MNCs, by spreading and intermingling their facilities and products globally will render the practice of international was obsolete. They know the case of the Atlantic Community which has vitually become a zone of peace because of the international corporate activity. It is unthinkable in our days to predict a war between the U.S.A. and Canada or between France and Germany.

The recent elections to European Parliament is an indicator of the good results that 'inter-dependency can produce and MNCs have played and are playing a big role in making the world interdependent. The MNCs supporters conclude, these are "ushering in a new golden era of peace and plenty," and that "the global corporations are mankind's (Humankind's) best hope for producing and distributing the riches of the earth."

B. *Arguments Against MNCs.* The critics of the MNCs particularly the scholars of the Third World countries, however, regard MNCs as instruments of neo-colonial control of the developed countries over the developing countries. These are profit earning exploiting agencies which cost much more than the services these under. Even in the home countries, the labour unions oppose these MNCs because of their ability to reduce employment opportunities in the parent countries by transferring the industries to developing countries where labour is cheap and unorganised. The main arguments against MNCs are as under:

1. *Agents of Unemployment.* The organised labour unions regard MNCs as agents of unemployment since their move their plants to areas of 'cheap labour'.
2. *Anti Worker.* Since multinational labour unions have not kept pace with multinational mangement, the MNCs can become much more resistant to strikes at the expense of general working conditions and compensation.
3. *Disasterous to National Industries.* The organised labour unions insist "that MNCs very often ignore and harm the interests of national industries in this environment of cut throat foreign competitions." MNCs flood the markets with goods produced by 'slave labour' in 'banana republics'.
4. *Anti Peace.* Barnet and Muller reject the thesis, and rightly so, that MNCs are fundamental agents of world peace and progress. They hold that on the contrary the present and projected strategies on global corporations offer little hope for solving the problems of mass starvation, mass unemployment and gross inequality.

5. MNCs are not only perpetuating the gap between the rich and poor countries but also increasing this gap in a big way by securing huge profits from the developing countries and transferring these to the parent developed countries.
6. The multinational corporations have paid little attention to the urgent human social, ecological and psychological needs. These breed economic inequalities, environmental pollution and psychological alienation. These concentrate solely on their profits and have little regard for the human needs and living conditions. They are almost as much and even more, exploitative than the traditional Zamindars and Jagirdars.
7. MNCs are agents of neo-colonial control of the rich countries over the poor countries. The former use these non-governmental profit organisations to influence the economies and policies of the latter.
8. Multinational corporations are harmful both for their host and home countries. As Barnet and Muller point out these "are colonising poor countries and progressively weakening and destabilising the rich countries, while becoming gargantuan themselves." These have in fact been engaged in an invasion over the economics and cultures of the Third World countries.

Thus, these are several strong and solid arguments against the role that MNCs have been playing as non-state profit-making business and industrial leviathans in contemporay international economic relations.

To sum up, we can say that the supporters of MNCs regard these as instruments of economic, industrial and technological development which are serving both are developed and developing countries. As such they hold that the need is to properly channelise the resources of these international giants for securing a world free from wars, under-development and poverty. The critics of MNCs, and the Third World Countries regard the emergence and growth of

MNCs as a big menance of contemporary times. They advocate strong and stringent measures against the MNCs for preventing them to act as instruments of Neo-colonialism. This can be done only by national and local regulations as MNCs, because of their powerful status, have become immune to the control of the United Nations and other international economic institutions.

The MNCs are the realities, may be hard realities, of contemporary international relations. No one can hope to eliminate these, nor one should try to put the hands of the clock back. What is needed is to introduce better regulation of MNCs with a view to prevent them from inflicting harm upon the humankind. These can pose and are in fact, to some extent, already posing a danger to the economic and power of the host as well as home countries. As non-state economies giants these can arm and limit the role of their parent nation-states in international relations by influencing the even controlling their policies laws in their own favour. These are already acting as road-blocs in the way of transfer of capital, technology and know-how from the developed to the developing world. Hence, the need is to initiate measures for controlling the activities of the MNCs with a view to make these instruments of modernisation and development and prevent them from developing into bigger and stronger means of Neo-colonialism and economic inequalities in the world.

Both, the supporters and critics of MNCs should realise that since these have already developed as powerful non-state actors in contemporary inter-national relations, every attempt should be made to harness these for serving as instruments of international peace, security and development. These should be prevented from harming the world, both the developed and developing. For this it is essential to end their present status as instruments operating outside national and international, legal and political jurisdictions.

GLOBALISATION OF ECONOMY AND POVERTY IN THIRD WORLD COUNTRIES

The relations between the developed and under-developed countries can be analysed under the following heads:

1. The Big Gap Between the Developed and Under-developed Nations. A very gap exists between the people of the developed countries and the people of the developing or under-developed countries. The former with less than 30% of world's population control more than 70% of world's wealth and income. The latter more than 70% of population live with less than 30% of resources and income. The per capita income of two dozen industrialised Countries is between \$3000 to \$6000 whereas that of hundred or more under-developed countries is about \$100. In the words of Jan Tinberger, "We have today 2/3rd of mankind living on less than 30 cents a day. We have today a situation where there are about one billion illiterate people around the world, although the world has both the means and technology to spread education. We have nearly 70% of the childern in the Third World suffering from malnutrition, although the world has the means to feed them. We have maldistribution of world's resources on the scale where the industrialized countries are consuming world's resources on a scale about 20 times more the resources than the poor countries. We have a situation where in the third world, millions of people toil under a boiling sun from morning till dusk for miserable rewards and premature death without dircovering the reasons why?" The wide gap between the developed and under-developed worlds seriously limits the scope of relations between them.

2. Ever Increasing Gap Between the Developed and the Under-developed. The gap that exists between the developed and the under-developed is further increasing at an alarming rate. The developed and rich nations are becoming richer and the under-developed and poor nations are becoming poorer, particularly after 1970. By virtue of being technologically advanced and industrially developed the rich are strengthening their control over international trade. UNCTAD and GATT have failed to prevent the continuously increasing gap between the rich and the poor. The record of UNCTAD clearly shows that the efforts of the developing countries to attain self-sustained growth have not received adequate support. The pattern of international trade still favours the developed countries. Despite bilateral and multilateral aid programmes, the gap between the developed and the developing countries is growing. The energy crisis, the falling exports, the stiff competition in world markets, the monopolistic role of the MNCs, the inadequacy of the Brettonwood system in contemporary times, the inadequate and limited economic and technological aid to the developing countries etc., have combined to make the poor live with poverty. A combination of the persistent monetary crisis, exacerbated by inflationary trends and balance of payment problems, continued deterioration in the terms of trade and aid, prevalent drought conditions aid above all the recent energy crisis have brought to the fore the array of grave economic and social problems for the Third World. The stark realities of economic conditions in the Third World are too grim to be ignored. The gap between the per capita incomes of the rich nations and the poor nations in widening. The share of the developing countries in world trade declined from 21.8% in 1960 to 17.6% in 1970. Though the report for 1980s appeared to be encouraging yet the continuance of trend towards decline in the world trade share of the developing countries continued to be there. The transfer of resources to the developing countries is continually declining while their external debt has increased by six times. The increase in the oil import bill of the developing countries has further limited their economic conditions.

3. Rich-poor Gap Widens Despite Growth. The gap between rich and poor nations has actually widened and poverty worsened despite a surge of world economic growth and notable social progress made by many developing countries.

Data generated for last 20 years show that per capita gross national product (GNP) rose significantly in industrial and rapidly industrialising countries and also increased in low income countries, the Washington based Institute said. Nonetheless the disparity in income between rich and poor countries had increased, the report said.

Although poverty was not as pervasive a problem in industrial countries as it was in developing countries, the 1980s saw a decline in living standards in industrial countries, including the United States, despite steady growth for most of the period. The results were striking because generally in the past, economic growth reduced poverty, the report siad. The report also highlighted the growing economic needs and problems of the Third World countries. The rich-poor trends were highlighted in set of indicators compiled by the World Resources Institutes as a way of measuring progress towards sustainable development.

4. Increased Global Interdependence. Despite the big gap between the economies of the developed and under-developed countries, the global interdependence has increased. Both the developed countries and the under-developed countries today find themselves in a stage of increased interdependence. In the words of Edward L. Morse, "Evidence for the existence of high level of inter-dependence in certain areas of the international system abounds. The recent global problems in energy resources, the frequent currency crises after 1967 and the suspicions raised by the (erstwhile) Soviet and American intentions in the Strategic Arms Limitations Task bear testimony to the fact the international and even predominantly domestic events have an increasingly deep impact on a growing number of political systems throughout the world." The developed countries find themselves dependent upon the under-developed countries for selling their goods and for purchasing raw materials. The under-developed countries continue to depend upon the developed countries mainly for: *(i)* securing economic and technological aid, *(ii)* selling their commodities, and *(iii)* securing access to advanced technology.

The Big Gap. However, due to the big gap that exists between the economic conditions of the developed and under-developed countries, the global into-dependences continues to be expolited by the rich for strengthening their economic conditions. The hope that the developed countries, which depend on the markets of developing countries especially for their manufactured exports world come forward for internation action of augmenting transfer of resources and liberalisation of trade, has proved to be wrong. The ardent belief of a number of international policy makers that appreciation of interdependence would enable the developed market economies to give more concessions to developing countries, has further proved to be wrong. In actual practice, the developed countries have failed to appreciate properly the inter-dependence and have continued to pursue their desired objectives in international trade and economy without without much regard for the perceptions and needs of the developing countries. Backed by three powerful weapons—technological, political and military power, the developed countries have maintained successfully their control and superior role over international trade even in the contemporary era of global inter-dependence. This has been been a source of great disadvantage for the developing countries.

Inter-Dependence. The need of the hour is that developed countries should realise fully the importance and absolute neutrality of global inter-dependence and must come forward to work for securing a more beneficial and equitable world economic and trading system. The developing countries are keen to secure development and for this regard a restructuring of the entire international economic system with a view to make it fair and just system as a total necessity. For this they want a comperhensive North-South dialogue and agreement. The developed countries, however, are not yet fully prepared to reconcile. They prefer to reform the existing economic institutions and instruments for somewhat accommodating the view of the developing countries.

5. Neo-Colonial Control of Developed Countries Over the Developing Countries. Despite the fact of global inter-dependence and the sovereign equal status of all the members of international community, the developing states continue to live under neo-colonialism. The dawn of independence and the resulting sovereign status has made them free politically and theoretically. Economically and in actual practice, they continue to be dependent upon the developed countries. Being poor, with object poverty and scarcity of essential goods as their assets, they find themselves dependent upon the developed states for securing foreign aid and help. Their present position is the result of the exploitation that they suffered during the past several centuries of their existence under the yoke of western imperialism-colonialism. The developed countries of today could develop only because of their ability and succes in exploiting the wealth and resources of their colonies, which have now become sovereign independent states—the developing countries. Even after the end of their imperial system, the developed countries have been maintaining a neo-colonial economic-political control over the economies and policies of the developing countries.

6. The Under-Developed World. The Third World, therefore, demands a total restructuring of interantional economic system in such a way as shall bestow in a fairer and just manner the gains of industrial, technological and economic development. It regards the creation of a new international economic order (NIEO) as the only effective and positive way of securing the development of the under-developed countries.

7. Neo-Colonial Control. The neo-colonial control of the developed countries over the developing countries continues to be a stark reality of contemporary international relations. Through several subtle devices, like foreign aid, military help, alliances, partnerships, interventions, multinational corporations, international economic institution, protectionist trade, this control is being exercised.

8. The Issue of NIEO. The Third World regards NIEO as the vital necessity of contemporary times as it alone can halt their fast deteriorating economic. In this age of global in interdependence any further squeeze and deterioration of the resources and markets of the under-developed countries is bound to be very harmful and even destructive of the economies of even the developed nations. Hence, NIEO can be of the greatest help and utility to both the developed and developing countries. The under-developed countries advocate that for the creation of a NIEO, the developed countries should come out to negotiate the issue. They advocate an immediate and serious North-South dialogue for this purpose.

9. Unwillingness of Developed Countries. The developed countries, on the other, are not willing to accept the abandonment of their existing strong economic position and control in international relations. The Existing system is helping them to maintain an economic and political control over the economic and policies of the under-developed countries. They do not want to part with their dominant position in the U.N.O. and other international economic institutions, like the World Bank. They advocate that through talks and adjustments the existing system and its institutions can be amended to accommodate some of the demands of the Third World.

10. NIEO. The developing countries, however, stand fully convinced of the fact that only a NIEO can meet their economic and developmental needs. They strongly oppose the attempts of the developed countries to perpetuate the existing system and to keep their neo-colonialistic control over the policies of the Third World. Faced with the continued opposition of the developed countries to the demand for NIEO though North-South dialogue and co-operation, the Third World countries have now come up with the concept of South-South cooperation and increased emphasis upon regional cooperation for development (RCD) among the developing countries. Several better developed Third World countries like India and Brazil, have decided to strengthen internal economic systems by finding internal solutions to their economic problems. This appears to be the best approach. However, all the developing countries cannot resort to this means because most of them are highly backward and poor. Even the South-South Co-operation and RCD are bound to be moderately successful because of the heavy constraints and big weaknesses of the economic systems of the under-developed countries. The concerted opposition from the developed countries is further destined to make the path difficult and problematic. The best alternative still continues to be a New International Economic Order. The developed countries are, however, not prepared to accept it as a priority and hence the relations between them and the developing countries are bound to remain tense and limited. The Third World is determined to get out of the system of neo-colonialism that has come to replace Imperialism and Colonialism, but the developed countries appear to be in no mood to accept an end to their dominance in international relations. Consequently, the North-South relations are destined to be problematic in the years to come.

11. The Economic Problems Compounded by the Recent Development in Eastern Europe and Republics of the Erstwhile USSR. The recent developments in Eastern European countries and their economic need as well as the economic needs of Russia and other republics of erstwhile USSR have tended to create more problems for the Third World countries. The disappearance of socialist bloc has made the developing countries more dependent upon the Western developed countries. The possibility of diversion of Western foreign aid to the former socialist states has been a source of concern for the developing countries. The chances for exploiting the economic dependency of the Third World countries by the developed countries have increased in the contemporary era of international relations.

12. Inadequacy of New GATT and WTO. The inadequacy of the new GATT and WTO agreements have been a further sources of strain on the relations between the developed and the developing countries. Now some of the developed countries have been trying to introduce a 'social clause' which is designed to act as a check upon the already limited export potentials of the Third World countries. In the name of prohibiting child labour the developed countries are traving to keep limited the chances of exporting such items as carpets.

13. Relations Between Both. Thus, the relations between the developed and under-developed countries continue to be strained and far from being satisfactory. The developed countries are maintaining, particularly in the sphere of economic and trade relations, a rigid big and exploitative control over the developing countries. The grim international economic situation, the energy crisis, the continued unproductive and harmful armament race, the faliure of the GATT and UNCTAD, the lack of success towards a North-South understanding over the issue of NIEO, the falilure of the United Nations to act out her role successfully, etc., have all combined to create a grim international situation in which the developing countries find themselves at the receiving end because of their poverty and dependence upon the developed countries. The developed countries too have formed G-15, but their poverty acts as a hindrance. The 1990s are destined to pose a bigger strain upon the economies of the developing countries because of *(1)* debt trap, *(2)* diversion of western aid towards Eastern European countries; *(3)* influationary pressures *(4)* and failure on the NIEO front. The failure of the developed countries to realise fully the developemental and economic needs of the new states has greatly disturbed and shocked the developing states. Today they stand determined to get out of the existing system with its clearcut neo-colonialist features and to secure a new international system based upon justice and equality.

IMF AND IRDB

The International Monetary Fund came into existence in December, 1945. Its chief objectives were stipulated in Article 1 of the agreement and include the following:

1. To promote International monetary co-operation through a permanent institution which provides the machinery for consultation and collaboration on international monetary problems.
2. To facilitate the expansion and balanced growth of international traded, and to contribute thereby to the promotion and maintenance of high levels of employment and development of the produce resources of all members as primary objectives of economic policy.
3. To promote exchange stabitity, to maintain orderly exchange arrangements among members and to avoid competitive exchange depraciation.
4. To assis in the establishment of a multilateral system of payment in respect of current transactions between members and in the elimination of foreign exchange restriction which hamper the growth of world trade.
5. To give confidence to members by making the Fund's resources available to them under adequate safeguards thus providing them with opportunity to correct maladjustments in their balance of payments without resorting to measures destructive of national or international prosperity.

The money for the fund comes through contributions made by the members. Each mamber contributes twenty-five per cent of its share gold and the remainder in the currency of its country.

Organization. The organization of the I.M.F. consists of a Board of Governors, Executive Directors and a Managing Director. There is also other staff to assist the organization. The real powers are vested in the Board of Governors which consists of one Governor and one Alternate appointed by member. Usually the Board holds one meeting in a year. The members of the Board are appointed for a term of 5 years. The members of the Fund have not been accorded equal status. The votes have been given to the members according to the weightage of their contributions. Thus U.S.A. and U.K. enjoy a weightage of 33 and 14 per cent respectively.

The Executive Directors constitute the executive body of the I.M.F. It consists of 20 members (originally 12). The five Directors are sent by the member states who contribute the largest quotas, while the others are elected by the Board of Governors. In electing these members due consideration is given to the geographical representation. The Executive Directors meet twice or thrice a week and are responsible for the operation of the fund throughout the year.

The Managing Director is the chief of the organisation and enjoy a position identical to the one enjoyed by the Secretary General. The main responsibility for the proper working of the Fund mainly rests with him. He is also responsible for the appointment of the staff of the Fund.

The organisation of the Fund has been greatly admired by Prof. Luard. He says: "Unlike in other Agencies, deliberative and decision-making powers are relatively clearly divided (between Governors and Directors). The independence and the calibre of the Managing Director and other Staff has also assisted in the process. Whatever the reasons, the Fund suffers less than other organizations from rancorous dabate and ill-organized discussions".

The members have a duty to keep the Fund fully informed about the domestic and international financial position. The Fund tries to help in eliminating short-term maladjustments by granting foreign exchange. But the funds granted can by used only for the purpose for which they are approved and in course of time the members are expected to buy back the amount of their own currency they sell to the Fund, *i.e.*, when their foreign exchange position improves or they acquire more gold. To ensure a perpectually revolving fund, it has been provided that the members must use half of each year's gain to buy its currency from the Fund.

During the initial years the I.M.F. could not work as per plan because most of the nations did not move towards multilateral payments system envisaged by the Fund. The 'dollar problem' also compelled the European countries to impose strict restrictions on import of goods from U.S.A. But after the establishment of the European Payments Union in 1950 (under which the European states provided a clearing system by which deficits with one country could be balanced by surplus with the other), the Fund introduced the system of 'stand-by-credits'. In the post-Suez crisis years the Fund was increasingly used to meet the strain on the payment positions of a number of countries. Further steps taken in this regard included the adoption of the principle of non-resident convertibility by a number of governments in 1958 under which pound sterling could be freely converted outside the sterling area into gold dollars or other currencies. The I.M.F. also increased the quotas and credit facilities. In 1968 the Fund introduced the scheme of Special Drawing Rights to solve the problem of liquidity. The fund also introduced the schemes of compensatory financing and financing of buffer stocks to increase assistance to the poor countries. In the wake of hike in the prices of oil in 1973 which created the problem of balance of payments deficits in most of the industrial and developing countries, the fund took special measures to assist the governments in difficulty and made available necessary money at low rates of interests.

Thus in the course of time the International Monetary Fund has come to play a vital role. According to Luard, "The degree to which the Fund's policies have evolved over the years, especially in the successful introduction of SDR system have brought a greater willingness to acknowledge its capacity to evolve with the time. Its technical abilities and the quality of its staff have been doubted".

INTERNATIONAL BANK FOR RE-CONSTRUCTION AND DEVELOPMENT (I.B.R.D.)

The International Bank for Re-construction and Development (IBRD) popularly knonw as World Bank, was set up for the purpose of assisting the less developed countries and regions in their development. Though the Bank was set up in December, 1945, it recognised as a specialised agency of the U.N. only in November, 1947. One of the main consideration with the statesmen in creating this Bank was that in the wake of World War II a large number of independent countries made their appearance. But most of these countries were at a very low level of development. The developed countries realised that in view of the interdependent nature of the world economy it was their duty to tackle the problem of under-developed regions. They thought this action desirable in their national interest too. The I.B.R.D. was created for this purpose. It may by noted that the membership of the Bank is open only to the sovereign states.

Purpose. Article 1 of Bretton Woods Agreement, which created the Bank, specifies the following purposes of the I.B.R.D.:

1. To assist in the reconstruction and development of territories of members by facilitating the investment of capital for productive purposes, including the restoration of economies destroyed by war and encouragement of development of productive facilities and resources in less developed countries.
2. To promote long-ranged balance growth of international trade and maintenance of equilibrium in balance of payments by encouraging international investment for the development of the productive resources of members.
3. To promote private foreign investment by means of guarantees and when private capital is not available on reasonable terms, to supplement private investment by providing finance for productive purposes on reasonable conditions.
4. To arrange the loans made or guaranteed by it in relation to international loans through other channels.
5. To conduct its operation with due regard to the effect of international investments on business conditions in the territories of members.

Organization. The organisation of I.B.R.D. consists of Board of Governors, the Executive Directors and the President. While all powers of the Bank are vested in the Board of Governors, the Board of Governors elect a Chairman every year. Each member has 250 votes, plus an additional vote for each share of the capital stock held by the nation which he represents. As countries like U.S.A. hold large number of shares they come to exercise great influence. The Board of Governors appoints a body of Executive Directors consisting of five members. The President is the ex-officio Chairman of the Executive Directors. These Executive Directors are appointed by the five largest stock-holders and not all the members. The President is the Chief Executive Officer of the Bank. He is assisted by other member of the staff.

Functions of I.B.R.D. The chief function of the Bank is to raise the levels of productivity. In initial stages the Bank gave money only for re-construction but after Europe and Asia got rehabilitated, the Bank started giving loans for development purposes. Thus it gave loans to Chiliean government for development of hydro-electric power and water resources; to Mexico for electric power development; to Brazil for expansion of hydro-electric power and telephone installations; to India for reconstruction and development of state owned railways and to Turkey for development of major ports and construction of grain storage facilities.

The Bank lends funds at moderate rate of interest to the countries which will have no difficulty in repaying the loan. Even after the loan has been granted the Bank can make sure that the money is being used as per terms of the contract.

In 1956, the International Finance Corporation was set up as an affiliate of the World Bank. The Corporation was expected to provide assistance to private enterprises projects in developing countries on commercial terms. The other important steps taken in this direction included the setting up of a Special Fund in 1958 and International Development Association in 1962. All these organisations provided fund at very soft terms. However, certain critics have alleged that during these years the Bank advanced loans mainly to the advanced countries and the less developed countries could not get any benefit.

The main reasons for this cautious approach on the part of the Bank have been put by Prof. Luard thus: "It was extermely conscious of the history of the pre-war years when a number of developing countries in difficulties had defaulted on their loans. It was concerned to reassure those investing in the Bank's bonds about the soundness of its lending policies. Conceived as a 'bank' it felt it necessary to think like a bank and talk like a bank. It applied strict banking notions to all projects, requiring firm assurance on the one hand that the projects themselves were sound, and on the other that the governments would not default on repayments".

A change in the Bank's policy took place after Woods took over as President. The Bank showed tendency to take greater risks. It not only lent money to the manufacturing industries but also advanced funds to India for the prupose of financing its imports. The Bank also rendered advisory services to the Member states. It sent missions to make comprehensive surveys of the economies of a number of countries with a view to advise them regarding fixation of priorities of different sectors of production. The Bank sent such missions to countries like India, Pakistan, Iraq, Jordan, Thailand, Ceylon etc. It also trained officials of various member states to enable them to implement the technical programmes more effectively.

It is often complained that by playing safe, the bank has disappointed those "who had counted on it as the major outside source of help to countries unable to finance their recovery". It finances only those projects which involved permanent addition to production capacity and where interest and repayment of loan could be easily foreseen. This was due to preponderous position of U.S.A., which determined the Bank's policy and decisions.

POLICY TOWARDS FOREIGN CAPITAL

In view of this low inflow of foreign investment, the Government of India has announced a liberal policy towards foreign capital. The new Industrial Policy announced in July 1991 contains the following provisions with regard to foreign investment:

(1) As against the past policy of considering all foreign investment on a case by case basis and that too within the

normal ceiling of 40 per cent of total equity investment, the new policy provides for automatic approval of direct foreign investment upto 51 per cent foreign equity holding in 34 specified high-priority, capital intensive, high technology industries provided the foreign equity covers the foreign exchange involved in importing capital goods and outflows on account of divident payments are balanced by export earnings over a period of seven years from the commencement of production;

(2) In order to avail of professional marketing activities for systematic exploration of world markets for foreign products, foreign equity holding upto 51 per cent will be permitted for trading companies as well;

(3) Foreign technology agreements are also liberalised for the 34 industries with firms left free to negotiate the terms of technology transfer based on their own commercial judgement and without the need for prior Government approval for hiring foreign technicians; and

(4) A special Board *viz.*, Foreign Investment Promotion Board has been set up to look into large foreign investment projects where higher foreign equity limit of more than 51 per cent may be permitted.

With an eye to attract Foreign Direct Investment (FDI) of $10 billion annually, the NDA Government, in a major policy shift, threw open (February 1, 2000) most of the Industrial sectors (barring defence, aeronautics, explosive, alcohol, tobacco products) for FDI an automatic route to NRIs and overseas corporate bodies. The main features of the latest liberalised FDI regime are: 100% FDI in *(a)* mining (including coal and lignite supply to private Indian power companies) prospecting of gold, silver diamonds and other minerals *(b)* pollution control-related equipment *(c)* films (in addition to high priority areas, export houses, trading houses, hotels and tourism-related industries, projects for electricity generation, transmission and distribution, roads and highways, parts and harbours and vehicular tunnels and bridges, which are already covered under automatic route): 74% FDI in *(a)* advertising *(b)* Bangalore international airport joint venture *(c)* prospecting and mining of gemstones.

FOREIGN INVESTMENT IN THE POST-LIBERALISATION PERIOD

The response to the new industrial policy and the liberalisation measures enunciated in that with respect to foreign investment has been encouraging. Inflow of foreign investment which was barely $133 million in 1991-92 and $559 million in 1992-93, jumped to $ 6008 million in 1996-97 after which it come down to $ 5025 million in 1997-98. Internal factors such as favourable growth prospects, exchange rate stability and bettter profit expectations compared to other industrial countries contributed to increased inflows.

The foreign capital inflow in India comes in two forms *viz.*, *(a)* Portfolio Investments and *(b)* Foreign Direct Investment (Foreign Collaborations). Portfolio investment has been the largest single source of foreign investment whose volume has increased from $4 million in 1991-92 to $3824 million in 1994-95 but then its flow was reduced to $3312 million in 1996-97 and $1828 million in 1997-98.

The other source of investment inflow is Foreign Direct Investment. Foreign investment under the equity participation schemes which was only $129 million in 1991-92 rose to $3197 million during 1997-98 and to $ 4.2 Billion in 1999-2000.

CONTRIBUTION OF PRIVATE SECTOR

Private Sector refers to that sphere of economy where there is private ownership and control over the means of production. Private owners utilise these means for maximum profits and in order to promote ones own interests. In India Private Sector can be conveniently divided into three parts:

- ***(i) Organised Sector.*** This includes large scale units and big industrial houses.
- ***(ii) Unorganised Sector.*** This includes individual units.
- ***(iii) Small Scale Units.*** In reality we mainly study the problems of the organised sector in the private sector, because these units are very large in regard to investment. Contribution of

small scale and unorganised sector is much less in the private sector. Hence we will limit our discussion only to the organised sector.

In India before freedom the story of industrial development is totally a story of private sector. It was in 1948, that under the first Industrial policy, the Public sector came into existence, and that too in a very limited manner. Only three industries were included in the public sector. 1956 policy extended the role of public sector, to some extent but still there was predominance of the private sector in the industrial structure of India. Only those important industries were kept in the public sector which were related to national security, infrastructure of the industrial development of the country and public utility, and could not be handed over to the private sector. All other industries were kept into the private sector. Thus it is clear, the government of India has accepted the importance of the private sector and adopted the mixed economy. Besides this government has been trying to extend and develop the private sector from time to time. In India, private sector has an important contribution in almost all type of industries.

PERFORMANCE OF THE PRIVATE SECTOR

We can consider the importance, contribution, and performance of the private sector, under these heads:

1. Capital Formation. Economic development of any depends upon the rate of capital formation. According to a survey of Economic Times Research Bureau, in 1970-71, total capital formation in the private sector was Rs.3911 crores at then current prices, which was raised up to Rs. 20,685 crores. In 1986-87 this quantity further increased to Rs. 37,734.

2. Savings. In the first plan savings were only Rs. 687 crores which was 35% of the total plan outlay. In the Sixth Plan savings increased upto 36,396 crores which was 37% of the outlay. In 1986-87 contribution of the private sector in the gross domestic savings was 5,089 crores.

3. Employment. A large part of the working population of India is engaged in various economic activities, such as agriculture, fishery, mining, building works, trade, Transport etc. As far as the statistics is concerned, figures are available only of those non-agricultural occupations which employ 10 or more persons. In 1961, number of persons, employed in private sector was 50.40 lakh, which raised up to 73 lakh in 1985 and in 1987 it became 73.57 lakh. This part in 28% of the organised sector.

4. Assets Growth. There was a tremendous growth in the assets of regulated organised sector. In 1963-64 total assets of the big 20 industrial houses of the country valued to Rs. 1,320 Crores, which, according to the Economic Times Research Bureau survey has grown up to Rs. 24,497.4 crores. The Bureau has also estimated the 101 big establishments have invested capital valued in 1987-79 to Rs. 6636 crores and in 1986-87, more than 32,000 crores.

5. Net Domestic Product. At the ten current rates in 1970-71 private sector contributed Rs. 29,630 crores in the net domestic product (which is 85.5% of the total product) This was increased upto 1,34,766 crores in 1984-85 (77.8% of the total product), in 1986-87 Rs. 1.63,401 crores (71.4% of total product.) Thus, in absolute terms it has increased but in relative terms it has decreased.

6. Profitability. Performance of the private sector can be evaluated on the basis of its profitability. Three types of profitability rates can be studied for this evaluation—*(i)* Ratio of total profit on invested capital, *(ii)* Ratio of total profit to net sales, and *(iii)* Ratio of Net-worth to net profit. In a recent survey of Economic Times Research Bureau has shown that the total quantity of profit of the big houses was Rs. 920 crores; their net sales were 536 crores and net worth, valued to Rs. 2702 crores. On these measures, the performance is appreciable.

PERFORMANCE OF SMALL SCALE PRIVATE SECTOR

Small scale sector has also developed under the private sector, a lot during 1973-74 to 1986-87, production of this sector has grown from Rs. 7200 crores to Rs. 72,250 crores. (Nearly 10 times.) Quantity of employment raised from 39.6 lakh to nearly 1 crore (2-1/2 Times). Production of this sector was 55% of the total industrial output in 1986-87. Contribution of this sector in exports was Rs. 2785 crores (21-16% of the total exports).

Thus the private sector (organised and Small Scale) has made significant contribution in the economic development of the country, despite its limited resources.

GLOBALIZATION, MERITS AND DEMERITS

Private Foreign Investment (PFI) possesses certain advantages which are discussed as under:

(1) PFI not only provides finance but also managerial, administrative and technical personnel, new technology, research and innovations in products and techniques of production which are in short supply in LDCs.

(2) This may, in turn, encourage local enterprise to invest more itself in ancillary industries or in collaboration with foreign enterprise. In fact, foreign entreprise encourages local enterprise in two ways: directly by fostering local entrprise with men, money, and material, and by imparting training and experience to its personnel; and indirectly by creating demand for ancillary or subsidiary services (like transport and training agents) which are uneconomical for private foreign enterprise to provide.

(3) PFI adds more value added to output in the recipient country than the return on capital from foreign investment. In this sense, the social returns are greater than the private returns on foreign investment.

(4) By bringing capital and foreign exchange PFI helps in filling the savings gap and the foreign exchange gap in order to achieve the goal of national economic development in LDCs.

(5) A part of the profits from direct foreign investment is generally ploughed back into the expansion, modernization or development of related industries.

(6) PFI also brings revenue to the government of an LDC when it taxes profits of foreign firms or gets royalties from concession agreements.

(7) PFI helps in raising productivity and hence the real wages of local labour. When foreign investment induced industrialization takes place, the real wages of the newly employed workers are higher than the real wages of workers in the rural sectors of the economy. If PFI is in export-oriented industries, it leads to much higher social benefit than it is in import-substitution industries. Because the former have large backward and forward linkage effects.

(8) Direct foreign investment also places of a burden in the balance of payments of an underdeveloped country in the early stage of development.For, the time lag between the starting of new business concerns and the reaping of profits is large. Moreover, profits are likely to be small in the earlier stages of production. Thus, the remittance of profits from direct investment brings less pressure on the balance of payments. If PFI mainly flows into agriculture and extractive industries with produce primary goods for export, it further helps in easing the balance of payments position of LDCs.

(9) Lastly, PFI flowing into a developing country also encourages its entrepreneurs to invest in other LDCs. Firms in India have started investing in Nepal, Uganda, Ethiopia and Kenya and othe LDCs while they are still borrowing from abroad.

DEMERITS OF PRIVATE FOREIGN INVESTMENT

PFI has certain disadvantages in the form of costs to the recipient country which tend to offset its benifits.

(1) The recipient country may be required to provide basic facilities like land, power and other public utilities, concessions in the form of tax holiday, development rebate, rebate on undistributed profits, additional depreciation allowance, subsidised inputs, etc. Such facilities and concessions involve cost in absorbing an LDC's resources that could be utilized elsewhere by the government.

(2) No doubt, PFI increases investment, employment, income and saving in LDCS, but it adversely affects income distribution when it competes with home investment. Capital and other resources may flow to foreign enterprises in preference to domestic enterprises. This may reduce profits in the later, thereby discouraging local enterprise.

(3) To attract PFI, LDCs have to provide sufficient facilities for transferring profits, dividends, interest and principal. If these payments lead to a net capital outflow, they create serious balance of payments difficulties. Thus the indirect costs of debt servicing and balance of payments adjustments create serious foreign exchange crisis, thereby adversely affecting the national economy.

(4) Many foreign concerns operating in LDCs, reserve all senior executive posts for their nationals and pay them very high salaries with many perks which are a huge drain on the resources of the recipient country. Moreover, the lavish spending habits of foreign national have an undesirable demonstration effect on the nationals of LDCs and create social tensions.

(5) PFI also involves costs in the form of a loss of demestic autonomy when foreign firms interfere in policy-making decision of the government of an LDC which favours the foreign enterprises. Such interference is usually resorted to by the multinational corporations.

(6) PFI brings in highly capital—intensive technologies which do not fit in the factor proportions of LDCs. Often obsolete and discarded machines and techniques are imported which involve high social costs in terms of replacement after a few years.

❐

12
New World Order

After renouncing the policy of isolationism in the early days of the twentieth century, the U.S.A. always fought the wars for establishing its hegemony. It fought the First World War to put an end to all wars. It fought the Second World War to make the world safe for democracy. It fought war against Iraq to establish a 'New World Order' made possible by the end of the cold war.

New World Order. 'People over the world, even the Americans, seemed utterly confused by president Bush's rhetoric on this term. It was on January 16,1991 in his speech, announcing hostilities with Iraq that President Bush declared that an opportunity had come for building a new world order "where the rule of law governs the conduct of nations", and "in which a credible United Nations can use its peace-keeping role to fulfil the promise and the vision of the UN's founders."

Hegemonistic Intentions of United States. But in the heart of its hearts, U.S.A. wants its hegemony. It wants to play as world's policemen. The Pentagon, while laying down the Defence Planning Guidelines for 1994-99 said "Our first objective is to pervent the re-emergence of a new rival, either on the territory of the former Soviet Union or elsewhere... This is a dominant consideration...to prevent any hostile power from dominating a region whose resources would, under consolidated control, be sufficient to generate global power.

There are three additional aspects to this objective. First, the US must show the leadership necessary to eastablish and protect a new order that holds the promise of convincing potential competitors that they need not aspire to a greater role or pursue a more aggressive posture to protect their legitimate interests. Second, in the non defence areas, we must account sufficiently for the interests of the advanced industrial to discourage them from challenging our leadership or seeking to overturn the established political or economic order. Finally, we must maintain the mechanism for deterring potential competitors from even aspiring to a larger regional or global role.

The second objective is to address sources of regional conflict and instability in such a way as to promote increasing respect for international law limit international violence, and encourage the spread of democratic forms of government and open economic systems...we will retain the prominent responsibility for the redressing selectively those wrongs which threaten not only our interests, but those of our allies or friends, or which could seriously unsettle international relations. Various types of US interests may be involved in such instances: access to vital raw materials, primarily Persian Gulf Oil, proliferation of weapons of mass destruction and ballistic missiles; threats to US citizens from terrorism or regional or local conflict, and threats to US from Soviet narcotics trafficking.

United Nations as an Instrument. For the realisation of these objectives it intends to use United Nations as an instrument. It wants UNO to act its instance. That is how in his capacity as a single player on the international stage, President Bush hijacked the United Nations. He made it an instrument of his national interest. It was made possible by the dramatic decline and fall of the Soviet Union which ceased to be an adversary. It could not afford to be an active player while there was political turmoil and economic fiasco at home. In addition to Soviet timidity, Chinese opportunism, West European disarray and Third World members of the Security Council facing economic and political crisis, made it possible for the United States to dictate terms. Consequently, the U.S. preferred to limit its diplomacy within the Security Council. The consensus in the Security Council over the resolution 678 authorising all 'necessary' means to free Kuwait was unprecedented but not surprising.

U.S. Efforts at Establishing NWO. There is a widespread belief, and rightly too, that the USA fought the Gulf war to make the oil of the region safe for itself-not only right now but in the times to come to contain Germany and Japan, the economic giants, from dominating the world stage. USA has enough oil for itself beneath its own soil and also in the backyard—the Caribbean and South American countries. It is Germany and Japan which are solely dependent upon the Arab oil. So, USA with its far off national interest, want a control over the Gulf Oil.

Not only that, the USA wants to contain India as well so as to checkmate its emergence as a regional power. India in the perception of USA, is highly constrained by ideological predilections and by the sentiments of its Muslim Constituency in that it as has no room for accommodating American view point. That is why the Bush Administration once again revived the Super 301 threat against India in order to force India to accept US laws on International business and commerce. That is how India stands nowhere in the new world order that President Bush envisages. Instead, it is Pakistan again which is expected to play a strategic role in the Gulf security structure. The first official indication to this effect came from Assistant Secretary of Defence, Henry Rowen, who in a Congress hearing said, "Pakistan can also contribute importantly to our interests in post-crisis security arrangements for the Gulf-Pakistan has longstanding military relations with all the Gulf States."

In the draft of Defence Planning Guidance for the fiscal years 1994-99, outlined on February 18, 1992. The American Pentagon, the highest policy framing agency, said: "We should discourage Indian hegemonistic aspirations over the other States in South Asia and on the Indian Ocean. With regard to Pakistan, a constructive US-Pakistan military relationship will be an important element in our strategy to promote stable conditions in South West Asia and Central Asia. We should therefore endeavour to re-build our military relationship given acceptable resolution of our nuclear concerns. ...We should work to have both countries, India and Pakistan, to adhere to the Nuclear Non-Proliferation Treaty and to place their nuclear energy facilities under International Atomic Energy Agency safeguards."

It appears that Saudi Arabia and Egypt will play an important role in the proposed security arrangements while Syria, Iran and Pakistan will be given a part in the military structure along with other members of Gulf Corporation Council Accordingly, Pakistan will be rearmed with high-tech weapons to play the allotted role. She will receive sophisticated weaponry, attack helicopters and missile systems. She will be provided with additional F-16 aircrafts and many hundred Ml-Al Abrams tanks. These are the highly sophisticated tanks with nuclear warhead capabilities and that the same time can withstand nuclear and chemical attacks.

The USA is not complacent on China as well It has singled out China as a major arms vendor in West Asia region and asked her to help prevent the arms race. President Bush has declared that it would be tragic if a new arms race were to develop in West Asia. And, James Baker, the Secretary of State, told Congerss that time had come to try to change the destructive pattern of military competition in the already over-militarised area. "But as the rhetories on arms control were still sounding, a campaign to promote arms sales abroad started", said Xinhun, the official Chinese News Agency. It added that "political influence usually goes along with the armament shipment," and said "after the Gulf War, the U.S. apparently thinks its leading role in the Gulf Area should not be challenged."

U.S. Realisation. The U.S.A. realises and rightly too that New World Order of its conception needs co-operation from other countries as well. That is why US sought India's order. US Secretary of State, James Baker's request to the Foreign Secretary Muchkund Dubey was to all intents and purposes a manifestation of Washington's irritation that since India became a member of the UN Security Council it has refused to be stream-rolled by the US-sponsored resolutions particularly with regard to Iraq.

It however, needs to be given a due thought since the US draft for permanent ceasefire in Iraq is no less than the Treaty of Versailles which became responsible for the birth of Nazi Hitler. Two of its provisions go far beyond the Iraq situation. The first pertains to the elimination of weapons of mass destruction in possession of or under development in Iraq-chemical, biological and nuclear. The second relates to reparations to be paid by Iraq as war damages to the nations which have a claim on Iraq. Restitution is no doubt allowed by international law but neither the USA in the case of Vietnam nor Israel in the case of Lebanon ever paid anything like that. The reparations extracted from Germany after the Versailles Treaty led to high inflation and mass unemployment in Germany resulting in another World War. Iraq has already paid a heavy price by remaining under bomb rain for over a month.

So, if President Bush means making all other nations fall in line, there is nothing new about this coveted new world order. He forgets that the new world order can not be made to order according to American specifications. In fact, the new world order means a system in which all the nations co-operate willingly, on the basis of equality and fair and equitable return on their raw materials and products. For the New order to be enduring, it must be based on justice, fairplay and harmonious relationship between the different segments of humanity. Human race cannot for long afford to remain divided into two segments—one consisting of developed and affluent nations and the other composed of poor, non-developed.

ECONOMIC IMPERIALISM

The leading states of the modern world have built their big economic empires. They have adopted this tendency since the end of the Second World War. The industrial states in their pursuit of economic progress and self-sufficiency have therefore tended to build their economic empires for the realisation of their industrial needs. A sharp competition for the exploitation of national resources to their utmost is witnessed between the states of the world. This competition has bound certain independent nations in the chains of economic dependence. These economic dependencies, may be classified into three distinct categories as under:

(a) Although most of these states have been nominally declared free, yet they are still bound with their ruling states in respect of their social and economic affairs.

(b) The Second Category of these economic dependencies (for example Pakistan and Indonesia) is the those who have duly attained their political and economic independence from their ruling states, but now due to their attempt for economic progress, have passed into the influence of new, rich and powerful states.

(c) The third category of such dependent states is of certain politically awakened states who in their competition for the acquisition of more and more power have turned into economic dependencies of big and powerful states. Thailand, Afghanistan are the examples of such dependent states whose economic resources are subsequently exploited according to the will of their ruling states.

A great number of economic dependencies which come in the first category have no doubt been declared free by their respective ruling states. Yet they still act on their instance and direction. After attainment of their freedom they cannot afford to discontinue political and economic relations with their old ruling states. But as soon as they grow rich, they tend to disconnect their usual relationship with their old ruling states. Not only that they are inclined towards becoming the satellite states of even more powerful and rich states of the world. For example Indonesia on being declared free by the Dutch Government in accepted the supremacy of China. Now it has started showing signs of its acceptance of Dollar Diplomacy practised by the U.S.A. It has been accepting Economic help form India also. Had India been an economically self-sufficient state it would have been in position to keep the neighbouring states under its economic influence. Contrary to India, Pakistan continued to remain an economic dependency of England even at the end of its political domination.

In the same way most of the central European states like Poland, Hungary, Bulgaria, Czechoslovakia and Romania have passed into the Soviet influence in order to safeguard their respective security and economic interests with the help of the Soviet Union. However, they have consequently come under Soviet influence. A number of Afro-Asian nations have been tending to conduct their economic and military affairs with the help of the United States. U.S.A. is the richest country of the world and it has turned to be the most powerful economic magnet in its relation to all other countries of the world. The capitalist power and the economic prosperity of U.S.A. has ever since been attracting various countries of the world, with the exclusion of certain strictly communist countries to come into its economic influence. Morocco and Tunisia have been declared independent by France, but they exist as economic dependencies of France who has still been stationing her armies in those North African countries.

In most of the cases it has been seen that the states on becoming free, tend to disconnect their political relations with the ruling state and establish fresh political and economic relations with another powerful state. At the end of the Second World War, all those spheres of military or economic control, which had been evacuated by England. France or Holland were taken over by the U.S.A. Even the Japanese colonies were not spared of the U.S. influence. Middle Eastern states to which had earlier been politically influenced by England and France were in due course brought under the influence of U.S. Dollar diplomacy.

The Soviet Government has now started to follow the foot-prints of U.S.A. in most of the backward countries of the world so as to win them over to its side. The Soviet Union is trying to gain the favour of Afro-Asian nations against U.S.A. The active foreign policy of Communist China which has made South and South East Asia as its target. The policy of economic control over the South East Asian countries following by China had led to the creation of serious animosities at the Northern and North Eastern borders of India in the name of Sino-Indian border dispute. The new colonial designs of China in Asia have caused an alarm not only in U.S.A. but also in U.S.S.R. and the Soviet relations with China have been considerably strained.

It is not difficult to know the number of those states which have been subject to economic control by other stronger nations. The states running their industries with the help of foreign capital and exchange turn into Economic dependencies of the respective powers.

It is, however, to be borne in mind that most of the economic institutions of any country are generally controlled by its own nationals. They conduct agriculture, retail trade and industry and exploit the natural resources of their country, while its major industries, exports and imports and industrial and agricultural outputs all are controlled by the foreign states. The foreigners exploit their mineral resources and control their trade centres and banks. Now only that they remain in charge of the chief managerial and technical posts in the industries.

The economic or political control spread by the Radical countries upon the developing regions of the world can easily be understood, but in case of the liberal and democratic nations this cannot be so easily perceived. Their control at even the border lines of such poor and weak countries cannot be easily detected. Sometimes the self-sufficient and powerful states allow the foreign enterprises to invest their capital in their countries, but under those circumstances their economic self-sufficiency can in no way be established.

These nations have developed Multi-National Corporations i.e., investors of different countries create a Joint Stock Company, float the concern and undertake enterprising in the development as well as developing countries. The presence of Multi-National Corporation in a developing country does not make it an economic dependence of one State. But this form is worst. Independent studies have observed that the presence of Multi-National Corporation always keep the political stability of the dependent nation in dock. People are the most sufferer of their exploitation and still they cannot launch a movement against them like the national liberation movements of the 1940's since the dominant economic power is invisible.

The Use of Force. The state government of any economic dependency is only outwardly a free and sovereign government. It is conducted by the powerful elements of the country, but in most cases it has been seen that the foreign nationals controlling the economic system of any country actually control nearly all departments of administration. This foreign control becomes much more distinct when most of the income of the national Government of any economic dependency is attained by it through those resources, which are controlled by foreign states on the basis of royalty. Such an instance may be found in Saudi Arabia. Sometimes the foreign states endeavour to establish their indirect control upon the weak and semi-developed states. They win the favour of the national leaders of such a state by pleasing them with bribes. In some cases semi-social relations are established between the political leaders of two different states of whom one happens to be very rich and resourceful while the other is generally a poor and semi-developed state. Their mutual relations also affects the conduct of their government in relations to one another. The managers and proprietors of the industries of weak and backward nations generally happen to be close friends of the foreign enterprisers. The foreign state economically dominating any other weak state thus succeeds in persuading to accept its economic policy. The state official too adopt only such a policy as might prove beneficial to their foreign supporters.

The economic dependencies may not be directly by the foreign states. The foreign states, mostly Western states do not prefer to directly extend their holds upon the administrative machinery of any national state. Contrary to it the countries of Eastern bloc mostly endeavour to recklessly influence the national government of a weak or a poor state, without any consideration of the world opinion. Once succeeding in their selfish attempt of influencing the other weak countries, the states of the Eastern bloc do not leave any loophole for them to extripate themselves from their impact. If any state of the Eastern bloc endeavours to affect some necessary amendments in its national policy, the remaining states of bloc with the Soviet Union at their leadership make an armed invasion against it.

The policy of Western states in relation to the other weak, and poor states, has been found to be mostly liberal. The after investing their capital in the foreign states aim only at their economic gains.

The foreigners trading with the so called economic dependencies to not take into consideration the weapons of foreign policies utilized by them. Their contenstations it the U.N. and their support or opposition to the other states. Even then the Western states actively influencing the administration of their economic dependencies always fear that they might not pass into the hands of Communist nations. The U.S.A. has attracted a good number of backward and poor states of the world to its own leadership on the basis of extending necessary economic, technical and armed help as a result of which the U.S. capitalism has been much successful in extending the sphere of its economic and military influence upon the weak and semi-developed states more than any other nation of the world. The states coming into the compass of the communist influence are comparatively lesser in number and they are in no way allowed to speak a single word against the conduct of Soviet foreign policy.

The Benefits of Indirect Control in the Process of New Colonialism. The indirect control upon the economically dominated state is of a great benefit to the dominating power. Most of the present economic dependencies had previously been politically dominated colonies of some or the other powerful state. The Imperial Power cared most to safeguard their colonial assests and their political and economic control over them. Therefore, the subject people were brutally treated since imperialism did not understand the language of equality. But in indirect form of economic domination compels the foreign not to untowardly suppress the popular will in exploiting the national resources of a weak and undeveloped country. The foreign capitalists therefore carefully manage to keep satisfied the labour class of their economically exploited state. The foreign powers keeping into consideration the safeguard of their own interest generally abstain from doing any harm to the national interests of their economic dependencies. Thus the nationals of the economic dependency cannot be in a position to spread hatred and jealously against its controlling foreign power. If by chance the people of an economic dependency become discontended against its controlling foreign states, they cannot even then hardly be in a position to harm the foreign interests.

The other benefit of the indirect control to the concerning foreign state is that it has to take into consideration nominal liability of the welfare of the people of their economic dependency. In case of any political colony, the responsibility of taking necessary care of the health and education of the people lies on the ruling state but in Economic dependencies all these responsiblities are borne by its national or local Government.

The foreign Government is generally not held responsible for the acting of its citizens carrying on their economic dependency. Truly enough the foreign elements present unlawful gratifications to the national state authorities of the economic dependency, evoke terror there and indulge in many sorts of untoward actions but the control of the poor state by their mother state being of indirect nature they cannot be legally held responsible by their own Government.

DISADVANTAGES OF INDIRECT CONTROL

(1) In the absence of direct control on the economic dependency the foreign Government is not able to easily satisfy its will on an alien soil. Although dominated by the foreign state in many respects the national Government of an economic dependency can very easily execute its will against the foreign interest of its superior power, without being effectively checked by the concerning foreign state Government. At the time of general election in any economically dominated weak state the foreign government can secretly side with the anti-national elements through the medium of its own countrymen who have settled in the said economic dependency. The foreign state cannot openly carry on any propaganda in its own favour or in the favour of its supported candidate at such occasions in the economic dependencies for the national government can under such circumstances instigate the countrymen to rise in severe revolt against those foreign elements and thus it can very well harm the foreign interests in its country, whereupon no armed action can be taken against it by the said foreign power.

(2) The states of America and Europe are guided by a singular feeling of superiortiy against the people of their economic dependencies and this creates a strong tension between the two states. These imperialist feelings are found in the European attitude since long. The Europeans do not even bear to see the spread of any civilization other than that of their own. The European industrialists and traders when they see that in spite of their investment of large capitals on the industries functioning in their Economic dependencies and statellite states the labourers do not work satisfactorily and do not care for their implied interests, they become all the more aggrieved and try to exploit their labourers and other national resources in the most obdurate and appropriating manner.

Partnership of the Foreign States in the Exploitation and Economic Profits of the So Called Satellite States and Economic Dependencies. The relations of a foreign state with its economic dependency can rarely be strained due to its indirect control over it while the Imperialist State is very liable to provoke the discontent and hatred of the people of their politically dominated colonies. The foreign control upon the economic dependencies is generally very less and therefore the foreign state is not so much defamed as happens in case of any imperial power. The European states do not make use of barbarous methods in exploiting the resources of their economic dependencies in spite of their feelings of supremacy. The foreign power can less exploit the resources of the foreign dependency than they can do those of their politically dominated colonies. The people of economic dependencies gain sufficiently by the national interests of their superior state for example the royalties, rents, taxes, profits and wages earned by a foreign state in her satellite States and economic dependencies fetch a considerable money income to them. The economic profit cannot be availed of by the political colonies of any Imperial state. It is also true that only the higher classes of the economic dependencies gain by that economic system controlled by the foreign while the standard of living of the ordinary people is not raised by such economic systems. The rich and higher class of society in these satellite states generally keep themselves engaged in protecting the foreign interests implied in its own country and at crucial periods it also helps the nations of the foreign state.

The higher as well as the lower classes of society living in powerful states are more beneficial. The prosperity of the U.S.A. and England is the result of their tactful measures of controlling economic colonies in various parts of the world. France and England for a long period of time extracted handsome monetary signs but their military, technical and economic control upon the Suez Canal Zone and when the nationalisation of the canal was done they tried to safeguard their interests in Suez Canal Zone, and their relations with the Egyptian Government became all the more strained. Similarly at the extinction of their colonial administration on the states of the Middle-East the Western states like England and France could realise that they had upto that time extracted sufficient monetary income from their colonial assets and become prosperous only due to the same.

Political colonialism and the new economic colonialism are not inconsistent in their effect. The states having political colonies can maintain also their economic dependencies. But the democratic minded people of U.S.A. are a great opponent of the political colonialism while they support the maintenence of economic dependencies. Even then there are political colonies and economic dependencies under the U.S. control. The People of U.S.A. had been engaged in their economic reconstruction and progress of their industries at the time when the European states were busy with their effective efforts of increasing their colonial assets. The U.S. Government felt an acute need of contracting with the foreign markets entered into the theatre of world affairs when the old Imperialist powers hed become tried of and fed up with their colonial pursuits. England and France, the two top ranking Imperial powers, had been dominating the world till the advent of Great War. Their power was broken by war. They could no more remain in a position of maintaining large armies and controlled their over-seas colonies. Thenceforth U.S.A. started championing the cause of their political freedom on the basis of self-determination. This mobilised the world opinion in favour of U.S.A. and various nations began to internationally respect the U.S.A. as their saviour. Further, they were openly helped by U.S.A. in their task of national reconstruction and economic progress so that they might pass into the U.S. influence.

BIPOLARITY

The Second World War was a source of big, deep and far reaching changes in the international structure. It ended the traditional power structure in international relations and ushered in a new power structure which, immediately after the conclusion of peace treaties, became a bipolar system and then gradually got transformed into a multipolar system. The loss of power suffered by the formerly powerful states, like Britain, France, Germany, Italy, Austria, Japan, Spain etc., and the rise of two very powerful states—U.S.A. and U.S.S.R. with Cold War and alliance politics in between them, led to the emergence of a bipolarity in international relations, and which by 1955, developed into a tight bipolarity.

(a) 'Pole' and 'Polarity'. Before examining the concept of Bipolarity, it is essential to know the meaning of 'pole' and 'polar system' or polarity in the context of international relations . A 'pole' in International Politics is popularly defined as a great or super power, and the standerd of determining such a status is generally military power. By 'polar system', as Robert E. Osgood and Robert W. Tucker write, we refer to "the number of centres of military power (whether individual states or coalitions) which are capable of substantially affecting the balance of power in an extensive area of the world, which are independently committed to the support of vital interests distinct from the interests of other centres and which, threfore, might go to war independently of other centres."

(b) Bipolarity: Meaning and Nature. Bipolarity or a bi-polar system is characterised by the existence of only two major powers, whose capabilities, generally comparable, are far beyond those of any other state within the system and each of which holds a vertical power structure which is the opponent of the other power structure. It is a system involving two opposing states or blocs and in which each regards the other as an adversary. Each sees the other as the one which threatens its security.

The bipolarity that emerged in the period immediately after World War II was characterised by the presence of two super actors whose power was far superior to the power of other states. Each super actor was engaged in the process of isolating and limiting the other. Each super actor, through a network of alliances, consolidated its power position and formulated its own bloc in international politics. The friends of the opponents were considered foes and *vice versa*. The conflict in international relations was interpreted as conflict between the two blocs.

Thus, in bipolarity, the international system stands-divided into two distinct blocs, each headed by a super power and supported by several other states which are committed to support the policies of their blocs. Under bipolarity, international conflict is always intensive because each antagonist sees any gain of power and security for the foes as a loss of power and tries to prevent such consequences. Both poles are hypersensitive to the slightest shifts of power. Each opposes all the moves of the other. The pushes and counter pushes are regularly practised for asserting their positions. Drawing lines between respective spheres of influence and then prescribing this territorial *status quo*, becomes the heart of the bi-polar system. As such we can say that politics under bipolarity is the politics of confrontation and recurrent crisis, and involves limited use of violence. Bipolarity provides little scope to the other parties to exercise their influence in international relations.

BIPOLARITY AND POST-WAR

The establishment of bipolarity in the international system of post war years was the direct consequence of the big and deep changes that World War II produced in the international power structure as well as due to the outbreak of cold war between U.S.S.R. and U.S.A.

1. End of its Isolationalism. The inability of Britain to carry out its former role in Europe, as became evident in its helplessness at the time of the crisis which developed in Greece and Turkey made it essential for U.S.A. to throw away isolationalism in favour of involvement in international politics.

2. Reduced Number of Great Powers. The numerical reduction of great powers from seven to two set the stage for the emergence of bipolarity in international relations. The Axis-powers—Germany, Italy, Japan, Austria etc., got totally shattered as a result of their defeat and the allied powers, though victorious, lost much in term of men, money and material.

3. Cold War and Alliance Politics. The net result was the outbreak of cold war in which America, through the Marshall Plan and U.S.S.R., through the COMECON stated their drives for increasing their respective influence in Europe. The Soviet success in Eastern Europe, where it could secure the establishment of socialist regimes and the American success in making the Western European nations accept Marshall Plan and democratic power umbrella (U.S. umbrella) created a ripe situation for the development of bipolarity in international politics.

4. Strong Sense of Competition in Political and Economic Spheres. The strong sense of political and economic competition that existed between Democratic U.S.A. and Communist U.S.S.R. compelled each to counter the possibility of growing influence of the other in world politics by attempting to increase its own sphere of influence in Europe and other parts of the globe.

5. Nuclear Arms Race. When the Soviet nuclear capability became known and there emerged a nuclear armament race between the two super powers, the stage got finally set for the division of the world into two hostile blocs each fearing the other. Infact, the cold war battle lines, as drawn in 1947, can be regarded as the foundations of the bi-polar system that subsequently emerged. Around this time the United States decided to pursue a broad scale policy of containment of communism and as a counter move the Soviet Union decided to work hard for spreading communism in other parts of the globe.

The Bipolarity Decade—1945-55. Between 1945-55 both the super powers were in a position to establish their respective blocs in world politics. This decade came to be described not only as a decade of bipolarity but also as a decade of tight biporlarity. In this era the dependence of almost all states (Non-aligned countries were still struggling to be conceptually clear about the nature and scope of their neutrality in cold war) upon either of the two super powers became a hard fact of international relations. Describing this situation, Toynbee characterised the world politics as: "Bipolarity" in which the U.S.A. and the U.S.S.R. had established their hegemony by dividing the whole world into two hemispheres. According to him, these countries of the two hemispheres were reduced to the position of either associates or satellites of two giant powers. In the world of Toynbee, "All the other states in the world today are in some measures dependent, most of them, on the United States and a few of them on Russia (USSR), but none completely independent of one or other of these two powers."

The Alliances of the Two Poles in the Era of Bipolarity. Many writers, like Steven Rosen and Walter S. Jones described 1945-55 years as a period of tight Bipolarity which saw such momentous events as the combat use of atomic energy, the attainment to nuclear capability by U.S.S.R., the establishment of a number of security alliance, particularly NATO, SEATO and the Warsaw Pact, the Berlin blocade, the rise of China as a communist power, Korean war and some other important events. This era witnessed the growth of intense Soviet-American rivalry and cold war interactions. During this period U.S.A. concluded eight major bilateral, trilateral and multilateral security alliances:

(i) O.A.S. 1947 (22 members),

(ii) N.A.T.O. 1949 (15 members),

(iii) Security Treaty with Japan 1951 (Bi-lateral),

(iv) A.N.Z.U.S. 1951 (Trilateral),

(v) Mutual Defence Pact with Phillipines 1951 (Bi-lateral),

(vi) Mutual Defence Treaty with the Republic of (South) Korea 1953 (Bi-lateral),

(vii) S.E.A.T.O., 1954 (Eight members), and

(viii) Mutual Defence Treaty with the Republic of China (Taiwan) 1954 (Bilateral).

Apart from these, although U.S.A. was not the member we can include the Baghdad Pact (1955), In it USA was very much in the pact through its ally—Britain. U.S.A. joined it is various committees and even used veto in them. U.S.A. contributed 20 per cent of its total expenditure. U.S.S.R. besides the Sino-Soviet Treaty of 1959, concluded a comprehensive security alliance of all the communist state—The Warsaw Pact. In between them U.S.A. and U.S.S.R. concluded alliances with sixty states and almost thirty non-self-governing areas. The popularity of these alliance and the super powers hold upon other states can be judged from the fact that at a time when the U.N. Membership was 59, the two alliance systems involved 60 states.

Nature of Bipolarity. Analysing the nature and impact of Bipolarity in international relations of 1945-55 period, Joseph Frankel well observed: "For a short while the trend seemed more or less inexorable. There was no place for neutrals in the bi-polar world, and both the Russians and the Americans regarded such states as India with the suspicion; both applied the maxim that he who is not with us is against us. The bi-polar character of the post-war world was revealed so suddenly that many people were blinded to other aspects of reality and became convinced that eventually the whole world become divided into two antagonistic blocs facing each other and that the bi-polar system would become fixed".

"The prospects seemed poor, both for mankind faced with the danger of an atomic holocaust and for the national states which seemed to be increasingly at the mercy of the super powers. The Soviet Union organised her empire rigidly and maintained sufficient troops in and near her satellites to ensure compliance: the Americans used subtler pressure, but their series of alliances amounted to no less than a counter empire, less hierarchical but nevertheless clearly centering around the United States."

EMERGING UNIPOLARITY

The bipolarity that had emerged during the first decade of the post-war period, got diluted in the post-1955 years and subsequently got transformed into multipolarity or, to be more precise bi-multipolarity existence of several major centres of power alongwith the two organised blocs of the two super powers. In the late sixties and seventies the emergence of China, France, Japan, West Germany, European community and NAM, India, Brazil, Nigeria, Egypt along with the two super powers and their respective bloc partners transformed the bi-polar international system into a bi-multipolar or polycentric international system. The new power structure definitely reduced the ability of the two super powers and their blocs to act decisively in international relations.

The bi-multipolar system continued to operate till late 1980s when several big and rapid changes in the U.S.S.R. and Eastern countries created a situation in which a unipolar system began emerging in the international relations. The subsequent disintegration of the U.S.S.R., the death of the Warsaw Pact, the end of Cold War, the liberalisation of Eastern Europe, the demolition of Berlin wall, and several other formidable changes created a situation of unipolarity in the international system. The dependence of Russia, the successor of former U.S.S.R., upon western particularly American economic aid, the weakness of Commonwealth to Independent States, the domestic involvement of unified Germany, the unwillingness of Britain and France to challenge the US role in the UN as well as in the world at large, the isolation of and strain upon the surviving communist regimes in China, Cuba and Vietnam, the continuance of NATO, the increasing US control over the UN Security Council, the increased US role as an international peace-keeper, the weakness suffered by NAM, the limitations of Japanese national power, the world as all countries now accept the principles of democracy, decentralisation, market economy and development, and several other such factors combined together to produce a virtual unipolarity in contemporary international relations.

The following factors were responsible for giving rise to unipolarity in international relations:

1. The end of cold war in international relations.
2. The disintegration of the U.S.S.R.
3. The liberalisation of Eastern countries.
4. The economic dependence of Russia and other republics of the former U.S.S.R., upon American and Western economic aid.
5. The emergence of the U.S.A. as the sole surviving power in the post-Cold War and post-U.S.S.R. world. The dominant role that the U.S.A. played in the Gulf War operations and willingness of almost all the major nations, for one reason or the other, to support the U.S. policies and moves in the United Nations and over different issues and policies, the strength gained by it due to the end to Cold War, disintegration of the U.S.S.R., and inability of other states to challenge its power, its ability to keep intact NATO even after the liquidation of Warsaw Pact, its increasing control over the United Nations, particularly its Security Council and its continued military economic, industrial and technological superiority all combined to strengthen the U.S. power in world politics. In the process unipolarity came to characterise the international system. Decision making at the global level started fully reflecting the increased U.S. role in world politics.
6. Japan has been a major economic power in the world. It, however, continues to abstain from developing its military power. It is almost getting involved in an economic cold war with the U.S.A. It wants to avoid and hence is not really been to challenge the U.S. power in international relations.

7. The demolition of Berlin wall and the unification of East Germany with West Germany and the consequent rise of a single United Germany. This development however, compelled Germany to concentrate upon the need for consolidation of the unity. German economy came under pressure resulting from the need to secure the economic development of its East German half.
8. The increased role of the United States of America in peace-keeping operations in the post-Gulf War world.
9. The universal acceptance of the principles of democracy, decentralisation, market economy, globalisation, denuclearisation, demilitarisation and development. The ideological unipolarity of the world gave strength to the emergence of unipolarism in the international system.
10. In the post-cold war world, the NAM has yet to revive its traditional role in world politics. The end of cold war which was followed by a disintegration of the U.S.S.R. produced several big and rapid changes in the international system. The changes came at a time when NAM was being headed by a self-destroying Yugoslavia and was struggling to meet internal pressures resulting from the policies of a group (Islamic states) of NAM countries. Under the circumstances NAM developed an inertia that led many scholars to observe that it has lost much of its relevance in the changed international system. Although NAM demonstrated its unity and continued relevance in September, 1992 at the time of the Tenth Summit of the Non-aligned countries, it also became evident that NAM was still to determine and take up its tasks in the post-cold war world. No one can deny that its ability to influence international decision making as well as to check the growing American role in the United Nations and in the World at large stand limited at the movement.
11. China as a surviving communist power now finds herself almost isolated. It has gone in the economic liberalisation at

a rapid speed, but still finds the path difficult. It has tried to mend its fences with India, Vietnam, Russia and Japan. It is trying its best to keep off growing pressure in favour of political liberalism. It has been developing trade relations with the U.S.A. but at the same time it fears the western attempts to export political liberalism. It is yet to get back Taiwan. It is due to get the liberalised Hongkong in 1995. Under the circumstances it is not prepared to challenge the U.S. power in world politics.

12. In the post-Cold war and post-Gulf war era of international relations, the U.N. Role, particularly its conflict-resolving and peace-keeping role has got invigorated. It stand reflected from the fact that presently it has been simultaneously undertaking peace-keeping operations in several different parts of the globe. However, alongwith this, it also reflects an increasing U.S. dominance of its decision-making. Almost all the U.N. Security Council decisions on Iraq, Libya, Bosnia, Serbian, votes on Human rights issues, vote on NPI and creation of Nuclear free zones etc.—or the U.N. General Assembly vote that Zionoism is not terrorism, all reflect the growing U.S. dominance over the United Nations. Several scholars even go to the extent of observing that the "UNO is behaving as a USO." We do not accept the validity of this observation but we do feel that American influence may control over the U.N. has been increasing in this post cold war and post—U.S.S.R. world.

With the status as the sole surviving super power in the world, the U.S.A. has gained a new validity and strength in the contemporary international system. Currently no other major international actor—Japan, Germany, France, Russia, China, European community, NAM and even the United Nations—has the ability to act as a major check upon the U.S. power. Ideological unity of the world has given an additional boost to the role of the U.S.A. in contemporary international system. Unipolarity or unipolarism is a new reality of international relations.

MULTIPOLARITY

Multipolarity involves the existence of a number of centres of powers in international relations. In the words of Wasby, "A Multipolar system includes a number of major states, typically at least five, of roughly equal power or capability." Multipolarity is characterised by restrained behaviour of the essential actors. As compared to Bipolarity's simple and rigid division, Multi-polarity involves a complex and flexible power structure. In it, no rigid distinction between friends and foes is enduringly made. Each pole views all other actors as potential adversaries or and potential allies. With a large number of great powers, states have adequate mobility to align and realign themselves. Many short term ad-hoc alliance are made from time to time. The hostilities are not allowed to become very intense. The degree of animosity among rivals/ competitors is quite less that the one which characterises bipolarity.

In Multipolarity, since the number of powerful actors is quite large, no single actor receives unduly large attention. In the opinion of Spainer John, "Whereas bipolar system is more prone to crisis and wars, the multipolar system, because of its flexibility and manoeuverability, is more likely to maintain peace". A similar view is expressed by Karl. W. Deutsch and J. David Singer that a multipolar system allows far less net conflict than the bipolar system.

TRANSFORMATION OF BIPOLARITY INTO MULTIPOLARITY POLY-CENTRISM IN POST-1955 PERIOD

The bi-polar system that came to emerge in post-war years and which developed into a tight bi-polar in fifties could remain in operation for nearly 10 years. By the late fifties it started developing several distinct tendencies towards transformation into a loose bi-polar system. In early fifties, the alliances of the two super power begin to 'loosen with internal conflicts and loss of confidence appearing in each bloc. Several fundamental changes that occurred around mid-1950s further encouraged the process of weakening of the alliances and the tightness of the alliance partnership began to dissipate.

I. Weakening of the Soviet Bloc. The Soviet bloc suffered setbacks due to the following developments:

(a) ***Ideological Conflict between USSR and China.*** The emergence of strong ideological differences between Khrushchev and Mao and the resulting conflict between Russia and China, gave a further blow to the influence of the former. The emergence of Sino-Soviet boundary dispute, the speed with which China began developing its independent nuclear capability, the emergence of Sino-US rapproachment in early 1970s, the Chinese entry into the United Nations and its new status as a veto power, and the continued Sino-Soviet differences over Afghanistan, Kampuchea and Sinkiang region were a source of pressure upon the Soviet Under its weight, the Soviet control over its allies developed.

(b) ***Strength of Forces of Nationalism in Yugoslavia and Some Other Pro-Soviet States.*** To begin with, the forces of nationalism started asserting themselves. In 1948, Yugoslavia was successful in freeing herself from the Soviet embrace. "The Soviet-Yugoslavia dispute", writes Frankel, "was misleadingly clad in an ideological garb but was in fact an assertion of national ambitions against Soviet tutelage". The success of Yugoslavia in asserting her independence regarding foreign policy decision-making can be legitimately described as the first crack in the Soviet bloc. Further, the Eastern European dissatisfaction with the Soviet control, force-shadowed a few years earlier in East Germany, climaxed with the Hungarian revolt in 1956. Though Russia was successful in containing the revolt yet the incidence gave a blow to Soviet control over her bloc.

(c) ***Liberation Waves in Eastern Europe.*** The experience with China made the U.S.S.R. conscious of the need to treat its Eastern European allies more accommodatingly. The existence of liberalisation movements in Poland and Czechoslovakia, and freedom of action exhibited by

Romania made the Soviet camp further weak. The trend towards increased co-operation between Western European and Eastern European states and the rise of Euro-Communism further reduced the Soviet grip over the communist states.

The weakness suffered by the Soviet bloc came to be a source of looseness in the bi-polar system and it was also responsible for the emergence of multipolarity in international relations.

II. Weakening of the American Bloc. The American bloc suffered setbacks due to the following developments:

(a) ***Suez Crisis and USA.*** In the mid-fifties the American bloc also began to develop cracks. In 1956, Britain and France got engaged in their abortive Suez expedition without consulting or informing U.S.A. This event appeared as the first crack in the American bloc.

(b) ***French Policies in 1960s.*** France, under General De Gaulle, got involved in the process of becoming an independent centre of power in world politics and this French policy clearly and definitely weakened the American control over her allies. The French decision to develop relations with communist countries, including China, inflicted a major blow to the American view of isolating the communists. Moreover, through has strong opposition to American policy in Vietnam, to British entry into the Common Market and to the American attempts at the intensive militarisation of Europe through the installation of Polaris Missiles in NATO countries. General De Gualle demonstrated a determination to free France from American influence. His call for the neutralisation of South East Asia and the threat, in 1966, to withdraw from NATO, further made the point clear. In order to make France an independent centre of power, General De Gaulle took the decision to develop independent nuclear capability. By the end of De Gaulle's era in French politics (1969), France had become firm on

the way to be a big nuclear power in world politics. The French policy in late sixties inflicted major cracks in the American bloc. The organisation and operationalisation of European communities was designed to check the growing US influence in Western Europe.

(c) ***Strengthening of Nationalism in Latin American States.*** The strength that the forces of nationalism gained in Latin America further loosened the American control over other states. Although U.S.A. continued to act successfully in maintaining its influence over the countries of the American continent, there came to be growing opposition to such American attempts. The rise of Cuba as a communist state further weakened the American hold over the continent.

III. Rise of Non-Alignment. The stand adopted by India and many other countries to remain aloof from the two power blocs, to pursue neutrality in Cold War and to maintain an independent role in international politics also helped the transformation of bipolarity into multipolarity. In the words of Frankel, "Particularly important was the stand adopted by India. With the background of their traditional tolerance, their abhorrence of polarities and of militarism, the Indians choose to stay out of the two rival blocs. They, with the Yugoslavia, offered a pattern of behaviour for other emerging states in Asia and the later also in Africa, who preferred to remain uncommitted (Non-aligned), 'Nasser' Egypt and Nkrumah's Ghana became prominent among the new comers who decided to follow non-alignment. Gradually, the concept of non-alignment started receiving more support and attention and by 1961, it developed into an international movement. The rise of non-alignment symbolised the rise of Third World and also of opposition to cold war an bipolarity. The success of non-alignment greatly weakened the bipolar system as nearly one half of mankind decided against joining the two rival blocs.

IV. The Expansion of the Nuclear Club. The super powers could retain their nuclear monopoly for a short time. Britain became the third country to secure capability in the fifties. In the sixties,

France and China were successful in acquiring nuclear capability and since then the two have been rapidly developing operational nuclear weapons. In 1974, India entered the nuclear club by successfully conducting a fully controlled PNE, but at the same time remaining committed to only peaceful and non-military exploitation of nuclear technology. Several other countries were in a position to exhibit their potentialities to be nuclear power. The expansion of the nuclear club contributed a lot to the development of multipolarity. Although the weapons produced by countries other than the two super powers did not materially affected the nuclear superiority of the U.S.A. and the U.S.S.R., yet these endowed their owners with much greater independence and flexibility in their foreign policies.

V. Rise of New States. Another factor which influenced the transformation of international system from bipolarity towards multipolarity was the rise of new states in world politics. Beginning in 1957, though more markedly after 1960, the, number of sovereign nations states registered a big increase. In a single year *i.e.*, 1960 as many as 17 new sovereign independent states were admitted to the United Nations and this process went on for almost 10 years. These new countries were committed to maintain their hard won independence and were very skeptical and suspicious of the powerful states. Consequently, they were not prepared to join any bloc as they felt that it would indirectly lead to a limitation of their freedom of action. The poverty and under development as well as the common sufferings that they suffered under the yoke of imperialism and colonialism made them opposed to the power-blocs. The attempts made by U.S.A. and the U.S.S.R. to won them into their camps made them more apprehensive of the power blocs and they decided to remain aloof, and tie themselves to neither of the two giants. They preferred to accept aid from either or both but without political strings. In order to protect their identities they started co-ordinating their roles in the U.N.O. and other international institutions. These states gradually began to form a multi-state group with potential collective influence. In the process there came to be developed a third force-the Third

World in international politics. The rise of Third World played a key role in making the international system multipolar in place of bipolar.

VI. Economic Integration of Western Europe. The big and rapid economic development registered by the Western European countries through orgainsed regional economic institutions like E.C.M., was also responsible for making Western Europe independent of American control and influence. These countries, through their economic development, developed the capacity to escape subordination to bi-polar politics. The economic prosperity through economic integration helped the Western European nations, particularly France, to challenge and American hegemony in international politics. The progress of economic and security co-operation among the European states, both Eastern and Western, diluted bipolarity in Europe.

VII. Rise of Japan and West Germany as Major Economic Powers. Within 30 years of the end of World War II, both Japan and West Germany were successful in not only overcoming the huge economic losses that they had suffered during war but also in registering stupendous success in industrial production and technological advancement. The rise of Japan and West Germany as two economic powers greatly influenced the process of emergence of multipolarity. Though militarily these states continue to be weak, yet they have come to be accepted as major actors in world politics. Technically they stand aligned with U.S.A. but in reality both have secured a degree of independence in conducting their foreign relations.

To this list can be added the rise of Eastern European states, demise of Warsaw Pact and the rise of a unified Germany in 1990. These developments made the power structure more polycentric.

Therefore, the collapse of the U.S.S.R., the emergence of the U.S.A. as a role surviving super power in the world, continued existence of NATO even after the liquidation of Warsaw Pact and the inability of Spain, Germany, France, Britain, Russia. NAM and other such centres of power of materially check time increased US power in world politics changed the international power structure into a unipolar stucture.

All these factors were in the main, responsible for the transformation of bipolarity into multipolarity in international relations of 1960-80. "The first decade after World War II". . as Hartman says "was the age of the super powers and bipolarity in international relations." However, since 1955 bipolarity began suffering a decline in favour of multipolarity or polycentrism. Undoubtedly, the era of tight bipolarity was over by 1965 when besides the two super powers, there came to be a number of centres of powers in the international system.

❐